CRYSTALS
COLOUR & CHAKRA

HEALING AND HARMONY FOR BODY, SPIRIT AND HOME

CRYSTALS
COLOUR & CHAKRA

learn to harness the transforming power of natural energies with practical
New Age techniques and over 1000 stunning photographs and artworks

SUE LILLY ■ SIMON LILLY ■ STELLA MARTIN ■ JOSEPHINE DE WINTER ■ GILL HALE

LORENZ BOOKS

This edition is published by Lorenz Books

Lorenz Books is an imprint of Anness Publishing Ltd
Hermes House, 88–89 Blackfriars Road, London SE1 8HA
tel. 020 7401 2077; fax 020 7633 9499
www.lorenzbooks.com; info@anness.com

© Anness Publishing Ltd 2006

UK agent: The Manning Partnership Ltd, 6 The Old Dairy, Melcombe Road, Bath BA2 3LR;
tel. 01225 478444; fax 01225 478440; sales@manning-partnership.co.uk

UK distributor: Grantham Book Services Ltd, Isaac Newton Way, Alma Park Industrial Estate, Grantham, Lincs NG31 9SD;
tel. 01476 541080; fax 01476 541061; orders@gbs.tbs-ltd.co.uk

North American agent/distributor: National Book Network, 4501 Forbes Boulevard, Suite 200, Lanham, MD 20706;
tel. 301 459 3366; fax 301 429 5746; www.nbnbooks.com

Australian agent/distributor: Pan Macmillan Australia, Level 18, St Martins Tower, 31 Market St, Sydney, NSW 2000;
tel. 1300 135 113; fax 1300 135 103; customer.service@macmillan.com.au

New Zealand agent/distributor: David Bateman Ltd, 30 Tarndale Grove, Off Bush Road, Albany, Auckland; tel. (09) 415 7664; fax (09) 415 8892

A CIP catalogue record for this book is available from the British Library.

Publisher: Joanna Lorenz
Editorial Director: Helen Sudell
Project Editors: Ann Kay and Joanne Rippin
Project Designers: Peter Clayman and Nigel Partridge
Copy-editing and new text for this edition: Judy Barratt

Crystal Healing, Colour Healing and The Chakras/pages 8–253
Authors: Sue and Simon Lilly
Special Photography: Michelle Garrett

Space Clearing/pages 254–331
Author: Stella Martin
Special Photography: Michelle Garrett

Altars and Shrines/pages 332–379
Author: Josephine de Winter
Special Photography: Michelle Garrett

Feng Shui/pages 380–495
Author: Gill Hale
Special Photography: John Freeman

Previously published in two separate volumes as *Crystal, Colour and Chakra Healing* and *Spiritual Home*

1 3 5 7 9 10 8 6 4 2

Publisher's note

Contents

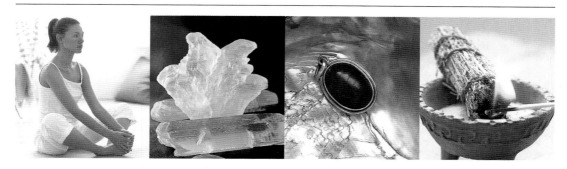

Introduction   6

Introduction

▽ As ideal examples of the universe's pattern-making and orderly structural harmony, crystals naturally bring clarity to the mind.

It sometimes seems that every day is faster, more hectic, and more stressful than the last. We often seem to have little time to be concerned about our state of physical health or our mental, spiritual or emotional wellbeing. Often the realization of how hard we are pushing ourselves comes only when we – finally – fall ill. Thankfully more and more of us are waking up to the realization that in order to deal more effectively with the pace of modern life, we need to find some balance – in our bodies, minds and spirits, and in our environments. This book provides a key practical reference to six of the most inspirational and effective methods for harmonizing our life and optimizing our wellbeing.

The first three sections look within at ways to treat the self in order to create a greater sense of harmony. The book opens with a practical guide to the healing power of crystals and stones. As well as describing the individual properties of some of the most important crystals available, this section teaches how to harness these properties, through certain 'layouts' (the positioning of crystals on or around the body) and through such techniques as dowsing with a crystal pendulum, and 'scanning' with a crystal to highlight areas of weak energy flow. The second section of the book focuses on the healing properties of colour, itself so important in the power of crystals.

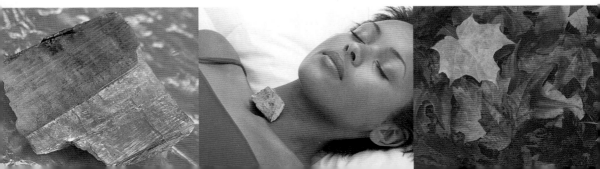

This section offers a comprehensive, hands-on guide to how the human body – including the mind, spirit and emotions – responds to colour. Learn about your own colour tendencies and what these mean, and discover how to use colour to heal yourself physically, emotionally and spiritually.

The third section of the book gives us a profound, practical insight into the power of the chakras – spinning wheels of energy that, according to ancient Indian belief, lie within our body and influence our state of wellbeing.

The second half of the book looks to heal body, mind and spirit through our environment. One of the most important things we can do for ourselves in this modern age is to create space to breathe and rest. Space clearing – the fourth section of the book – shows how we can learn from philosophies such as Zen Buddhism and Ayurvedic medicine (among others) to rid our environment of negativity and turn it back into a tranquil, spiritual place in which every aspect of ourselves can flourish. In the fifth section we learn how to create altars and shrines – dedicated spaces, away from the hustle of modern life, where we can go to meditate, pray, or simply to rest. Altars are not only for those of us with a particular religion. When they are personalized, these spaces can provide us with a focus for our energy to let the stress of everyday life slip away. All the themes of the book – colour, energy and space – are brought together in its final section on the basic principles of Feng Shui. Use this section to create a positive environment in which to live to your full potential.

△ Working with Nature's array of colours in an informed way can bring out the creative side in all of us.

Crystal Healing

Thousands of years ago humankind began mining rocks buried deep within the earth's crust. Some of these rocks were used to build sacred monuments, such as the Great Pyramids in Egypt. Others were seen to be more precious – perhaps they were beautifully coloured, such as orange carnelian, or perhaps they offered the magic of solidified light, such as clear quartz. Soon the ancients began mining the rocks to make talismans and amulets – protective artefacts and jewellery that might be owned or worn to ward off evil spirits, bring luck, strength, prosperity or wealth, or even to ensure a safe passage into the afterlife. We have no way of knowing whether or not ancient peoples had knowledge of the health-giving properties of crystals, but now – several thousand years on – we know from endless accounts of effective treatments that crystals have a remarkable power to heal body, mind and spirit. This section explores how crystals are formed, and explains the different ways in which we can harness their power to optimize our wellbeing, including how to use them to re-balance our chakras – spinning wheels of energy that lie within us. Then, grouping the crystals by colour, we take a practical look at their specific effects on the mind, body and spirit.

The world
of crystals

Crystals remind us of the structures

upon which our universe is built. All

matter, everything that is physical and

solid, owes its existence to the

organizing properties of crystals.

In the beginning

In all parts of the world, and from the dawn of history, crystals have been regarded as belonging to the heavens, as gifts from the spirit worlds. Their colour and brilliance have set them apart from everything else on earth. Today we know that the story of crystals is indeed the story of the creation of the universe.

Astronomers believe that after the initial expansion of the universe from its original point, clouds of hydrogen, the simplest form of matter, began to cluster together. In time, within these vast balls of hydrogen, the pressures became so great that atoms began to fuse together, releasing a huge amount of energy. These glowing spheres became the first stars. Within these stars hydrogen continued to fuse to become helium and, as the burning continued, increasingly heavy elements were formed, such as nitrogen, oxygen, carbon, iron, lead and gold.

As the first stars eventually died, some exploded sending these new elements careering throughout space where gravity created new stars and planets from them. Our own solar system and the Milky Way formed in this way. Lighter gas clouds, the remains of countless stars, were drawn towards the young sun, while the heavier elements settled into orbits further away, gradually coalescing to become the planets.

the earth

Earth formed at a distance from the sun that allowed both light and heavy elements to combine. The larger atoms sank downwards to create the planet's core of iron and nickel. The core is probably surrounded by a layer

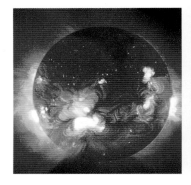

△ Every element in the universe that makes up physical matter was formed within the stars.

▽ Throughout universal space the same raw materials come together to form crystals.

△ The apparent stability and continuity of the planet is in reality a constant cycle of erosion, deposition and metamorphosis.

its composition is altered. The change it undergoes gives it the name metamorphic rock. Crystals can be found in all types of rocks where conditions for their formation are right. As superheated gases and liquids rise to the surface, they begin to cool in the cracks and crevices of the surrounding rock, crystallizing into sparkling and coloured minerals. Harder minerals, such as diamonds and rubies, form at high temperatures in areas of volcanic activity. The crystals that form in sedimentary rock are usually much softer like gypsum and halite (common salt).

The same chemical elements appear throughout the whole of the universe. Given the right conditions, atoms of these different elements can come together to form new substances. Minerals are combinations of different elements that form the building blocks of all physical matter. All minerals, for example halite (sodium chloride – rock salt) and quartz (silicon dioxide – rock crystal), are composed of the same sorts of atoms in the same proportions.

of molten metal. This layer, or mantle, around the planet comprises the greatest volume of the earth. It is 2,900km (1,800 miles) thick and composed of many layers of fluid, swirling rock. The outermost layer is the crust, a thin layer of rock that makes up the earth's continents.

The earth's crust forms less than 1 per cent of its total mass and is less than 40km (25 miles) thick over most of its surface. The distance from the surface of the planet to its centre is 6,391km (3,971 miles), yet the deepest humans have been able to drill is 8km (5 miles).

The earth's crust formed from super-heated rocks such as granite and basalt, that welled up through cracks in the surface layers either to spread out in vast domes called basoliths, or as volcanic eruptions. Rocks formed in this way are called igneous, meaning formed by fire. Millennia of erosion by wind and water wore these igneous rocks to dust. Carried downstream

by rivers, this dust was deposited at the bottom of the sea where it became compressed and eventually turned to rock again. This type of rock is called sedimentary, after the way it has been formed.

Wherever either igneous or sedimentary rock is subjected to extremes of heat or pressure by movements of the earth's crust,

▽ Without the constant movement of the earth's crust many crystals would not be formed out of the sedimentary rock that lies beneath the sea.

The nature of crystals

All minerals will form crystals, though the conditions for their growth varies from mineral to mineral. Crystals begin to grow when the right amounts of their constituent atoms are present, usually in the form of a liquid or gas, but sometimes as a solid, in conditions that allow the atoms to move into those patterns where they are in the best possible state of equilibrium with each other. Heat and pressure ensure that the atoms have the maximum movement and energy to locate these positions before conditions change.

CRYSTAL TOOLS

The first tools were made from stones such as flint and obsidian. Much later, once smelting techniques were discovered, tools and weapons were crafted from metals such as bronze and iron. Today's sophisticated technology makes use of some of the hardest elements on the planet – gemstones. Always valued as things of beauty, mystery and magic, crystals are now also prized as components in precision tools.

▽ In today's high-tech industries crystals are used in sophisticated automated tools.

structure

Once the basic pattern has been taken up by a few atoms, called the 'unit cell' of a crystal, other atoms quickly repeat the arrangement and build up the crystal lattice, the characteristic pattern of atoms unique to each mineral.

A crystal will continue to grow in this way until the exterior conditions alter or the available raw material of atoms is used up. Once formed, crystals are the most stable and organized forms of matter in the

△ These crystals are used in industry. Clockwise from top left, ruby (corundum), two pieces of tourmaline, garnet, chalcopyrite and kunzite.

universe. Their 'ideal' structure means that they often display unique qualities that make them both useful and attractive. A crystal's physical form is the expression of its interior atomic arrangement. Crystals of any given mineral always display the same relationship of symmetrical faces, and each face will meet in flat planes at the same angle. Due

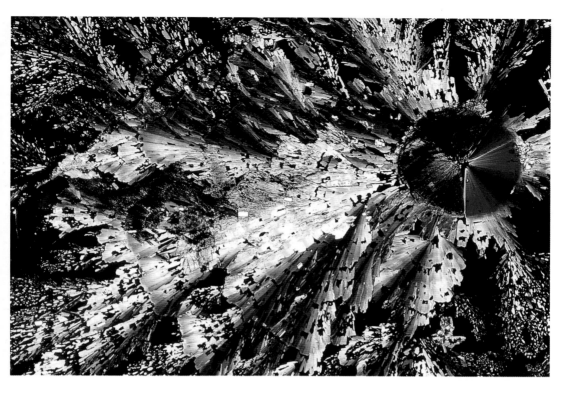

▽ Every crystal is unique in size and shape, yet all crystals of the same mineral share an identical atomic lattice structure.

to different growing circumstances no two crystals will be identical, but they will all show these characteristic features.

△ How light rays refract, reflect and move through crystal structures largely determines what colours a crystal will exhibit.

colour

Although crystals are the most perfect arrangements of matter, small imperfections are present within the lattice structure of most crystals, and in fact these anomalies are often the very things that make them so useful to us. Crystals usually get their colour from the presence of a minute amount of another substance, which distorts the lattice and deflects or alters the light rays as they pass through it. Thus quartz, which is transparent, can appear violet coloured when iron atoms are present, and pink coloured with titanium or manganese. It becomes smoky brown when the lattice is subjected to natural radiation from radioactive elements such as uranium, or intense gamma rays from space and ultraviolet radiation from the sun. Internal fractures and dislocations within the lattice can also create wonderful plays of colour and light, which make some minerals valuable as gemstones.

▽ Quartz crystal carries the properties of its elemental constituents: silicon and oxygen.

The power of crystals

Crystals are objects of beauty, fascination and mystery. They never lose their beauty so they can be treasured, hoarded and exchanged. They can become an expression of wealth. Fine examples of crystals are rare and difficult to find, which is why they have become symbols of high rank, royalty and even divinity.

magical properties

The beauty of crystals makes them a natural choice in personal adornment or the decoration of precious objects. Their uniqueness imbues them with magical power: the power to protect, to enhance, to strengthen, to uplift. They have been used as amulets to ward off harm, as talismans to encourage virtues, as magical guardians to heal, and as tools to interpret messages from the spirit world. The attraction they hold transcends time and place. Many people are keen to own their birthstone, and to discover which stone will encourage love or wealth. With the much larger range of stones from all around the world available today everyone has a favourite, and is drawn to crystals for their particular qualities of warmth, subtlety or sparkle.

▽ Many people simply collect crystals and gemstones for their visual appeal.

△ Natural magic, in contrast to the complex rituals of ceremonial magic, has always used the unique properties of crystals.

decoration and placement

Large crystal clusters are increasingly found in homes and offices. Their visual complexity and their wonderful colours make them ideal to gaze at while the mind relaxes a little. The beneficial energy that they may bring to the observer or the room they are in is an added bonus.

Crystals can be placed in the home according to Feng Shui, the traditional Chinese art of arranging objects, for the enhancement of positivity. The Chinese believe that they bring orderliness and clarity into life.

the spiritual healing paradigm

Crystals and gemstones have a long tradition of being used for healing. In contemporary practice there are two main ways in which they are used, both of which have parallels in much older traditions across the world. The first method can be called the 'spiritual healing paradigm'. Here crystals, especially clear quartz stones, are used to channel,

are used. The second method of crystal healing can be called the 'resonance placement paradigm'.

the resonance placement paradigm

This method doesn't require belief in the spirit worlds or in any kind of energy coming from elsewhere, but relies only on the power of the crystals themselves, and the healing intuition of an individual. Many different stones may be used, each one chosen for a particular beneficial effect on the patient. Placed on or around the body, the colour, shape and composition of the stones are thought to create a resonance that encourages healing to take place. This system parallels the magical, talismanic practices of carrying gemstones, as well as the Ayurvedic traditions of India in which stones are chosen to bring the most harmonious energy to each individual.

direct and amplify energy from the healer, or from the spiritual realms with which the healer works. Healing energy is mentally directed through the stone, which amplifies and clarifies the healing potential. Some North American Indian healers use quartz in this way to diagnose a problem and then remove it. In these instances the crystal may or may not come into contact with the patient. Very often only one or two crystals

△ **In all periods of history, crystals have been regarded as magical and otherworldly.**

▽ **As ideal examples of the universe's pattern-making and orderly structural harmony, crystals naturally bring clarity to the mind.**

▽ **The clarity of crystal can be felt to positively influence the space within which it is placed.**

Getting to know your crystals

Each human being is completely unique, and we will all respond to a specific crystal's energy in a different way. Getting to know each crystal in your own collection is very important. It is more helpful to learn how to get to know the feel of an individual stone than to learn what other collectors or crystal experts have to say about it. What the body senses or knows, our intuition can be trained to access. The most effective healer uses information from a combination of sources, but the most important source is the physical and mental personal experience of healer and patient.

learning a new stone

Once you have gathered together a small collection of crystals you need to begin to learn their potential. Cleanse all new stones well before working with them. Begin by holding a new stone in one hand for a

moment or two, then in the other. Notice how you are feeling. Remember that all the information you can get from the crystal's energy will be registered inside you. Get used to recognizing changes of feeling in your body, emotions and mind.

◁ Taking time to examine your crystals creates a strong intuitive energy link that will be useful in healing situations. It isn't necessary to always have new insights or experiences in this process.

△ Lay out your entire collection on a neutral coloured background. Gazing quietly at a selection of stones will help identify the effect that each stone creates.

After holding the stone for a moment, place it away from you and simply gaze at it. Pick it up once more and notice any changes within you. Close your eyes and simply sit with the stone, then, once more, place it away from you. By such processes you will gradually see a pattern emerging. Once you have established your own responses to a stone you will be able to begin by experience and experiment to find out whether your own response is shared by other people.

The next stage of getting to know your crystals is to place a stone at an energy sensitive spot such as a chakra. This can give you some further insight. Place the stone for a minute or two on each chakra in turn and take notes on your responses. You might find that some places, and some stones, are a lot more sensitive than others.

Keep a stone with you for a while to deepen your connection with it, especially if it is a new one. Putting one under your pillow or next to you when you sleep may produce significant dreams, particularly if you have a clear intention before you fall asleep that you wish to learn the properties of a stone. Again, make a note of these experiences. Carry a stone around with you for a few days and then leave it at home for a while. As you repeat this process you may notice changes in how you feel, or behave or in how others are behaving towards you.

▽ **Holding a stone to a chakra point will show you how it may modify the energy of that centre.**

MEDITATION WITH THE SENSES

Sit quietly with the stone you wish to explore just in front of you. Close your eyes and quieten your mind by focusing your attention on your breathing for a minute or two.

1 Pick up the crystal and hold it comfortably in your hands.

2 Imagine your awareness spiralling down into the stone, as it opens up and lets you explore it.

3 First see how, in your imagination, the inside of the stone feels. Is there a sense of texture, a change of temperature, a sense of space or restriction?

4 Is there any sense of sound? If the energy within the crystal were expressed as sound, how would it seem to you?

5 Breathe in the energy in your imagination. Does it remind you of anything? Is there a fragrance at all? Is there a quality of taste?

6 Visualize that you open the eyes of your imagination and that you can see the energy of the crystal around you. This may take any form, pattern, landscape, or figure.

7 When you have explored the stone enough simply close off your inner senses and bring your awareness back to your body and the sounds that are around you.

8 Complete the grounding process by seeing all aspects of your awareness spiralling back out of the stone and into your body.

9 Make a note of your experiences.

Cleansing crystals

Crystals need to be protected from physical damage, but also from energetic imbalances. Crystals can register a wide range of vibrations, from electricity and magnetism, to sound, emotions and thoughts. The natural coherence of crystal can eventually dissipate imbalances within the lattice but the following cleansing techniques speed this process and ensure only positive energy is present in healing situations.

Every cleansing method has advantages and disadvantages. You will quickly learn to determine the most useful method for your situation. It is better to regularly cleanse the crystals you are working with rather than letting imbalances accumulate over time.

cleansing with water and salt

With the exception of a few water-soluble minerals, each new crystal should be washed before you use it. Use a little soapy water to remove dust and fingerprints. Water will

▽ **Use whichever cleansing techniques you find most effective and practical. You will soon learn to recognize the feel of a cleansed stone.**

also cleanse your stones of energy imbalances. Another method is to hold the stones in cold running water and then leave them to dry naturally. Visualizing the flow of water drawing away all imbalances as you cleanse can speed up the process.

Salt water is often suggested as a medium for clearing crystal energies. Although effective, it can be difficult to remove all traces of salt from the tiny crevices in the crystal, and salt will damage the surface of many softer stones. Dry sea salt piled around each stone and left for a day is a good alternative. Either use small dishes for each stone or nestle each stone in its own little mound of salt on a large flat plate.

cleansing with sound

Resonant sound from a tuning fork, metal bowl or bell rapidly vibrates the physical structure of the crystal allowing it quickly to 'shake off' any intrusive energies. Simply hold a struck bell or tuning fork close to your stones, or place one or two crystals in the bottom of a Tibetan singing bowl, and run the wooden handle around the rim.

△ **Use a clear intention that your chosen method will cleanse your stones, to speed the process.**

▽ **Mineralogy reference books will tell you which stones can be placed in water.**

◁ Dry sea salt, without any extra additives, draws out negative energies. Throw the salt away after use.

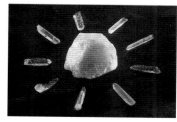

△ Surrounding a crystal with other cleansed stones, or placing the stone on a large cluster or bed of crystal, is an effective cleansing method.

▽ Incense cones or sticks make sufficient smoke for cleansing as well as grains, resins and herbs.

enlivening crystals

To enliven a very tired crystal, it may be necessary to bury it in clay or the earth – but always be sure to mark the spot well! Leave in place for a day to a week before returning to check on progress.

energy cleansing

After cleaning, it is important to remove any energy imbalances your crystal may have accumulated. Over time crystals can be affected by strong negative emotions or electromagnetic pollution. Such a stone will feel lifeless, dull or unpleasant in some way no matter what its appearance. Energy cleansing can be done in many ways. The simplest method is to use incense smoke or a smudge stick with traditional cleansing herbs and pass the stone through the smoke until you feel it clear.

Sandalwood, frankincense, juniper and sage have a long history of use simply because they were found to be powerful purifying herbs. Experiment to find those that work best for your stones.

Get into the habit of cleansing your healing stones before and after use – and don't forget to cleanse any large decorative crystals you may have around your home from time to time.

Crystals and chakras

Gemstones were traditionally used to alleviate the physical symptoms of illness. Today, crystal healing focuses on removing the underlying energy imbalances that may eventually lead to physical problems. In modern complementary therapies, as well as many traditional forms of healing, the person is seen as a complex interaction of different sorts of energy systems. Though not so apparent as the physical body, these energy systems influence every aspect of our lives and they can be clearly felt by anyone trained to notice the subtle differences and states they produce.

△ Tiger's Eye is a variety of quartz that works well at the solar plexus chakra.

Ancient Indian seers perceived seven chakras – vortices of spinning energy along the spinal column, each with its own functions for maintaining health. They found exercises and meditations to regulate and enhance each chakra to promote spiritual wellbeing.

chakras and colours

The chakra system was simplified in the West and a single rainbow colour was attributed to each of the seven chakras. The colour correspondences of the chakra system can be combined with the colour of

△ Ruby, like all red stones, helps to energize and balance the first chakra at the base of the spine.

▽ Carnelian is coloured bright orange by iron particles. It helps balance the sacral chakra.

△ Moss agate is a green stone that works in harmony with the heart chakra.

▽ Turquoise is among the most-used light blue stones, which work with the throat chakra.

△ Sapphire is a deep blue crystal that works well at the brow chakra in the centre of the forehead.

▽ Purple stones, such as sugilite, can help to balance the crown chakra.

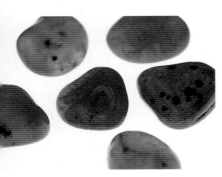

crystals for a simple healing system. Through observation, intuition or dowsing, a crystal therapist can determine which of the chakras need re-balancing to restore

equilibrium to the system as a whole. Appropriate crystals can be placed around the energy centre, and, by the colour or some other balancing aspect of the crystal,

that chakra will be brought back to a healthier functioning. This is an effective way of releasing physical, emotional and mental stress.

SIMPLE CHAKRA HEALING

Crystals that are the same colour as a chakra will enhance its natural qualities, whatever the situation. For a simple chakra balancing therapy, place one stone of the appropriate colour on each chakra area for a few minutes.

Use small tumbled stones or crystal points. Choose your stones and arrange them in sequence beside where you will be lying. When you are ready, you can easily pick up the stones and place them on your body without them falling off. If you prefer to sit, you will need small pieces of surgical tape to hold each stone in position on your body.

1 The first or base chakra is at the base of the spine. Use a black or red stone between your legs to balance physical energy, motivation and practicality, and to promote a sense of reality.

2 The second or sacral chakra is in the lower abdomen, below the navel. Use an orange stone here to balance creativity, and to release stress and blocks in your life that prevent enjoyment.

3 The third or solar plexus chakra is close to the bottom of the ribcage. Use a yellow or gold stone in this position to

clear your thoughts, reduce anxiety and improve confidence.

4 The fourth or heart chakra is in the centre of the chest. Use a green stone here to balance your relationship with others and the world, to increase calm and create a sense of direction in life.

5 The fifth chakra is at the throat. Use a light blue stone here to ease communication difficulties, express yourself and bring peacefulness.

6 The sixth is the brow chakra in the centre of the forehead. Use a dark blue or indigo stone here, to increase understanding, access ideas and promote intuitive skills and memory.

7 The seventh chakra is the crown, situated just a little way above the top of the head. A violet stone placed in this position integrates and balances all aspects of the self – physical, mental, emotional and spiritual.

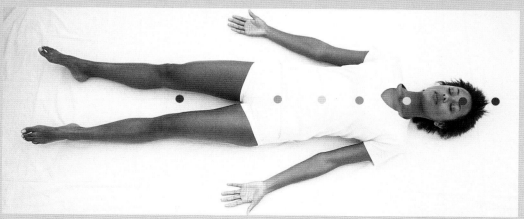

Subtle bodies

The subtle bodies are non-physical aspects of each human being surrounding and interpenetrating the body. They constitute what is usually called the aura. Each level of the aura can be thought of as the individual seen from a slightly different energy vibration – like listening to the different instruments playing in an orchestra.

different levels

Closest to the physical body in frequency is the etheric body, an exact double of the body and a template for the physical organs and systems. On a finer level is the emotional body, often perceived as a swirl of ever-changing colours that alters with our moods. The mental body contains thought processes, ideas and beliefs we hold about ourselves and the world. It usually appears as a yellow glow and can be bright around the head during concentration. The

▽ Dowsing can be used to choose the most appropriate crystal for healing. With the most useful stone or stones, the pendulum will rotate, while with others it will remain stationary.

finer vibrational subtle bodies contain the energy patterns of our spiritual natures and are less bound by rules of time and space.

Like the chakra system, the subtle bodies have a complex interaction and flow between them. When this is disrupted in some way it can create knock-on effects that may lead to the symptoms of stress and disease. Disruption in a subtle body can be likened to a storm that fails to dissipate and upsets the weather patterns for miles around – an El Niño in the body! The subtle bodies can also be imagined as many layers of glass letting light into a room. Dirt and dust accumulating on one layer will cast shadows on all the others and into the room itself. Crystals can be a very effective tool for removing these energy disruptions.

Subtle bodies are made up of fine energy frequencies so we need some way to detect them and then make accurate assessments of their condition. Using a crystal pendulum is the simplest method, amplifying the body's innate understanding of these subtle fields. Crystal pendulums will also help to restore most imbalances as they are located.

▽ Any crystal can be used for dowsing but it is best to start with a stone that has a broad healing ability such as clear quartz or amethyst.

FIVE-LINE CLEARING

This is a technique that can be used to restore balance to all the subtle bodies. It is not necessary to know what imbalances are being cleared where the pendulum begins to move away from the neutral swing. All subtle bodies interpenetrate and affect each other. An area of imbalance may be at only one level or it may move through many different layers. Simply focus on the pendulum movement and move steadily up the body on each line.

This technique is an excellent way to help others. A clear quartz or amethyst will give the best results because they act on very broad levels, and work as all-purpose healers. Stones such as garnet or lapis lazuli will focus their balancing abilities in more precise ways.

To help you to make the correct movements with the pendulum, imagine five lines running down your partner's body: one in the centre – the midline – and two either side, running parallel. The inner two lines should be within the outline of the body, the outer two lines are just outside the physical body.

1 Put the crystal pendulum into a neutral backwards and forwards swing. With the patient lying down, suspend the pendulum a few centimetres above the body at the midline, in the centre of the body, just below the feet.

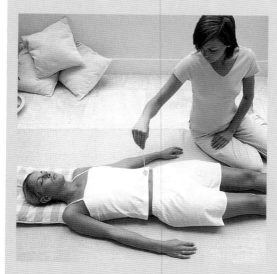

2 Slowly move the swinging pendulum up the midline. Wherever there is a movement away from the neutral swing, stay there until the pendulum returns to normal. Move up the midline until you reach the top of the head.

3 Start the process again, this time moving the pendulum up one side of the body, and then the other. Finally, move the pendulum up the fourth and fifth lines, just to the outside of the physical body.

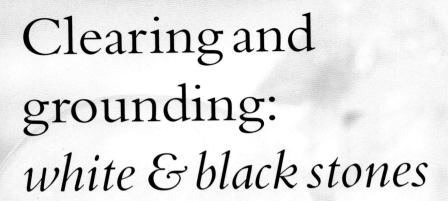

Clearing and grounding:
white & black stones

Stones that are clear or white in colour have the
ability to bring clarity and purity to the aura.
This makes them very useful healing tools.
Black and other dark coloured stones help to
integrate the healing that has taken place so that
we can feel the practical effects of the process.
They help to strengthen and stabilize our
fundamental energies.

Clear quartz – solidified light

Quartz (SiO_2) is the commonest and most widespread mineral in the earth's crust. It is a component of many types of rock and a constituent of many different minerals. The purest variety of quartz is known as rock crystal and has the clarity, transparency and coolness of ice.

Quartz can form as magnificent clusters of crystal, as gigantic single crystals and as massive aggregates. Impurities and inclusions of other minerals give the quartz family the greatest variety of any crystal. Quartz is very weather-resistant and with the erosion of bedrock it finds its way down rivers where it becomes the main component of river and seashore pebbles – as well as of sands and gravels.

△ Clear quartz is completely transparent and colourless except for internal fractures and microscopic bubbles of gas or water that appear as milky areas.

▽ Quartz can form in a huge variety of beautiful clusters, aggregates and single stones.

DIRECTING ENERGY

A single quartz crystal anywhere within the aura will help to bring balance. It often helps to visualize the flow of energy you want and place the quartz appropriately. A quartz point above the head and another between the feet creates a useful flow up or down the body. Points facing downwards have a grounding effect. Points turned upwards give a feeling and quality of expansion. Another method is to hold pointed quartz in your hands. The left hand (in right-handed people) is receptive and absorbing, the right is projecting and energizing. It's the other way round for left-handed people.

1 Hold a quartz point inwards with your absorbing hand and another with its point outwards in your energizing hand to create a flow through the body that balances and clears energy blocks.
2 Change the direction of the crystals after a few minutes and see how you feel.

◁ Transparent, clear crystals have always held immense fascination. To hold solid matter and yet be able to see through it is a truly magical experience.

types of clear quartz

Clear quartz normally grows long six-sided crystals, meeting at a natural point or termination. Opposite the termination, the base of the crystal grows from 'massive quartz', which consists of microscopic crystals, or a bedrock of some other mineral. Quartz with its point towards the body has a tendency to energize, whereas quartz with points away from the body releases or discharges excess or unwanted energy. Large flat crystals called tabular quartz also act as rapid transporters and transmuters of energy. Rough pieces, tumbled and smooth-polished quartz give a less directional, more diffuse effect that can be useful for gently infusing energy at one place.

Some quartz crystal shapes can focus or amplify energy many times above the usual. Laser wands are so called because they have slightly bent sides that narrow significantly towards a small termination. Energy

△ Herkimer diamonds, placed under a pillow at night, can help to encourage lucid dreaming.

entering the base becomes compressed and more energetic as it moves up the crystal towards the tip. These crystals can be powerful healing tools.

Herkimer diamonds

The most brilliant quartz crystals are called Herkimer diamonds. First found in Herkimer County, New York State, USA they are particularly clear and bright. They are powerful cleansers renowned for their ability to enhance subtle perceptions. Herkimer diamonds encourage stabilization and a dynamic exchange of energy.

Clear quartz, of any shape, is very useful in crystal work because it amplifies and increases the harmony of all energies with which it is brought into contact. The coherence of rock crystal strengthens all the energy systems of the body, bringing stability and calmness to the mind. It can also direct energy from one site to another.

THE SEAL OF SOLOMON

One of the simplest and most widely applicable layouts using clear quartz is called the Seal of Solomon. Some stones may need to be taped in place, some may be on and some off the body. This layout can also be used for localized healing – simply repeat the process with crystals placed around the area that you feel needs help.

1 Choose six natural crystals of equal size and arrange them, evenly spaced, in a hexagon shape around the body. Start off with the points facing outwards, this will help to release stresses and imbalances.

2 After a few minutes, turn the crystals round so the points face inwards. This re-energizes the body at every level.

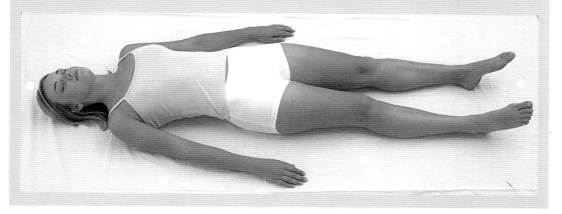

Moonstone and selenite – moonlight and water

Moonstone and selenite each have a soft, luminescent quality and are associated with both moonlight and water because of the way the light plays on their surface.

moonstone

A variety of the common mineral feldspar, moonstone ($KASi_3O_8$) has a soft, lustrous translucence of white, yellow or pink. Moonstone can sometimes have a rich play of colour, in which case it is called rainbow moonstone. In India, moonstone has long been regarded as the perfect gemstone for women. It is well known for easing menstrual cramps and other constrictions

△ Moonstone is recognized by its translucent sheen, no matter what colour it may be.

▽ Selenite is a very soft stone made up of thin layers of gypsum that diffuse the light.

within the female reproductive system – carry a moonstone in your hip pocket to help relieve the symptoms of PMT. It is understood that emotional stress upsets the body's natural fluid balance. Moonstone helps to balance all fluid systems in the body, such as the lymphatic and digestive systems.

Emotional states are linked to the element of water, which is ruled by the moon. This is why the moon's gemstone is able to work so effectively in these areas.

△ Holding a piece of selenite helps to drain any negativity from the body.

Moonstone will gently stabilize all emotional states and help to release any stress and tension. These qualities link moonstone to the sacral chakra, which is a focus for emotional tension. Moonstone also works well at the solar plexus, where emotional stress can disrupt the nervous system and the digestion of food.

MOON NET

To experience the soothing effects of moonstone, choose five pieces of about the same size.

1 Place one moonstone on the front of each hipbone. You may need to tape the stones in place. Place another moonstone on the front in the dip of each shoulder.

2 Place one just touching the top of the head.

3 After a little while there will be a deep relaxation and a soothing energy washing through the body. After five to ten minutes, remove the stones and remain easy for a little while. Creativity and intuition may also be enhanced.

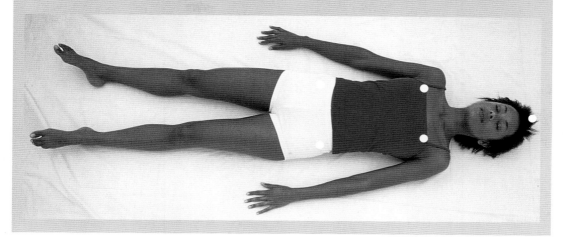

selenite

A clear transparent form of gypsum, selenite ($CaSO_4.2H_2O$) is a very soft mineral easily scratched by a fingernail. Gypsum is so water-sensitive that even a change of humidity can make it bend. The thin layers or stripes visible in selenite create its moon-like luminescence. Such a delicate mineral needs careful care and handling, but it is well worth the effort. Few other crystals have the ability to effortlessly remove unwanted energies from the subtle bodies. Selenite combines the soothing effects of moonstone with the energy shifting properties of crystals with parallel striations (stripes). Whenever there are build-ups of energy, such as inflammation and pain, selenite brings a cooling release.

clearing negativity

Selenite is a very common mineral that crystallizes in long blade-like shapes. Although it can be tumbled and shaped into wands or spheres, it is really so delicate that the finest quality stones should be collector's pieces rather than used in everyday healing.

When a stressful experience seems to be locked into the mind or the emotions, causing continual repetition of the same thoughts or feelings, selenite can be used to break that negative cycle.

Sit quietly for a moment and observe where the energy of the experience seems to be located. Somewhere in the body there will be an unusual sense of heaviness or dullness, or possibly an ache of some kind. Take a few minutes to see how sensations and thoughts revolve around the area. The selenite can now be used to drain the negative energy away. Either place the crystal on that spot and visualize the stone drawing away the source of stress, or hold the selenite in your hands and visualize the negative energy flowing and concentrating into the crystal and then rapidly streaming outwards to a place where it can be of use.

All soft minerals absorb imbalances rapidly and will need good cleaning after use. Do not use water with selenite. Sound or incense smoke cleansing will be effective.

▽ **Moonstone works where there is emotional or physical tension or blocks in energy flow.**

Other white and clear stones

Transparent or clear stones exhibit the qualities of amplifying and clarifying. White stones can show the same characteristics, but they tend to be gentler in their actions. Milky quartz, for example, has the same structure as rock crystal, but the presence of many microscopic air bubbles reflects all light back from the interior. Milky quartz has a gentle energizing and soothing effect that radiates out into its surroundings.

Some agates, particularly Botswana agate, have a high proportion of white or light blue-grey banding. These are created by different sized quartz crystals, impurities and

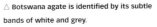

△ Botswana agate is identified by its subtle bands of white and grey.

◁ Milky quartz may seem less attractive than the clear variety but it is equally helpful as a healing tool.

▽ Agate slices show the formation of the crystal as different bands of coloured quartz.

air bubbles. Botswana agate is a gentle cleanser and can be used to good effect where there are feelings of constriction.

diamond

The strength and brilliance of diamond (C_4) has made it the world's most valuable gemstone. Diamonds are octahedral crystals of pure carbon found in many colours as well as clear. Most single diamonds are found in soil deposits along river banks. Large deposits of diamonds, found in hard igneous rock, are rare and difficult to work.

Diamonds were first mined in quantity in South Africa in the 19th century, and South African mines have produced more diamonds than any others throughout history. Most coloured diamonds are used in industry: less than a quarter of all finds are of the completely transparent quality that is required by the gem trade. This means that coloured diamond crystals are reasonably priced, though they are still quite difficult to obtain.

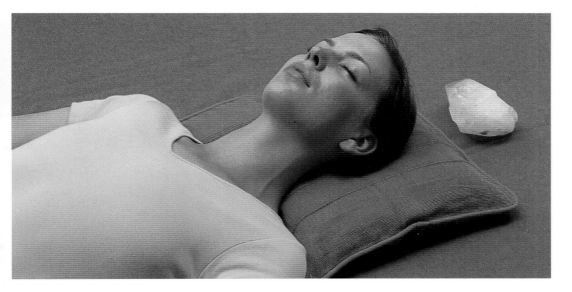

△ Clear stones have a natural affinity with the crown chakra. Both are able to reflect the whole spectrum of energy.

Diamond is primarily an amplifier of energy and is best used to enhance the properties of other stones. It is also a very effective detoxifying stone, effective at removing stagnant and inappropriate energies from the body. Diamond has a natural affinity with the crown chakra and has been found to help realign the bones of the head, the jaw and spine. It can be used to adjust small imbalances in the bones of the skull that may have been created after dental work, for example.

other transparent stones

Most crystals have a natural transparent form though this may be quite rare, as the impurities that enter a crystal lattice only need to be present in minute amounts to create colour. The clear form of any mineral can be used at the crown chakra above the top of the head. Simply placing the stone here will stimulate all the energy bodies and help remove imbalances.

Danburite ($CaB_2Si_2O_8$) is a brilliant clear stone that forms wedge-shaped crystals with parallel striations like those in topaz. It is light and fairly fragile, but is a useful activating and cleansing stone that amplifies and brightens the energies of other stones.

Apophyllite ($KCa_4 Si_8O_{20}(F,OH) . 8H_2O$) has greater brilliance than danburite but is even softer and lighter. The crystals tend to be cube-based or pyramidal with bright shiny surfaces. Apophyllite allows us to become more aware of subtle perceptions and can be an effective meditation crystal, expanding awareness while helping release blocks and stresses. The green variety encourages awareness of levels within nature.

Softer still is calcite ($CaCO_3$), a very common mineral that can sometimes be found as perfectly transparent crystals known as Iceland spar. All calcite is a good remover of stagnant energy and this too can be a useful meditation tool.

▽ Danburite is light and brilliant, amplifying the energy of stones around it.

▽ Apophyllite is mined in Poona, western India. It can be brilliantly clear or translucent green.

▽ Calcite, when perfectly clear, is called Iceland Spar. It commonly forms rhomboidal prisms.

Smoky quartz – the solidifier

Smoky quartz (SiO_2) ranges from a light golden brown to deep black. Even when it is very dark, smoky quartz nearly always remains translucent. The colour is thought to be derived from natural sources of radioactivity close to where the crystals are formed. Smoky quartz carries the same basic energy as clear quartz but absorbs and stores it rather than radiating it. This gives the crystal a quietening and calming quality that makes it a help in focusing energy internally. The absorbing quality of smoky quartz makes it an excellent stone for meditation as it stabilizes the body and mind.

▷ **Smoky quartz is much less common than the clear, milky, or gem-quality varieties.**

TO BRING CALM

Smoky quartz, with its quiet, calming energy is an effective grounding stone. As it draws energy towards itself it can remove imbalances from the subtle energy bodies, gently dissolving and transmuting negativity. This simple stone placement will help to collect all sorts of scattered and confused energies. It helps bring emotional calm and clarity of mind and allows any overabundance of energy to flow out into the earth.

1 Use two smoky quartz crystals. If possible use crystals that have natural points (terminations). This helps to move the energy in the most appropriate direction. Place one with its point down the body at the base of the throat where the collarbones meet the breastbone.

2 Place the other with its point downwards between the legs, either between the knees or between the feet. Stay like this for five minutes or until you feel fully grounded.

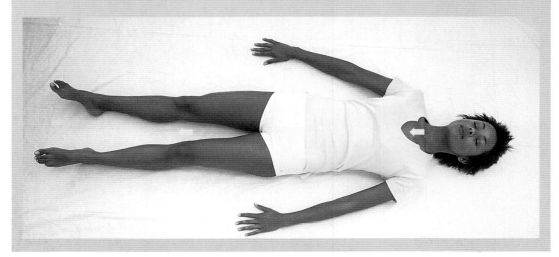

GROUNDING STONES

The placement of a grounding stone during and after a crystal healing session, or holding one in your hand, really helps to integrate the changes into the physical body. Without proper grounding any benefits may disappear as soon as normal activity resumes. Grounding stones can be placed at any of the following locations:

1 At groin points on the front of the hips
2 At or near the base of the spine
3 Between the legs
4 By the insides of the knees
5 Between the feet
6 Below each foot

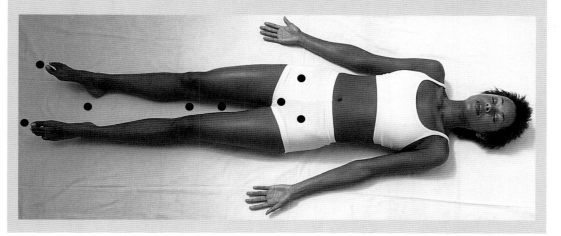

achieving stability

Balance in life is essential. Outward, dynamic change needs to be countered by stability, focus and centredness. As most healing work is concerned with the removal of inappropriate energy it tends to initiate deep levels of energy adjustment throughout many subtle systems of the body. Any rearrangement of energy, no matter how beneficial eventually, can create turbulence in everyday life, bringing confusion, emotional instability and lack of focus. To avoid this discomfort, healers take care to emphasize grounding and centring techniques to act as an anchor, stabilizing and balancing the changes that healing creates. Grounding ensures a firm contact with the energies of the planet so that excess energy can be conducted away from the body. It focuses on the present moment, practicality and connectedness to reality.

Being centred suggests that the focus of awareness is balanced within the whole body – rather than just being in the head. There is awareness of the world outside, yet there is no confusion or distraction. It is not possible to be grounded effectively without being centred, and it is not possible to be centred unless our energies are grounded.

The first chakra at the base of the spine is concerned with centring and grounding. Techniques that direct energy and attention to this point and to points on the legs and feet are naturally grounding. Red, brown and black stones all help in directing and stabilizing energy in the body.

◁ Confusion and anxiety can be rapidly reduced by holding a grounding stone.

▷ Red stones can also help to achieve stability, and can be used with black stones for grounding.

Black tourmaline – alignment

Extremely useful for protecting and grounding personal energy, tourmaline $(Na(Mg,Fe,Li,Mn,Al)_3Al_6(BO_3)_3Si_6O_{18}(OH, F)_4)$ can be found in nearly every colour and the same crystal will often contain several different colours. Black tourmaline is known as schorl. It is easy to recognize with its long, thin striated sides with three

▷ Tourmaline commonly crystallizes alongside quartz and often interpenetrates it. Tourmaline quartz (or tourmalated quartz) combines the qualities of both stones, clearing and grounding, energizing and protecting.

EARTH NET

A strong energy connection to the earth is a prerequisite for effective grounding and protective support. An energy net using eight black tourmalines can be used to reinforce this support, and can be particularly useful after moving house or travelling. Indeed, there have been reports that black tourmaline can reduce the effects of jetlag. One of the effects of tourmaline particularly emphasized in this layout is the ability to help the bones realign themselves. Tensions in bone and muscle are relaxed and physical balance improves. Tinnitus, the continuous ringing of the ears, has many causes, but misaligned skull bones can add to the problem. Wearing tourmaline earrings has been found to help this.

1 Use a green cloth as a background to lie on, or a white sheet for second choice. If possible arrange it so that your head will be to the north.
2 Put four tourmalines pointing inwards in a cross – one above the head, one between the feet and the others at either side, midway down the body.
3 Place the remaining four tourmalines just to the right of the others at an angle of about 20 degrees, so all are aligned to the same imaginary point in the centre of the body.
4 Remain in the energy net for five to ten minutes, then when you have removed the crystals spend at least 15 minutes resting before returning to normal activity.

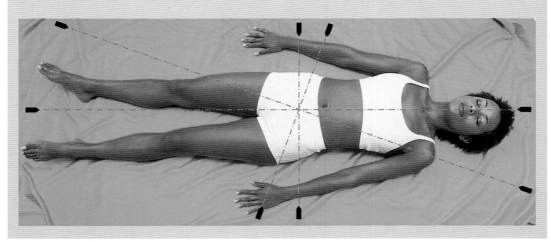

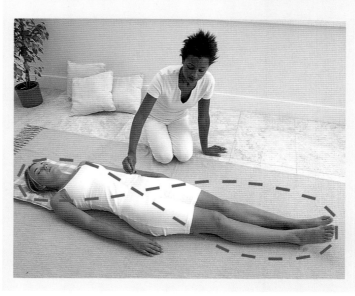

◁ Far left: tourmaline earrings can help in a wide range of situations, protecting the energy of the wearer. Tourmaline is thought to be able to help ease the symptoms of tinnitus.

◁ After using crystals for a healing session they should always be cleaned. Place tourmalines in a bowl of fresh water and leave for 2–3 hours.

faces giving it a triangular cross-section. When tourmaline is heated, it produces a positive electrical charge at one end and a negative charge at the other, making it a useful switching device in a lot of heat sensitive equipment.

energy focus

As a grounding stone, black tourmaline can be used whenever energies are scattered and confused. It will very quickly bring the awareness back to the present moment. Because of this, the stone gives strong protection against negativity of all sorts. A negative influence is anything that superimposes itself and overrides the individual's own energy field to create imbalance. A crystal that reinforces personal energy will help against these disruptive effects. Black tourmaline deflects negativity back into the earth, rather than absorbing the energy into itself, where it would accumulate and interfere with its efficiency.

TOURMALINE CIRCUIT

Crystals that have parallel striations running along their lengths tend to be very good at moving energy from one place to another, releasing blocks and tensions in the body. Sometimes the same problem resurfaces many times because a hidden, underlying block prevents effective healing. A pattern of black tourmaline crystals can clear away these deep levels of imbalance. Some stones in the pattern will be on the torso and hips, others will be put next to the head, shoulders, legs and feet. The number of crystals available to you will limit how and where they can be placed. Use dark tourmaline crystals – either black or very dark green. Alternatively, use smoky quartz.

1 Place the stones, all pointing in the same direction, in a figure of eight over and around your partner's body.

2 Emphasize the flow by tracing over the pattern with your hand, while holding another crystal.

3 After a few minutes within the pattern, remove the stones. Use another grounding stone to settle the energies before ending the session.

Obsidian – delving deep

Obsidian is volcanic glass that solidifies so rapidly from lava that it does not have time to form crystals. Although non-crystalline, obsidian often contains very small crystals of other minerals, particularly quartz, feldspar and iron compounds. These microcrystals can create variations of colour and lustre as light is reflected off them. The random scattering of light rays makes most obsidian black in appearance. Clusters of feldspar crystals create white or grey patches in snowflake obsidian. Iron minerals give the red-brown colour to mahogany obsidian, while densely packed crystals create a rainbow lustre or iridescence.

Obsidian is an effective grounding stone, but its most useful attribute is the ability to draw hidden imbalances to the surface and

▷ **Obsidian is black volcanic glass – ideal for transforming energy patterns.**

OBSIDIAN NET

This particular obsidian layout will allow the energies needed for cleansing and transformation to be gently integrated into the subtle bodies. Repeating this procedure regularly will bring about significant changes. You will need five obsidians and a red or black cloth to lie on.

1 Place one obsidian above the top of the head; two level with the neck/shoulder area; and two at the feet.
2 Lie within the net for three or four minutes. Then take as much time as you need before resuming normal activity, and sip a little water to help integration.

HOW TO SCRY

You will need an obsidian sphere (the size of the sphere does not matter), a black or dark-coloured cloth and a candle. The surface and structure of obsidian quietens normal thought processes, enabling the scryer temporarily to leave behind the rules of time and space. Set your obsidian sphere at a comfortable viewing distance from you. Surrounding the back of the stone with a dark cloth will help to prevent visual distractions.

Make sure that there are no reflections to distract you – dim light is best – such as the light of a single candle. Scrying involves all the senses, so don't expect to see visual imagery in the ball.

1 Gaze steadily at the sphere, without strain, looking through the stone as if it were a window.

2 Frame a clear intention of what it is you wish to discover, then relax. You will feel the answer as a thought rather than an image.

△ Sipping a little water after any crystal healing will help to integrate the effects and ground and centre your energies.

release them. This needs to be done with some care as most hidden things are buried because they are uncomfortable to face. There are times when outdated patterns need to be broken to release the energy that is being wasted in supporting them. Obsidian is ideal when a transformation is needed, bringing fiery energy from deep within the earth to purify and cleanse.

scrying

Obsidian was one of the traditional materials used for scrying – seeing into the future. Scrying, or crystal gazing, is a worldwide practice that is used to reveal all sorts of information unknown to the conscious mind of the scryer. It has been known to reveal the causes and cures of illness, to explore and communicate with the spirit worlds and to foretell future events or disclose the truth of the past.

Other black stones

Black stones have a solidifying and grounding effect on the human energy system. They increase our awareness of immediate reality and physicality.

haematite

This stone is a very common oxide of iron (Fe_2O_3). Large crystalline masses of haematite have an attractive silver sheen and are often cut for use in jewellery, though the stone is very brittle. Haematite is the main source of iron for industry, but there is also a soft variety formed in sedimentary rocks known as red ochre. This is the most ancient of precious materials, regarded the world over as a symbol of life-energy – the blood of the earth – and it is much sought after as a pigment.

Haematite is an energizer of the physical body but its primary use is as a grounding stone. Wearing or holding a piece of haematite will bring most people's awareness back to the body and the present almost instantly. Some individuals, however, find

▽ **Haematite is one of the most effective grounding stones available.**

RESTORING NATURAL BALANCE
We live in a very intense, artificially created electromagnetic environment. Treatment with a pendulum of lodestone or magnetite ensures that we do not suffer from the ill effects of strong electric fields. It is particularly useful for people who are over-sensitive to chemicals, who work with computers or other sources of electrical equipment or who are easily fatigued. Place a magnetite crystal or lodestone pendulum within a silver spiral on a length of cord or chain. Hold the stone a few centimetres above the body, and the pendulum will begin to rotate wherever there is an electromagnetic stress in the energy field. Hold the pendulum still until the rotation stops. The imbalance has now been removed.

Carrying a grounding stone will also help to prevent the unwanted accumulation of electromagnetic resonance. Holding the hands under cold running water, having a shower, wearing natural cloth and standing on the earth with bare feet are other ways of restoring natural balance.

▽ **A lodestone pendulum will rotate when it approaches electromagnetic imbalances.**

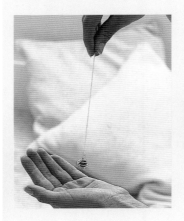

▽ **A build-up of electromagnetic stress can be dissipated by running water.**

that haematite has too energizing an effect and will need some less potent stone to ground them effectively.

magnetite and lodestone

Another iron ore, magnetite (Fe_3O_4) has the highest proportion of iron to be found in any mineral, making it very important commercially. Magnetite forms metallic grey octahedral crystals. Lodestone is the name given to the magnetic iron ore in its massive (microcrystalline) form. Lodestone and magnetite are extremely useful healing tools. They can align the chakras and subtle bodies allowing rapid release of stress and tension.

Because of their composition (iron and oxygen) and because they have a strong magnetic field, magnetite and lodestone both help to align us with the earth's own electromagnetic fields. This has a very

▽ An octahedral crystal of magnetite (far left) with a piece of lodestone within a spring spiral ready for pendulum use.

△ Jet is found washed up on shorelines after it has been dislodged from ancient seabeds.

grounding effect and brings an increased sense of belonging and security. The many energies along the spine can be strengthened by placing a small lodestone near the base chakra and another at the base of the skull. When you are healing someone, move a single stone slowly along their back a few centimetres above the spine. Take time to hold the stone still over areas that feel particularly sensitive or are uncomfortable.

jet

Like coal, jet is fossilized wood. Jet is formed when ancient waterlogged wood is compacted by vast pressure below the sea. It is found in several parts of the world. Like amber, jet produces static electricity when rubbed. This lightweight dark brown or black shiny gemstone exhibits grounding properties associated with its colour and the supportive, balancing qualities of the original source, trees. Valued for its protecting and comforting qualities in the 19th century, it was worn during mourning.

USING JET TO ENERGIZE THE CHAKRAS

Jet placed by the lower spine energizes the base chakra. When placed higher up the body it can draw energy from the base into those areas. Jet is valuable in chakra balancing, particularly if the upper chakras are under-energized when compared to the lower centres. Indications of this sort of imbalance are: plenty of energy and drive, but inability to use it creatively; confusion; frustration.

1 Place grounding stones under the feet and between the legs. At the groin points, use two black or red stones to stabilize the base chakra.
2 Place jet on under-energized areas and check after a few minutes if the balance is better.
3 Repeating this regularly for five minutes at a time will help to alleviate imbalance.

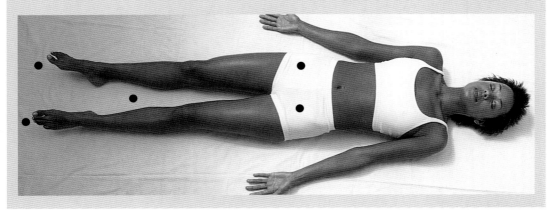

Energizing and organizing: *red, orange & yellow stones*

Crystals from the warm end of the colour spectrum help to balance the first three chakras and release pent-up energy in the heart chakra. Stability, creativity and clear thinking, as well as the flow of life-energy through the physical body, can all be enhanced with their help.

Garnet – stone of fire

A large and chemically diverse group of silicate minerals, garnets come in a variety of colours, a rich wine-red being the most familiar. All stones of this colour used to be known as carbuncles, from the Latin *carbunculus* meaning small, red-hot coal.

Garnets form at very high temperatures in many different rocks, often in those altered by close proximity to volcanic activity. As it is a hard mineral, garnet survives erosion and is found in riverbeds and gravels. Its hardness and durability makes garnet ideal for abrasives and polishing.

There are many green, orange and brown garnets but the red varieties are the most useful in crystal healing work. Garnet is the finest energizing stone for the body. Especially when cut, it can amplify and energize the properties of other stones. Cut faceted stones of most crystals increase the liveliness of the stone and can act like a lens, focusing light with more intensity.

The fiery garnet can be placed wherever a lack of energy exists. It can act as a 'starter motor' for the body's repair mechanisms, so

▽ Tumbled garnets can be so dark as almost to show no colour, but the dense weight gives a clue to their identity.

very often garnet needs to be in place for just a short while to do its work. Where there is an area of underactive or stagnant energy, place a garnet at the centre of the body and surround it with four clear quartz crystals, points facing outwards, to help increase energy and distribute it.

△ The name garnet derives from the Greek word for pomegranate. The small, bright red crystals resemble the seeds of that fruit.

▽ A garnet surrounded by clear quartz points, with points facing outwards, will rebalance a 'cool' spot in the aura.

BODY SCANNING

Identifying areas of poor energy flow is a useful skill to learn. It relies upon the healer's sensitivity to slight changes in the patient's aura. Everyone will have different ways of registering energy changes, so just be attentive. Low energy can often feel like a dip, hollow or emptiness in the aura. It may feel cool or somehow 'wrong'. You may sense the difference in your hand or arm or be struck by an intuitive thought or emotional impression. If you are not sure of your assessment, just repeat the body scan a few more times. Even without consciously registering it, the body scan will give you enough information at deeper levels of the mind to place healing stones appropriately. Learn to trust your intuition. Using grounding stones will help reduce any doubt.

1 First sensitize your hands by rubbing them together or rolling a clear quartz crystal between your palms. Now bring your palms together slowly from a distance, and you should feel a tingling or a pressure as your hands come closer together. Gently 'bouncing' the space between your palms helps to build up your energy aura and your sensitivity to other energy fields.

2 Starting from near the feet and moving upwards, use one hand to slowly sweep a few centimetres above the patient's body. Your intention is to locate areas of blocked energy or under-energy. Simply move your hand through the aura and be open to any changes you may feel.

3 Where you have identified low energy, place a red, orange or yellow stone, whichever feels most appropriate, for a few minutes. Then, remove the stones and repeat the body scan. There should now be an improvement in the energy field. If a few areas of imbalance remain make a note of them and then repeat the process after a few days.

▽ Before beginning any kind of scan, sensitize your own hands, and centre and ground your energies.

▽ To increase your sensitivity in a scan, hold a clear quartz crystal in your scanning hand.

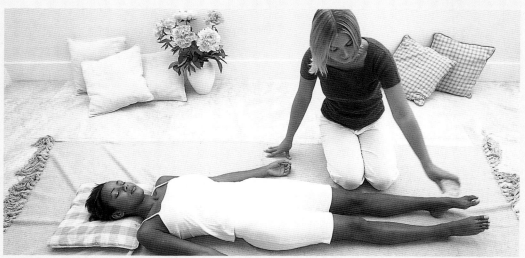

Ruby – motivation and action

Ruby is the red variety of the very hard mineral corundum (aluminium oxide, Al_2O_3), which takes its colour from traces of chromium and forms characteristic barrel-shaped crystals. Ruby has a long history of use as a gemstone, though until recently, because of its hardness, the stone was not faceted but was always polished into a domed, cabochon shape. In Ayurvedic Indian healing traditions ruby is the stone of the sun.

the heart

As the sun is the centre of the solar system so the heart is the centre of the physical body. Ruby balances the heart, enhancing its function and the circulation of the blood and improving the quality of thought and feeling associated with the heart – confidence, security, self-esteem and our relationship with others. Ruby acts by energizing us at the very centre of our being. It balances by reminding us of the

△ Ruby has a hexagonal cross-section and usually forms barrel-shaped crystals.

◁ Polished ruby shows metal-like striations across its surface. Only the finest gem-quality rubies are translucent and deep red.

vast reservoirs of energy within us that can enable us to succeed in any venture where we have full trust in our own abilities.

Red is the energy of gravity, pulling things together and establishing reality. Red is also the colour relating to the creation of matter and its manifestation. So it makes sense that a red stone such as ruby can help us to achieve our goals, particularly as ruby has such a connection with the heart, the seat of our desires.

RELEASING THE HEART'S POTENTIAL

This net will help release pent-up energy in the heart, remove guilt and unworthiness, and reveal your true strengths and potential. If possible have a white sheet to lie on, this encourages a gentle cleansing of negative emotions. Place a small ruby crystal at the heart chakra in the middle of the chest. Place 12 clear quartz crystals, points outwards, equally spaced around the body. Lie in the net for about five minutes.

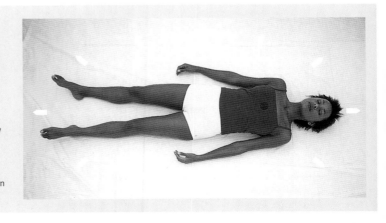

▷ **A ruby that has been polished into a traditional cabochon shape.**

Often in life the heart suffers pain because we feel unable to fulfil our wishes or desires. After pain such as this we often create barriers in an attempt to prevent future hurt. Unfortunately, what this really does is just separates us further from the source of our own power and courage.

Crystal healing techniques are ideal to help us solve such long-standing difficulties and barriers in our lives. Regular practice for five or ten minutes once or twice a week will begin to bring about positive change without having to revisit, and perhaps open, old wounds. In a situation where there is a loss of personal power, taking the initiative to help yourself is very important.

SUN NET

When there is a fear of failure, the heart, whose natural energy needs to expand outwards and experience life, becomes restricted. Then there is a lack of security, which comes from having lost the sense of being centred in the self. This happens at a mental and emotional level, but can also manifest in physical symptoms such as poor circulation, cold hands and feet and other upsets to the temperature regulation of the body. Ruby can be an ideal healing stone in these circumstances. To amplify and integrate the energy of the sun net lie on a yellow cloth.

This net will be gently energizing, bringing focus and clarity to the mind and emotions. It can be useful to help regulate the circulatory system and usually produces a gentle warming sensation. Use six small ruby crystals – stones that are not of gem quality are inexpensive and fine to use.
1 Place one ruby crystal above the head and one below the feet in the middle.
2 Place one ruby crystal next to each arm and one next to each knee so that the six stones are all evenly spaced around the body. Stay in this position for five to ten minutes.

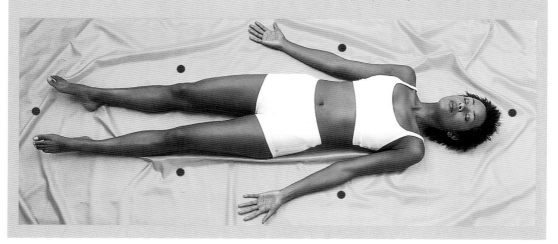

Other red stones

Every red stone will give an energizing, activating and warming quality. Differences of crystal shape, quality of colour and chemical composition will affect the way each stone is experienced.

red jasper

This stone is actually a form of quartz (SiO_2) that crystallizes from hot solutions and is changed several times by reheating. This process produces a wide range of internal colour and patterning that makes jasper a valuable gemstone. Unlike other microcrystalline quartzes, jasper has a strong permanent colour created by iron minerals.

As an opaque, massive variety of quartz, red jasper focuses on solidity and grounding. It is an ideal stone to balance the base chakra. Jasper will always emphasize practical, down-to-earth solutions, which, like each piece of the stone, are unique to the individual. Jasper can also be coloured by impurities that turn it yellow and green.

▽ Red coral helps to balance the base chakra, regulating physical strength, and the skeletal and circulatory systems.

△ Each piece of jasper is unique in its patterning and colour. Fractures in older crystals are refilled with quartz of a slightly different colour.

red coral

The earth's surviving natural growths of red coral ($CaCO_3$) are now largely protected from exploitation but this strikingly coloured organic secretion, the home of colonies of tiny sea creatures, has long been regarded as a precious gemstone. In Ayurvedic tradition red coral is the best stone for the energies of the planet Mars. In Asia and America turquoise and red coral have been put together in wonderful designs for ceremonial and decorative jewellery. Old red coral beads can still be found, though imitations are very common.

Coral primarily acts as a balance for the emotions – its watery origins suggest this function – and it will work well for the maintenance of energy levels, enthusiasm and practicality.

fire opal

Opal ($SiO_2.nH_2O$) forms when hot silica-rich solutions fill the crevices of sedimentary rock. It is quartz with a high water content. All opals work well to balance the emotions. Fire opal is a deep orange-red, due to iron and manganese, which suggests a warming, activating quality. It is useful in emotional situations where there has been exhaustion, withdrawal and 'switching off'.

spinel

Iron and chromium impurities often give spinel ($MgAl_2O_4$) a deep ruby red coloration. Many of the famous larger 'rubies' of the world are, in fact, spinels. Spinels commonly form spiky octahedral crystals, which give them their name – 'little thorns' in Italian. The brown or orange-red varieties encourage the energizing properties of the base chakra. Spinel may also help with detoxification as its red energy will focus on powerfully cleansing energy blocks.

zircon

With a relatively recent history of use in jewellery making, zircon ($ZrSiO_4$) has clear varieties that can be cut and polished to the

◁ Red coral is useful for balancing the emotions and for maintaining enthusiasm.

▽ Like many red crystals, red calcite takes its colour from iron atoms in the surrounding rock. It has a smooth, energizing effect.

brilliance of diamond. The yellow-red variety is traditionally known as 'jacinth' or 'hyacinth' and has always been popular in the Far East. Today zircon is important for its constituent, the rare metal zirconium – a hard, heat-resistant metal that is used in industry as an anticorrosive and abrasive.

As a healing stone, zircon exhibits some of the useful spiritual properties of red stones. Like red crystals, such as red calcite, red zircon warms the subtle bodies, helping to prevent the stagnant conditions of listlessness, melancholy and depression. Zircon can also help to ground and clarify spiritual experiences and will ease any tensions that may have arisen in the mind from psychic or visionary experiences. Zircon reminds us that vibrations of red energy are needed to maintain stability at all levels. Red energy provides fuel for our mental, emotional and physical wellbeing.

▽ Fire opal is one of the less common varieties. It is unmistakable, with a dense orange-red glow.

▽ Spinel usually forms small crystals with a characteristic double pyramid shape.

▽ Zircon crystals have a dull, red, metallic lustre and usually have clearly defined faces.

Rose quartz – healing the emotions

Rose quartz (SiO_2) is an important crystal for removing blocked emotional stress. It is generally considered to encourage love and harmony. It is true that the vibration of pink does reduce aggression and promote understanding and empathy, but it is a mistake to think that because of this wearing a rose quartz will make you feel happier.

emotional release

If there is suppression of barely controlled emotions, rose quartz will quite likely stir up a lot of turbulence. In such circumstances – and the majority of us have significant amounts of unresolved emotional stress – rose quartz can act like a safety valve, allowing a sudden release of emotional

▽ Emotions are complex and many layered things. You may need to use a variety of different stones to effectively release emotional stresses.

pressure. This can be an uncomfortable experience without understanding and guidance, and a little self-defeating if it creates further anxiety.

The guideline with rose quartz, as it should be with every crystal, is to explore the stone carefully and, if discomfort arises, change the approach. Our bodies are usually quite willing to correct imbalances gently, as long as they are provided with an appropriate stimulus. Stressful events tend to get frozen into repeating time-loops of memory in the body's muscles, as well as in the mind and emotional responses. Crystal healing is one of the most effective ways of allowing this trapped energy to release safely.

Emotional stress can become locked in any part of the body, and where it settles tension develops, restricting the local flow of energy. Starved of life-energy, these blocked areas become more susceptible to

CALMING THE EMOTIONS

The heart chakra is the centre of many of the body's energies and this is where we feel emotional hurt. This simple layout of stones will relax and ease any unexpected emotional upsets. It is also beneficial when used on a regular basis to prevent stress building up.

1 Place a small piece of rose quartz on the heart chakra in the centre of the chest.
2 Surround the rose quartz with four clear quartz crystals with points initially facing outwards. This will help to release stress.
3 Place a pointed citrine or smoky quartz over the second chakra below the navel, with its point downwards. This will have a gentle grounding and stabilizing effect and will also help to release any of the more long-term stresses that might be lodged in this centre.
4 Place an amethyst quartz crystal in the centre of the forehead. This will help to calm the mind and will encourage a degree of mental detachment from any emotional recall.

Lie in this calming layout for five to ten minutes or until you become aware of a feeling of relaxation and balance.

STRESS RELEASE POINTS

For the rapid, safe release of particular stresses, place small rose quartz stones on the slightly raised bumps to the sides of the forehead. You may need to tape the stones in place. Remembering the stressful event will begin the release process, which will be complete when you feel a change of emotion or a return of equilibrium. Placing a grounding stone by the feet and a balancing stone at the heart or solar plexus chakra may also help.

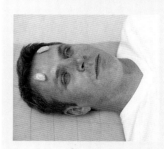

△ Rose quartz is useful to reduce any build-up of emotional stress and tension, and is also felt to encourage love and harmony.

▷ Keeping some rose quartz at your bedside can sometimes be effective as an aid to restful sleep.

illness. When the illness then causes pain and discomfort, the problem can be made worse by anger, irritation or disgust directed by the suffering person at their own affliction, as well as the draining emotions of fear, self-doubt and denial.

Local pain and inflammation can respond well to the placement of rose quartz as it calms and restores life-energy to the area. The addition of clear quartz points around the rose quartz, points directed away from the area, will also help remove imbalances.

Rhodonite and rhodocrosite – clearing and balancing

Two minerals rich in manganese form crystals of a beautiful pink. Rhodonite and rhodocrosite are both valuable in helping to bring balance to the emotions.

rhodonite

Named at the beginning of the 19th century after its colour – a rich rose pink – rhodonite $((Mn^{+2},Fe^{+2},Mg,Ca)SiO_3)$ is a hard, massive mineral, important in industry for its high manganese content. Rhodonite has become a popular semi-precious stone, especially the deep pink pieces patterned with dark brown or black oxides. It is cut as cabochons and carved into decorative ornaments.

Where the soft shades of translucent rose quartz may seem too gentle or soft, the balance of colours within rhodonite suggests a more robust and energetic character. The deep pink to magenta colours reflect the practical, down-to-earth vibration of caring

▽ **Rhodonite combines the pink of emotional balance with the red and brown of a practical approach to life.**

for oneself, having confidence and a sense of self-worth while remaining aware of the needs of others. The black or brown veins and patterns anchor rhodonite's energy into the solidity of the base chakra and through that to the earth itself. Because of its combination of colours, rhodonite works well at the base and sacral chakras. In emotional healing situations it complements and stabilizes the release initiated by rose quartz. Rhodonite will restore a sense of equilibrium without stifling the release processes that are underway. Always remember that grounding stones will quickly restore balance to a volatile emotional state.

Rhodonite can help to remove doubts about self-worth that prevent us from striving to achieve desired goals in life. A great deal of stress is created when personal ambitions are restrained or diverted. The entire structure of an individual's life energy can become distorted, leading to resentment, anger and aggression that may seem to have no apparent cause. Where

△ **Wearing a pendant of rhodocrosite can help to encourage a more positive view of oneself.**

these emotions are present rhodonite will help to divert the build-up of energy in positive and safe directions. Rhodonite used as a pendulum, wand or body sweep will identify the main areas of tension. Combined with blue stones, rhodonite will help us to find a way of achieving our ambitions.

rhodocrosite

This stone can sometimes be mistaken for its close relation rhodonite. Both are manganese ores, but rhodocrosite $(MnCO_3)$ often has additions of calcium, magnesium and iron. Whereas rhodonite is granular and opaque, rhodocrosite can be transparent or, more commonly, translucent. It usually forms in banded zones of pink, red, peach

▷ Rhodocrosite crystallizes in shaded bands of pink, cream and peach. Large crystals form translucent deep salmon-pink rhomboids.

and cream. Such a coloration lets rhodocrosite work on the base, sacral and solar plexus chakras, helping to blend their energies particularly where there is disruption due to emotional stress.

Poor self-worth and lack of self-confidence can manifest as problems in the digestive and reproductive systems. Anxiety creates tension in the stomach and pelvic areas, which can interfere with normal functioning. Particularly where there are emotional issues revolving around sexuality and fertility, rhodocrosite can help to ease negative perceptions.

In situations where there may be fear for one's safety, whether it is real or imagined, wearing a deep pink stone will help to reduce any anxiety and tension that themselves may create inappropriate reactions to those around you. Breathing through the stone, visualizing pink light around you, and allowing tensions to drain through the soles of the feet all help to achieve equanimity.

▽ Rhodonite or rhodocrosite can help to identify areas of emotional tension.

STRESS RELEASE THROUGH BREATHING

Where obvious tension exists in the body, focusing the healing energy of pink light can help you to relax at a deep level. Use any kind of pink stone for this.

1 Place the stone on or near the area. Take a moment to let the awareness centre on that part of the body.

2 Now as you take a slow breath in, imagine that the air is focusing directly through the pink stone and right into the centre of the tension. Coloured by the pink stone, your breath will slowly begin to dissolve the pain and sorrow hidden there.

3 Each time you breathe out, feel the tensions melt and relax. Continue this for a minute or two, then lie quietly.

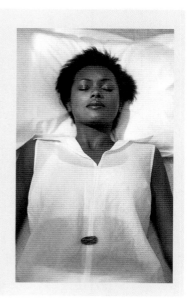

Other pink stones

If ever there is any doubt about which crystal will resolve an imbalance, consider using a pink stone of some kind. This will always allow deep healing to take place. Pink stones not only help to clear emotional stress, they can also be powerfully protective, expressing as they do the energy of unconditional or universal love, perhaps more accurately called compassion. This quality of non-judgemental, unequivocal understanding and acceptance is a result of deep experience of the underlying unity of life. When this unity is felt there can be no fear, and without fear, aggression melts away.

kunzite

A pink variety of the mineral spodumene, (the green form of spodumene is hiddenite) kunzite ($LiAlSi_2O_6$) is coloured by manganese. Kunzite can be identified by the parallel striations that run the length of the crystal and by the fact that the colour is more intense when viewed down the cross section of its main axis. Gem-quality kunzite can be transparent and clear, while low-grade stones when tumbled are opaque lavender-pink. Kunzite is an excellent protector of the heart chakra and of the integrity of the emotions. Emotional energy is such a powerful force that sensitive people

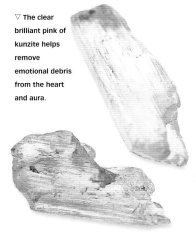

▽ **The clear brilliant pink of kunzite helps remove emotional debris from the heart and aura.**

WAYS TO RELEASE NEGATIVITY

When you feel that you have acquired an uncomfortable or intrusive energy from outside yourself, or even if you are finding it difficult to let go of a certain emotional state, you can use kunzite to release negativity. In both these methods, the discordant energy becomes neutralized and harmless on passing through the crystalline structure of the 'exit' crystal. Make sure that all the stones you use are well cleansed before and after use to help them maintain their efficiency.

1 Sit quietly and simply observe the energy patterns you wish to get rid of. Then take a kunzite crystal in both hands and imagine all the unwanted energy, thoughts or emotions are draining out of your body through the stone as if it were a stream of water.

2 A variation of this can be to hold a kunzite or clear quartz in your left hand and another in your right hand. Visualize cleansing energy entering through the left and sweeping away unwanted energy through the right.

This layout can be used when there is a feeling of energies 'stuck' within the personal aura. Emotions or memories may be repeating in an obsessive loop, or there may be a 'bad taste' from an unpleasant experience that you want to dispel.
1 Place a smoky quartz or a piece of kunzite between your feet pointing down and away from your body. Place a clear quartz or kunzite above the crown of the head pointing inwards. A third kunzite can be placed on the area where the negativity is most clearly felt.
2 Alternatively place the kunzite at each chakra point for a minute or two, starting with the brow and moving down the body to the sacral chakra.

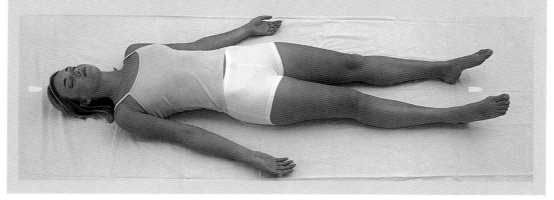

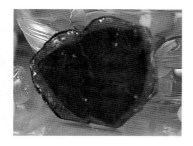

△ Rubellite is red tourmaline and is one of the most attractive of pink crystals.

▽ Lepidolite, or lithium mica, is a sparkly pink stone often found with rubellite embedded within it. It can support self-confidence and the clearing of emotional debris such as guilt.

can unwittingly pick up emotional debris from others. This can lead to unexpected mood swings and out-of-character behaviour. Placing or wearing a piece of kunzite by the heart for a while can help to sweep away this kind of negativity and any unwanted energy. Kunzite can be used as a release from any powerfully charged experience – such as a film, a song that gets stuck in the mind, or a hurtful remark.

If simply wearing a piece of kunzite is not sufficient, reinforce your intention with your imagination. This can be done in several ways, depending on what stones are available.

rubellite

One of the most beautiful pink crystals is red tourmaline, also called rubellite. Its colour ranges from a delicate pink to a rhubarb red. Usually the crystals are translucent, but occasionally they can be very dense and almost opaque.

With all types of tourmaline the density of colour changes slightly depending on the angle of view. This is caused by light rays becoming polarized as they pass through the crystal lattice. Like kunzite, rubellite has parallel striations along its length, which help it to act as an energy conduit. It also

△ The complex makeup of tourmaline means that it can contain many colours within a single crystal. 'Watermelon' combines red and green, a perfect heart chakra balancer.

has great strengthening and protecting effects on the heart chakra. Rubellite provides an excellent way to balance the emotions when there is either too much aggression (caused by fear or nervous irritation from external or internal imbalances) or too much passivity (caused by a poor level of self-esteem). Rubellite is sometimes found embedded in lepidolite, a stone which shares its qualities.

Often tourmaline combines shades of both red and green. This complex variety is called 'watermelon' tourmaline, and it holds the best combination of colours to balance the heart chakra and the emotions.

Carnelian and rutilated quartz – healing the wounds

Orange stones can often be effective repairers of the body, encouraging a rapid release of stress. Carnelian and rutilated quartz both encourage the body's own powers of regeneration.

carnelian

A variety of chalcedony, carnelian (SiO_2) is a microcrystalline quartz formed from the dissolving of other minerals containing silicates. Chalcedony does not have the crystalline lattice usually found in quartz. Instead, it is made up of closely packed fibres arranged in concentric layers or parallel bands. This stone gets its warm colour from the presence of iron oxides. It is often translucent, showing colours ranging from pale orange to a deep orange-red. As iron is a very common metal in the earth's crust, carnelian is found around the world. The

▷ **Carnelian is a warming stone that links well to the creative energy of the sacral chakra.**

ENERGY NET FOR HEALING THE ETHERIC BODY

Use this net regularly for five minutes at a time to help release trauma from deep in the body. It may sometimes bring old symptoms or pain to the surface before they can be completely removed. You will need six tumbled carnelians and an orange cloth to lie on.

1 Place one carnelian at the top of the head and one at either side of the body at the level of sacral chakra.

2 Place another stone between the legs at mid-calf level and another below it near the ankles. Place the sixth stone at the base of the throat.

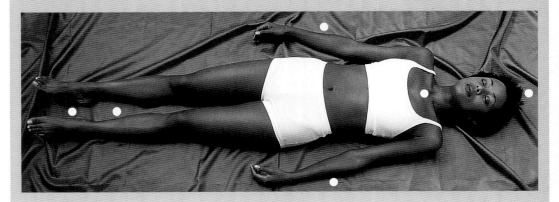

finest examples are used in jewellery – gem quality stones are traditionally known as 'sard'. Carnelian is one of the most useful stones for healing the etheric body when trauma and stress have accumulated to disturb physical functioning. Most will experience carnelian as a gentle soothing energy, though in some circumstances where it feels uncomfortable, the addition of some cooling green or blue stones may help.

rutilated quartz

This is clear or smoky quartz that contains fine thread-like crystals of rutile, titanium dioxide (TiO_2). Rutile is a metallic, needle-shaped crystal that can have a remarkable deep red colour. In quartz it is usually straw coloured – a lustrous gold to golden brown. Titanium is a non-corroding, extremely strong and light metal so it is no surprise that rutilated quartz can help to knit together and strengthen tissues that have been strained or damaged. Like many long,

△ **Two pointed quartz crystals either side of the affected area, with the points facing each other, will diffuse a painful build-up of energy.**

▽ **Each crystal of rutilated quartz is different. Some have a few very long and fine threads of rutile running through them, which help repair nerve damage or connect energy pathways from different parts of the body. Other examples have tightly packed interwoven layers of rutile that might prove more effective in tissue repair.**

TO EASE PAIN

Pain is a useful indicator of damaged tissue. Without that sensation we might not necessarily know that a problem exists. However, it is useful to be able to lower the levels of pain when they are very high. Pain is a concentration of energy, so by diffusing that energy the experience of pain can often be lessened. For repair of damaged physical tissue there must be a nourishing flow of energy to that area.

1 To ease the emotional stress of the situation, and to help repair be more rapid and complete, use pink, orange or yellow stones at the sacral chakra or solar plexus, with perhaps an addition of violet stones at the brow or crown chakra to establish calm.

2 To bring a cooling, quietening energy, place cool coloured stones, green, blue and violet, on or near a painful or inflamed area.

3 To speed the repair of tissues, such as pulled muscles and broken bones, place rutilated quartz on or around the affected area. This will encourage the torn tissues to rejoin and heal.

thin crystals, rutile is an excellent energy shifter and will help remove energy blocks. Its golden colour suggests that rutilated quartz can reorganize and integrate scattered energy fields.

Very often symptoms of physical pain can be eased when the energy flow within the meridian system is repaired. Detailed knowledge of these energy channels is not necessary – simply placing rutilated quartz or clear quartz crystal points at either side of the painful area, points facing each other, will often bring relief.

Use your hand to scan over the area so that you can feel the flow of energy. The appropriate direction of flow will feel different from any other direction. If needed, the flow can be encouraged by sweeping over the area with a hand-held crystal.

Other orange healers

Copper and topaz share the ability to create a healing flow of energy through the body. For an even more gentle, clear orange energy, orange calcite is perhaps the coolest and most soothing of the orange stones.

These stones are ideal for helping internal emotional pressures that largely arise from unresolved situations or subtle, unnoticed sources in the environment, such as subsonic vibration or conflict with people around you. Pressure can also be caused by the wrong food or drink, ionization in the air prior to a storm, planetary influences and so on. Like a pressure cooker, energy begins to build up and, with no means of release, turbulence increases until an explosion of some kind restores the equilibrium. To avoid explosions, which can be a sudden, unwarranted loss of temper or could even develop into a nervous breakdown, you need to safely ground and release the unwanted energy.

RELEASING UNWANTED ENERGY

The following layout with orange stones can be used in acute cases of frustration or where there is a long term difficulty with a personal situation. The treatment helps to stimulate the creative flow of the sacral chakra and grounds any excess energy through the feet. Use any orange stones in this layout. Remain in position for ten to 12 minutes.

1 Place one stone below the left foot.
2 Place another below the right foot.
3 Place a third stone a couple of centimetres below the navel.
4 Place a fourth stone a centimetre or so above the navel.

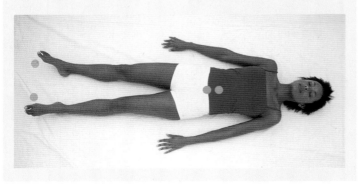

△ Golden topaz is associated with qualities of leadership and self-assurance. It can, however, be rather susceptible to absorbing energy, so needs regular cleansing if worn.

topaz

Found in many degrees of colours from completely clear to green or blue, topaz ($Al_2SiO_4(F,OH)_2$) is best known in its rich golden-yellow and orange-pink varieties. The colour is caused by traces of iron or chromium and may change in sunlight, becoming stronger or more faded.

In any of its colours topaz is good to use when the physical body is tense and emotions are volatile. It encourages the relaxation of rigid areas. Topaz will charge up any area it is focused on and can also be used to draw off excess or negative energy.

For a more grounded and gentler effect, tiger's eye (SiO_2 variety) can be used instead. This stone will also help the individual to integrate and become comfortable in challenging social situations.

▷ Water is able to hold the energy patterns of
crystals placed in it.

copper

Metals can sometimes be found in a pure
unmixed state in the earth, as nuggets or
amalgamations known as native metals. All
the precious and semi-precious metals have
useful healing qualities, though sometimes
they may be prohibitively expensive. Copper
(Cu), a metallic red-orange that oxidizes to
green, is a great conductor of energy. It is
well known to be of benefit to rheumatic
sufferers and its use can reduce inflammation
of all sorts. Copper helps the flow of energy
between all systems in the body and brings
a stability and flexibility that protect against
stress. When there is an energy build-up and
an increasing sense of internal emotional or
nervous pressure, copper can aid the flow
of energy to safely release or ground it.

gem waters and essences

Releasing stress and trauma can be a long-
term process. Using techniques to maintain
the momentum between crystal healing
sessions can speed the healing considerably.
Gem waters and gem essences offer easy and
effective ways of doing this and are simple
to make and use. The energy patterns held
in the water will only be released as and
when the body requires.

▽ Emotional turbulence, over-emotional states or
irritability can be eased with copper.

TO MAKE GEM WATER OR ESSENCE

When you are preparing to make a
gem water or essence, choose a
cleansed and washed sample of
crystal. Members of the quartz family
such as carnelian, and similar, harder
minerals are ideal. Avoid very soft,
water-soluble or potentially toxic
minerals. Once you have made your
gem water or essence, pour the water
into a more permanent container such
as an amber glass bottle and preserve
it with alcohol or cider vinegar. Add a
few drops to drinking water as required
or rub on pulse points.

1 To make a gem water, place the crystal
in a clean, plain glass or bowl and cover
with spring water. Leave overnight and
drink in the morning or take sips
throughout the day.

2 To make a gem essence, place the
stone in a clear glass bowl, cover it with
spring water and put it in direct sunlight
for at least two hours. This imprints the
quality of the mineral on the water.

▽ Rub a drop of essence or gem water on
pulse points for healing energy.

▽ Drink gem water within a day, while gem
essences can be kept for much longer.

Citrine – sun and the mind

One of the rarer varieties of quartz, citrine (SiO_2) forms from recrystallized quartz solution where nearby oxidized iron impurities become included in the atomic structure. These impurities create the characteristic golden-yellow coloration of citrine. The finest quality of citrine is transparent lemon or golden yellow. More commonly, crystals are golden brown to orange-brown with milky white areas. Most citrine these days is made by gently heating poor quality amethyst, turning it golden. This process can also occur naturally in metamorphic environments.

Whatever its origin, citrine quartz is invaluable as a healing stone. The range of colours allows it to work as a grounding stone (browns), as a balancer of the sacral

▷ **Citrine quartz is a translucent variety that shows a range of colours from brown to yellow.**

CLARITY OF MIND LAYOUT

This energy net uses citrine to help clarity of mind, communication skills, adaptability and energy levels. It may quickly feel uncomfortable unless you really need the extra energy. Begin with short sessions of five to six minutes, and practise regularly, especially if you are studying. You will need three citrines, three clear quartz and a yellow cloth.

1 Place one citrine at the solar plexus, point down. Hold the other two citrines in the hands, points away from the body.
2 Place one clear quartz on the forehead with the point towards the top of the head. Tape the remaining clear quartz stones on the top of each foot, between the tendons of the second and third toes.

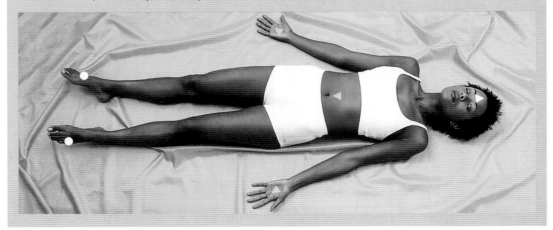

A CHAKRA GOAL BALANCING

This exercise can be used to help a friend or partner. A chakra goal balance uses crystals that will bring each of the chakras into balance and release the stresses related to the issue being looked at. Repeat the process regularly.

1 Encourage your friend or partner to share her problems and concerns with you, then together decide on a phrase or short sentence that sums up her intention.

2 Help her to intuitively select a stone for each chakra that will both balance the energy and also support the process of achieving the desired goal. When all the stones have been chosen, settle your friend in a comfortable position.

3 Place a stone on each chakra. Leave for five to ten minutes. Take away the stones, ground and centre her energies.

4 After the healing session give your friend a piece of citrine to take with her; this will help to keep confidence high and reduce any emotional turbulence the release may cause. When you repeat the process, new stones should be selected.

chakra (oranges) and as a support for the energies of the solar plexus chakra (yellows). Citrine is gently warming, soothing and integrating. Working in harmony with the solar plexus chakra, it is effective at increasing self-confidence and the achievement of personal goals. This crystal smoothes away areas of irritation and friction, creating more optimism and relaxation through the body, emotions and mind. Thought processes especially are helped with citrine – the grounding qualities prevent the build-up of anxieties, the oranges encourage a flow of creativity

and the bright yellows calm the digestive system. Citrine has a calming effect on the nervous system, bringing clearer thought and improved memory.

The solar plexus chakra, with which yellow stones work so effectively, is the seat of our sense of personal power. From this centre arise our beliefs or doubts in ourselves. From here, confidence or anxieties, optimism or fear modify all our beliefs and our behaviour. Working with yellow stones like citrine can be an effective way to strengthen the positive aspects and release the fears within the body.

goal balancing

Bad experiences, fear and anxiety often prevent us from achieving goals we would dearly love to reach. Removing the stresses that are linked to specific activities and personal behaviour patterns is one of the most rewarding techniques available to crystal healers.

There are many different ways of goal balancing. For example, with a pendulum it is possible to focus your intention on removing those stresses connected with the problem. The pendulum recognizes and releases only those related energy blocks.

Other yellow stones

There is a crossover between crystals that work on the second and third chakras – the orange and yellow coloured stones. Citrine, topaz and tiger's eye, for example, will work well at either location depending on the exact shade of the stone.

The solar plexus chakra is especially important because it interfaces with many of the body's systems. The digestive system, the nervous system, the immune system, the brain and its memory function, all depend upon the solar plexus. The solar plexus is also the centre of emotional stability, the seat of personal power, hope and optimism.

Crystal healing is one of the best ways to release the tension that affects the solar plexus, causing stomach problems. Yellow stones help to support positivity and access reserves of personal initiative.

▷ Tiger's eye can be used at the base, sacral and solar plexus chakras, depending on the precise mix of colour in each stone.

▽ Nuggets of pure gold are rare. A very small piece of gold could be attached to a slab of clear quartz to enable its use in crystal healing sessions.

△ The beautiful, warm, glowing colour of amber echoes the gently activating effect it has on the body.

▽ The bright gold colour of iron pyrites from a distance resembles gold, hence its popular name, fool's gold. It is, however, an indicator that gold-bearing rocks could be nearby.

amber

Not strictly a mineral or a crystal, amber ($C_{10}H_{16}O+H_2S$) is fossilized tree resin more than four million years old. It can be brown, orange, yellow, green or red, perfectly clear or contain bits of debris from when it oozed from the bark of ancient pine trees. Amber containing whole preserved insects tends to be highly valued and is often imitated with plastic or resin. It can be worked very easily with abrasive papers and reheated to melt small fragments together into larger pieces, producing so-called Russian amber.

Amber is a soothing stone that is useful for correcting imbalances in the nervous system, or when there is a need for gentle activation and energizing. Amber can be helpful for detoxification and reduces confusion and anxiety.

iron pyrites

With its high sulphur content, iron pyrites (FeS_2) can have beneficial effects on the digestive system, helping with the elimination of toxins. More commonly known as fool's gold, pyrites forms brilliant

▷ Gold jewellery will have some beneficial effects on the energies of the body.

▽ Yellow coloured stones help to reduce tension in the solar plexus and encourage relaxation and positive attitudes.

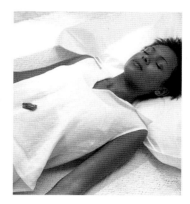

golden metallic crystals, often perfect cubes. As an iron ore, it is gently grounding, helping recovery from flights of anxiety and other emotionally charged imaginings that contribute to depression and frustration. If anxiety is a factor in digestive problems, pyrites can help reduce tension.

other yellow stones

A commonly occurring native metal, though usually in quantities so small as to be uneconomical to retrieve, gold has been sought after and treasured since the Stone

▽ Sunstone is a variety of feldspar with a yellow-orange colour and a brilliant play of light. It is of the same family as moonstone.

Age. Forming from gold-bearing rocks or in hot water solution it is usually found near to granite rock masses and in quartz veins. As these erode the grains of gold are deposited in river gravels.

Gold rarely crystallizes but forms thin plates, wires and grains. Nuggets are very uncommon. Gold is not often used in crystal healing, simply because natural examples large enough to be practical are rare. Small flakes of gold can be found in mineralogical shops boxed for display.

Like the other elemental metals, silver and copper, gold is a great conductor of energy, helping to harmonize many of the different levels within the body. Creating easy energy flow, gold is helpful in releasing stress from the nervous system, increasing the efficiency of the brain and the ability to repair damaged tissues. The immune system is strengthened by gold's positive effect on the heart chakra and thymus gland. In the absence of a piece of native gold, a clean piece of 24 carat jewellery can be used.

Stones such as fluorite, feldspar, beryl and tourmaline all have yellow varieties that can play a part in rebalancing the solar plexus chakra. Those stones with a warm orange-yellow work best with the digestive system and will be relaxing. The stones with a more lemon yellow colour will be effective in clearing the mind and nervous system, encouraging clarity and mental alertness.

Balance and peace:
green & blue stones

Crystals with the cooler colours of
blue and green all tend to encourage
a sense of balanced calm and a quality
of peacefulness. These crystals work
well with the energies of the heart and
throat chakras.

Green stones – balancing the heart

There are a great many minerals and crystals with a green coloration. All work very well to balance the heart chakra energies and introduce stabilizing and calming influences.

green aventurine

A member of the quartz family, green aventurine (SiO_2) is one of the best overall balancing stones for the heart, because it acts without creating any turbulence or sudden release. Aventurine forms when quartz is subjected to heat and pressure, causing it to melt and resolidify, usually as large slabs, with inclusions of other minerals. It is these inclusions that give aventurine its colour. Green aventurine resembles green jasper but contains fuschite mica or sparkling fragments of haematite and pyrite, which catch the light and make it easy to distinguish from other similar stones. The inclusions have a slight grounding effect that increases the stabilizing qualities of the stone.

▽ Aventurine is a massive form of quartz that can be found in a range of colours from emerald to very pale green.

△ Bloodstone of the finest quality is a dark green with bright red spots and splashes. It can also contain areas of grey, yellow and orange.

bloodstone

Another green member of the quartz family, bloodstone (SiO_2) is well known for its beneficial effects on the heart and circulation. In the past it was believed to be effective in staunching wounds and soldiers

△ Verdelite can be distinguished from similar coloured stones because, like all tourmalines, the colour alters slightly with the angle of viewing.

used to carry a piece with them into battle. Heliotrope, as bloodstone is also called, is a type of chalcedony with the same structure as jasper. The green colour is caused by small crystals of actinolite, while the prominent bright red spots and streaks derive from iron oxides that were present as the solution crystallized. With a combination of red and green, bloodstone can work with both the base and heart chakras, bringing either a sufficient energy or a sufficient calmness.

verdelite

Green tourmaline ($Na(Mg,Fe,Li,Mn,Al)_3Al_6(BO_3)Si_6O_{18}(OH,F)_4$) is also known as verdelite. The green colour, which can vary from very light to almost black, is brought about by higher than usual amounts of sodium in the structure of the stone.

All tourmalines help to re-align the physical structures of the body and our connection to the energies of the planet. Its green colour attunes verdelite more to the heart chakra and to a relationship with the natural world. Like many green minerals, verdelite increases our receptivity allowing greater harmony with the surroundings.

BALANCING THE HEART'S ENERGIES

The heart is the balance point for our entire energy system. Creating balance and stability in the heart makes it easier for other imbalances elsewhere to be corrected. Balancing the heart brings a life-supporting calm inside us, and an ability to relate positively to the world around us. The following layout of crystals helps to stabilize all the energies of the heart.

Beneath the heart chakra is another small energy centre that is particularly concerned with holding and bringing to fruition our most cherished wishes and desires. A Herkimer diamond placed just under the heart (pictured right) will help access this energy, bringing a sense of clarity and direction when there is confusion.

1 For the layout shown below, first place a small rose quartz crystal at the centre of the chest.

2 Then take four green tourmalines, and make a cross along the axis of the body around the rose quartz. Clear quartz can be used here if tourmalines are unavailable. It is important that, if the stones have natural points, these are all placed so that they are facing outwards.

3 Between the four tourmalines make a second diagonal cross using smoky quartz crystals. Again, if these have natural points they should face outwards. This pattern will release stress from the heart while balancing and grounding its energies. The outward pointing stones ensure that a relaxing calm is established. Stay in this heart layout for five to ten minutes. Use grounding stones if necessary afterwards.

4 For a variation of this layout, if you want to bring full potential closer within your reach, then you can add a Herkimer diamond underneath the layout.

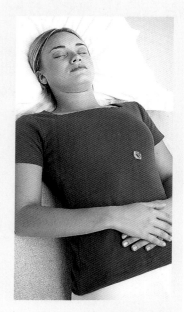

Green crystals and the space of nature

Green is the colour of nature, the energy of expansion and space. The heart chakra establishes our own inner space and our relationship to everything in the world around us. Green stones and crystals can help to create the fine balance that we need in order to live harmoniously with the world without suppressing our own desires. Green crystals can also help to break down some of the barriers that keep us feeling trapped within our circumstances and the limits of our abilities.

moss agate

Common symptoms of feeling trapped are tightness in the chest and breathing difficulties. Moss agate, a form of chalcedony, with coloured inclusions resembling trees, ferns or moss, can help to relieve the tensions that underlie these problems. Within the translucent or transparent quartz, which usually has a blue or yellow tinge, crystal growths of manganese oxides, hornblende or iron in various shades of green and brown suggest the ability to grow and expand. The inclusions often look like the fine structures within the lungs, suggesting freedom to breathe. Moss agate encourages a sense of increased confidence and optimism, allowing a much greater relationship with the world of nature.

▽ Moss agate can be a useful calming stone for feelings of confinement and confusion.

jade

By connecting us to our physical instincts and earth energies, jade ($NaAlSi_2O_6$) increases the sense of belonging. Thus jade is an antidote to over-intellectual spiritualism – it calms the arrogance that sees the physical world as inferior to the flights of fancy the mind can conjure up.

emerald

This stone is a gem-quality green variety of the mineral beryl ($Be_3Al_2Si_6O_{18}$). It balances the heart, speeds up detoxification and brings calm by removing hidden fears. Like many green stones, emerald can be a helpful aid to meditation.

healing the garden

Green stones have a natural affinity with growing plants and they can be used to heal the energies of a garden. Simply place stones where you feel extra help is needed. Walk round your garden, allowing yourself to be receptive to energy changes. You will almost certainly be drawn to spots that feel dull or heavy in some way. This process is similar to scanning a body and is corrected in the same way by the placement of appropriate stones. Minerals with a significant copper content, such as turquoise, malachite and chrysocolla, can all encourage plant growth.

▽ Jade has been widely used for rituals and is linked to ancestor spirits and the gods.

△ Green stones make a space calm and restful for contemplation and meditation.

making space

Healing the heart can never truly be accomplished if whenever we reduce stress, we return immediately to a hectic and stressful life. For anything to grow, space is needed. If we wish to get more from life, sometimes it is necessary to do less instead of trying to cram more things in.

▽ Emerald of gem quality is rare and expensive but impure pieces work in healing just as well.

A SMALL CALM SPACE

Finding a few minutes once a day to be silent in your own company will help you to see opportunities and new solutions that would improve the quality of your life. Crystals can help to bring balance into our energy systems but it is up to us to maintain and build upon that state of balance.

Use some green stones to bring some of the qualities of nature into your home. Set a small space aside in a corner or on a table. Keep it clear of everyday clutter, and arrange some of your favourite green stones there, together with a beautiful plant and a candle, or other items that help you feel calm and relaxed.

1 Take two minutes a day to sit and look at the stones. Sit comfortably in front of them, light the candle or burn some incense.

2 Take up one or two of the stones and hold them in your hands, close your eyes and relax. You are making space in your mind, your emotions and your life for new things to enter.

3 Open your eyes to look again at the stones and then close them again and think of the space you are creating in your mind. Repeat if you wish.

4 When you have finished, return the stones to their place.

▽ ▷ **The energy of any room in the home can be enlivened by having a small quiet space somewhere within it**.

Green stones strengthen the main quality of the heart chakra, which is to grow and expand in a harmonious manner in such a way as to fulfil the individual's core needs. Personal space and freedom to be oneself are essential for wellbeing and health. We can use crystals to help us achieve our goals in life, both by giving us quiet in order to see things more clearly and by encouraging the growth of qualities we need.

Before goals can be reached, it is necessary to clarify as much as possible what those goals are. A reminder of your aim keeps your attention focused in the right direction without becoming obsessive. Set aside a space that can be dedicated to your wishes. Have a representation of your goal; a picture, photograph or phrase. For example, if the goal is to pass your driving test, a picture of a car can be the centrepiece. Then choose crystals to encourage qualities that are needed for you to succeed. Encourage optimism and clarity with yellow crystals, calm with green stones, ability to learn with blue, co-ordination with violet. A clear quartz crystal can reinforce your intention if it is programmed.

▽ **This space is dedicated to a wish for personal control and confidence. The yellow crystals will help to encourage optimism and reduce anxiety.**

GREEN BREATHING
This exercise easily creates a meditative state. Using a green crystal as a focus of attention naturally calms the mind and acts as a support to the entire process. Sit in a comfortable position and take a minute to settle yourself. Have a green stone in front of you – the type is not important.
1 Look at the stone, letting your eyes rest on it gently. Keep looking at the stone and let your mind be aware of your breathing.
2 After a few minutes, close your eyes and imagine you are breathing in the colour green. If you get distracted, open your eyes and gaze at the stone for a while longer, then close your eyes and breathe in the colour again.
3 When you are ready, put the stone aside and relax for a minute before returning to normal activity.

▷ Exposing a clear quartz crystal to a range of coloured lights is an effective way of programming it, or modifying its energy.

programming a crystal

To direct a crystal's energy towards a specific, clearly defined goal you need to programme it. This will always be most effective when your intention matches the natural quality of the crystal. Programming a blue crystal to radiate red energy is possible, for example, but will go against the flow of energy that crystal possesses. Always get to know a crystal well before you consider modifying its function with programming. Remember that a crystal that has always been used for its healing energy will always be better suited to healing rather than being used as a meditation stone. A meditation crystal will come to enhance and amplify the energies of the meditator each time it is used, and so will be less useful as a healing stone.

There are two ways to programme a crystal. The first way is by exposure to a type of energy, such as a light source. A clear quartz that is exposed for a prolonged amount of time to red light, for example, will after a while begin to resonate to that red frequency.

The second programming technique is to redirect the stone's energy through strong intention and affirmation. Hold the stone in your hands, or to your heart or brow, and project your intention into the centre of the crystal. Repeat this process several times until you intuitively feel that the crystal can now hold and broadcast the thought or intention. For sucessful programming, it is important that the intention you project is as clear and precise as possible. Vague or muddled desires bring vague results.

Once it is programmed, place the crystal carefully in a space where it can be seen, to remind you of your goals.

To remove the programming repeat the process with the intention that the stone reverts to its normal state. Cleanse the crystal and thank it for its help.

GREEN HEART

This exercise will calm the heart.

1 Put a green stone at your heart. Hold a clear quartz crystal in your left hand, point inwards. Hold another clear quartz in your right hand, point outwards, away from the body.

2 Visualize a flow of energy from your left hand to your heart and from your heart to your right hand and out of your body. Feel calm energy filling you and tension draining away.

3 Change the quartz points around so the flow moves in the other direction. Repeat the process.

4 After five minutes put down the quartz points and experience the calm green energy at the heart chakra. If there is somewhere else that is in pain or in need of extra calming energy, put the green stone there, instead of at the heart.

Expansion into the beyond – stones from space

Tons of dust land on the planet from space every year but it is rare to find larger fragments, even though meteorites have crashed into the earth since its creation. Metallic meteorites consisting mainly of iron and nickel are more common than rocky meteorites that have a composition similar to igneous rock. Many meteorites are thought to be the remnants of a planet that once orbited between Mars and Jupiter, a space now occupied by the asteroid belt.

tektites

Even more mysterious than meteorites are tektites, a group of minerals found scattered around the globe whose exact origins are unknown. Tektites may be glassy meteorites but it is more likely that they formed millions of years ago when large meteorites struck the earth, melting rock in huge explosions of energy. The strange shapes of tektites are evocative of such cataclysmic events. Very often they have pitted, rippled or cratered surfaces and form pebble, teardrop or elongated extruded fragments. They are usually black-brown. In one area in the Czech Republic tektites are a brilliant green, and there they are called moldavites.

moldavites

These are much sought after, even though they are rarely found in large pieces. Moldavite is an excellent amplifying stone,

▷ Meteorites remind us of the vastness of the universe and the possibilities of the unknown.

MOLDAVITE NET

If you are lucky enough to have nine moldavite pieces you can try the following crystal net. This energy net will help expand awareness beyond its normal physical limitations. It will help connect you to the energy of the earth, and through its core energy out into the wider universe. This layout will help relax tensions in the chest, easing feelings of constriction and confusion. It will also help clarify your goals and directions in life. Moldavite can give a powerful and sometimes disorientating experience. Make sure you spend

no longer than ten minutes in this net and ground yourself thoroughly when finished.

1 On either side of the body between the head and solar plexus put three moldavites, evenly spaced.

2 Position another moldavite midway between and below your feet.

3 Place one above the top of your head.

4 The last moldavite goes on the brow chakra in the centre of the forehead.

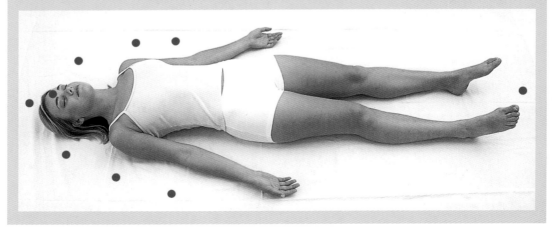

EXPLORING MOLDAVITE

The energy of moldavite definitely seems to be unearthly at times, as befits a stone created from the meeting of earth and outer space. Comfortable exploration of moldavite's potential can be helped with this layout.

1 Use eight pieces of amethyst or eight pieces of clear quartz. If they have terminations, place these so they are facing inwards towards the body.

2 Once these are in place, place the moldavite on your heart, throat or brow chakra. Experiment with the moldavite on different chakras to see how your experiences alter.

3 After a maximum of ten minutes remove the moldavite and replace it with a grounding stone, such as haematite or black tourmaline. Another grounding stone can be added near the feet if necessary.

4 When you are ready, remove all the stones and relax for at least five minutes before resuming normal activities.

enhancing the properties of other stones placed with it. It usually feels expansive and enlivening and it may cause sensations of movement or sudden changes of energy and awareness, such as heat or flashes of imagery across the mind. It is well worth sitting for a time with a piece of moldavite and just allowing these tides of energy to come and go. If you wish to explore more deeply, place a piece of moldavite at your heart, throat or brow chakra and surround your body with clear quartz or amethyst. Keep a good grounding stone nearby for when you have finished. Do not place too much meaning on your experiences. Simply accept.

When exploring the qualities of crystals in this way remember to make notes of your experiences afterwards. Over time certain themes and types of imagery will emerge and these may suggest how the crystal is interacting with your own energy systems.

With stone such as moldavite there can be a powerful amplifying effect. This makes them useful in the exploration of other sorts of crystal. Green stones in general, and moldavite in particular, seem to enhance our natural sensitivity and psychic skills, particularly if we have learned the value of entering a quiet, receptive, calm state on a regular basis.

◁ **Moldavite has a characteristic bottle-green colour and a rippled or pitted surface pattern.**

▷ **Although attractive in its natural shapes, moldavite is also used in jewellery.**

Turquoise and aquamarine – joy and the immune system

Activating and strengthening the body's own defences naturally improves quality of life, bringing an increased sense of optimism and happiness. Both turquoise and aquamarine can be used for this purpose. Happiness is one of the greatest antibiotics available to us. It rapidly creates balance in the blood chemistry and hormones, releasing stress and flushing out damaging toxins.

turquoise

A hydrated basic phosphate of aluminium and copper, turquoise ($CuAl_6(PO_4)_4(OH)_8.4H_2O$) is of medium hardness, and the colour – which varies – can alter when exposed to light or chemicals. Despite its lack of stability it has been used throughout the world as an important gemstone.

In North American Indian traditions, in China and Tibet, as well as in Europe, turquoise has a reputation for protection. There is a belief that the stone will become paler when its owner is in danger. Certainly it will react to chemicals secreted from the skin as well as to oils or perfumes being worn. Because of its susceptibility, the colour of turquoise is often stabilized with wax or resin. In the southwestern US, turquoise was often powdered and presented as an offering

△ Turquoise is one of the most universal and oldest of gemstone amulets worn for protection.

▽ Turquoise is a soft mineral. Often in jewellery making it is crushed to a powder and mixed with resin, to make a more robust-coloured stone.

INCREASING LIFE-ENERGY

The thymus gland is located between the heart and throat chakras. It is an important organ of the immune system and at energetic levels regulates the amount of life-energy, or *prana*, within the body. All turquoise-coloured stones placed around this area will help to regulate and balance the thymus.

◁ Aquamarine is so-named from its colour resembling the sea. It was once prized as a protection from shipwreck.

to the spirits. In Central and South America it was used to decorate offerings to the gods. The delicate sky-blue tones suggest its affinity to the heavens – sky that has fallen to earth.

The colour of turquoise has a strengthening and supporting effect on the thymus gland, which is located just below the throat where the collarbones meet. This gland is one of the main organs of the immune system. In complementary medicine, it is of vital importance to the levels of life-energy available in the body.

Turquoise encourages the functions of this gland and so increases available energy, protecting the body from negativity.

aquamarine

Blue-green in colour, aquamarine ($Be_3Al_2Si_6O_{18}$) is a variety of the mineral beryl, which can form very large crystals up to several metres long. Many of the finest crystals are found in Brazil, and it is a good source of the light metal beryllium, which is used in alloys. Aquamarine is excellent for energizing the immune system and is useful in the recovery from debilitating illnesses, where it provides an energy boost, helping the body to get rid of the underlying causes of disease. Whereas turquoise is an absorbing stone with gentle actions, aquamarine can be stimulating and purifying. Occasionally it may appear to exacerbate symptoms as they are lifted from the subtle bodies. If this occurs, use it with a stone that will ease the process such as kyanite or selenite.

An important quality of the thymus, located midway between the heart and throat, is the expression of uniqueness. Repressing our natural qualities suppresses life-energy, leading to stress and susceptibility to illness. If you are in a situation where you cannot be yourself, use aquamarine to find a positive way to express your individuality. Aquamarine can help clear localized areas of imbalance and dulled energy. Placing it on or near an infected or inflamed area will help to release the difficulties that hamper the body's defence systems.

TURQUOISE LAYOUT

Use this layout when healing energies are required or there is a lack of self-confidence. Turquoise stimulates the natural protective energies of the body, citrine reduces fear and balances the body's functions.

1 Place a turquoise just below the collarbones.
2 Place a bright yellow citrine at the solar plexus.
3 Place a rose quartz at the navel to calm and stabilize the emotions.

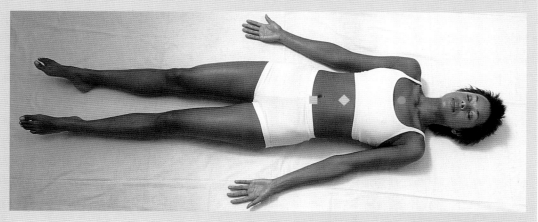

Amazonite and chrysocolla – self-expression and creativity

Turquoise stones help to combine and harmonize the energies of the heart and throat chakras, easing the flow of personal expression and individuality. Amazonite and chrysocolla improve communication on many different levels.

amazonite

A variety of the common mineral feldspar, amazonite ($KAlSi_3O_8$) has been used for centuries in jewellery and ornamentation because of its fine blue-green colour. Characteristic to amazonite is a streaky parallel patterning of different shadings, caused by the presence of lead, the impurity of which creates the intense colour.

Like turquoise, amazonite can sometimes be more blue and sometimes more green in colour, and this makes it useful both at the heart chakra and the throat chakra – but of special value for the thymus gland midway between them both.

Amazonite is particularly effective at activating the qualities of self-expression,

confidence, leadership and communication. Like many green and turquoise stones, amazonite may also help to enhance psychic skills, in particular the ability to receive images from the past. This ability is known as 'far memory'. The images received often relate to, or are symbolic of, current preoccupations and parallel or reflect the current goals of the viewer. Whether these

△ **Amazonite often shows streaks of different greens along its central axis. It forms clearly defined block-like crystals.**

far memories are actually past life information, or come from another subconscious source, their impressions can be useful in encouraging us to locate, order and pursue our unique path in life.

AMAZONITE NET

An energy net of six pieces of amazonite can be used to release skills hidden deep within our genetic memory. It can also help the recall of distant personal memories, throwing light on repeating patterns of behaviour. This helps to clarify what prevents us from achieving our goals time and again, so that steps can be taken to remove hidden blocks. Place six amazonites evenly around the body: one above the head, one below the feet and two at either side. Allow five to ten minutes for a session.

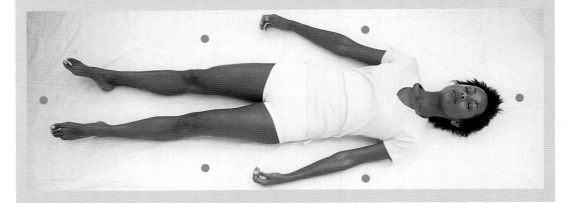

▷ Those who work creatively may benefit from chrysocolla, as it releases tension in the upper body and helps the flow of creative expression.

▽ Its effects on the thoracic cavity and throat make chrysocolla of benefit to singers.

chrysocolla

A delicate and very beautiful mineral, chrysocolla ($(Cu,Al_2)H_2Si_2O_5(OH)_4.nH_2O$) is formed from solutions of copper, silica and water. Because it occurs near copper deposits it can be found intermixed with other copper-rich minerals such as turquoise, azurite, malachite and cuprite. Chrysocolla often intergrows with quartz, which makes it slightly more durable, though still soft. In this form it is called gem silica. A variety of chrysocolla mixed equally with turquoise and azurite–malachite has a deeper, even blue-green colour and is known as Eilat stone. This variety is named for the region on the Sinai Peninsula where it was mined in the time of King Solomon.

Chrysocolla helps to balance the whole region of the chest, lungs, throat and neck. It cools and calms inflamed areas, stimulating the immune system and quietening the mind. The mix of greens and blues acts on the heart and throat chakras, reaching up to the deeper blue of the brow chakra and the related minor chakra at the base of the skull, the medulla oblongata. This small energy point is important for regulating and directing psychic information and energy from other levels of existence. It clears away blockages in the emotions and belief systems, which cause confusion and failure.

Placing a piece of chrysocolla at the heart or throat, at the base of the skull or in the centre of the forehead can create a rearrangement of energies that results in a clearer view of issues. For particular problems, begin with a clear intention or a situation you wish to understand better. Focus clearly for a moment on that thought and then relax. The chrysocolla will help to bring resolutions to your conscious mind.

At a physical level, chrysocolla encourages relaxation and balance, allowing the green energies of the heart, with all its strength of feeling, to be manifested and expressed through the blue energies of the throat chakra and the voice.

◁ Chrysocolla can have strong areas of green next to rich, deep turquoise and blue. Its irregular and flaky appearance in natural form helps to identify it from other similarly coloured minerals.

Blue lace agate and celestite – touching the clouds

Light blue stones, such as blue lace agate and celestite, are used to introduce a calming influence in situations where cool, peaceful energy is required.

blue lace agate

This is one of the most striking varieties of quartz. The rich blue bands in blue lace agate (SiO_2) are created by larger quartz crystals intergrowing through chalcedony, which originally seeped as solution into cavities within volcanic rock. This natural blue agate is not commonly found, so it tends to be rather more expensive than other agates. Because of its microscopic structure, all agate is very porous and will take up dyes easily. Dyed agate is relatively easy to identify as all its bands are shades of one colour, whereas natural samples have some variation created by the different impurities in the surrounding rocks where they crystallize.

Few crystals have the soft, gentle energy of lace agate. It can be used anywhere that needs calming and cooling. Blue stones encourage the flow of energy and have a natural affinity with the throat chakra, our

means of communication and expression. When the flow of communication is stifled, internal pressure builds up. Unexpressed, this energy can become resentment, anger and aggression; unable to flow, the blue vibration becomes red energy that will eventually explode. Blue stones can help to ease the pressure and release the energy.

△ All agates are a microcrystalline quartz in massive form only, though sometimes small crystals can be seen within the layers.

▽ A feeling of pressure is often felt at the throat when emotional stress is being released. A piece of blue lace agate placed at the base of the throat will quickly ease and release the energy.

▽ When polished, blue lace agate reveals undulating bands of blues and milky greys.

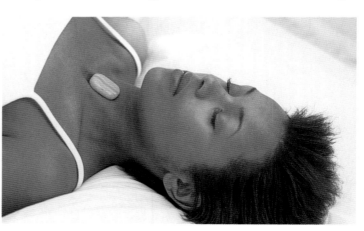

celestite

Also known as celestine, celestite ($SrSO_4$) is a soft blue or grey mineral that has been used for centuries as an ingredient in fireworks and rescue flares. The strontium content burns with a bright crimson flame.

The finest celestite crystals come from Madagascar and are a beautiful sky-blue colour, hence the mineral name. Celestite has an uplifting, calming and expansive quality, making it good for contemplation and meditation. It is effective at lifting heavy moods and sadness as well as balancing the throat chakra. The ethereal quality of celestite crystals often helps the mind to travel beyond its normal perspective, promoting inspiration and intuitive leaps.

▷ **Celestite is easily damaged as it is very soft, so keep it away from harder stones in a collection.**

ETHER NET

Using an energy net with seven small clusters of celestite and a white cloth will help you tune into spiritual states as well as encouraging communication skills and artistic creativity. Ether is the fifth element, the element of space. Within its fine substance are all the possibilities of creation. Lying in this energy net can provide a deep rest from the cares of the world, and an effective way to lighten heavy emotional burdens. It can also help dissolve negative patterns that have become attached to the auric field.

Lay out the seven clusters on the white cloth, one above the head, one at either side of the feet and the others evenly spaced between. Lie in the net for five to ten minutes.

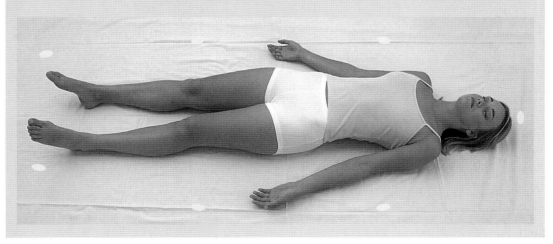

Healing and beyond:
deep blue & violet stones

With deeper blue and violet crystals
the potential for change and growth
of awareness greatly increases as our
inherent abilities and buried talents
emerge to enrich our lives. These stones
attune to the brow and crown chakras.

Deep blue stones – lapis lazuli and sodalite

There are many deep blue minerals available, all of which can help us to regain a state of quiet peaceful awareness, in which we become more receptive to all sorts of information and communication.

lapis lazuli

A rare gemstone that has always been highly prized, lapis lazuli $((Na,Ca)_8(Al.Si)_{12}O_{24}(S,SO_4))$ forms only where limestone comes into contact with calcite and pyrites. Metamorphic conditions produce a new mineral, lazurite, which has an intense blue coloration. Lapis lazuli is a rock comprising several minerals: lazurite embedded in calcite and pyrites. Afghanistan has always been the best source.

▽ The rich blues of lapis lazuli were once ground to a fine powder and used as pigment.

Lapis lazuli works well with the whole area of the upper chest, throat and head. It can be very quietening initially, but this is often the prelude to deep cleansing at many different levels. Lapis can help those who are shy or introverted to communicate and express themselves. It can also benefit those who project their voices, such as teachers, singers and sales personnel.

Like other deep blue and violet stones, lapis lazuli attunes to the throat and brow chakras and enlivens communication, the processes of thought and memory. The energy of lapis lazuli is not comfortable for everyone, provoking detachment and floating into uncharted depths. This apparent emptiness, when patiently absorbed, reveals a wealth of information and solutions to problems. It can also reveal past errors and bring up unresolved fears.

△ The peaceful, calm presence of lapis lazuli brings a lively silence to a meditation room and aids thought processes.

sodalite

This mineral can be easily confused in appearance with lapis lazuli. Indeed, sodalite $(Na_4Al_3Si_3O_{12}Cl)$ can often be found as one of the minerals making up lapis. The main differences are a slight variation of blue – lapis is more brilliant, sodalite darker. Lapis contains specks of golden iron pyrites and has a speckling of different colours, while sodalite has thin veins of white running through it. Sodalite is named from its high sodium content. It is a useful stone for the brow chakra. It can be less penetrating in its energy than lapis lazuli, but can help nevertheless to access fine levels of intuitive knowledge and promote understanding of ideas and concepts. It is therefore a useful stone for the student and the philosopher.

Physically sodalite will, like all dark blue stones, have a sedating and quietening effect on overactive systems, particularly the nervous system and the lymphatic system,

◁ A flow of fine levels of information is suggested by the web-like structure and veins of colours within sodalite.

▽Sodalite promotes understanding and is helpful placed close by when studying.

which is suggested by the web of fine white veins throughout the stone. This visual characteristic also reflects the ability of sodalite to strengthen communication, particularly in groups.

Dark blue stones should be used sparingly with those suffering from depressive states as the colour can exaggerate the condition. Choose activating, warm coloured stones to encourage optimism and dynamism.

LAYOUT FOR INCREASING EASE

Sometimes there is a feeling of unease, of things being not quite right without any apparent symptoms of illness or upset in your life. Because of its potent cleansing energy lapis lazuli can be used to alleviate this in a simple procedure that can be remarkably powerful.

1 Place a clear quartz, point upwards, above the crown of the head. Place a smoky quartz, point down, between the feet.
2 At the centre of the brow place a piece of lapis lazuli. Remain in the layout for five to ten minutes and repeat for a few days if necessary.

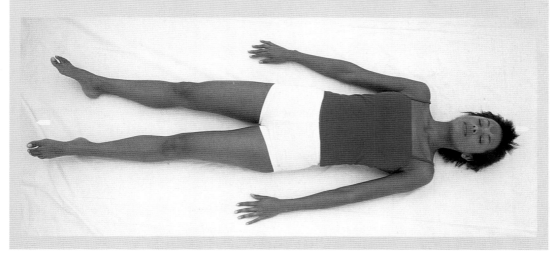

Other blue stones – intuition

Becoming a good crystal healer requires a degree of knowledge about tools and techniques, but most of all it is necessary to have confidence in your own intuitive abilities. Crystals can be described only in general terms – each person will react slightly differently to a given stone. The ideal stone for one person may not have any effect on another. Intuition lets the crystal worker choose the most appropriate stone for each case.

guided by instinct

Intuition is the sum of information that is received by the mind at levels of awareness that we do not usually access. Though an important factor in our everyday lives, intuitive choices usually go unnoticed. Often they are things we 'just do' without any conscious justification.

Paying attention to where our awareness moves – where the eyes may be resting, what the hands are doing, the sorts of thoughts in our mind, how the body is feeling – is important. It's also useful to take note of the actions we perform 'by mistake', like picking up a stone other than the one intended, or having a stone fall out of place time after time – all these are clues to intuitive knowledge. Intuition rarely operates at the level of spoken thoughts – it is necessary to have a quiet mind so that these subtle impressions are not drowned out by our usual mental chatter. This is why developing a regular meditation practice and removing our own stress is important. Taking time to experience calmness and clarity increases the likelihood of noticing what is really happening around us.

Regardless of how large or small your collection of stones, intuition will guide you to choose the most appropriate crystals for the work you are doing. When you go to select stones for a healing, notice those that first catch your eye. See if, when you pick up the stones, there is an instant of hesitation before you select a particular crystal.

USING INTUITION IN CRYSTAL HEALING

Noticing your instinctive actions, thoughts and feelings greatly increases the effectiveness of a crystal healing session. Be aware of hesitation before or after placing a stone – you may need to adjust the position. Notice if there is a feeling of rightness or completion when all the stones have been placed. If there is not, maybe

another stone needs adding or some other change should be made.

Working with crystals teaches you to become aware of slight changes in your mental and physical state. When working with others, scan quickly across the patient's body to discover how they feel. Then note which crystal or group of stones comes immediately to mind. Practise your sensitivity all the time, not only with hand scans but also with visual scans. Remember that the individual energy field is greater than the physical body. When you quickly scan someone – does the energy feel balanced? Is there a sense of being top or base-heavy? Do you sense grey areas or energy hollows?

◁ Intuition develops at its own pace. Regular work with crystals will ensure accuracy.

▽ Focus on maintaining a relaxed awareness rather than on any desired outcome.

△ Regardless of how large or small your collection, intuition will guide you to choose the most appropriate crystals.

▽ Indicolite is the blue-green variety of tourmaline ideal for working on the upper chakras and wherever a peaceful flow of energy is needed.

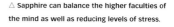

△ Sapphire can balance the higher faculties of the mind as well as reducing levels of stress.

deep blue crystals

Crystals of a deep blue colour will stimulate the latent abilities of subtle perception and intuitive skills. Stones with striations will speed the flow of information, as well as initiating levels of peacefulness through which information can be recognized. Blue tourmaline, also known as indicolite, will energize and balance throat, brow and crown chakras in this way.

Kyanite (Al_2SiO_5) is a blue variety of the mineral disthene, which forms thin blade-like crystals. Kyanite is a very effective energy conduit that can balance most systems in the subtle anatomy. It can quickly create great stillness and tranquillity, which makes it ideal for meditation.

Corundum (Al_2O_3) can often be found in the same rock as kyanite. The presence of iron and titanium colours corundum blue, creating the stone we call sapphire. Forming hard, barrel-shaped or hexagonal crystals, sapphire will enhance the functions of the higher levels of consciousness, reduce tension and bring calm, especially to the crown and solar plexus chakras.

▽ Kyanite forms fan-like clusters or blades of thin crystal ideal for restoring energy balance.

Amethyst and other violet stones

Violet stones have a natural affinity to the crown chakra just above the top of the head. This chakra relates to functions of the brain and mind, but most of all it is the master control centre for the whole chakra system. Violet stones combine the vibrations of practical, down-to-earth red energy with the energy of blue – the expansive, spacious, undefined flow of peace. Combining the two extremes allows violet stones to bring a state of balance wherever it is required, while having a special focus on the workings of the mind.

amethyst

A violet form of quartz, amethyst (SiO_2 + Fe) has always been prized as a beautiful gemstone and master healer. Coloured by

▷ **Clusters and geodes of amethyst are ideal for placing in rooms as a focus for healing and peace.**

AMETHYST HEALING NET

The amethyst net is an excellent method to explore the qualities of other crystals. It also aids any deep healing work and is especially useful for creating calm.

1 To enhance the effect of this net, lie on a yellow or violet cloth. Place eight amethyst crystals evenly spaced around the body, with one below the feet and one above the head. If you have amethyst points, place them so they face inwards. Have the stones you want to investigate close at hand.

2 When you are settled in the amethyst net, experiment by placing a stone at your brow chakra (or any other chakra point you want to try). Finish off all exploratory sessions holding a piece of black tourmaline to ground and centre.

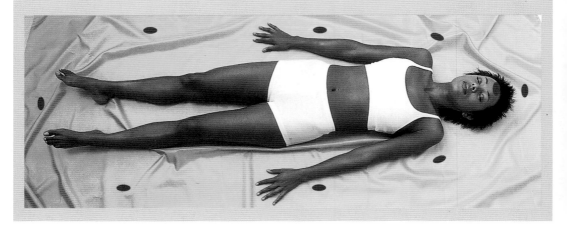

△ Fluorite is characterized by internal bands of colour and clearly visible planes of cleavage.

▽ First found in Japan, then South Africa, sugilite has become a popular stone for quality jewellery.

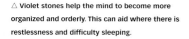

△ Violet stones help the mind to become more organized and orderly. This can aid where there is restlessness and difficulty sleeping.

▽ Dynamic rest and effortless action are the characteristic qualities that violet stones can bring to our lives.

iron, amethyst tends to form geodes of densely packed short crystals all pointing inwards towards the centre of the hollow. Colour varies from very dark, almost black, through purple to a delicate violet. Amethyst is calming and stabilizing to all areas, particularly the mind. It can be a useful stone to reduce restlessness, irritation and worry. Amethyst balances brow and crown chakras but can be used anywhere. Held or placed upon the forehead or above the crown, it is helpful for meditation. The combination of the grounding effects of red together with the expansive quality of blue allows amethyst to be an effective guide in the exploration of different states of being.

fluorite

A common mineral found in metamorphic rock, fluorite (CaF_2) has many uses in industry and is the main source of fluorine gas. Fluorite often has bands of different colours running through it, making it a popular decorative stone despite its softness and fragility. Common colours are blues and violets, green, yellow and clear. Fluorite is particularly useful as a balancer of brow and crown chakras – though it will help to integrate spiritual energies in a balanced way to any level of the body. It will encourage orderliness and structure and is especially helpful at improving levels of physical co-ordination and mental agility.

sugilite

A stone that was only discovered in the first half of the 20th century, sugilite (KNa_2 $(Fe^{2+},Mn^{2+},Al)_2Li_3Si_{12}O_{30}$) is another purple mineral that helps the co-ordination of the left and right hemispheres of the brain. The nervous system is balanced by this stone and it helps sensitive individuals who feel unable to keep up with the changes within society and technology. This inability can create confusion and alienation or can manifest as allergy problems. Sugilite helps integration with the everyday world, and can help prevent a withdrawal from it.

Multi-coloured stones – unlimited possibilities

Crystals displaying more than one colour can be especially useful for healing as they will introduce a mixture of colour energies simultaneously. A combination of red and green, for example, will be energizing but in a very organized way. Red-and-green stones, such as bloodstone or ruby in zoisite, can energize the heart chakra and calm the base chakra. A combination of complementary colours (red-green; blue-orange; violet-yellow; black-white) very effectively harmonizes and integrates related chakra energies and can help energy flow better throughout the whole system.

Azurite-malachite and chrysocolla display different shades of blue and green and therefore broadly balance the area of the throat and chest. Where one colour predominates, that will be the main energy involved, and other colours present will modify that primary focus. So a bloodstone will work mainly at a green level, lapis lazuli at a blue level and so on.

Some crystals display a whole rainbow spectrum of colours. These stones naturally attune to the very rarefied levels of energy above the crown chakra. They can also be used in the same way as white or clear stones, bringing in the whole potential of the spectrum of light. The colour in many of these multi-coloured stones is created by light refracting off their internal structures – microcrystals, fractures, inclusions and so on. Their appearance changes depending on how the light catches them, giving them an extra liveliness. Organic gems such as mother of pearl and abalone exemplify this very well.

opal

A member of the quartz family, opal ($SiO_2.nH_2O$) crystallizes in a slightly different form and has a high

water content. Its watery quality and great range of colours aligns the stone naturally with the emotions and emotional balance. The opal will work with emotions in the area of its dominant colour.

Brown, black or dark blue opals will work well with the lower chakras and are particularly effective at releasing tensions in the reproductive system, being useful for painful periods and PMT. Fire opal, a bright orange colour, will energize and help recovery after emotional upset. Water opal, which is colourless with a sheen of rainbow colours, can help to stabilize mood swings and energize the subtle systems of the body.

◁ **The high water content and microscopic structure of opal gives it a unique variety of rainbow colours and patterns.**

△ **Stones that combine red and green, such as ruby in zoisite, shown here, or bloodstone, help to enliven with their polarity of energy, both the heart and base chakras.**

labradorite

A variety of feldspar, labradorite ($(Na,Ca)Al_{1-2}Si_{3-2}O_8$) looks dull grey until light hits the inclusions of magnetite crystals. The iridescence created is a vivid mix of peacock blues, yellows, oranges and greens. Like all stones with a vivid play of rainbow light, labradorite can inspire many different levels of energy and awareness. It brings energy into the body and works well with any of the chakras.

One of labradorite's most important characteristics is the ability to protect the auric field and prevent energy being drained by other people. This sort of energy drain is usually an unconscious process between people who are in a close relationship of some kind – family members or co-workers – where one person habitually absorbs the energy they need from the other. This leaves

▽ Ametrine can be useful for easing worries, increasing creative imagination, restoring balance to the digestion and improving memory.

89

healing and beyond

ametrine, azurite-malachite

Amethyst, when subjected to heat, turns golden yellow. Where the heating is uneven or localized there may be areas of yellow next to the original violet colour. This variation is known as ametrine. A combination of violet and yellow is ideal for balancing anxiety, fear and nervousness as it affects the solar plexus and brow chakras. Azurite is a deep blue copper mineral that gradually breaks down to form green malachite. Both are therefore often found together.

△ The play of colour in labradorite helps to disperse enervating external energies to maintain personal energy integrity. A white variety is known as spectrolite or rainbow moonstone.

▽ Azurite-malachite is a good stone to calm the heart and emotions, restoring a sense of peace.

the second person feeling tired and drained, put-upon or overwhelmed. Wearing or carrying a piece of labradorite effectively prevents this excessive loss of energy. There may have to be some changes in the relationship as it comes to terms with a new balance of energies.

▽ Abalone shell is formed from layers of crystallized calcium carbonate, a substance known as nacre.

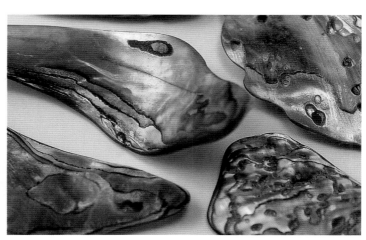

Colour Healing

Most of us will have experienced the sensation of feeling energized by wearing our favourite colour, soothed by gazing at blue water or uplifted by the sight of lush green grass. The influence of colour over our mind, body, spirit and emotions provides the basis for colour healing. We experience colour when light is refracted through, or reflected by, an object at a certain frequency or wavelength. Scientists believe that we each experience colour according to our own individual physical and psychological make-up – what one person sees as bright red might be seen by another as, say, orange. In colour therapy, practitioners believe that our experience of colour is a direct reflection of our state of health. This being the case, they then use colour to correct any imbalances in our wellbeing. This part of the book unravels the influence of colour – and light – in our everyday lives. It looks in detail at the seven colours of the spectrum, showing how each can have a profound impact on our mind, body and emotions. It then explains how, through techniques such as meditation and visualization, and even through eating foods in certain colour combinations, we can begin to use colour to optimize our wellbeing and to heal ourselves.

Colour fundamentals

Colour is a universal language. Everything under the sun is affected by colour. Plants, animals, bacteria, chemical reactions, all exhibit changes of behaviour when exposed to different colours. It is also a subconscious language that we use instinctively in every area of our lives.

Natural environments

The human characteristic of adaptability allows us to successfully inhabit all sorts of environments. Whether living in a forest or a desert, people adapt to the unique qualities of their surroundings. We get used to the colours and shapes around us, which is why a change of scene, such as a holiday, makes us sharply, refreshingly aware of many different details of colour, light and shape. Colour plays a big part in creating the ambience and mood of a place because its vibrational energy charges our emotions and energy levels.

the calm of nature

When escaping from the crowded and grey environment of towns and cities, most people experience a noticeable relaxation and lifting of mood as the green of nature fills their vision. Walking through woodland where the light is predominantly filtered through green leaves creates a sense of calm in the emotions and an expansive, increased sense of connection with our surroundings.

△ **Inside a wood or forest the trees alter the quality of light to something completely different from the one that exists outside it.**

The feeling of relaxation and the renewed sense of mental perspective during and after a country walk is so common that few will stop to think about it when the walk is over, but they will subconsciously feel profound benefits from the experience.

holiday happiness

Many people enjoy relaxing by the seaside in summer. The predominant colours are the blues of the sea and sky, which introduce a feeling of expansiveness and peace. Turquoise tempers the deeper blues with an extra sense of calm and comfort. The golden yellow of sand and sunlight energize the body's systems, helping to restore balanced functioning by reducing anxiety and stress levels, and creating happiness and clarity in the mind. It is no wonder with today's hectic lifestyle that two weeks doing

▽ **When we dream of holidays, the first image that often comes to mind is a beach. The yellows and blues of the seaside revitalize our energies.**

△ Deserts provide endless variations of a few colours and their calm stillness has inspired visionaries and mystics for centuries.

special places

Colour in the landscape separates and defines special places. The white cliffs of Dover symbolize more than simply the end of the land of England. Their very starkness suggests both a barrier of otherworldliness, a mystical separation from the mainland of Europe and – when seen from afar – an invitation to explore new possibilities.

In Australia, Uluru (Ayer's Rock) is sacred to the Aborigine peoples, not just because of its shape and size, but because of the amazing red coloration the rock has, especially at sunset. The colour of blood, the energy of life and heat, it rises dramatically out of the vast landscape and is regarded by the Aboriginals as the birthplace of the gods. In the south-west states of America, the canyons, especially the Painted Canyon, were held in the same awe by the people living in the region because the powerful colour symbolism was so suggestive of the generative forces of life. In the same way certain mountains – Mt Shasta in California, Mt Fuji in Japan and Mt Kailash in the Tibetan Himalayas – are held in awe as focuses of power and transcendence because their white peaks dominate the landscape and evoke the purity of the heavenly realms.

▽ Uluru, formerly known as Ayer's Rock, in Australia is a perfect example of how the natural colour of rock can take on magical and sacred significance for the people who live near it.

△ Archaeological evidence shows that our earliest ancestors felt exactly the same as we do about flowers, offering tokens made from them at important ceremonies and life-events.

nothing and simply being on a beach in the sunshine is regarded by many as the perfect holiday, and one which they will repeat each year with unfailing regularity.

The same colour combination of blues and golds occurs in many desert or near-desert conditions and it is perhaps significant that in the past many people have sought the deserts of the world as places of mysticism, for contemplation, visions and religious inspiration. With such isolation, very few distractions and the stimulus of blues, golds and yellows directly affecting the function of the nervous system, such places encourage the deepest thought.

Nature's use of colour

In the natural world colour is used in two main ways: to hide and to reveal. Considering that full colour vision is a very rare development in the animal world it is surprising how sophisticated nature's use of colour can be.

the seeing world

In the simplest of eyes there is only the ability to distinguish between light and dark. In creatures that live in darkness, for example in the depths of the ocean, colour vision is not as important as other sensory mechanisms for identifying electromagnetic radiations such as electric currents. But where there is sunlight, colour vision does become important. Experiments have shown that though many insects are sensitive only to green, blue and violet light, they can see beyond the human range, well into ultraviolet. Birds, dogs and cats have different degrees of colour recognition depending on the importance of sight

△ Bees' eyes see different frequencies of light from those that the human eye is able to recognize. Ultraviolet frequencies play a vital role in the bee's ability to locate flowers.

△ The male peacock has evolved a fabulous display of tail feathers to attract a mate.

▽ The courtship and mating rituals of birds rely heavily on dramatic displays of colour in the male's plumage.

compared with their other sensing mechanisms. Owls and hawks need acute visual sensitivity to movement, while dogs rely less on colour vision because their highly effective sense of smell is their dominant sense for gathering information. Full-spectrum colour is seen by the higher vertebrates, including humans, as well as a few unexpected animals, such as tortoises and the octopus.

The eye is not the only mechanism for recording light and colour, nor does the greatest use of colour belong to those creatures with the best colour vision. The eye is simply a specialist organ for recording colour and light. Light is an energy and its vibrations can create many changes in physical matter. It is thought that within the human skin there are specialist cells that have a great sensitivity to light, and that it is possible to notice subtle changes that take place when these are exposed to colours. It seems that this method of sensing increases when there is impairment of vision.

Plants have no specialized organs for colour recognition as such, yet colour is employed magnificently as a communication device. Bees and other insects are drawn to flowers by their colour and this ensures the fertilization of seeds and the continuation of the species. As it ripens, fruit accumulates sugars, so changing colour to indicate that it has become edible to animals. The animals then eat the fruit and spread the seeds through their droppings.

▽ Some animals use colour to imitate aggressive species as a form of protection. Some butterflies, for example, have large eye-like markings.

colour prevailing in a habitat. So, for example, the ragged vertical stripes of the zebra help it to blend into the tall grasses of the African plains, by disguising its size and shape. Some creatures have the ability to change colour very quickly, to achieve an almost perfect match with their background. The slow-moving chameleon has an amazing range of colour changes as does the bottom-feeding flatfish, the plaice. Both of these creatures are virtually impossible to see until they move. Perhaps the most unusual and striking use of colour is the protective warning or camouflage device of the squid, which has evolved a complex and beautiful language of expression and mood by sending constantly changing waves of rippling colours across its body.

▽ No colouring is accidental or superficial, it is a survival strategy, an evolutionary advantage that all creatures, such as this jellyfish, utilize.

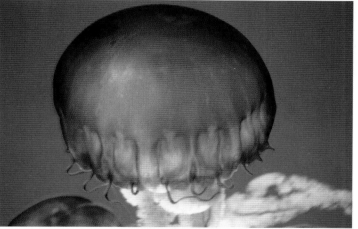

warning signals

In some creatures bright and striking colour displays are used to attract a mate or to act as a warning of aggressive superiority. The male peacock displays its fan of wonderful tail feathers when trying to attract the attentions of a female and to demonstrate superiority to a potential rival. In insects and snakes, bold, distinctive markings, such as the yellow and black stripes of the wasp, are recognized as danger signals by other species. This colour strategy can be so effective that even some completely non-toxic and harmless animals mimic the coloration of a poisonous or dangerous species to avoid unwanted attention from predators. The eye and face patterns on the wings of some butterflies and moths mimic the aggressive displays of much larger animals to much the same effect.

camouflage

Using colour to blend with the surroundings is a common strategy. Camouflage often mimics the light and

▷ The chameleon has developed special pigment cells that rapidly blend with its surroundings to disguise it from predators who rely on sight.

Climate, culture and colour

Although the physical effects of colour are biologically constant, people living in different climates understand and interpret colour in ways that can differ, and even oppose each other. Colour becomes a language of tribe and culture, and to members of the tribe the messages of colour are easy to read on a subconscious level. However, these colour messages mean little or nothing to people from a different culture. The energy of colour remains constant but the significance of that energy changes.

black and white

For people of the northern hemisphere, the north is a region of ice and snow where the sun never travels. The north therefore is associated with the white of snow or the black of winter and night. In the southern hemisphere, however, winter weather comes from Antarctica, from the south, and therefore white and black are linked to the south rather than the north. This affects other colours and elements accordingly.

In Europe, for example, death has traditionally been associated with the colour black. Funeral cortèges use black cars, and coffin bearers and mourners dress in black. In China, however, mourners wear white, because white is the colour of winter when all things return to the earth in a dormant state. In fact, traditionally minded Chinese will avoid wearing white, because it reminds them of the death shroud, whereas in the West, white is associated with innocence.

red and white

There are some colour combinations that seem to have the same resonance in most parts of the world. Two of the colours most frequently found together are red and white, symbolizing the polarities of male and female. In Tibetan symbolism and in some pagan traditions, red is the colour of the female Sun, white the male Moon. The two together are the power of creation, the union of opposites, the joining of Heaven

and Earth. Right across the northern hemisphere, in the Arctic and temperate zones, these colours appear each autumn after the fertilizing rains, in the form of the fly agaric mushroom, characterized by its red top and white spots. The fly agaric is a favourite food of the reindeer of Lapland, and the native Sami peoples of that region observed the apparent intoxication that the animals showed after eating the fungi. The Sami, along with every Siberian tribe, woodland American Indians and others, learned to dry and eat small portions of the mushroom in order to enter exalted altered states of reality, the realms of the spirits and gods. Ceremonial costumes of red, decorated with white polka dots, were worn by the shamans and healers of these peoples and still are today.

It is interesting that the Western image of Father Christmas retains all the symbolism of the Arctic shaman: dressed in red and white, he is drawn in his sleigh by reindeer, and he travels across the sky-worlds to bring the magic of gifts to his people in their time of hardship – the depths of winter.

◁ White has become traditional for Western weddings where it is regarded as a symbol of purity and new beginnings.

green

In Western Europe forests dominated the landscape for thousands of years. The colour green was always associated with the wildness of nature, the power of growth and of freedom. The woodland world was believed to be inhabited by spirits, elves and fairies, who were often dressed in green. The dominant energy, the intelligence of nature, was represented by the Green Man – a fusion of human and plant life. In the Arabic world, green is the sacred colour of Islam. In a landscape that is dominated by desert and arid wilderness, green is the colour of oases, providers of life, food, water and shelter. To the Arabic mind, green represents the refuge of heavenly paradise. In the West, green is the force and wildness of nature.

▽ Each figure in this Tibetan mandala is identified by its colour, denoting the exact energy each manifestation displays to the meditator.

△ In Peru traditional clothing tends to be as bright and colourful as possible.

traditional uses of colour

Mankind's use of colour grew from the needs and limitations of the environment. The first colours were of the earth – the red,

△ Bold colours and extravagant designs have characterized war dress for millennia. Colour is used to threaten the opposition and create a sense of unity among warriors on the same side.

ochre and black of cave paintings created from ground-up iron-bearing rocks and clays, and soot. Red ochre is the earliest dye used worldwide, and sacred red is found in burial chambers in most parts of the world.

development of dyes

Plant dyes provide a range of browns, yellows, blues and greens. The rarity of a colour or the difficulty of producing a dye quickened the birth of the fashion industry. Only the rich and powerful used the expensive colours, which became symbols of privilege and power. Blue was difficult to produce so the plant woad was precious and its use probably had spiritual significance to the ancient Britons and Picts who were famed for its use. In the long history of the Roman Empire, the most prestigious colour was purple, extracted from the shells of Mediterranean shellfish, by a secret process originally known only to the Phoenician traders of the eastern seaboard. Wearing purple robes was the exclusive right of the emperor. Lesser nobles were ranked by the precise widths of purple stripe that they were allowed to wear on their togas. Wearing too much purple was a serious offence.

display and concealment

Colour is used in dress to display and to conceal, as it is in nature. Tartans show a mix of the practical and social uses of colour. Woven tartans have been found on mummies in the Taklamakan desert of Mongolia, though today this cloth is more often associated with Scotland and Ireland.

The choice and blend of colours as well as the pattern of warp and weave in Scottish tartans are unique to each clan or tribal grouping, and no clan would dream of wearing another's tartan. Every tartan has

▷ In this Byzantine mosaic each figure's rank and status is identified by the amount of purple worn. The central figure is the Emperor Justinian, dressed all in purple.

several variations of colour and pattern – for example, hunting tartans use a blend of tones to act as a camouflage in the Highland landscape. Dress tartans have bright reds and yellows, and are worn at social occasions.

group identity

While hunters favour camouflage, warriors aim for maximum display. Colour can be a means of identification, and an aggressive statement, so red is a common military colour. The bright red uniform that the British Infantry wore for hundreds of years was worn to intimidate. Other groups, such as the Masai, also dress warriors in red.

Traditional clothing around the world tends to reflect tribal unity. To an outsider the group may be perceived as dressing alike, but to the insider there are subtle differences that clearly denote rank and status.

Colour co-ordination

An instinct for harmonizing and co-ordinating colour is a gift that some people are born with, but the rest of us can manage if we follow a few guidelines. In practice, shades, tones and tints that work well together do so because of their natural visual relationship, and there are simple rules to mixing and matching colour.

When similar colours are placed next to each other, each loses some of its vibrant qualities. Complementary colours, those opposite to each other on the colour wheel, will augment each other's qualities. Colours that are next but one to each other on the

▽ Colour in nature, designed for survival, often makes harmonious juxtapositions that are borrowed by fashion designers.

HOW COLOURS ARE DEFINED
• A hue is the quality of a colour that enables us to classify it as red, green, yellow etc.
• A tint is a hue with white added.
• A shade is a hue with black added.
• A tone is a hue with grey added. Tints look good together, as do shades or tones, but mixing tints, shades and tones does not always work well.

True Colour Wheel, present pleasing combinations that are often employed as tints by interior designers to create a comfortable space.

colour categories
Carol Jackson, the author of the book *Colour Me Beautiful*, formulated categories of colour into a practical and easy to use system, based upon the four elements (fire, earth, air and water) and the seasons (spring, summer, autumn and winter). She applied the colour groupings to décor, furnishings, clothes and make-up.

△ Plants naturally grow together in swathes of the same species. Garden designers develop this theme of group planting to create stunning displays.

Spring colours are those linked to the water element. They feature warm and light tints, and no dark colours. Spring colours include turquoise, lilac, peach, coral, scarlet, violet, emerald, sunshine yellow, cream and sand. All the colours in this category are clear and almost delicate. They create a joyful and nurturing ambience.

Summer colours, linked to the air element, are all tones (that is, they have a lot of grey in them). This range of colours is

▽ Colours that appear with the season's changes become associated with the qualities of that time of year, and are reflected in our clothes.

▷ The colour wheel here is often described as the True Colour Wheel. This presentation of colour was put together by Sir Isaac Newton and has been used by many famous colour workers, such as Goethe and Steiner. It shows the complementary colour to red as turquoise. In the Artist's Colour Wheel, not shown here, the complementary colour to red is shown as green.

red

orange

magenta

yellow

green

violet

blue

turquoise

◁ When it comes to choices in fashion, no one system will suit everyone. Colouring and personality are factors to consider but the colours should also 'feel' right to wear.

△ Experiment with a wide range of colours in your clothing, and don't be afraid to mix strong shades together if that's what feels right.

▽ Try dressing in a colour range that complements your natural colouring and also dress in a contrasting style to compare. See how your behaviour is modified.

very subtle and includes maroon, rose, powder blue, sage green, pale yellow, lavender, plum, oyster and taupe. This is a 'middle-of-the-road' selection, that includes darker colours, but not heavy colours. Summer colours have an elegance that is also cool and contained.

Autumn colours are related to the fire element. These are warm colours. All are shades, which means they have black in them. They include mustard, olive green, flame, peacock, burnt orange, teal and burgundy. These colours are very rich and striking. They suggest maturity and depth.

Winter colours are connected with the earth element and feature a big contrast between hues, tints and shades. Winter colours include black, white, magenta, cyan, purple, lemon, silver, indigo, royal blue and jade. None of these colours are subtle, they are all bold and powerful.

These colour groupings can also reflect psychological personality types, not simply a person's natural colouring or skin type. For example, winter colours are often favoured by people with strong business sense, confidence and a practical nature. Spring colours, on the other hand, are popular with those of an artistic, sensitive and quiet disposition.

There can also be a strong second preference in colour groupings. Occasionally the second preference can be useful in choosing clothes that are designed to create a particular effect, for a presentation or interview for example. However, wearing colours to impress people may feel rather uncomfortable compared to wearing your natural, instinctive choice. Both men and women can use these colour categories for choosing clothes, and women often use it too when selecting make-up.

Colour for commercial use

Colour affects everyone at an unconscious level, that is, below the awareness of normal everyday thought. So politicians, businesses and advertisers have learned to manipulate the desired response by using the language of colour. Careful use of colour can bypass the viewer's ability to discriminate or make instant critical judgements.

advertising

The human eye can distinguish between hundreds of shades of colour, and each shade elicits a slightly different emotional and behavioural response. The advertising industry exploits this ability and constantly bombards us with subliminal messages through the use of colour. As those who work with hypnosis and auto-suggestion know well, subliminal messages, because they are not recognized by the conscious mind, can have a profound effect on our behaviour and attitudes. It is the advertisers' job to select the most appropriate colours for their product 'message' as well as an image that is uniquely identifiable. The right colour or combination of colours can make all the difference to product sales.

△ Retail outlets depend on being seen and recognized. Colours and logos that can be seen from a long way have a distinct advantage.

▽ An effective interior design will match the colour and shape of a room to its function, creating an ideal atmosphere. Muted colours and soft lighting will promote relaxation in this restaurant's customers.

colour manipulation

Red is the key colour in products that suggest energy, vigour, excitement and speed. Fast food outlets very often combine a bright red with yellow or white in their logos and décor. Bright yellow stimulates the digestive system, so we feel hungry, while white combined with red suggests clean, efficient service. Using bright red and a creamy white as interior colours in eating places ensures that customers are focused on the business of eating rather than on socializing. Whites and greys also prevent people from relaxing and becoming too comfortable. On the other hand, in up-market restaurants, dark, rich reds are often combined with subdued lighting to create an atmosphere of comfort and security. This encourages people to talk quietly or intimately, while taking time over a meal. Orange or yellow walls in eating places make for a convivial and a lively atmosphere, with more bustle and noise. These colours are often used in bars, bistros and coffee houses to create an ideal atmosphere for chatter and socializing.

Blue suggests sobriety, control and responsibility, and is used in products where a sense of stability and authority is required.

◁ This interior, though at first glance abstract and random, draws the eye to a reception area by using warm, more welcoming colours.

▽ Warm colours in a bar setting often encourage relaxation and enjoyment.

colour fundamentals

Light or mid-blue is rarely used in food advertising as we tend to associate it with decay in that context. Dark blue labelling combined with a rich yellow or gold is often effective in the promotion of specialist gourmet foods, suggesting a certain level of detachment and even superiority from the everyday. The qualities associated with blue make it a popular colour for the interiors of public service buildings such as banks, where it helps to keep a subdued, serious and unemotional ambience.

Green colours and tones are used to promote products that suggest freshness, and naturalness. Often green coloured packaging will form part of a claim made by the manufactuer that the product will bring health benefits. Dark greens and mid tones are used in preference to olive and yellow greens, as these lighter green colours may suggest and even at times create feelings of unease and nausea.

colour at work

There is ample evidence, both anecdotal and researched, that colour is an important factor in every environment. The same pale greens that can suggest nausea in food environments, especially the sallower shades,

are often used in large public meeting spaces and corridors where people need to be encouraged to keep on the move rather than loiter and socialize. The wrong colour combinations in an office, greys and cool blues for example, or browns and tans, not

▽ In this office colours have been kept cool to encourage quiet efficiency, but avoid the sedating effect of dark blues.

only affect the mood of the staff but can also reduce profits, while creams and pale tones can create a rather uninvolved attitude from the workforce. Yellows, oranges and peachy pinks with turquoise and warm shades of green can transform a company's workforce and productivity from mediocre to efficient.

Colour should never be thoughtlessly applied. It is a vibrant, life-sustaining energy that should be used with care and skill.

Colour inside the home

The home, whatever its shape and size, always becomes a reflection of the people who live in it. Our own space speaks volumes about our personal tastes and attitudes. Becoming more conscious of the effects of colour on behaviour, and learning what colours reflect our own energies, makes us better able to choose the right colours for our home.

Recommendations about using colour in the home, like all opinions of what is considered fashionable, are usually very culturally specific and change from one year to the next. Formulas can be helpful, but

they should never supersede personal choice. In general, colours with red in them will warm up a cool space, such as a north-facing room. Warm colours will also make a space feel smaller. Colours with blues in them will make a room feel cool and appear larger. Dark hues will reduce the apparent size of the space and light hues will make it seem larger than it is.

entrance halls

Hallways are the first rooms entered in many homes. They are rarely large enough to be a living space and so can be treated as a transition between the outside world and the inner privacy of the rooms beyond. Hallways immediately reflect how we wish to be seen by the world. They can be extremely formal or simply act as a storage space. Colours here will suggest whether the hall is a barrier or a welcome sign. White or cream is often chosen as a neutral colour that acts as an emotional air-lock. Rich, deep colours, whether warm or cool, will create a strong impression of personality and a clear boundary to demarcate territory.

The colour used in an entrance hall will directly affect the visitor, so choose wisely. Strong reds are energizing while slightly

▽ Subdued earth tones are enlivened here with the use of complementary blues and yellows.

△ Tints of orange, creams and browns create a spacious feel while bringing a quality of warmth.

▽ The cool blues here create spaciousness and neatness. Stairs and banisters in red and yellow articulate depth and distance in a practical way.

△ A mix of yellow and green items in a kitchen that is decorated in neutral colours creates a bright and cheerful room.

muted reds (with a hint of brown) suggest solid, powerful and practical comfort. Pinks, depending on the tint, offer a warm, friendly, non-threatening atmosphere. Blues are calming and sedating, useful for city homes where the outside world is noisy and hectic. A deep blue will help to cool over-stressed and over-stimulated nervous systems, generating relaxation and a sense of peace and quiet. Greens and browns suggest the natural world, though here it is very important which shades and tones are used. A strong, bright green can look fine in nature where light levels are so complex that they create a huge variety of subtle shades. Follow nature's example and imitate the diffusion of light by using a range of tones and shades of greens, rather than one strong block of colour.

kitchens and bathrooms

Utilitarian rooms like the kitchen and bathroom need colours that harmonize with their functions. For example, it is a good idea for bathrooms to be painted in warm tones – yellows, pinks and oranges. These give a comfortable, relaxing brightness and reflect the energies of cleansing and caring. Yellow in the kitchen, on the other hand, can be over-stimulating to the digestive system unless tempered by other colours, such as blues and greens. Red can heighten emotions and can cause recklessness and a lack of consideration, whereas warm shades of terracotta connect to the practical earthiness of cooking and baking.

Blues and white are cool and efficient. They are not the best main colours for a kitchen that is a social space as well as an area of food preparation, but their clean freshness together makes them ideal as a colour for plates and other crockery. Cool colours in both rooms could be enhanced by the addition of a strong third colour to offset them. A luxurious space can be created by adding gold or a rich green to a stark blue and white setting.

Modern design's trend for wide expanses of stainless steel in kitchens is practical in commercial premises but can give an empty, unemotional feel to a family room that should be warm and welcoming.

△ It is important to choose the appropriate shade of colour in decoration. A warm yellow in a kitchen is refreshing, a yellow that has more green in it may create the opposite effect.

◁ Bathrooms in bright, warm colours are enlivening and uplifting – as well as feeling both relaxing and cleansing.

▽ Blue and white are classic colours to use in a bathroom, and in a room where there is plenty of natural light will bring a sense of clean tidiness without overwhelming coldness.

△ This choice of colours will allow feelings of comfort, restfulness and a certain dreaminess to develop – ideal for a quiet space.

▽ Warm tones on large areas keep a space comfortable while spots of brighter colour bring individuality and visual interest.

△ Brown promotes calm but this corner would benefit from a splash of yellow to add life.

living rooms

The only golden colour rule in the home is that if you dislike a particular colour – you should change it. Living in an atmosphere that you find disturbing in any way does not support health and wellbeing.

The main living area in the house needs to be a reflection of the owner's personality and should also be flexible enough to remain comfortable and generate a positive influence throughout all sorts of activities

▽ A collection of items with a range of complementary tones and hues creates a balance of energy, both visually and emotionally.

highlights of these colours will add depth and equilibrium to the home, maintaining a healthy balance of vibration.

Acquiring small items, such as cushions, throws or ornaments, that can be changed or their placement in the space rearranged, can be far more practical and flexible than adjusting large areas of colour in a room to

reflect the energies of the people using it. Careful use of single coloured items can enhance a particular space. These items can be of similar tones or can be complementary colours for a subtle approach. Choosing contrasting colours can add a much more dramatic effect that draws attention to a particular area of the room.

INSTANT COLOUR

Keeping the main colour in the living area neutral means that it is a lot easier to change your surroundings from a cool, calm environment to a rich vibrant one, simply by swapping fabrics and soft furnishings. Add to this an adjustment in lighting, or even the addition of a few candles, and you have a cost-effective way of adjusting the overall ambience to suit your needs.

▽ **Even though complementary colours from the artist's colour wheel are used here, the red by its very nature is more dominant, bringing energy into a neutral white area.**

▽ **Blues with a hint of pink or violet have the quality of a warm summer sky and are inviting rather than isolating. A vase of vibrant orange flowers adds to the warmth.**

△ Greens in nature display variation with the constant play of light. Indoors, greens are best in subtle, tempered shades.

and moods. A background colour chosen from a pale version of one's favourite colour will be generally supportive and in harmony with the individual's energy field. If more than one person lives in a space a neutral tone can be chosen, or a compromise needs to be found so that everyone feels equally comfortable. For example, if one person's favourite colour is green and their partner's is blue, a turquoise colour scheme might be a good choice. Or, a complementary colour could be chosen, in this case a peach, gold or a pink tone.

Many people's choice of colours follows a similar pattern to other preferences in life. We prefer certain types of music and food, for example, but few of us would be happy just eating one thing all the time or listening endlessly to one piece of music. The same is true with colour. You may prefer tones that are within the turquoise through light blue to violet range of the spectrum, sometimes tending towards turquoise, other times towards magenta. If so, it is less likely that a yellow or red would appear in your colour scheme, but nonetheless, a few

▽ A calm blue background can be quickly enlivened with temporary elements if you are in need of some stimulation and energy.

▽ Chair covers that can be changed allow you to alter the feel of a space to suit your preferences at different times.

bedrooms

Perhaps the most important room in the house for most people is the bedroom, as this is where we spend the longest periods of time. These rooms are also our most individual and personal spaces so we need to be as comfortable in them as possible. Even a favourite colour can become a depressing influence if there is not a balance with other colours.

▽ Cool colours in a bedroom are perfect as they encourage the mind to quieten down and release the hectic activities of the day.

△ Blues and whites, especially with a hint of violet or purple, are quietening, restful colours that help the body's natural sleep rhythms.

Colour favourites can also change quite quickly, especially with a greater awareness of the energy of colour vibrations. Generally speaking, colours that are restful and calming are better in bedrooms. Remember that the colour on the walls and fabrics will be having some effect on your energies even when you have your eyes shut. Muted and mixed tones are probably preferable to strong, bold colours. Blues calm the mind and lower the body's levels of activity, naturally encouraging sleep. Yellows, on the other hand, may be overstimulating – fine for waking up in the morning but not so good for getting a good night's rest. Pale violets will encourage relaxing, dreamy states and pale pinks will give a feeling of security.

▽ Pink and violet hues are light and calming and are good healing and recuperating colours.

▷ **Creative spaces are often made more effective when there is a range of colour energies – this encourages play but not necessarily mental focus.**

▽ **A splash of yellow would bring a note of clarity and inspiration to this bland work area.**

studies and workrooms

Work rooms such as studies and offices should reflect and complement the energy of the activity. Mental clarity and inspiration, for example, are promoted by bright yellow. and small amounts of yellow like a lampstand or letter rack, work just as well as yellow walls or curtains. Even a sheet of yellow card that can be placed in view can

be very effective when you are feeling particularly tired. Cool blues are useful for calming down thought processes so that intuition and new ideas can emerge. In a busy space, where there is high energy and a fast pace, the presence of some blue can help to keep a peaceful ambience.

For physical dexterity and practical work, reds and oranges provide energy and focus, balanced by complementary greens to encourage calmness of mind and emotions. These colours are ideal combinations for sewing, painting and other creative arts, as they provide a comfortable space where work can be carried out for long periods.

◁ **Your own character will determine whether you work more effectively in an energizing or a sedating environment.**

The colour palette

Each colour has a set of clearly defined influences and meanings, which can be invaluable in understanding the world around us and our behaviour patterns. These qualities can also be used to create particular impressions on others. A desired image or a subtle message can be sent with colour much more effectively than with words.

Red

Red is the colour with the longest wavelength. It is the nearest visible light to infrared in the electromagnetic spectrum. Infrared waves (with longer wavelengths) produce heat, and very hot objects become visibly red. Even rocks will become red when they are heated sufficiently. This is seen in volcanic eruptions when lava pours out on to the surface of the earth.

living red

Instinctively, the occurrence of red makes us wary, as we connect it with heat and the potential danger of burning. Red lights are

△ Red is the colour of heat and burning, and the dramatic sight of red-hot objects or fire provokes instinctive fear and caution.

▽ The effect of red on the eye is quite unusual. For the colour to be seen, the eye itself makes internal adjustments. This alteration means that we see red objects as closer than they really are.

built into artificial fires to help simulate the cosiness of a real fire. Too much heat and red burns, but at the right level it supports our lives and gives us comfort.

Being the colour of blood, red has symbolic links with living and life. Spilling or losing blood brings illness and death. Wearing red, eating red foods and surrounding yourself with red increases the body's ability to absorb iron, the metal that is responsible for the colour of haemoglobin in the blood. The presence of haemoglobin allows the blood to absorb oxygen in the lungs and to transport that life-giving oxygen to the cells of the body.

Physical activity and the energy that supports it also has a red vibration. If speed, danger, daring or courage are involved, the red quality of the activity increases. Mountaineers, racing car drivers and stuntmen all have 'red' careers.

feeling red

Phrases like 'red light district' and 'scarlet woman' aptly describe the sexual nature of red. Some aspects of red behaviour are not socially acceptable. Red together with black is associated with evil, for example in the archetypal 'red devil' of medieval artists.

△ The cliché of what the red sports car is thought to represent sums up the dynamic, direct, self-absorbed quality of red energy.

PUT RED IN YOUR LIFE WHEN THERE IS ...
• a lack of enthusiasm and interest in life
• a lack of energy and a feeling of over-tiredness
• an inability to make your dreams a practical reality
• a feeling of insecurity, unwarranted fear, or anxiety

◁ **When a woman wears the colour red, it has an immediacy and boldness. It says 'I am here, notice me' and is closely associated with sex appeal, and also with illicit passion.**

who abuse it. These people often display some of the negative qualities that are associated with red – selfishness and an interest only in personal, rather than global, survival and short-term security.

To be healthy in a long-term sense, we need the colour red to reconnect ourselves to the planet and support it as it supports us. For our personal development, the role involves taking responsibility for our own wellbeing and survival as part of humanity as a whole, not being separate from it. Although often seen as a 'green' issue, global and local conservation is also about survival, which is a red issue. Red and green issues are intrinsically linked, as they are complementary colours.

USING RED
If you want to come across as a bold and dynamic person, wear a red scarf or tie. This is especially effective if you have an event coming up at which your confidence needs a boost, such as an interview or a presentation. You might also find this useful for a social occasion when you feel nervous about some new people.

Blatant expression of emotion is not always easy to handle, whether it is sexuality, passion, anger or aggression. When expressing red emotions, the heart beats faster, the capillaries dilate and the skin becomes flushed and feels warm.

Red is thought of as an immediate colour. This affects the thinking processes, causing restlessness and impatience. Red can result in very selfish behaviour, a focus on personal needs and survival above everything else. Sometimes the drive to survive is what fuels

◁ **Red can easily lead to excess as its own nature is impulsive and reckless. Drunken behaviour exemplifies many qualities of too much red energy.**

impulsive actions and rash comments. When these traits are managed well they create capable business people who are innovators and entrepreneurs, preferring to move from one project to another, getting an operation on its feet then moving on. They are gifted with being able to manifest new ideas. Often people with red traits are also renowned for their daring exploits, and they can be somewhat extrovert and boastful about their skills.

Red brings focus to the physicality of life, to the process of living. The colour is symbolic of what we need to survive. Life should be grabbed and lived with a sense of immediacy. Without red we become listless and out of touch with reality and we fail to live our dreams in this world. Without the foundation that red gives us we just daydream of escaping into fantasy worlds.

Red keeps us rooted in the red energy of our planet. People who become detached or divorced from the planet tend to be those

Orange

While red is associated with fiery heat, orange is more closely linked to the benign warmth of the sun and of fire. Like fire, orange energy displays some sense of direction and purpose – it moves along those pathways which fuel its own existence. Orange is certainly dynamic, but more thoughtful and controlled than explosive red. As a mixture of red and yellow, orange blends the properties of both primary colours. (The secondary colours – orange, green and violet – are also able to balance contrasting energies.) Curiosity is one of the driving characteristics of the orange vibration and this brings exploration and creativity, particularly on a practical level.

△ Orange warms without burning. The light of sunrise and sunset encourages a sensitivity to creative ideas and contemplative thought.

▷ A fox cub illustrates how orange promotes exploration, play and creativity.

▽ Orange combines the new energy of red with the organizing qualities of yellow.

PUT ORANGE IN YOUR LIFE WHEN THERE IS ...

• a feeling of bleakness and boredom, particularly where there is a sense that time is really dragging
• a lack of interest in what is going on around you, even to the degree of disdaining to become involved in any way
• a resentment of changes in familiar routines and an obsessive need to have things in their 'proper' place
• over-seriousness – taking oneself too seriously, being unable to see humour and playfulness in life
• a fear of experiencing pleasure through the senses and of enjoying sensuality
• an inability to let go of the past. This can be especially apparent after an accident or shock where the mind continually revolves around the issues involved – the 'what if ...' and 'if only I had done this instead of that ...'
• a problem with blocked experiences in life, such as a decrease in personal creativity

playing at life

While red is a focusing or self-centred energy, orange reaches out to see what it feels like to be somewhere else – it is the toddler trying to grasp and wanting to taste everything. Orange is learning to experience the world with a sense of play and enjoyment.

Strangely, surveys have often found orange to be the least popular of colours (the favourites being green and blue). Exploring and reaching out can sometimes be painful. We learn that stroking a cat's fur is enjoyable and fun, but pulling a cat's whiskers can lead to the pain of a swift retaliation. Learning by exploring is somewhat risky, full of unknowns – this is the element of excitement, but it can also bring shock and stress. Yet because the orange energy is purposeful and has an instinct for moving on, it can creatively remove blocks to restriction and stagnation.

Orange represents instinctive rather than intellectual or thought-out problem solving. Orange energy often manifests itself

△ **Orange peel – washed first, or from organic sources – makes a soothing tea that aids digestion and helps to relax the body and release any feelings of stress.**

when someone is working on the design of their garden. It can also emerge through a potter working clay, or an artist roughing out a sketch, or a poet scribbling ideas. Even doodling on a pad while listening to someone on the telephone is exhibiting the natural urge to explore through creativity – to allow a flow of energy to balance the sense of identity characterized by red.

A balance of orange energy brings a willingness to get involved, to 'get one's hands dirty' with practical exploration. It gives the ability to fill time creatively and to be aware of the needs of the body. Without orange energy, attention tends to get drawn to the head, filling our lives with ideas, thoughts and theories. Orange enables us to put these thought processes into practice in the world in a creative way, and to enjoy the experience of doing so.

USING ORANGE
In times of stress, or after a shock or a surprise, wearing shades of orange can help the body to return to a state of balance.

Yellow

Yellow is a bright, sunny colour. Most people will recognize the sensation of warmth and vitality when looking at a strong, pure yellow. Like the energy of a bright, sunny morning yellow brings clarity and awareness. As with all colours, different yellows will create markedly different responses. An orange-yellow or golden colour imparts a sense of establishment, of solidity and assuredness, a rich, round sensation of inner warmth. A clean, light yellow seems to clear the mind while keeping it alert and active

PUT YELLOW IN YOUR LIFE WHEN THERE IS ...

- confusion and indecision
- fear and anxiety caused by unknown factors leading to nervous and digestive disorders
- a weak and confused immune system – frequent minor illnesses, intolerances and allergies to foods and other substances
- nervous exhaustion, nervous breakdown, 'burn out', panic attacks, hot flushes
- poor memory, inability to concentrate or study
- tendency to Seasonal Affective Disorder (SAD) or lethargy and depression in dull weather
- digestive difficulties, malabsorption of food

△ The light of the morning sun is stimulating and enlivening to plants and daytime creatures.

▽ Yellow enriches, lightens and activates many of the systems of the body. It tends to encourage orderliness and clarity.

in a state of readiness. An acid yellow can be stimulating and enlivening, a shade of yellow that has just a touch of green, however, will create a degree of discomfort, disorientation and even nausea.

decisive yellow

The functions of the yellow vibration have to do with decision-making, with what to do in any given situation. Decisions rely on information, but more importantly on the ability to select bits of information that are relevant. Discrimination, knowing what is what, is a 'yellow' skill upon which we constantly rely for our wellbeing, physically as well as mentally.

The digestive system, the immune system and the nervous system all reflect yellow frequencies. The functions of the digestive system are to break down, identify and absorb those substances that the body requires for maintenance and growth, and to eliminate from the system those substances that are harmful or unnecessary. The

▷ The colour yellow is naturally associated with the sun itself, and so with its life-giving and sustaining energies. Lemons and yellow flowers are instant reminders of these qualities and an easy way to access them.

▽ Honey, the concentrated energy of sunlight turned into nectar sugars by plants and processed by bees, has many yellow qualities: it helps the digestive system, is gently energizing and is a powerful immune system booster.

immune system works in a similar way. Its various organs and defences are able to identify and destroy cells that are in the wrong place or have come into the body from outside, such as bacteria and viruses.

The digestive system and the immune system rely on correct decisions about what is useful and what is dangerous. Both need qualities of intelligence, memory and discrimination. If for some reason, such as stress, the systems fail to work as well as they should, mistakes are made: the digestion may not absorb nutrients that are needed and the immune system may identify harmless substances as dangerous, creating intolerance or allergic reactions.

The nervous system relays information to the brain, which then categorizes, interprets and acts upon the signals. Correct identification of priorities leads to an easy relationship with the world. When this yellow function is lacking, confusion and indecision creep in. Fear and worry are the consequence of an imbalance of yellow energy, when wrong information and a lack of clear and logical thought result in an inability to act positively.

Society in the West is currently very focused on the yellow qualities of acquisition of knowledge, organization, structure and information exchange. The senses are continually bombarded with information, and large amounts of yellow energy are used up. However, people in this work environment spend the day in artificial light and are badly lacking in the yellow energy of sunlight. As a result, they need additional yellow from food, furnishings and sunlight to help keep the balance in their busy lives.

◁ Eating outside in natural sunlight improves digestion and gives a feeling of wellbeing.

USING YELLOW

When working at a computer use a yellow mouse mat to improve your concentration and stay alert.

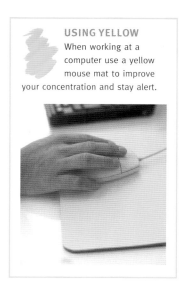

Green

Green is the colour of nature, the colour of the plant kingdoms. The human eye has its greatest sensitivity in the range of frequencies we perceive as green. Perhaps this skill evolved during mankind's early development as a forest dweller. The qualities of green are characterized by balance, and indeed green itself is found midway in the spectrum. Whereas the reds and yellows are warm colours, and the blues and violets are cool, green can be seen as either, depending on the shade.

△ Personal space and a sense of freedom helps to relax emotional and physical tensions. We respond to such views by taking a deep breath.

▽ The human eye recognizes more variation of colour in green than in any other colour. Individual choice can therefore be very particular.

green growth

The power of nature is green power. Green stands for growth and the desire to expand and increase. Yet growth requires change, and change means that what has been must disappear to be replaced by what is to come. The process of life is the process of transformation from one state to another, the death of one form giving birth to another. Balance and a sense of order must be present for growth. Growth is an expansion of

△ The need to expand, grow and increase is a core quality of green energy expressed in nature.

orderliness that must be sustainable, with each stage acting as a foundation for the next period of expansion.

green relationships

The colour green is the vibration of relationships, because in growing and expanding we meet others in the world around us.

△ **For people who work and live away from a natural environment, gardens and urban parks help to restore balance and perspective. Even a simple window box can have this effect.**

USING GREEN
When there is a sense
of thwarted ambition,
restriction or being
trapped by external circumstances,
surrounding yourself with greens,
or taking a walk in green gardens
will restore equilibrium.

Learning how to relate to others is a skill of balancing our needs with the needs of the other person. If it is possible to develop a mutually agreeable relationship of caring and sharing, both lives are enriched and expanded – our interaction with the world is broadened. When a relationship is formed that is negative, manipulative or unpleasant in some way – very often because one person is trying to gain power and control over the other (a negative green tendency) – then

our own potential for understanding the world is curtailed and restricted.

Green energy inevitably has to do with the pushing out of boundaries, of growing beyond what is known. Because it is expansive it must develop relationships with those things around it, but it must also have a degree of power and control.

The power of green can be expressed in a harmonious way, as in an ecological balance where all elements are accommodated and mutually supportive, or it can be destructive to everything around it, simply absorbing or taking over, enforcing new order on others. The energy that green creates is the energy of finding direction and new paths. Green enables us to find the means to the desired end; it provides the power to accomplish rather than power to dominate. In this way green shows how to balance difficult extremes to enable progress to be made.

Blue

Blue is the colour of distance. When artists of the early Renaissance began to consider how to represent perspective, they employed the simple observation that in nature the further away an object was in space, the more blue it appeared. When we think of blue in this way it is associated with looking beyond what is in the immediate environment – and the colour itself also has the effect of stretching the perceptions outwards to the unknown.

▽ The peaceful, restful energy of blue has almost universal popularity, and imbues the qualities of steadiness and reliability.

△ The blues that are found in the sea and sky help to free the mind from its normal activity.

communicative blue

There are two aspects of blue. On the one hand there is the experience of going beyond what is known – the active search for information or detail – and on the other hand the experience of rest and peacefulness, simply being happy to be alive without any particular focus of thought.

In some respects these seem to be contradictory qualities but in fact the uniting factor is the desire for equilibrium. For example, the teacher is better informed than the student. Communication allows the student to learn what the teacher knows. The teaching will stop when the teacher and student know the same information. This is a new state of equilibrium and peace that will continue until a new source of information is found and interaction begins again. All kinds of communication, like talking, listening, learning and the exchange

USING BLUE
Blue will help the easy flow of communication whether it is with other people or listening to your own thoughts and feelings. To help remember a speech, write your notes on blue paper.

▷ Using the colour blue in a situation of relaxation and repose will encourage quiet communication and feelings of peace.

of information and viewpoints are blue activities. So too, are the expressive arts – not just the performing arts such as acting, singing and music, but any art form that seeks to communicate with other people. Any of the five senses can be used to tell the story or carry the message.

Although blue is the colour of communication and the flow of energy it is a cool vibration. We can understand this property when we consider that redness or heat is often caused by a concentration or build-up of energy that cannot flow freely. Thus inflammation – a red, energetic state – in the body can be reduced by cooling the area down by using a blue vibration. This will counteract the red quality, or will help to remove the block and to create a flow of energy, thus enabling the area to return to normal functioning.

▽ Blue encourages an effective flow of peace and understanding. Many compassionate deities are associated with blue. The robes of the Virgin Mary are predominately blue indicating her ability to hear and respond to humanity.

distant emotions

The sense of distance gives blue a quality of detachment and devotion. Gazing into the sky naturally brings a sense of peace. The colour blue somehow seems to free the mind from its normal activity, removing us slightly from involvement with thought, emotion or physical action. A 'cool' personality avoids getting caught up in emotional turmoil or any particular belief. That impersonal quality is like the blue of the distant mountains, not overwhelmed by detail or closeness, but offering the possibility of greater perspectives. Blue is also linked to devotion. This is the quality of the vibration that can be understood as a constant stream of energy or communication towards the source of devotion, which is usually a powerful, universal focus of great depth such as the Virgin Mary, Krishna or Shiva – all of whom are associated with the colour blue.

Without some injection of blue in our lives helping the flow of information and energy, we will inevitably experience frustration, disappointment and lack of progress in whatever we do.

PUT BLUE IN YOUR LIFE WHEN THERE IS ...

• a need to calm agitated, excitable, or chaotic states
• a need to communicate clearly
• a need for help with new information or in seeing information in context
• a need for peace, detachment, solitude and rest

Indigo

There is a different quality to the experience of looking at a cloudless blue sky and a midnight blue sky. The indigo of the midnight sky amplifies the characteristics of blue in a profound, resonant way. At a physical level, while blue is a quietening and cooling colour, indigo is sedating. In a depressed state indigo is to be avoided as it can easily deepen the mood.

how indigo works

In a way, indigo turns blue energy inwards: while blue promotes some form of communication between people, indigo creates an internal communication in an individual that might manifest as profound thought processes, new insights, philosophy and

△ The midnight sky has an infinite depth that reflects the timeless quality of indigo light.

PUT INDIGO IN YOUR LIFE WHEN THERE IS ...

• a need to focus on personal issues, beliefs and ideas
• a need to develop sensitivity to the inner senses and intuition
• a need to cool and quieten normal mental processes
• a need to relieve physical, mental and emotional pain

• inability or difficulty in assimilating and understanding new concepts or philosophies
• a need for temporary relief and removal from everyday problems and difficult experiences in life
• a need for space and a desire for a period of solitude

intuition. The flow of blue can be fast, but the flow of indigo can be almost instantaneous, often leading to the sensation of inspiration 'coming out of the blue', with no previous development or build-up of thoughts and ideas. Intuition and sudden clarity of awareness, startling realizations and innovative concepts occur in the 'supercooled' state of indigo.

The depths of indigo may seem unfathomable and mysterious, but they can yield useful perceptions. Indigo is related to clairvoyance, clairsentience and clairaudience (clear seeing, feeling and hearing) and other psychic skills.

▽ Indigo pigment was derived from azurite and lapis lazuli and was an expensive commodity. Woad is one of the few vegetable dyes to produce the same deep blue colour.

△ The wonderful stained glass windows of Chartres cathedral in France are a masterpiece of medieval design, bathing the interior with a deep blue light that heightens the sensitivities and elevates awareness from the mundane world.

▽ Blueberries and sloes are some of the indigo foods that can be found growing wild.

△ In an indigo state of awareness, the stillness of the mind is unperturbed by thoughts that come and go – like fish moving through deep water.

profound indigo

The deep, directionless depths of indigo can sedate the conscious mind to a degree where more subtle, delicate perceptions can be registered. Blue energy is the skill of language and eloquence personified in the talker. Indigo energy definitely belongs to the listener. Blue energy can be frivolous and superficial, but indigo energy never fails to be profound and significant.

The internal quality of indigo and the enhanced sense of removal from normal, everyday communication can mean that those using a lot of indigo energy are able to step away from how the world is usually seen and come up with new and startling ways of thinking. The inventor has these qualities, going beyond the consensus view of what is possible while often appearing to be socially out of step or isolated. The internalizing qualities of indigo make it an ideal colour to use in contemplative and spiritual contexts, particularly in solitary meditations, and in visualization, where the inner senses are given a higher importance than the physical senses. Without the qualities provided by indigo we would need to find other resources to help provide deep quiet in our lives.

USING INDIGO
To find peace for reflection, look up at the clear night sky. Contemplation and deep meditation come easier in the indigo depths of night. Night-time is often when inspirations and solutions to problems naturally arise.

Violet

Violet is the colour at the opposite end of the rainbow spectrum to red. A combination of blue and red, it can be seen both as a completion and as the beginning of another cycle of vibratory energy, the rest of which ascends beyond the visible spectrum. Violet is the door to the unseen, both in terms of the electromagnetic spectrum and in human experience.

how violet works

The key to understanding the energy of violet is to see how its component colours work together.

Red is a focusing, concentrating, dynamic and activating energy, while blue is a cooling, quietening and expansive energy. Violet brings a new dynamism to the unfocused expansion of blue and a stabilizing energy to the frenetic activity of red. The rather undirected spaciousness of blue is made practical by the addition of

◁ Aubergines (eggplants) are part of the Solanaceae family, which also includes deadly nightshade and tobacco, and contain toxic alkaloids, which can distort our perception of reality, a very violet characteristic.

△ Healing is represented by the colour violet – the blue giving detachment and the ability to be devoted to the flow of energy, and the red supplying motivation to be of use to others.

the red. Concepts and ideas are thus better able to find some real application in the world. The energy that red brings allows more creative qualities to emerge from the blue, so violet is associated with the imagination and with inspiration.

violet and fantasy

The difficulty with the world of violet energy is that it can become very self-contained. The red and blue make such a balanced whole that it is easy not to look

△ The silhouette of an industrial landscape, beautifully etched on a violet sky, illustrates this colour's ability to combine and balance the practical with the ideal, dreams with reality.

◁ Violet energy ranges from blue with a hint of red, to purple, where the red and blue are more equally mixed.

▷ Quiet, meditative spaces can benefit from a touch of violet colour.

△ **Violet encourages the flow of the imagination and the integration of ideas, or it can degenerate into daydreams and fantasy.**

beyond it. Where this happens, imagination transforms into fantasy, and inspiration becomes fanaticism. Violet energy, because it seems to extend beyond our current knowledge into the unknown, can trap the spiritual dreamer in a fantastic world of miraculous happenings and unrealistic wishful thinking. Here the practical world and all its tangible solidity is rejected in favour of a make-believe, usually very selfish, sense of personal evolution or spiritual progress.

▷ **Violet and purple suggest luxury, even today, a lasting memory of the time when these colours were exclusive to the rich.**

If the lure of the glamorous unknown can be avoided, violet energy can become one of the most effective colours to bring balance and healing in any situation. It helps to integrate energies at every level and as healing requires the building up of new systems (red energy), according to accurate information (blue energy), violet can speed both physical and emotional recovery.

Violet is an important energy to those who use the blue and indigo skills of psychic perception, because it helps to supply the grounding energy for the work. Without the anchoring abilities of red, the use of subtle perceptions can seriously imbalance and exhaust the life-energy of the practitioner.

The skill of integration is aided by violet. As the colour combines opposite energies, it can help people who need to work with an array of disparate things. Violet is often associated with the richness and diversity of ceremony, perhaps originating from its ability to psychologically balance the minds

and actions of the participants. Violet is often thought to be the most spiritual of all colours. In bygone days, violet dye was expensive and reserved for the priesthood and the rich. In practice, though, no colour is more spiritual than any other.

USING VIOLET
Lavender is a traditional remedy for insomnia or restlessness at night. It is also one of the most versatile essential oils for scratches, burns, headaches and worry. Dried lavender flowers beside the bed, or a drop of oil on the pillow, will encourage peaceful sleep.

White and black

When people speak of opposites it is usually in terms of black and white. Strictly speaking neither are colours – simply characteristics of the presence or absence of light. As in all polarities, black and white cannot be defined without each other. Like day and night, white and black are part of an unceasing definition of existence.

white absolutes

The presence of white is what humans perceive as the entire visible light spectrum seen

▷ Coal and soot consist of black carbon – one of the earliest used pigments.

together – the complete energy of light. In this sense it stands for wholeness and completion – nothing has been taken out, everything is present. In many cultures white is associated with purity and cleanliness, openness and truth – everything is shown in bright light, nothing is hidden. This is why white is often used to denote holiness. White is also the colour of bone and the snow of winter, so for some, the energy of white relates to the starkness of death and endings. Both of these interpretations – purity and death – are connected by the act of setting things

USING BLACK

If you want to become inconspicuous, consider dressing in black. Black can be inconspicuous, or it can make a bold statement of mystery and self-control. Black clothes often say: 'notice my presence but don't intrude into my space'.

△ Light and shade, black and white, the zebra takes advantage of random contrasting patterns to disappear into its surroundings.

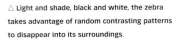

◁ Black and white are associated with viewpoints where no mutual ground can be found yet neither can exist without the other.

apart from normal life, creating a sense of specialness. Entering or leaving the world, white signifies beginnings and the end of one cycle that enables another to start.

White is uncompromising. Everything is clear, open and explicitly manifest. It has a cold quality. White can be of use when clarity is needed in life. But it can also take on a hint of the other colours around it and so acts like a mirror to the energies that are in proximity. This can make it a rather uncomfortable colour for those who do not wish to have their hidden feelings reflected back to them. As a vibration of purification,

△ **Where there is light and three-dimensional form there is shadow, each defines the other.**

me!' Black withdraws, refusing to take a stand or be noticed. White is the energy of completion, an expanse outwards. Black is the energy of gestation and of preparation. Black has often been associated with the energies of the earth and the fertile soil. The rich earth from which all life and sustenance springs is the same earth where the dead are placed.

In a way, both white and black reflect the particular beliefs of the individual. White can be seen negatively as blankness, and positively as a clean slate, offering a new beginning. In times of fear and uncertainty, black is a threatening unknown, a silence in which our own terrors and nightmares can be amplified. But at other times, black may simply be experienced as a restful emptiness that allows many different possibilities to emerge and disappear again.

white can help to clarify all aspects of life, giving the energy to sweep away blocks in physical, emotional and mental patterns. There are no degrees of white, and its action can be as uncompromising and rapid as a flash of blinding light. White gives the potential to move towards every other colour, as it allows development in any direction. It is a good choice for new beginnings.

black contrasts

White reflects all aspects of light, but black absorbs all aspects of light. So while white reveals, black conceals. In the simplicity of symbolism white is translated as whole, holy and good, so black inevitably becomes linked to the hidden, fearful and bad experiences. Black is the fear of a starless, moonless night where everything is unseen and unknown and anything might be hiding out there to wish us harm. Where white is the colour of emergence, of birth and change, black is the colour of continuity, of withdrawal from definition, of the hidden. White continually makes its presence felt: it shouts 'I am here, look at

▽ **Black can be seen as a threatening colour, representing a cloak over what lies beneath or within. At other times it is mysterious, allowing a sense of potential or possibility. It is the energy of gestation and preparation.**

USING WHITE

White has the ability to clear away all clutter, all extraneous noise. Fresh starts and new beginnings all benefit from its energy. Looking at a picture of snow-clad mountains brings clarity and freshness to a mind that feels crowded.

Turquoise and pink

USING TURQUOISE
Throughout the world turquoise stones have been used as protective amulets for promoting health and guarding against harm. A large proportion of everyone's energy comes from the turquoise motivation to experience life to the full. Wear turquoise jewellery to give yourself confidence and strength. Turquoise has a strengthening influence on all systems of the body bringing a sense of inner confidence.

Turquoise is a blend of green and blue. It is so named because the Turks were fond of the colour and decorated many of their buildings with turquoise ceramic glazed tiles. Turquoise has the calming, expansive nature of green and the cool, quiet flow of blue. It can bring to mind a particular quality in the sky before or after sunset, a calm, warm sea, a beautiful lagoon, a pure mountain stream or distant hills in the mellow light of late summer.

functions of turquoise

The energy of turquoise allows the expression of our wishes. The green quality of growth is added to the blue quality of communication. Turquoise is the colour of the desire for freedom to be a unique individual. The blue ingredient ensures that, whatever the need may be in the heart of the individual, it will communicate itself and be recognized for what it is. Turquoise

△ Turquoise and pink are both blends of colours that can be warm and cool. Both balance and strengthen life-energy at many levels.

▽ The Turks were skilled tilemakers and with access to the mines of Persia they were able to use turquoise pigments to great effect.

▽ Turquoise is a copper ore with varying degrees of blue and green. Each mine produces a slight variation of colour.

also represents the exploration of information through feelings and emotions. This creates the possibility for new interpretations of established ways for doing things, of new uses for old ideas.

Space and freedom are essential for every living creature. Restriction of natural behav-

iour patterns and the inability to find a place in the community cause a rapid build-up of stress and toxins in the body. This leads to a decrease in energy and greater susceptibility to disease. Turquoise can help when there is low energy, a lack of interest in life, a failure to fit in with the surroundings or a lack of courage to strike out on your own.

◁ Dark pink, bubble-gum pink and magenta are much more stimulating than pale tints. They provide the energy to make changes to improve one's life and are dynamic and assertive.

functions of pink

Pink is red and white combined in varying degrees. The quality of the energy will depend on how much red vibration is present. White is the potential for fullness, and red is the motivation to achieve that potential, so pink is a colour that promotes both these energies together.

Pink gives an underlying confidence to existence, it provides a level of support that means that it has the ability to neutralize any negative or destructive tendencies. Aggressive behaviour patterns arise where there is fear at an emotional level, or friction at a physical or mental level. Pink

provides sufficient energy to move out of that negative state and enough clarity to recognize and clear away misconceptions.

Deep shades of pink that veer towards magenta have proved to be extremely effective in situations of disorder and violence, such as in prisons and police cells. In places such as these, a limited exposure to pink

light rapidly defuses aggressive attitudes and behaviour. These deeper shades of pink can also help to improve self-confidence and assertiveness, while pink's paler shades are more protective, promoting peace and being supportive of self-acceptance and feelings of self-worth.

Pink is sometimes seen only as a soft, feminine colour, a colour representing the qualities of caring and tenderness. It will also help to take the heat out of any turbulent or aggressive situation. The dynamic mix of red and white is a useful balance of male and female energies that can also be valuable as a healing colour, reducing the effects of disease as well as the fear and anguish disease can cause. Pink can help where other colours may have drawbacks, as it fundamentally supports the integrity of an individual.

▽ Pink promotes relaxation and acceptance of where one is in life without false views or feelings of complacency.

USING PINK

In any aggressive or threatening situation, or where there are simple misunderstandings leading to anger, visualizing pink around everyone can help to calm the mood and reduce tension.

Brown and grey

Brown clothes were worn by the large majority of manual workers until the introduction of blue denim. As a mix of the primary colours, brown can blend into many surroundings. It is a disguise that shows no preference, no specific direction or attitude. It can be used very effectively to hide the true nature of the individual. Grey clothes are the favoured uniform of managers, businessmen and politicians. Grey reflects the desire to project coolness of mind, emotional stability and the ability to look down on the rest of the world with a detached neutrality. It epitomizes the myth of efficiency.

practical brown

Brown is a mixture of red, yellow and blue. Like every colour, brown has a wide range of shades and tones, each having a different effect. It is primarily a colour of the earth and the natural world. Brown acts as a solid background colour, a base upon which other, more striking colours can arise. As a combination, brown is neutral and non-threatening. Its warm tones are comfortable and familiar.

The red content makes brown a colour of practical energy and this mixed with the mental qualities of yellow and blue can encourage study and focus of the mind. However, in too great a quantity brown can also have a dulling effect, as it lacks the overall clarity to break out of established patterns of behaviour. Brown gives a state of solidity and reality from which one can grow. It suggests reliability and the desire to remain in the background, unnoticed.

In the traditional surroundings of an oak-panelled library or study, brown aids the transformation of inspiration and thoughts into practical, everyday reality. Discoveries and inventions need time devoted to painstaking detail, and involve going over the same set of ideas repeatedly until a solution emerges. Brown acts as a supporting colour in this process.

◁ Brown is a warm, comfortable colour, reflecting wholesomeness, naturalness and dependability.

▽ Deer, like other forest or woodland animals, use their brown hides or coats to blend into the background and become virtually invisible.

▽ Brown is a varying mixture of red, yellow and blue. It can range from a burnt orange tone to a chocolate brown with hints of red and purple.

> ### USING BROWN
> Brown in the home can be overbearing. Adding a few richer colours to brown wooden furniture and neutral coloured floor coverings will create a warm, stable atmosphere where it is easy to feel comfortable for long periods.

neutral grey

Grey is the true neutral colour. It is usually thought of as a combination of white and black, but a mixture of any complementary colours will produce grey. Grey is the colour of void, of emptiness, lack of movement, lack of emotion, lack of warmth, lack of any identifying characteristics in fact. Because of this, grey can be restful. If it contains a high proportion of white it will tend to take on the qualities of surrounding colours. If it has a greater amount of black, it can feel very heavy and depressing. Grey lacks information and this has a numbing effect on the mind, though not in a particularly peaceful way, as with blue or indigo. Indeed the inability to see into the colour can be reminiscent of the experience of fear or terror where decision-making processes seem frozen and even time stands still. With its emptiness, boredom and lack of direction, grey has an enervating and draining effect: its neutrality prevents us from moving towards an energetic state.

Unlike brown, grey has no connection to the solid earth or the life of nature.

▽ Grey pigments appear to be that colour because they scatter all light that hits them in a random way.

◁ Where grey skies are common they can have an oppressing influence on people as it reduces the intensity and effect of all other colours.

Immovable stone and cloudy skies reflect the impersonal, implacable nature of grey. Grey has a detached, isolated and unemotional feel. While brown suggests a down-to-earth practicality, grey has a cool, calculating mental neutrality, an unwillingness to get one's hands dirty.

Grey clothes can suggest that the wearer wishes to remain unsullied or uninvolved, but they can also suggest sophistication – being cool. When placed next to other colours, grey does have a cooling effect. It is moderating and stabilizing, making neighbouring colours stand out while muting their vibrational energy.

▽ Grey clothes suggest efficiency and are often used in the business world. Grey can also suggest a lack of imagination, however.

USING GREY

Grey clothing will emphasize neutrality. However, too much grey, or a wrong shade, will suggest lack of character, lack of initiative and extreme detachment. A hint of another colour that reflects individual preference will make all the difference: efficient, well-behaved but with personality. If you want to emphasize your willingness to comply, wear grey.

Self-healing
with colour

An understanding of how the body uses the language of colour helps an individual to discover their personal colour needs. Selecting from a range of coloured, everyday items can enhance wellbeing and help to provide harmony and clarity in life.

Human responses to colour

The only real difference between coloured light and any other radiation of the electromagnetic spectrum is that we can see it. Under the light of the sun, which reaches the earth with greatest strength in the visible spectrum, humankind has evolved to respond and make use of colour. The fact that the warm colours of reds and oranges activate and stimulate us while the cool colours of blues and violets calm us, probably derives from the biological triggers of daylight and nightfall.

eyes and light

Our eyes serve not only as a sense organ but also directly stimulate vitally important, fundamental and very primitive parts of the nervous system located deep in the brain. The hypothalamus, pituitary and pineal glands are all extremely light sensitive. Light reaching these areas of the brain has an immediate effect on the involuntary autonomic nervous system, changing our physical, mental and emotional states. The human eye is a complex and sophisticated

△ It is thought that our sensitivity to colour has evolved over time, in order to respond to the changing conditions of sunlight in our world.

sensing device. Light passes through the transparent lens and stimulates the retina at the back of the eyeball, which consists of specialized light-sensitive cells called rods and cones. The rods are sensitive to blue and green and work in dim light. The cones work best in daylight and are sensitive to different colours depending on the pigments

△ The human eye is one of the most complex structures in the whole animal kingdom, the product of millions of years of evolution.

◁ The warm colours in fire combine with the physical sense of heat, and promote feelings of warmth and comfort.

tors and healers can therefore find ways of using colour to manipulate our responses – for better or worse. Colour, as well as the amount of full-spectrum sunlight, has been shown to initiate profound changes in the nervous system. We are all moved by colour whether we are aware of the process or not, but increasing our knowledge of how colour influences us can help us to be aware of any attempts to manipulate us.

they contain. These photoelectric cells, when stimulated, send electrical impulses via the optic nerve into the brain where they are interpreted. The process of vision is primarily a function of the brain, for the eyes 'see' only a small area of the world at any one time. The eyeballs move very rapidly, 50 to 70 times a second, scanning the field of vision. It is the visual cortex in the brain that makes sense of this information and tells us what we are seeing.

△ Colour is the food of our emotions. It reflects our thoughts and moods consciously and unconsciously. Combinations of bright, festive colours, for example, are powerfully attractive, particularly to young children.

the energy of light

Light impulses do not go just to the visual cortex in the brain. Some nerves go from the retina directly to the hypothalamus, a small organ that regulates most of the life-sustaining functions of the body, such as control of the autonomic nervous system, energy levels, internal temperature, cycles of rest and activity, growth, circulation, breathing, reproduction and the emotions. The hypothalamus directly affects the pituitary gland, which is the major controlling organ for the endocrine system and all its hormonal secretions. Light from the eyes also directly affects the pineal gland, which modifies our behaviour patterns according to the amount of light it receives. The pineal gland regulates our energy so that we can remain in balance with our environment. The correspondences between the endocrine glands and the subtle energy systems of the body, indicate that colour affects all levels of our being.

The eyes are thus not simply a source of information about the world around us, they also allow light energy to be carried to the centre of the brain where it can create profound changes at the level of cellular function, physical activity, emotional and mental states. Advertisers, interior decora-

▽ Although we think of colour as a decorative, superficial thing, our choices and reactions are dictated by the energy each wavelength exerts on important areas of the unconscious brain.

NATURAL LIGHT
It has been recommended that people spend at least 20 minutes outside in direct sunlight every day. If you wear glasses or contact lenses it is also a good idea to remove them for five or ten minutes every few hours, in order to get the benefit of natural light.

Light as healer

The sun is the motor that drives this world. A change to the energy we receive on the surface of the earth is like a change in gear that speeds up or slows down all life processes. It is not a matter of choice – life has evolved to take advantage of the energy of the sun and so is automatically connected to its cycles.

cycles of light

At sunrise, the sun low on the horizon is red. As it climbs into the sky, the widening angle with our point on the earth's surface allows more orange and then yellow light to reach the ground. Experimentation has clearly shown that red light increases blood pressure, pulse rate and breathing rate, and that these functions are further increased in orange light, reaching their peak in yellow light. The human physiological response to light has evolved so that the rising sun stimulates us into activity and alertness.

▽ Only the comparatively recent introduction of artificial lighting has changed our patterns of rest and activity, triggered by sunrise and sunset.

△ Sun, moon and stars are the earliest deities in many religions. Light is a universal metaphor for enlightenment and spiritual fulfilment.

Other experiments have shown a decrease in blood pressure, pulse rate and breathing rate when people are exposed to green light. Relaxation increases with blue light and is at its fullest in complete darkness. White light has been found to have similar quietening effects to blue light. As daylight fades the subduing green light changes to the blue of evening, then the

△ Energy levels, hormone activity and mood are all automatically regulated according to the quality of light.

darkness of night, with perhaps only the moon for illumination. Night is the natural time of rest and reflection. Emotionally and physiologically we respond to colours as they fit the times of the day, just as our distant forebears did before artificial light sources were available.

light reaction in cells

Studies with plants grown under different colours and ranges of light have demonstrated that the wrong kind of light can seriously damage their growth and health. Full-spectrum natural sunlight with normal levels of ultraviolet light (which is filtered out by most types of glass) is essential to maintain the normal, healthy functioning of plant cells. The same has been found with animal cells. Filtering light or exposure to a single colour for long periods causes cells to function abnormally and even eventually die. These studies seem to suggest that humans, as well as plants, need a balanced environment of light and colour. Until 1879 when the electric light bulb was invented, most people lived and worked outdoors in natural light. Now more and more people spend a large proportion of their lives in enclosed environments exposed to artificial light and completely cut off from the sun.

△ All life has evolved to take advantage of the different qualities of sunlight through the year.

When full-spectrum, balanced fluorescent lighting was tested in schools against normal white tubes, there appeared to be a significant decrease in irritability, hyperactivity and fatigue in students after just one month. Interestingly, there also seemed to be a correlation between poor quality lighting and the amount of tooth decay!

The reduction of sunlight on a cloudy day or, more profoundly, in the long months of winter, significantly changes the mood of most people, but for some, the lack of sunlight can be seriously debilitating. Seasonal Affective Disorder (or SAD) causes mood swings, low energy levels and depression that begins as the days grow shorter and only gradually improves with the onset of spring. Effective treatment is by exposure each day to several hours of bright full-spec-

trum light that resembles sunlight and which resets the chemical balance within the pineal gland, the organ that is disrupted. Without sufficient exposure to the full spectrum of light from the sun, the finely balanced chemical reactions in our bodies tend to falter, leaving us prone to ill health.

△ An indoor lifestyle may be a factor in our lack of health and sense of wellbeing, spending time outside will counteract this.

▽ During the long winter months the grey rainy weather in some countries can contribute to feelings of seasonal depression.

Single colour guidance

Our instinctive emotional response to colour can tell us a lot about ourselves. It reflects back to us how we are functioning. It can show life-long tendencies, immediate situations or a potential direction in personal development. Sometimes certain colours stay with us as favourites for many years. This is reflected in the colours we choose to paint our home, inside and out, and the predominant colours in our wardrobe. It is possible to interpret these colour preferences through their known correspondences to our physical, emotional, mental and even spiritual state.

colour choice

Given a range of colours to choose from, the process of self-reflection and self-revelation can begin. The simplest approach is to make spontaneous choices:

* Which colour do you like the most?
* Which colour do you like the least?

The colour you like the most will, as likely as not, be present in your home or in

▽ Sometimes our instinctive choice of food reflects our energy needs of the moment.

△ Coloured candies can be used as a way of identifying colour energies that are lacking.

▷ Flowers, with their vibrant colour and variety of shape, are an excellent way to introduce a balancing colour into the surroundings.

your clothes. It may also be a colour that you need to help you in a current situation. By looking at the full range of correspondences for that colour, as discussed earlier in this book, you may get insight into a new direction in life. However, if the colour you have chosen is an absolute favourite and you have no desire to reflect on other choices, you may have become stuck in particular habit patterns. Again, look at the correspondences for that colour to see what these habits might be.

The colour you like least will suggest areas of your life that may require attention and healing. Each colour has positive as well as negative attributes, so it is a good idea to bring the positive energy of a colour you dislike into your life to create balance. Do this through new activities, the choice of food, by wearing that colour in clothing or adding it to your surroundings.

The process of self-analysis through colour can be developed a step further by deciding, before you make your choices, what each choice will represent. For exam-

ple, a series of three choices could be selected to show:

1 What your physical needs are now (e.g. activities, food, clothes)
2 What your emotional needs are now (e.g. peace, space, fun, company)
3 What your mental needs are now (e.g. time to study, standing up for yourself)

how to do it

1 Collect together a selection of different coloured items, for example ribbon lengths, pieces of card or buttons so that you have at least one of each colour of the rainbow plus a selection of other colours.
2 Lay the items out at random on a plain background.
3 Close your eyes and have in your mind your first question.
4 Relax, open your eyes and pick up the colour that you are immediately, and instinctively drawn to.
5 Repeat these steps for each of your questions in turn.

what does it mean?

The colour that you have instinctively selected will give you the answer in the language of colour. You can then introduce the colour energy into your life by whichever means seem appropriate. The colour choices may highlight some aspects of your life that have not been clear to you. This process can bring issues to the surface so they can be looked at and healed.

taking it further

You can invent any number of permutations for a series of questions or choices. For example:

1 Where am I now?
2 What are my main difficulties?
3 What is at the root of those difficulties?
4 What are my priority needs?
5 What is the next possible step and the way forward?

The colour choices can be interpreted through colour correspondences and then introduced into your life using the information in this book.

▽ Use collections of differently coloured items, such as ribbons or pieces of fabric, for single colour guidance exercises.

CHOOSING COLOURS

Try not to think about the choice you make. Just pay attention to where your eyes settle as soon as they are open. For a moment or two you may find your eyes just scan over the colours, but soon they will focus on one in particular.

△ Lay out all your colours so that your eyes can easily scan all of them at the same time.

△ Close your eyes, take a moment to relax, and think of the area you wish to investigate.

△ When you feel ready, open your eyes and pick the colour that first draws your attention.

single colour assessment

A simple way to determine your day-to-day colour needs is to carry out a single colour assessment. This process can be done as often as you like. Sit quietly with these pages open in front of you and go through the steps below one by one.

how to assess yourself

1 Cover the chart showing the keys to colours with a sheet of paper. This helps to stop the logical and judgemental part of the mind from interfering with the instinctive choice of colour.

2 Note down on a piece of paper the number of choices you will make and what each will represent. For example, a one-colour choice could represent what you most need today; a two-colour choice could reveal firstly a problem you are encountering, and secondly, a possible solution.

3 With the framework decided, close your eyes. For each choice, open your eyes and record the colour that your eyes are immediately drawn to.

▽ **Relax before starting a single colour assessment and remember that you are being guided towards a colour by your intuition.**

4 Repeat the process for each choice, then look up the correspondences on the chart.
5 Consider the questions and phrases linked to each of your colour choices, and where appropriate, decide to bring that colour more into your life.

▷ **Any coloured items can be used for colour assessment. The important thing is to decide on an appropriate framework of questions.**

KEYS TO COLOURS	
Colour	**Key phrases and questions that may help you to focus ideas**
Dark red	Need to keep your feet on the ground What is taking your attention away from where it needs to be?
Red	Need to take action, now What is stopping you doing what is necessary?
Orange	Need to let go of old, worn out ideas, things, emotions What is blocking you? What are you allowing to block your way?
Gold	Need to relax, enjoy life What is making you doubt yourself?
Yellow	Need to start thinking clearly What are you afraid of?
Olive green	Need to reassess where you are going What hidden factors are stopping your growth?
Green	Need for space to gain fresh perspective What is restricting you?
Turquoise	Need to put into words exactly what you feel What are your strengths?
Light blue	Need to talk to people around you What do you need to express to others?
Dark blue	Need for peace and time on your own What are you so close to that you cannot see clearly what is happening?
Violet	Need to heal yourself What are you sacrificing to appear as a 'good' or 'helpful' person?
Black	Need to be quiet and listen What are you wanting to hide from?
White	Need to make some changes What is painful to look at in the real world?
Pink	Need to look after yourself more What thoughts do you have about yourself that are too critical?
Magenta	Need to take time out to repair all levels of yourself What have you been overdoing at the expense of your own health?
Brown	Need to focus on the practicalities of life In what areas of your life have you been too dreamy?
Grey	Need to disappear into the background What do you want to hide and why?

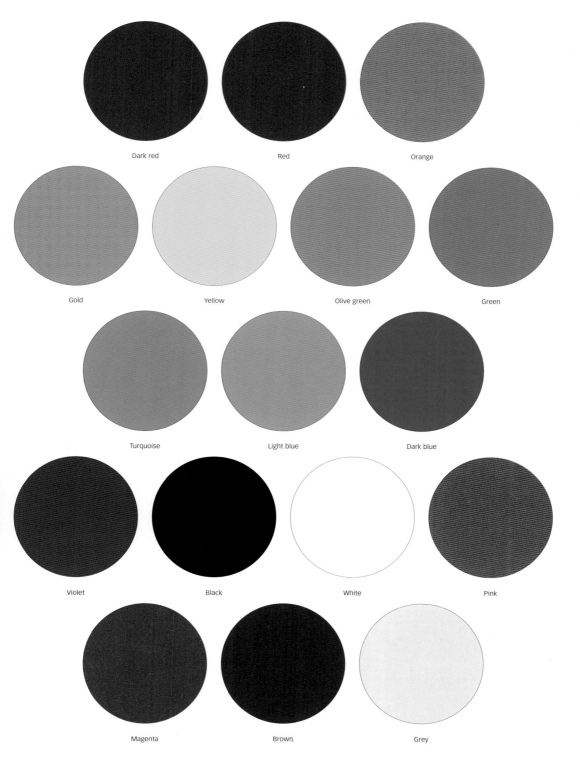

Dark red

Red

Orange

Gold

Yellow

Olive green

Green

Turquoise

Light blue

Dark blue

Violet

Black

White

Pink

Magenta

Brown

Grey

Specific colour placement

In certain situations it is helpful to introduce specific colours into the environment for immediate short-term effect. This can often be more effective than redecorating whole rooms, or enthusiastically pursuing certain foods or activities. Once the situation changes, the colour can be removed until it is needed again in the future.

everyday uses of colour

When you use visualization techniques for relaxation and stress removal, it can sometimes be difficult to return to everyday activities or focus on practical tasks, especially if your experience has been deep. The same problem sometimes occurs in people who meditate regularly, as returning to the realities of the world can be disruptive. A rich red object such as a cushion or a piece of fabric can help. After relaxation or meditation, try gazing at the colour red for about a minute. This will integrate the benefits of meditation into your body and prepare you to return to the normal world.

Students studying for examinations will find the process less tiring and generally more effective if they introduce a shade of yellow into their study-space. An acid yellow will keep the mind alert, while sunshine yellow combines alertness with relaxation.

▽ **Small areas of bright colour, like cushion covers, are excellent ways to temporarily bring colour energy into a room.**

colour and reading difficulties

American psychologist Helen Irlen introduced the idea of reading through coloured overlays in 1988. Her attention was drawn to a type of dyslexia called SSS or Scotopic Sensitivity Syndrome. People with this difficulty are very light-sensitive. They have trouble dealing with high contrasts, such as black and white, find that letters and numbers 'move' on the page and have difficulty with groups of letters or numbers. They also

△ **Having a red object in a meditation space helps to ground spiritual energies at a practical level. Tibetan monks often wear red shawls or robes for this purpose.**

have a poor attention span. Irlen has devised a series of tests for people with reading difficulties which enables her to help them by recommending reading through different coloured overlays or tinted spectacle lenses. These measures can alleviate, or even sometimes remove the problem entirely. Irlen's

THE WORK OF BARBARA MEISTER VITALE

Barbara Meister Vitale, a well-known educator and lecturer in the USA, has used colour in her work since 1970. During her research with children and the way they learn, she has concluded that:

• Lots of different coloured pieces of material in the classroom help to reduce hyperactivity and increase children's attention span.

• Children behave differently when dressed in different coloured clothes.

• Using several different coloured pens and coloured paper increases children's learning skills and aids their ability to recall.

• Using a blue light helps both adults and children in their reading and studying.

• People with reading difficulties respond well when a transparent colour overlay is placed on their reading material.

• The effect of colour is unique to each individual. It might be their favourite colour, or its complementary colour, that is most helpful to them.

△ **Bringing colour into a space is more than a design or fashion whim. Colour has an impact on every activity around it.**

▽ **Study can be helped by having objects of lemon yellow around that help the memory functions of the brain. If exam-stress is a problem, a bright golden yellow encourages relaxation and reduces nervousness.**

work has centred on people with SSS, who make up approximately one-fifth of those with dyslexia or other identified learning difficulties. Irlen believes, however, that her findings could benefit a much wider section of people, and that about one-fifth of the general population could benefit from reading through colour. There is medical evidence to suggest that wearing coloured lenses can also reduce the incidence of migraine by up to 80%.

The benefits of using colour in health and in education are only now being investigated scientifically. Perhaps in the future these inexpensive and simple tools could help in many situations, and may well transform many peoples lives.

Rainbow diet

Each of us has colours that we prefer and some that we dislike. Any reaction of an emotional nature to colour, either positive or negative, can indicate how colour can be used to promote healing and wellbeing.

A balance of attractive colours in the food we eat plays a large part in a healthy diet. But few people recognize their instinctive reaction to the colour of food, or notice that they get drawn towards that colour in a foodstore or marketplace. Manufacturers of convenience foods play on this reaction, which is why many packaged foods contain dyes and colourings to tempt our palate.

The effect of a food is not always gauged by the colour we see; its colour-related action or quality is also important. One of the qualities of orange is to eliminate toxins. Brown rice and oats are good detoxifiers, so can be described as having an

△ **Fresh fruit and vegetables provide a banquet of colours to feast the eyes and tempt the poorest of appetites.**

orange action. Often the body tries to direct us to the foods we need to rebalance our health. It is worth observing the types of food that appeal to someone after an illness or shock. Allowed a free choice we will always tend to be drawn to the foods we need by colour as much as by smell or taste but we rarely recognise or allow ourselves to follow through and eat the foods.

CHOOSING FOOD BY COLOUR

- Foods that display our favourite colours will always be needed because they give us the particular energy that supports our body's function.
- Foods belonging to the least-favourite, or even hated, colours will provide the nutrition and colour energy that we are lacking.
- Food colours that we are attracted to temporarily reflect the immediate nutritional needs of the body.
- If you have problems that correspond to certain colours, you may wish to introduce foods of that colour into your diet to help your body with its healing.

▽ **Unprocessed natural sugars could be thought of as better for us than the white, processed varieties. We do, however, get enough sugar for our daily needs from eating fruits and vegetables without having to add it to other foods.**

RED FOODS AND FOODS THAT WORK IN A RED WAY

Red foods are generally rich in minerals and provide good sources of protein. They are good for increasing levels of vitality. Red deficiencies are shown through low energy levels, anaemia, light-headedness and lack of stamina.

Foods have different kinds of colour energy, one is its obvious outwards appearance, the colour it actually is, another is the inherent energy it supplies. Chocolate is a good example of this, although not red in colour it is an important red-energy food because of the instant energy it supplies. In appearance watercress and parsley are both green foods, but their high levels of minerals give them a red quality. Red wine is red in colour and provides iron, but its high alcohol level means that it also provides violet energy, so it can be classed in either colour category.

△ Redcurrants are widely used to accompany rich, red foods, such as meat and game.

△ Chocolate is an important red-energy food as it gives instant energy.

Red fruits	Strawberries, raspberries, cherries
Red vegetables	Red cabbage, beetroot, radishes, peppers, onions, tomatoes, chillies, watercress, parsley
Other red foods	Meat, pulses, nuts, fish
Red vitamins	B12 (vital for the absorption of iron)
Red minerals	Iron (helps the blood to carry oxygen), magnesium (good for nerve responses, cell energy, hormones, healthy bones), zinc (good for fertility; healthy hair, skin and nails)
Other red nutrients	Fatty acids (improve function of cells and promote healthy blood, skin, hair and nails)
Red non-foods (foods with little or no nutritional value)	Red wine (stimulates and relaxes in moderation), coffee (stimulates the adrenals, diuretic), chocolate (gives instant energy), sugar, the ultimate non-food (very addictive but gives instant short-lived energy, followed by a big energy 'low')

◁ Red foods can be very attractive when energies are low or following periods of illness.

▽ Soft red fruit is many people's favourite way of absorbing red energy and natural sugars.

ORANGE FOODS AND FOODS THAT WORK IN AN ORANGE WAY

Orange foods help with the release of toxins and stress from the body, they support the reproductive system and encourage creativity at all levels. Orange deficiencies are shown in constipation, artist's block, difficulties with fertility and stiffness of the joints. Orange foods help with the release

Orange fruits	Oranges, peaches, apricots
Orange vegetables	Pumpkin, peppers, carrots
Other orange foods	Brown rice, sesame seeds, oats (provides roughage which is mucilaginous and gentle), shellfish
Orange vitamins	Vitamin A (for healthy eyes, skin, stable energy levels), vitamin C (strengthens cells and blood vessels, helps absorption of iron)
Orange minerals	Calcium (for muscle relaxation and healthy bones), copper (helps absorption of iron, improves flexibility of arteries), selenium (free-radical scavenger, helps reduce the effects of ageing), zinc (for healthy reproductive organs).

◁ Seafood is rich in many trace minerals and Omega 3 fatty acids that support the reproductive system.

▷ Oranges contain the key nutrient vitamin C and carotenoids that support the body in healing the effects of disease and ageing.

foods into a system that is tired or toxic is easier for the body to handle than the strong, direct energy of red foods that could appear on first glance to be the solution.

▽ The vitamin C and zinc in raw carrots provide an excellent combination to help the body detoxify metals and other pollutants.

of toxins and stress from the body by encouraging the system to become more efficient in the natural elimination and excretory processes. This, in turn, aids relaxation and the release of stress as the body lets go of unwanted and waste products.

Orange foods contain key nutrients that support and maintain the reproductive systems. These foods can also aid the flow of creativity on other levels too.

Lack of orange and orange-energy foods can be evident in physical constipation, but also in stagnation in other areas, such as artist's block and stiffness in muscles and joints. Introducing orange or orange-energy

◁ We are often attracted to orange foods when our bodies need to release significant amounts of stress or toxicity.

YELLOW FOODS AND FOODS THAT WORK IN A YELLOW WAY

The sun gives us our main source of yellow during daylight hours, but as modern life uses up the yellow vibration in dealing with pollution, chemicals, living indoors and high stress levels, yellow foods are needed in large amounts by much of the industrialized world's population.

Lack of yellow leads to irritability, tension, poor memory, restlessness, inefficient absorption of nutrients, digestive problems,

▷ Bananas are rich in potassium that helps to maintain healthy muscles. Grapefruit and lemons help to fight infections.

▽ Yellow foods are a useful addition to the diet for those who are studying, or coping with worries that they can do little about.

a drop in immunity, a tendency towards hot flushes, feelings of depression, and inability to make decisions.

Problems with learning, concentration and memory can indicate a lack of yellow energy in the body. Sometimes this lack is made worse by the modern lifestyle, lighting and high levels of stress. However, recent research into learning and attention difficulties has concluded that fish oils (Omega 3 fatty acids) have a crucial role in the internal body chemistry. The systems of people experiencing these problems seem to be unable to assimilate these vital nutrients correctly. This indicates that what were once thought of as behavioural problems are actually nutritional difficulties. Giving children experiencing these problems daily supplements of fatty acids – a yellow food – resulted in significant improvement in over 40 per cent of cases, confirming research.

▽ Grains that are made into flours form the staple diets of most cultures.

Yellow fruits	Lemon, bananas, grapefruit
Yellow vegetables	Grains (rice, corn, wheat, rye etc.), peppers, pumpkins
Other yellow foods	Eggs, fish, oils, food rich in fatty acids
Yellow vitamins	Vitamin A (for healthy tissues, blood, eyes and immune system), vitamin B complex (helps the body to convert food into energy, support nerves and muscles), vitamin D (for absorption of calcium, promotes healthy muscles, nerves and parathyroid), vitamin E (antioxidant, good for healthy tissues and wound repair)
Yellow minerals	Sodium and potassium (for healthy blood pressure, cell function, smooth muscle function), selenium (for smooth skin, protects blood cells), phosphorus (for healthy bones, teeth, kidneys, nerves and energy levels), iodine (for balanced function of thyroid, healthy arteries), chromium (helps metabolism of sugars and the function of the pancreas), molybdenum (facilitates use of iron and fats), manganese (stabilizes hormones, improves nerve function)
Yellow non-foods	Food additives (interfere with natural digestive processes), alcohol (depletes the liver of nutrients, overworks the pancreas), sugar (overworks the pancreas)

▷ One serving a day of green leafy, raw vegetables is thought to be the minimum for a healthy body.

GREEN FOODS AND FOODS THAT WORK IN A GREEN WAY

Food that is green, or that works in a green way, tends to be rich in vitamins and minerals, though these can be lost in cooking or storage. Some parts of the world do not support the growing of fresh green foods, so people living in these places have to find

△ Dark, leafy greens are some of the best sources of vitamins and anti-oxidants, that help us to deal with old or dysfunctional cells throughout the body.

▽ Green foods calm our emotions, by providing the nutrients that the body uses to balance all of our energies.

other sources of green nutrients. The Inuit people of northern Canada, for example, live on a diet almost entirely based on fish and fish products, which supply the green energy they need. All minerals act in a green way and all therapeutic herbs, as well as culinary ones, also come under this heading.

Lack of a green vibration creates depression, a feeling of being trapped, breathing difficulties and a lack of self-value. Being in a large space, in the open air, and among natural surroundings is a quick way to bring a green vibration into your life if you feel your green food intake is insufficient.

Eating foods in their natural season, or where possible, foods grown locally, allow the body to settle into the rhythms and patterns of our immediate surroundings.

Many leafy green foods are categorized as bitters by nutritionalists as they stimulate the liver and help to keep the whole of the digestive system in balance.

Green fruits	Apples, pears, avocados, green grapes, limes, kiwi fruit
Green vegetables	Cabbage, calabrese, broccoli, kale, sprouts, green beans, peas, leeks, spinach
Other green foods	Most culinary herbs – marjoram, basil, oregano
Vitamins/minerals	All vitamins and minerals

Blue and violet fruits	Plums, blueberries, black grapes
Blue energy vegetables	Kelp and all seaweed products, asparagus
Violet vegetables	Purple sprouting broccoli, aubergines
Violet energy herbs	St John's wort (acts on the pineal gland)
Blue and violet energy vitamins	Vitamin E (stabilizes oxygen in the body, improves pituitary gland function)
Blue energy minerals	Iodine (enhances the function of the thyroid gland)
Violet energy minerals	Potassium (stabilizes electrolytes in the body, keeps oxygen supplied to the brain)

BLUE AND VIOLET FOODS AND FOODS THAT WORK IN A BLUE AND VIOLET WAY

There are very few foods that are blue or violet coloured. However, some foods work in a blue or violet way. Blue foods are useful when the voice, glands and organs of the neck, and communication skills need help. Violet vibration foods have a remarkable effect on the workings of the mind.

negative violet effects

Food additives and colourings serve to create illusion (a violet function) and relate to the shelf-life or appearance of foods. Some

△ Good crops of asparagus need special fertilizers, usually seaweed or from a seaweed source, to ensure an adequate supply of iodine.

▽ Dark-coloured grapes produce varying shades of red wine. The violet qualities of otherworldliness are encountered when drinking too much.

▷ Purple and violet foods bring unusual colouring to dishes or culinary displays.

additives also have an addictive quality, a trait that also belongs to a violet vibration. Both alcohol and sugar belong in this violet category when they are used in excess to escape from the reality of the world. Alcohol in particular is often the socially acceptable face of addiction and escapism.

Genetically modified foods also reflect a violet vibration because of the false idealism associated with their production. They are being upheld as the solution to world hunger, when in reality, there is already more than enough food to go around, but it is not being shared and distributed appropriately.

healers and intoxicants

Plants that have a violet resonance have long been used in healing all over the world. When used carefully under experienced supervision they can open the consciousness to other realms of experience. The use of intoxicants is a topic where cultures clash and legal entanglements abound, creating confusion and subversion which are strong violet traits.

In Meso-American traditions, a small cactus plant called peyote (*Lophophora williamsii*) is ritually harvested

and widely used for its mind-expanding effects in religious and healing ceremonies.

Throughout the region of the Amazon basin a vine grows called ayahuasca (*Banesteriopsis caapi*) that is collected from the forest, cut into small sections and boiled for many hours with combinations of other plants. Ayahuasca too, is an intoxicant used in healing and religious ceremonies, though it requires a special preliminary diet to give maximum benefit. Both ayahuasca and peyote are valued as purifiers of the body and are used to remove the causes of infection and illness.

Basil, the common pot-herb, used in Mediterranean cooking, has specific and therapeutic effects when taken in small amounts. Drunk as a tea, it can help relax the body while keeping the mind alert.

▽ Purple basil belongs to the same family as holy basil, which is used in the Indian subcontinent as a sacred herb of meditation.

Colour therapies

Colour has been used as a therapeutic tool for thousands of years. Today many of the traditional uses of colour for healing have changed little. The original practices have created a firm foundation for new ideas and applications of colour in the quest for health and wellbeing.

Theories of colour healing

Colour has always been associated with certain types of energy that are useful to both the healer and the magician. In the Middle Ages, colour was one of the correspondences used in magic along with planets, elements, spirits and angelic beings, metals, herbs, shapes and numbers. Tibetan and Chinese traditional medicine requires knowledge of the relationship between the colours of the elements and the compass directions to balance health. Yet it was only in the 19th century that science began to verify the healing possibilities of colour.

The German natural philosopher J.W. von Goethe (1749–1832) greatly influenced 19th-century ideas about light and colour. His book *Die Farben Lehre* (*The Theory of Colour*), published in 1810, combined scientific observation with metaphysical concepts, describing colour as an interplay

△ As an artist and scientist, Goethe was an important influence on colour theory.

of the polarities of light and dark. Goethe saw colour as an expression of spirituality and a way of expressing the inner nature of humanity. His thinking influenced artists such as Turner and teachers like Rudolf Steiner, who became influential in forming the colour theories of the 20th century.

During the 19th century there was an increasing interest in the healing properties of light. In 1851 Jacob Lorber wrote *The Healing Power of Sunlight*, which advocated exposing diseased parts of the body to the sun's rays as well as taking sun-charged mineral water and even sun-energized salt and other substances for speedier healing. In 1877 the American physician Dr Seth

▽ As in the 19th century, sunlight is still seen as part of the healing process today, and is often used as a therapeutic tool.

◁ Blue light has been found to significantly reduce the pain of a form of arthritis – the longer the exposure the better the results.

▽ Gradual and consistent exposure to yellow light decreases blood pressure and heart rate and increases energy and endurance.

Pancoast published *Blue and Red Lights*, in which he discussed using coloured filters to alter the body's function. He found that red filtered light would energize the nervous system while blue would sedate it. A year later, in *The Principles of Light and Colour*, another American physician, Dr Edwin Babitt, focused on the healing properties of the three primary colours. He began by creating small cabinets through which he shone filtered sunlight on to his patients. He later developed ways of projecting electric light through filters on to the patient. Babitt also recommended his patients should drink solarized water charged with coloured and filtered light. Many thought him a miracle worker, as he would frequently treat the most stubborn ailments with success.

Dinshah Ghadiali, a scientist who was born in India in 1873, devised a complete system of healing involving colour. He proposed that sound, coloured light, magnetism and heat were all different frequencies of one single energy. He correlated colour and other vibrations directly to specific areas of the body and its functions. In 1939 he published his theories in *The Spectro-Chrome Metry Encyclopedia*. He proposed that just as every chemical substance showed a unique spectral analysis, which means that each substance absorbs and reflects different frequencies of light energy, so the body would absorb and reflect colours depending on its state of health. Ghadiali also devised a machine that projected colour.

At the beginning of the 20th century in the USA, optometrist Dr Harry R. Spitter developed a colour healing system he called syntonics. He founded the College of Syntonic Optometry in 1933, where he

▽ Transparent coloured filters are an important tool in colour therapy that can be used to carry specific energies.

taught that light shone through precise combinations of 31 colour filters directly into the eyes could have profound healing effects on many aspects of the glandular and nervous systems, as well as significantly improving vision. Spitter's work was continued and developed after his death by Jacob Liberman, who uses a system of 20 coloured filters in holistic healing.

The use of colour and light as healing tools faded into the background as the use of new drugs became more widespread. Pharmaceutical drugs became available to treat conditions where sunlight and fresh air had been recommended. As more drugs arrived, the knowledge of utilizing light, colour and other natural resources to heal was no longer used. Recently, the popularity of colour and light as healing tools has increased, particularly as the limits of pharmacology and the complex difficulties of certain diseases are being recognized.

Colour essences

Many of the pioneers of colour healing found that their patients benefited from drinking water charged with natural sunlight or specific wavelengths of colour. Some theorized that the atomic structure of the water was somehow altered and given particular life-enhancing properties. These theories hold renewed interest for scientists today. Medical researchers are currently investigating techniques to target specific light frequencies on diseased tissue to restore normal functioning to the cells.

Colour essences are regaining popularity as vibrational healers. They contain nothing other than water that has been subtly energized and altered by the action of natural sunlight through a coloured filter.

△ The purity of single coloured light that is shown in a rainbow is what makes colour essences such a powerful healing tool.

▽ Medieval doctors would often use the early morning dew gathered from flowers, knowing that it possessed unique balancing properties.

They are easy to make and, like all vibrational remedies, have the advantage of being self-regulating. This means that the body will only make use of the energy within the essence if it is appropriate. Vibrational healing seems to work by reminding the body of its natural state of balance, which it needs to return to after some stress or shock.

Although simple to make, colour essences can be effective tools for healing. Rapid release of stress can sometimes feel uncomfortable. If this is experienced, simply reduce or stop using the essence for a day or two. Taking essences last thing at night and immediately on waking is a good way to bring a person back to a state of balance.

▷ Water can be charged with a colour using sunlight. Take a glass of water and surround it with a coloured gel and cut a disc from another piece to cover the top. Make sure the glass is surrounded then leave it in direct sunlight for two hours.

TO MAKE A VIBRATIONAL ESSENCE

YOU WILL NEED
- Clean drinking water, spring water or mineral water is best
- A plain glass container
- Colour gels from theatrical lighting suppliers or other coloured filters
- Brown glass storage bottles
- Labels
- A preservative, such as alcohol, cider vinegar or vegetable glycerine

METHOD
1 Pour the water into the glass vessel. Stand it on a colour filter of your choice and cover it with another filter in the same colour. (Colour gels can be made into cones or laid across the top of the vessel.) Leave the vessel in bright natural sunlight for at least two hours.
2 If you are going to keep the essence for future use it will need to be bottled – preferably in brown (neutral amber) glass to reduce exposure to light.
3 It is a good idea to add a preservative to your essence to keep it stable unless you are going to use it immediately. A 50/50 mix of energized water and alcohol such as brandy or vodka will

▽ Using a diffuser spray with water and a couple of drops of essence can quickly bring a colour vibration to a whole space.

keep for many months. Cider vinegar, honey or vegetable glycerine can also be used as preservatives if you can't use alcohol.

USES
- Drink a little each day in water. If kept in a dropper bottle, the essence can be taken as and when you need it, either directly dropped into the mouth or mixed with a little water.
- Drops can be placed straight on to pulse points at the wrists, side of the neck or on the forehead.
- Add colour essence to a diffuser sprayer filled with water. Spray around the room or around the body for immediate effect.
- Rub a drop or two on to the affected area, or the related chakra point.
- Add a drop or two to bath water or massage oil.
- Add a few drops to water in an oil burner, with or without the additions of essential oils.

△ Taking a few drops of a colour essence three or four times a day can quickly restore balanced energy.

▽ Rubbing a drop of essence into an area of imbalance can speed up the healing process.

Plants and colour

All over the world plants have been used to help keep the body healthy and to fight disease. Today, herbalism is still the most practical source of healthcare for a majority of the planet's population. Many of the herbs that are in common use indicate by their colour, shape, habit and popular associations how they can be used in healing. The name given to this information is the Doctrine of Signatures, and it has been used as a guide to healers for centuries.

△ The sunflower is sacred to the sun in its native Mexico, and its seeds have been used to treat cold, damp illnesses such as coughs and colds.

▷ Flower essences are a simple way to use plants' energetic and vibrational properties.

flower essences

Paracelsus, the 16th-century Swiss physician and occultist, is believed to have used the dew of flowers for his healing practice and there is some evidence that flower waters were also an integral part of Tibetan medical practices.

Early in the 20th century the gifted homeopath Dr Edward Bach made his own important discoveries about the healing properties of flower essences. He energized

▷ Essential oils are made from the concentrated extracts of plants. They can often be linked to colour energies and used alongside other colour healing techniques.

water with sunlight and flowers or other plant parts to create a set of 38 remedies. They were designed to rebalance the emotional disharmony that Bach saw as underlying all diseases. Dr Bach was often drawn to choose his remedies by the colour as well as other qualities of the plant. Flower essences are now made all around the world to help people bring balance into their lives, and colour plays an important part in explaining how they work.

energizing flowers

Red flowers often boost energy levels, for example, scarlet pimpernel (*Anagallis arvensis*) is a bright red, ground hugging plant whose flowers open only in sunshine. It used to be a popular remedy for heavy moods and depression, but today the flower essence of scarlet pimpernel is more often employed to energize and clear deep-seated blocks. The elm tree has tiny deep red and purple flowers, and their flower essence helps to clear the body and mind when

▽ Red coloured plants and flowers often have rich, heady perfumes that can be sensual, energizing and grounding.

fatigue and confusion have set in. Here the red stimulates the energy reserves and the purple balances the mind.

calming flowers

Blue flowers will often bring a sense of peace and help with communication and expression. Forget-me-not (*Myosotis arvensis*) can aid memory and help those who feel isolated and cut off from deeper levels of experience. Sage (*Salvia officinalis*) has violet-blue flowers that suggest it will be effective in the areas of the head and throat, and the leaves make an antiseptic gargle. The essential oil used very sparingly can help with certain types of headache. The flower essence helps to give a broader outlook on life and balances the mind.

Double colour healing

Single colours are very effective healing and assessment tools. However, if two colours are used in combination, both the healing and the assessment capacities increase. In the last 30 years three systems have developed that make use of the double-colour technique for healing – AuraSoma, AuraLight and AvaTara. All consist of coloured oil floating on top of a different coloured water in clear bottles. Cards can also be used as double-colour healing and assessment tools. They may have windows of theatrical spotlight gels or stained glass, or be simply printed with blocks of colour.

With all colour combinations, the top colour represents the conscious, the present and the most apparent energies. The lower colour represents the underlying factors, the past or roots of the situation and associated unconscious issues.

how to use a double-colour system

As with single colour selection, just pick the combination that appeals to you most. Your choice will reflect your current situation. Each of the colours is then interpreted through its correspondences. Try also selecting the combination you like the least, as this will reflect areas that may need a different kind of attention.

Sometimes several combinations may be chosen. The first choice can represent the roots of the present situation, the second choice can indicate the difficulties encountered, and the third choice can show the primary healing requirements.

△ Bottles of dual-coloured liquid capture the attention easily, regardless of any understanding of colour healing.

▽ Colour rarely appears isolated in nature. Combinations of colour build up complex and specific effects, affecting moods and thoughts.

examples of double-colour selection

choice 1 – yellow over red – the roots of the situation

• Physically this could indicate the possibility of tension or digestive difficulties (yellow) with a need for activity or initiative (red).

• Emotionally this may show that fear or anxiety (yellow) is being fed by anger or passion (red).

• Mentally, there is a need for clear, logical choices (yellow) to begin new projects (red).

• Spiritually there may be a need to get to know yourself better (yellow) in order to become more secure and grounded in the world (red).

choice 2 – green over blue – the difficulties encountered

• Physically there may be breathing problems (green), and some communication difficulties (blue).

• Emotionally, there might be a feeling of being confined (green) by ideas and beliefs (blue).

• Mentally, there is a definite need for space (green) to find peace (blue).

• Spiritually, there is a desire to go your own way (green) in a natural flow (blue).

choice 3 – violet over turquoise – primary healing requirements

• Physically, there is a need to be in quiet and harmonious surroundings (violet) so

that you can settle down and just be yourself (turquoise).

• Emotionally, consider cutting away illusion and delusion (violet) to find where the truth is for you (turquoise).

• Mentally, you need to gain inspiration (violet) from your own resources (turquoise).

• Spiritually, there is a need to heal yourself in order to feel at one with life (violet) and be able to express yourself freely (turquoise).

how double colours can heal

In a healing situation, once the choices have been made and discussed, issues often rise to the surface. Colour has a habit of bringing to the attention facets of life that have remained hidden. This gives an opportunity for healing. One way to bring healing is to have contact with the chosen combinations for a few minutes. If bottles are being used, they can be held or placed around the body.

◁ Your choices can be held up to the light or close to the body, for the healing effect of colour to be absorbed.

△ Selection from a range of double-colours elicits deep levels of information about a person's needs and direction in life. The choice of bottle will be made on an intuitive level.

The oil and water constituents of the bottles can also be massaged into the hands, feet or other appropriate places. If the combination is a light gel, it can be projected on to the body, or on to a wall to be looked at. The constituents of the combinations can also be introduced through diet, lifestyle or through your surroundings.

In the third example given here, the primary requirements were shown to be violet over turquoise. This could suggest spending quiet periods alone, and also introducing violet and turquoise items temporarily into the living space. Wearing two of the appropriate colours can be an immediate way to bring those energies into your life. This could be through single coloured separates or by wearing ties or scarves of the colours. Even such simple changes can have profound effects.

Colour and shape

Philosophers and mystics have always been interested in exploring the origins of creation. Eastern and Western thinkers have traditionally used light and colour combined with geometric shapes to help define the forces of the universe in symbolic terms.

sacred shapes

The science of geometry is the basic patterning of all matter in creation. In Classical Greece the philosopher Plato devised a system of representing the elements with coloured geometric forms, in an attempt to explain the building blocks of all existence, including spiritual realities. Platonic Solids define how to form physical matter, because they represent the only way atoms can pack together. Like the elements and colours,

energy interacts to form physical matter. The Platonic Solids, therefore, encapsulate our understanding of the universe.

At around the same time that Plato was working, Indian philosophers were also choosing different shapes and colours to represent the elements. They called the elements and their symbols tattvas, literally: those things that possess distinction.

Shape holds and defines colour, giving it solidity and presence, while colour imparts different qualities to shape. A viewer reacts differently to a blue triangle and a red triangle. A yellow circle feels different to a yellow square. The human brain's response to various stimuli has allowed the non-verbal language of symbolism to develop in every culture.

▽ A set of Platonic Solids cut out of clear quartz: (left to right) cube of Earth; octahedron of Air; tetrahedron of Fire; dodecahedron of Ether; and icosahedron of Water.

△ Shape as well as colour contains specific energies. These are harnessed especially in religious buildings to enhance the spiritual qualities of the surroundings.

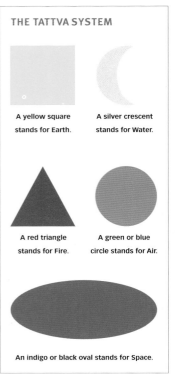

THE TATTVA SYSTEM

A yellow square
stands for Earth.

A silver crescent
stands for Water.

A red triangle
stands for Fire.

A green or blue
circle stands for Air.

An indigo or black oval stands for Space.

Colour therapists such as Theo Gimbel and Howard and Dorothy Sun have introduced shape into their colour healing work. Theo Gimbel shines coloured light through shaped apertures on to the body to help restore balance to its subtle energy systems. The Suns assess their patients' wellbeing after asking them to choose from a range of coloured shapes based on the Platonic solids. This gives an accurate profile of both personality and situation. Similar assessment techniques are continuing to be developed as it becomes more widely understood that our instinctive choices of colour and shape can accurately indicate underlying factors in our lives.

Mary Hykel Hunt, a Welsh psychologist and colour worker, is in a unique position

△ The forms of classical Indian architecture are precisely proportioned to reflect the elemental shapes of the tattvas, such as the crescent, square, cone and sphere.

WHAT'S IN A NAME?

Ask a friend, colleague or family member if you can look at their name for colours and shapes. Sit quietly, thinking about the name, and intuit what colours and shapes seem to be present in it.

Let us imagine that the name you're thinking about is Kathy. You might feel that the name is made up of a three-dimensional blue rectangle (or double cube) followed by a red circle, a brown cube and a yellow crescent.

The three-dimensional rectangle or double cube represents Earth, coloured with the blue of communication. It suggests someone with practical communication skills. The cube again represents Earth, this time coloured brown for practicality and focus. This shows creative and nurturing skills put to practical use.

The circle represents Air, coloured red for activity. This activates or energizes communication.

The crescent represents Water, coloured yellow to show thought processes, anxiety and joy. This hints at the emotions that lie behind the practical activity, and suggests that there may be some problems with self-criticism.

to explore the relationship between shape, colour and personality. From birth she has been synaesthetic, that is, her senses of sight and sound are combined so that she experiences colour and shape with each sound she hears. This has enabled Hykel Hunt to train others to explore the innate ability we all have of translating one sense into another. Hykel Hunt's workshops provide people with a whole series of symbols, similar to the tattvas, with which to intuitively explore the energy make-up of the world around them.

People's names provide a rich source of intuitive exploration. Hykel Hunt teaches how to intuit coloured shapes from the sound of someone's name and then to use those colours and shapes to discover the

skills and gifts of that person. The more you try to link colour, shape and sound, the more successful and confident you will become. Try the name visualization exercise in a group of people, and you will find remarkably similar results.

This suggests that people can successfully tap into their innate skills with a little practice and encouragement. It also backs up the findings of the Indian and Greek philosophers, who saw correlations and correspondences between colour, shape and human experience.

Colour visualization

In Tibetan meditation practices, different aspects of energy are visualized as spheres of coloured light. Visual imagery of many sorts is a major part of Tibetan spiritual techniques, along with the use of breath control, sound and posture.

Complex visualizations take practice to achieve, but the focus required is itself of benefit, by taking the mind away from everyday concerns. In all visualization exercises it is important to remember that cinema-like clarity and detail are not necessary to achieve success. Simply reading through an exercise begins to create the right emotional picture.

energy sphere visualization

The following exercise is designed to integrate the inner and outer worlds by bringing the colours of the directions into the heart. This leads to a balance of harmony

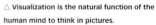

△ Visualization is the natural function of the human mind to think in pictures.

with one's surroundings and restores equilibrium in the body, mind and emotions.

1 Sit in a comfortable position, facing the east. Imagine a deep blue lotus with four petals resting at its centre.

2 In the heart of the flower is a luminous clear sphere of light, like crystal. It reflects the blue of the petals and represents the element of space (ether).

3 Before the lotus is a yellow sphere, representing the east, the earth element.

4 To your left, the north, is a green sphere, the air element.

5 Behind you is a red sphere of the west, the fire element.

6 To the right of you is a blue sphere of the south, the water element.

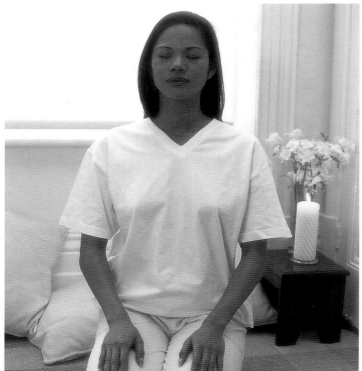

◁ Visualizing specific colours around you, in the compass directions, then visualizing blue and white flowing through you, is exceptionally relaxing and healing.

rainbow breathing

This is a simple but effective way of bringing colour energies into your body to restore balance when there has been stress, or to identify which colour energies you are most in need of absorbing.

1 Take a minute to relax and calm your mind with your eyes closed.

2 Imagine the air around you is a rich, deep red. As you breathe in, your whole body fills with red energy. Continue breathing in the red light until you feel you have sufficient, then breathe out the red light through your feet or your spine, into the earth.

3 Next, imagine the air becomes a vibrant, warm orange colour. Breathe in the orange energy in the same way. When you have

△▽ Imagining an object of the same colour as the one you are visualizing will help to create a clearer image. Look at a bright coloured flower and imagine yourself breathing in the colour.

completed the process and breathed it out to the earth, continue with the other colours of the spectrum: yellow, green, blue, indigo and violet.

If you have need for a particular colour energy, concentrate on that visualization and take notice of how it seems to move around the body. Make sure the light goes to every part of your body by paying attention to areas that are difficult to visualize.

protecting the heart of all things

This is a visualization exercise that is extremely valuable when we face difficult circumstances in our lives. It helps to remove fear, which is the cause of all other negative reactions, both from ourselves and from the people around us. Doing this exercise can also help to reduce anger, aggression, irritation and misunderstanding.

1 Right at the centre of your heart chakra, in the middle of your chest, imagine a spark of bright pink light.

2 Keep your imagination on that spark of

△ The visualization of pink light has a calming, integrating and healing effect on yourself and your surroundings.

light strong and gradually see it radiating out through the body in a strong pink glow.

3 The spark of pink energy is like a sun in your heart and its light completely fills your body and then continues to expand outwards in a pink halo of light surrounding everything around you.

4 As it touches others, the pink star at their own heart sparks into life, so that the pink energy gets stronger the more people around you it contacts.

5 At the end of the visualization, allow your attention to return to the pink star at your heart, as the surrounding colour fades gently away.

If when you begin the visualization, you see a different colour, allow that to be your focus. It may be more appropriate to the energy of the situation you find yourself in, even if you feel the colours you see to be negative or hostile.

Colour in meditation

Colour is a very powerful tool in all meditation exercises because it has a profound effect on the nervous system, no matter what else may be happening on the surface levels of the mind. Here are two meditation exercises that use colour in different ways. When you use them make sure you are sitting or lying in a comfortable position, with no risk of disturbance or distraction.

absorbing the lights of perfection

One of the main practices in Tibetan Buddhism is to visualize a teacher or enlightened being, such as a buddha, and absorb their enlightened qualities into one's own body in the form of coloured light. The nature or form of the visualized being is not as important as the confidence and faith of the meditator. The being represents all those who have taught us, looked after us, and wished us well in our lives.

The following exercise is calming and clarifying and helps to bring the energy of the mind into its natural state of relaxed quietness. It helps to establish a continual connection to your true nature.

1 Sit quietly for a minute or two. Consider all the teachers and spiritual beings who have inspired you with the qualities of clarity, compassion and truth. Visualize their presence in front of you as a glorious bright

▽ **Feel the coloured lights at brow, throat and heart dissolving all negativity and bringing clarity and peace.**

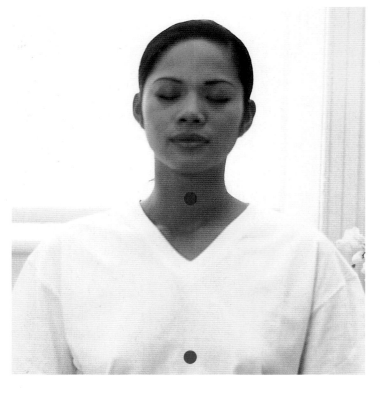

light suffused with translucent rainbow colours. Within the light is a figure representing all the wisdom of the universe.

2 From the forehead of the figure, a clear white beam enters your forehead and fills your body with light, cleansing all heaviness and negativity from your body.

3 From the throat of the figure of light emerges a ray of ruby red, which enters your own throat. From there, it fills your body and cleanses negativity from your senses.

4 Now from the heart of the figure of light flows a ray of shimmering deep blue, entering your own heart and pervading your whole body, clearing away negativity from your mind.

5 As you have shared the purifying colour vibrations from the being of light, you have merged together so that now there is no distinction, no difference between your energy and the clear compassionate light of the universe.

a tattva meditation

Using the tattvic shapes, the traditional Hindu symbols of the elements, can be an effective way to balance personal energies. Many variations are possible but the aim is to absorb the quality of each element and integrate it into the body.

For this meditation you need to focus on each tattva in turn or concentrate on those you feel need more balance. As you visualize the shape within your body, feel your inbreath entering the symbol, charging it with energy. As you breath out imagine it removing imbalance from that area.

Alternatively, you can place a representation of a particular tattva in front of you on a white wall. As you breathe naturally, imagine that you are breathing in the energy of the element represented by the colour and shape.

The yellow square of Earth sits with its base upon the base of the spine. It can be used when energy is low and there is a lack of motivation.

△ Gazing at an elemental tattva shape lets you understand the quality of energy of shape and colour and will balance the element in your body.

▷ Working with coloured shapes on card can be an intuitive way of selecting and balancing your needs at the moment.

The silver-white crescent of the Water element sits between the navel and the pubic bone within the top of the pelvis. Use it when there is indecision, excess of emotion or a feeling of heaviness.

The red triangle of Fire sits pointing downwards from the base of the ribcage towards the navel. It is useful to calm anger, irritation and exhaustion.

The blue circle of Air is in the centre of the chest. It will help focus concentration, reducing agitation and scattered thoughts.

The midnight blue or black egg of Ether or Space sits within the throat. It can soothe feelings of emptiness and uselessness.

The Chakras

According to ancient Indian belief, as well as our physical body we have a body of energy, known as the 'subtle body'. This is made up of myriad channels called nadis through which flows prana, or life-force (chi in Chinese medicine). The most important of the nadis is the sushumna nadi, which runs from the top of the head to the navel. Along the sushumna nadi spin seven 'wheels' of energy, known as chakras. Each chakra is said to spin at a certain frequency, each has a specific colour and mantra (sacred sound), and each has particular associations with parts of the physical body. When we are healthy and our body, mind, spirit and emotions are in balance, prana flows freely through the subtle body and the chakras spin brightly and at the right frequencies. However, when we are ill, upset, stressed or otherwise out of kilter, energy becomes blocked and the chakras become unbalanced – some may be overburdened with excess prana, others may be lacking. This section of the book explains more about the nature of chakras and their specific associations in the physical body. It then takes each of the seven chakras in turn to show how, through techniques such as meditation and postural exercise, we can correct any chakra imbalances to live healthier, more fulfilling lives.

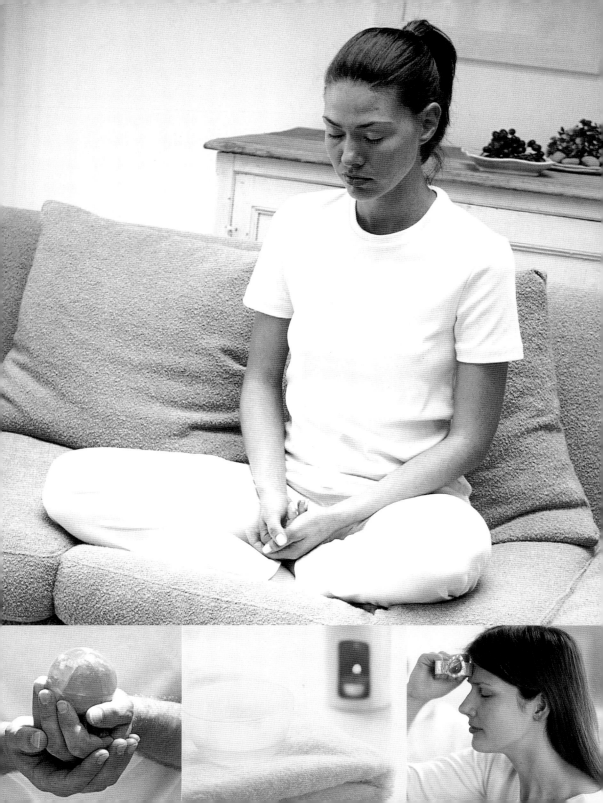

The chakra system

"In the body there are many kinds of channels, which are very extensive. The sage must understand them in order to understand his own body… Running transversely, up and down, they exist in the body joined together like a wheel, dependent on the life-force and linked to the breath of the body."

From the Shiva-Svarodaya Tantra, traditional Indian teaching on the subtle anatomy of the body.

What are chakras?

Over the last five thousand years, sages, philosophers and mystics have described the subtle energies in our environment and within our bodies in many different ways. Several systems have developed to explain them in the context of other philosophical backgrounds. However, it was generally agreed that wherever dynamic energies meet together in nature they form spinning circular patterns, or vortices. On a small scale this can be seen in tiny spiral eddies on the surfaces of streams and rivers; on a large scale in the movements of cloud systems that create cyclones and anticyclones.

The seers of ancient India perceived similar vortices within the energy of the human body. They described these in the Vedas, the primary source of all Hindu cosmology and philosophy, codified around 3000 BC. According to the Vedic seers, wherever two or more channels of subtle energy meet, there is a vortex, which they named 'chakra', meaning 'wheel'. Because these energy concentrations appeared to them to be funnel-shaped, multi-coloured and related to spiritual qualities, they became associated with the sacred lotus.

Where major energy flows coincide – on the midline of the body in the front of the spinal column – the seers of India saw seven main chakras that seemed to mirror both health and the spiritual state. These seven

△ **Wherever different streams of energy converge, a spiralling dynamic funnel, or vortex, is created, as in this cloud formation.**

chakras were like multi-dimensional gateways that would allow the individual to access different experiences and states of consciousness. The use of visualization, sound, chant, meditation and exercise to activate, cleanse and integrate these seven chakras became an important part of spiritual practice, especially in the Himalayan regions of India, Nepal and Tibet. Under guidance from an experienced teacher, each student was taught the appropriate methods to activate and integrate every part of the chakra system in a safe and balanced way.

Though everyone is likely to experience problems and energy stresses in different parts of the body and mind, our individual strengths and weaknesses are unique to us. In the same way, each chakra deals with particular areas of function, but the quality of the energy will vary from person to person. The skill of the teacher is to identify how to clear the energy pathways as the blocks reveal themselves.

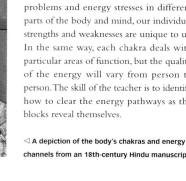

◁ **A depiction of the body's chakras and energy channels from an 18th-century Hindu manuscript.**

△ The spirals of nature mirror the vortices in the human body, which are formed when two or more channels of energy meet.

▽ The Vedic seers could perceive the structure of the cosmos and had startling knowledge of its true nature. In the same way, they were able to understand how cosmic energies manifested themselves within the human body.

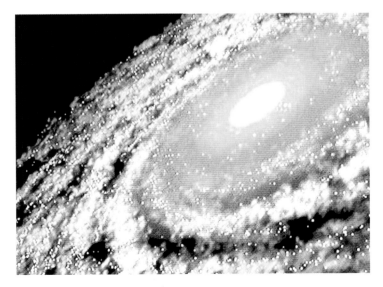

chakras today

Many of the original Vedic texts discuss the development of psychic skill and supernatural power that arises from spiritual exercises. This connection with the spirit world attracted the attention of 19th-century Western thinkers, many of whom had become interested in oriental mysticism. As movements such as Spiritualism and Theosophy developed, the Vedas were translated into Western languages. These translations emphasized the development of the higher chakras, and the desire to go beyond, or escape from, the bonds of the physical world. This bias echoed the trends of theosophical thinking, and usefully avoided what were viewed as embarrassing sexual techniques involving the three lower chakras. This false division into lower (or mundane) and higher (or spiritual) chakras misses the point that is continually reiterated in the original texts: that all chakras are of equal practical value.

Today our way of understanding the chakras is different again. Since the 1970s the seven chakras have been seen as fitting in with the other sets of sacred sevens, and have become particularly associated with the seven rainbow colours, with each chakra having its own colour. Although this is a modern departure it works very well, combining as it does an easy-to-remember colour code with the qualities and functions of each chakra. It is important to remember, however, that whichever system is used, classical or modern, it is really no more than a partial description of a complex set of energy interactions that make up the human mind, body and spirit.

Chakra imagery

Whatever their correlation to physical structures within the body, chakras are entirely non-physical. The mind, rather than the sense organs, is the traditional tool for accessing, exploring and balancing the energy of each chakra. The main features of each chakra are described here as in the original Vedic texts, as they would be visualized by a meditator. Each chakra is symbolized by layers of imagery, including a particular animal, and a god and a goddess whose form and attributes encapsulate the inherent qualities that arise when the chakra is functioning in a balanced way.

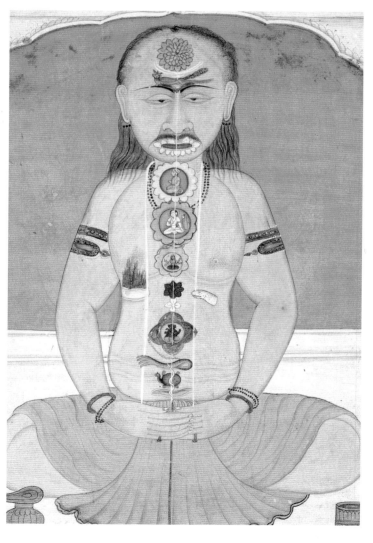

◁ **An Indian depiction of the chakras, each with their god or goddess depicted within.**

muladhara

This is the base chakra and its name means 'foundation'. It has four vermillion petals around a yellow square. The yellow square represents the element of Earth and the petals represent the four directions: north, south, east and west. The animal form representing the base chakra is a seven-trunked elephant, associated with solidity and assuredness. The elephant's trunks represent the sacred sevens, the chakras, planets, colours, notes and behavioural aspects which each of us must work with in the world. On the elephant's back rests the bija, or seed, mantra – the sound that stimulates the energy of this chakra – Lam. The god and goddess images show attributes of fearlessness and stillness.

svadistana

The sacral chakra, whose name means 'sweetness', has six red petals. It represents the Water element. The sacral chakra's animal is a crocodile, which represents its sensuous, watery and deceptively strong energy. On the crocodile rests the bija mantra Vam. The images of the god and goddess display peaceful emotions.

manipura

The solar plexus chakra's name means 'city of gems'. Ten luminous blue petals surround a downward-pointing red triangle, symbol of the Fire element. The animal is a ram: headstrong and direct, his fiery nature controls the group of which he is the leader. The deities represent control over anger and control of energy. The bija mantra is Ram.

anahata

The name of the fourth, or heart, chakra means 'unstruck'. Twelve deep red lotus petals surround a hexagram or six-pointed star of grey-green, representing the element

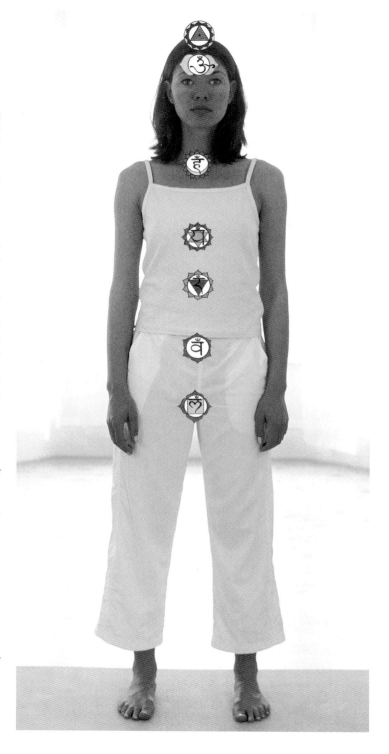

▷ The chakras are usually mapped in a vertical line running up the spinal column, corresponding to the physical structures to which they relate.

of Air. The animal is a black antelope, leaping with joy. It shows the sensitive, aware and curious nature of the heart chakra. On the back of the antelope rests the bija mantra Yam. The sound here controls breath and life-energy. The deities represent the arts and harmony in both inner and outer worlds.

vishuddha

This is the throat chakra, and its name means 'pure'. It has a circle of 16 lavender or smoky purple petals enclosing a silver crescent and the white circle of the full moon. This represents the ether or space, where all the elements dissolve into their refined essence, akasha, the pure cosmic sound. The animal is an elephant, the colour of clouds. His single trunk represents sound and he carries the memory of all past knowledge. He carries the bija mantra Ham, which empowers his voice. The deities represent the union of the elements, dreams of inspiration and higher knowledge.

ajña

The brow chakra's name means 'command'. It has two petals of luminescent pearly blue. Within a white column (the 'colour of light') is a representation of unified consciousness – a combined male and female deity. There is no animal here for the bija mantra, Aum, to rest on, so it rests on the finest quality of sound itself, known as nada. The goddess of this chakra embodies unconditional truth.

sahasrara

The 'thousand-petalled' crown chakra is at the top of the head. It is sometimes described as formless, sometimes as a moonlike sphere above which is an umbrella of a thousand petals with all the colours of the rainbow. The bija mantra is the 'nng' sound, known as Visarga. This is the breath-like sound that ends all previous bija mantras. It rests upon the bindu, the first moment of creation in the relative universe.

Physical correspondences

Because they cannot be seen by normal means, the chakras and the nadis – their related system of subtle channels – are represented by diagrams and other symbolic maps of the body. This is necessary to clarify the relationship between the subtle centres and the physical organs and structures with which we are familiar. However, mapping the chakras in this way can lead to a very static, inflexible and two-dimensional view of what is an elegant, dynamic and ever-changing interaction of energies.

Being non-physical, influencing matter but not consisting of matter, chakras are not bound by the laws of matter. In classical texts the chakras and nadis are considered to be expressions of consciousness. Time and

△ Chakras provide the underlying orderliness of our being. Those with clairvoyant sight see them at every level, from physical to most subtle.

▽ A diagrammatic view of the chakras helps to identify their physical correspondences, though it does not reflect their interactive nature.

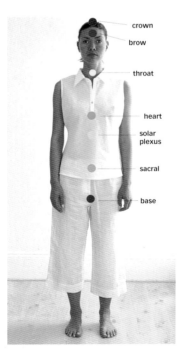

- crown
- brow
- throat
- heart
- solar plexus
- sacral
- base

space, three-dimensional existence and scale have little relevance, except as a way to understand the chakras in familiar terms.

Around each chakra, echoing its function, are one of the main endocrine glands, a concentration of nerves known as a plexus, and concentrations of blood vessels and lymph nodes. There is some difference of opinion as to which physical system is related to which chakra, but most healers follow the correspondences described below.

the base chakra

Located at the base of the spine, the base chakra is sometimes represented as a vortex with a downward opening. In some systems it is related to the testicles or ovaries, in others to the adrenal glands. Although physically a long way from the base, the adrenal glands reflect the survival instinct of this chakra. The concentration of nerves in this area is called the coccygeal plexus.

the sacral chakra

The second chakra, sometimes called the sex chakra, is located in the lower abdomen, between the navel and the pubic bone. It is related to the sacral vertebrae in the spine, the sacral plexus of nerves and the sex glands – the ovaries and testicles. This chakra is associated with emotions and sensuality.

the solar plexus chakra

The third chakra is located on the front of the body between the bottom of the ribcage (diaphragm) and the navel. It is concerned with personal energy and power and is associated with the adrenal glands and the pancreas. The solar plexus chakra is named after the complex of nerves found here and is connected to the lumbar vertebrae.

THE LIMBIC SYSTEM

Deep in the centre of the brain lies a complex series of organs known as the limbic system. Within it, the pineal and pituitary glands control all the hormone systems of the body – in the same way that the crown chakra regulates the chakra system. Modern Vedic seers have linked each part of the limbic system with the functions and energies of the planetary influences in our lives: microcosm and macrocosm can exist at the level of neuroscience, as can the concept of the non-physical chakras.

▽ The pineal (left) and pituitary, or master, gland (right) are very small organs that control the body's hormone-releasing systems.

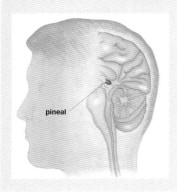

pineal

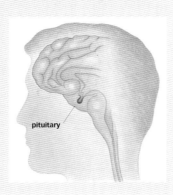

pituitary

unseen, subtle forces, or spiritual powers, that control the existence of physical matter.

Like seed crystals dropped into a saturated solution, concentrations of dynamic orderliness, or points of consciousness, act as a template for the accretion of physical matter and the development of the systems of the human body. The chakras can be understood as working in the same way as planetary bodies in a solar system. Each, by its placement and qualities, attracts free floating matter and maintains it in its orbit.

Seen as concentrations of consciousness or crystallized mind, the physical systems of the body cannot be separated from the subtler structures. The body, mind and emotions are all extensions of chakra function. Changes at one level will bring automatic changes at every other level. Dysfunction at the physical level is echoed in the function of the chakras, and stress in the chakras can be felt as discomfort at the level of mind, body or emotion.

the heart chakra

The fourth chakra is the heart, located in the centre of the chest, associated with the thoracic vertebrae of the spine. The related gland is the thymus, a small gland above the heart vital for growth and the maintenance of the immune system. Two nerve centres are found here – the pulmonary plexus and the cardiac plexus. This chakra deals with love and relationships.

the throat chakra

The fifth, or throat, chakra is located near the cervical vertebrae and the base of the throat. It manifests communications and creativity. The thyroid and parathyroid glands (which control the body's metabolic rate and mineral levels) and the pharyngeal plexus are found here.

the brow chakra

The sixth chakra is the brow, located in the centre of the forehead. This is linked to the pineal gland that maintains cycles of activity and rest, and to the carotid plexus of nerves. The brow chakra directs intuition, insight and imagination.

the crown chakra

The seventh chakra, the crown, is located just above the top of the head and influences all the higher brain functions. It is connected to the pituitary, the gland that controls the whole endocrine (hormone) system. The entire cerebral cortex is influenced by this centre. The crown is associated with knowledge and understanding.

subtle forces

The modern study of embryology has yet to uncover the mechanisms by which original cells, which are identical and undifferentiated, migrate to certain places in the embryo and begin to form specialized organs. In complementary medicine and the holistic philosophies of non-Western cultures, it is the

▷ The endocrine glands maintain hormone balance in the body. Energy levels, emotional states and reactions to external and internal conditions are under their direct control. They can be seen as representatives of the chakras at a physical level.

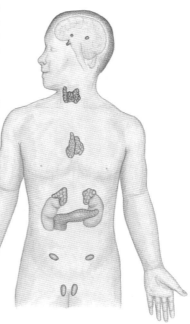

Cycles of nature

In the original Indian texts the chakras are related to a series of milestones in life. Each chakra and its function represent a stage of development and growth. Each stage can be seen as a time in which certain skills are developed. The precise shift from one stage of development to another will vary from individual to individual. The stages may overlap, but in some cases, where stress or trauma disrupts the chakra energy, this may create an underlying problem for subsequent growth. If one function remains underdeveloped, all the others dependent on it will have a built-in dysfunction.

conception and birth

The base chakra relates to the creation of the physical body, so it represents a stage of growth that begins at conception and continues until around the age of one year. The immediate, powerful energy of the base chakra is evident in the speed of growth and the primary need to survive. An infant during this time is dependent on others for its food, warmth and shelter. This period helps to anchor the individual into the physical world.

the developing baby

The sacral chakra begins to activate consciously at about six months and its effects last to around the age of two years. The feedback in this time comes from pleasure and gratification. The distinction between the child and the mother begins to become more apparent. Being given space to explore existence without negative reinforcement or verbal reprimand helps to build confidence in being a separate individual.

▽ All chakras are present in the growing child but during natural development energy focuses at certain centres.

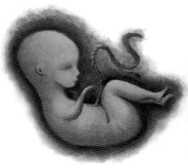

◁ From the moment of conception, consciousness coalesces around the energy of the chakras. The primary needs of survival and nutrition are the first focuses of each new life.

the small child

The onset of the activity of the solar plexus chakra is commonly referred to as the 'terrible twos'. It starts at around 18 months and lasts until the child is about four years old. This is when language develops, together with an understanding of the passing of time. Maintaining the balance between freedom and discipline is crucial at this age. Lack of restraining discipline creates an overpowering, egotistic child, whereas too much control will stop any sense of autonomy developing.

the child

The heart chakra covers the period from four to seven years and is characterized by relationships outside the immediate family. Relating helps to build self-esteem and self-acceptance. If love and relationships are always seen as being conditional – that is,

▽ Shared, co-operative creativity flourishes when the sacral and throat chakras have developed in a balanced way. Problems can arise if other chakras do not work in harmony.

having an emotional price-tag attached – the underlying feelings of guilt and grief caused by not receiving enough love can create great difficulties through life.

the pre-pubescent

The development of the throat chakra between the ages of seven and 12 marks the beginning of the stage of self-expression. If the lower chakra energies have been integrated to a reasonable extent, confidence can be gained from a firm emotional base. Through the throat chakra, this is given back to the community and family, sometimes in plays and perfomances.

the adolescent

The brow chakra covers the adolescent years, when the young person should be encouraged to reflect on the patterns in their own and others' lives. This is the first of several key stages when it is possible to re-invent and readjust the role that an individual sees themselves playing in the world.

the adult

The crown chakra becomes active between 20 and 27 years, as the individual fully reacts and interacts with the world. Sometimes this stage stays dormant, because it relates to questions like 'Why am I here?' and statements like 'There must be more to life than this.' These issues may never be looked at. On the other hand, the action of exploring them may be the beginning of a radical change of life and work. Having gone through a whole cycle, the

process begins again with the base chakra. Just as, in musical scales, each octave returns to the start note, the chakra cycle can repeat many times in a single life. The fact that this cycle renews itself periodically gives us opportunities to heal and repair ourselves. This enables us gradually to strengthen the energy within our chakra system and express more of our potential.

▷ As adults, we pass through successive cycles of the chakra system, continuing our own spiritual growth while also perhaps fostering the development of children.

Nadis, kundalini and minor chakras

The seven main chakras are only part of a much larger complex of subtle energies that make up the individual human being. For example, there are many other chakras throughout the body, all of which are expressions of different kinds of consciousness and energy. The physical disciplines, such as hatha yoga – the use of specific postures to encourage spiritual development and health – and mudra – the holding of specific hand positions – have developed to make use of the energy of these smaller chakras and the channels that link them together.

Surrounding each chakra are the main channels of energy, called nadis, that flow from the centre and interact with the rest of the body. Nadis are related to some aspects of the autonomic nervous system, and also to the meridian channels identified in traditional Chinese medicine, but they are of a much finer subtle substance.

There are said to be, in total, 72,000 nadis. Fourteen are named and described in detail, and of these three are of prime importance: the ida, the pingala and the sushumna. These three main channels run parallel to the body's physical axis of the spinal column.

The sushumna is the central channel, and the most important. This is the channel that yogis seek to cleanse and into which they direct energy to achieve realization. As the Tibetan teacher Lama Sangwa said: 'By causing the winds (pranas) and subtle drops (elements) to enter into the central channel, bliss arises and the body itself becomes the source of enlightened awareness.'

Ida, the left channel, carries a lunar energy that is nourishing and purifying.

▽ This traditional image, called Sri Chakra, is a schematic representation of the main energy components of the human body.

▷ The sushumna is the central channel from which the chakras emerge. Weaving from side to side are the Ida and Pingala, the sun and moon channels.

▷ The caduceus represents the Staff of Hermes, the Greek Messenger of the Gods. It was adopted as the symbol for healing and bears a striking resemblance to the three main nadis of the human body.

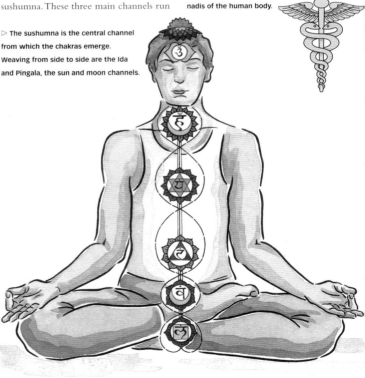

NADI SODHANA

Purification of physical and subtle energies in the body helps to clear the nadis, strengthens the chakras and begins to free up the primal energy of kundalini. A safe, well-balanced exercise for this is a breathing exercise (or pranayama) known as nadi sodhana. This exercise helps to balance the energy in the left and right channels (ida and pingala) and is calming and relaxing.

1 Sit comfortably with a straight spine. (If sitting in a chair, plant your feet flat on the floor.) Tuck your chin in so that the back of your neck is straight. Sit for a moment with your hands on your knees and calm your body and mind.

2 With the right ring finger, close off your left nostril by gentle pressure to the fleshy part and inhale slowly and deeply through the right nostril.

3 Now use your right thumb to close the right nostril, releasing the left nostril, breathing out through the left nostril, slowly and deeply.

4 Keep the right thumb in place and now breathe in through the left nostril. At the end of the breath, close the left nostril with the right ring finger again.

5 Now breathe out slowly through the right nostril.

6 Repeat the whole sequence of breaths ten times.

△ The lotus petals round each chakra represent the nadis that distribute that chakra's energy through the body. Each chakra and nadi are expressions of the individual's core life-energy held within the three central channels.

Pingala, the channel on the right side of the sushumna, is said to carry solar energy. The three channels are sometimes represented as running parallel to each other, while in other depictions the solar and lunar channels are seen weaving between the chakras until all three meet at the brow chakra.

The fundamental life energy of the individual is thought to reside in a quiet state within the base chakra. This force is called kundalini, which means 'coiled up'. As the chakras and their nadis are cleansed of stress and other energy blockages, more of the kundalini energy is able to move freely through the body. As this energy is pure consciousness, its awakened state can create various degrees of realization or enlightenment in the individual.

Many of the main chakras located on the central channel have smaller associated energy centres. For example, the muladhara at the base of the spine has related centres at the groin points, the knees and the soles of the feet. All these minor chakras help to ground and balance the physical energies. The heart chakra, anahata, has a smaller chakra inside it, which is represented as having eight petals. This is the spiritual heart, the anandakanda, whose eight channels represent the emotions.

Chakras in other therapies

Although the chakras are non-physical, they influence physical functioning. Their subtle channels, the nadis, interface with many systems, both energetic and material.

The original theory of the chakras was holistic. It set out a coherent system of psycho-spiritual development that automatically included the health and wellbeing of the physical body. Blocks and stresses caused by ignorance and inappropriate belief systems were believed to produce physical illness and spiritual suffering. Nowadays, complementary and alternative therapies are again seeking to work with a unified holistic vision of the human being. For this reason, integrated and self-contained systems like the chakras are again becoming useful models for healing.

yoga

Followers of the original Indian spiritual traditions worked with the chakra energies through physical exercise. Hatha yoga

▽ Hatha yoga is effective because it directly influences the chakra system. Holding a posture ensures that the nadis, the chakras and the muscles all work to bring specific functions of the system into balance.

positions (asanas) are designed to tone the physical body and stimulate the chakras and their nadis. They will do this automatically, though it is useful to follow a sequence of asanas that works through each of the chakras in turn.

sound

Used to restore balance to the body, sound therapy is often focused on the chakras. Each area of the physical system is made up of different densities of tissue and hollow cavities. Sound, either produced externally by a therapist or internally by the patient, resonates with different areas of the body according to the tone that is being made. Blocks in the emotions, the physical body and within the chakras can be loosened and released very effectively by sound. Resonant instruments such as didgeridoos, tuning forks, bells, gongs and singing bowls can all be placed close to chakra points.

Toning, which uses the resonant voice to make particular sounds, is also commonly used to release blocks. For example a resonant 'mmm' sound vibrates the bones of the head and the brow chakra, while an open 'aaah' sound relaxes the diaphragm and energizes the solar plexus.

△ Sound vibrates the physical structures of the body, and its subtle qualities also help to balance or clear the chakras and nadis.

▽ Colour therapy harnesses light, the subtlest of all physical energies. Specific colours can be used to help energize and heal particular chakras.

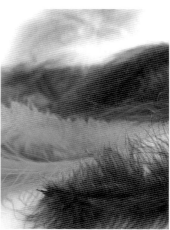

colour therapy

The original yogic exercises placed great emphasis on visualization. This often involved building up exact and powerfully coloured shapes and patterns, each of which created specific changes within the brain function and caused energy channels to activate around particular chakras.

Today colour therapy offers healers a valuable way of working directly with chakras. There are many ways of introducing colour into the human energy system. Shining coloured light directly on the chakra, over the whole body or through the eyes all create physical, emotional and mental changes. Visualization and imagination techniques involving colour are also often used. The body affects the mind and the mind affects the body, and as the ancient yogis and seers of all cultures discovered, energy flows where the attention of the mind is directed. This energy is the same as prana, or life-energy, so naturally it can be effective in bringing health to an area needing attention.

▽ Crystal therapy uses the combination of colour and resonance – the energy unique to each type of stone – to rebalance the chakra centres.

△ Even therapies that do not specifically focus on the main chakra points have a profound influence on them. Any release of stress takes the burden off the chakra system as a whole.

crystal healing

In crystal healing the seven main chakras are often the primary areas of stone placement. The organized structure of natural minerals has been found to have a beneficial and quick-acting effect on balancing the chakras. After an initial assessment, during which the quality of energy in each chakra is determined, stones are placed on and around each centre. The stones very often follow the Western colour correspondences, so that red stones will naturally enhance the qualities of the base chakra, orange stones those of the sacral chakra, and so on. From this starting point the therapist can modify the approach to release stress and correct under- and overactive chakra states.

healing by touch

Spiritual or hands-on healers may focus their healing attention at chakra points where they sense energy flowing with a significantly greater or lesser intensity than elsewhere. Because chakras are energy gateways that allow a flow of energy both inwards and outwards, they are natural focuses for a great many developing types of holistic therapy.

Discover your own chakra energy

Chakra energies are forever changing, interacting, balancing and rebalancing. From hour to hour and minute to minute as our activities alter, we move from concentration, to remembering, to physical coordination skills, to relaxing. As we do so, different chakras become more or less dominant. As individuals we each have a predisposition to certain chakras being more dominant than others. If we enjoy physical activity and have a practical, hands-on job, this will focus our energies at the first and second chakras. On the other hand, with an occupation that focuses on organizational skills and ideas, the solar plexus and brow chakras will inevitably become more significant.

Our life circumstances also alter the flow and interactions the chakras have with each other and with the environment. For example, if we are naturally comfortable working in socially complex interpersonal relationships – a heart chakra state – and then have to spend time where there is little chance to interact with others, or where our relationship skills are not valued, then this inevitably requires us to 'change gear' and focus our chakra energies in different ways. If we can identify the chakras that need

▽ **Give yourself time to think about the questions before you choose your answer.**

balancing, we can help ourselves a great deal in our journey towards our full potential and wellbeing.

Chakra dominance is not in itself a problem. However, where a major imbalance occurs, one or more chakras begin to take over the roles more properly belonging to others. This overburdens the dominant chakras and atrophies the others. We can survive for a long time in this false equilibrium, but it is like having a toolkit where only the hammer is used whatever the job. Often it is an accumulation of stresses and trauma in a chakra that reduces its effectiveness. If this is not remedied the system will naturally compensate by diverting energy to areas that are still working. This is the state of false equilibrium that most people cope with in their lives.

the questionnaire

In the following questionnaire there are seven options open to you for each question posed. Jot down the number of each reply on a sheet of paper. Pick more than one choice if it seems appropriate.

Now see how many times you recorded each number. Each refers to a chakra: 1 the base chakra, 2 the sacral chakra, 3 the solar plexus chakra, 4 the heart chakra, 5 the throat chakra, 6 the brow chakra and 7 the crown chakra. If you look at your score, you will be able to see which chakras are dominant for you.

For example, if you have two answers of number 1, two of 2, six of 3, two of 4, three of 5, one of 6 and three of 7, you will see that the third chakra, the solar plexus, is dominant. This is where most of your energy is focused. Although dominant, the solar plexus chakra needs the most attention and healing. Chakras 1, 2 and 6 (base, sacral and brow) have little focus of attention, so they too, may need healing and energizing.

▷ **If some of your chakras are overburdened your system will not be functioning properly.**

THE QUESTIONNAIRE

1 Which area(s) of your body concern you the most?
❶ feet and legs
❷ between waist and hips
❸ waist
❹ chest
❺ neck and shoulders
❻ face
❼ head

2 Which area(s) of your body do you dislike?
❶ feet and legs
❷ between waist and hips
❸ waist
❹ chest
❺ neck and shoulders
❻ face
❼ head

3 Which area(s) of your body are you proud of?
❶ feet and legs
❷ between waist and hips
❸ waist
❹ chest
❺ neck and shoulders
❻ face
❼ head

4 Which area(s) of your body are affected by major health issues?
❶ feet and legs
❷ between waist and hips
❸ waist
❹ chest
❺ neck and shoulders
❻ face
❼ head

5 Which area(s) of the body are affected most by minor health issues?
❶ feet and legs
❷ between waist and hips
❸ waist
❹ chest
❺ neck and shoulders
❻ face
❼ head

6 Which colour(s) do you like the most?
❶ red
❷ orange
❸ yellow
❹ green
❺ blue
❻ dark blue
❼ violet

7 Which colour(s) do you like the least?
❶ red
❷ orange
❸ yellow
❹ green
❺ blue
❻ dark blue
❼ violet

8 Which are your favourite foods?
❶ meat/fish/pulses
❷ rice/orange fruits
❸ wheat/yellow fruits
❹ green fruit and vegetables

9 Which sort of exercises or interests attract you?
❶ fast action
❷ dancing/painting
❸ crosswords/puzzles
❹ anything outside
❺ drama/singing
❻ mystery/crime novels
❼ doing nothing

10 What sort of people do you look up to or admire?
❶ sportspeople
❷ artists/musicians
❸ intellectuals
❹ conservationists
❺ speakers/politicians
❻ inventors
❼ mystics/religious figures

11 What sort of person do you think of yourself as?
❶ get on with things
❷ creative

❸ thinker/worrier
❹ emotional
❺ chatterbox
❻ quiet
❼ daydreamer

12 What emotions do you consider are uppermost in you life?
❶ passionate
❷ easy-going
❸ contented
❹ caring, sharing
❺ loyal
❻ helpfully distant
❼ sympathetic

13 What emotions do you have that you would like to change?
❶ temper
❷ possessiveness
❸ confusion
❹ insecurity
❺ needing things to be 'black or white'
❻ feeling separate from others
❼ not saying 'no'

14 If you get angry, what is your most common reaction?
❶ rage/tantrums
❷ sullen resentment
❸ get frightened
❹ blame yourself
❺ keep quiet
❻ withdraw
❼ imagine nothing happened

15 What are you most afraid of?
❶ dying
❷ lack of sensation
❸ things you don't understand
❹ being alone
❺ having no-one to talk to
❻ losing your way
❼ difficult situations

16 Which of these describes the way you prefer to learn?
❶ fast
❷ slowly
❸ quickly but forget
❹ through feelings
❺ by rote
❻ instinctively
❼ can't be bothered

17 What best describes your reaction to situations?
❶ enthusiastic
❷ go with the flow
❸ think things through
❹ see how things feel
❺ ask a lot of questions
❻ see the patterns then act
❼ drift along

18 If you are criticized or reprimanded, what is your usual response?
❶ anger
❷ resentment
❸ fear
❹ self-blame
❺ verbal riposte
❻ think about it
❼ denial

19 How would you describe your favourite books, films, video games?
❶ combat action
❷ art
❸ skill, intellectual
❹ romances
❺ courtroom dramas
❻ detective stories
❼ spiritual or self development

20 Which category best describes your friends?
❶ competitive
❷ creative
❸ intellectual
❹ loving
❺ idealistic
❻ rebellious
❼ spiritual

Chakras of manifestation

Once you have completed the questionnaire on the previous page you can use the following chapters to find appropriate ways to heal and balance the chakras that need attention. This chapter covers the first two chakras, the base and the sacral. They ensure the stability of the individual at every level of body, mind and spirit.

Base chakra – foundation of energy

Matter requires stability and structure in order to exist. Energy must be organized and maintained in the face of all sorts of opposing forces in the universe. The force of gravity is the energy of compression and its focus is the basis of the first chakra, located at the bottom of the spine. This is the rock upon which the whole of the chakra system, the subtle energies and the physical body rely, and without which disorder soon arises.

The Sanskrit name for the base chakra is muladhara, which means 'root'. The foundation of our life is the physical body

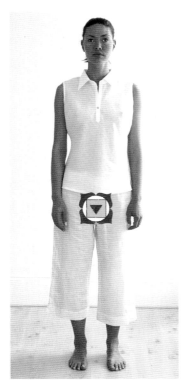

▽ The muladhara chakra ensures our physical existence, nourishing and energizing the whole chakra system.

△ Placing too much value on thought processes, of knowing rather than feeling, can create an imbalance that isolates us from the planet.

△ Our sense of self, and desire to live, are the hidden roots of our existence; this is the ground of our being that sustains us constantly.

and its ability to use energy to sustain itself. Survival is the key activity of the base chakra, which deals with life at the level of practicality. The base chakra is the closest energy centre to the Earth and it links us to the planet itself.

head in the clouds

The base chakra is what links 'us' – the consciousness sitting up there in the head commenting on everything that's going on – with our bodies. Many ancient cultures saw the mind or soul as located in the heart. The West puts emphasis on the head, the seat of the rational thinking mind, and often views the body as an awkward nuisance. With such a dissociation, the natural connections with physical reality and the sense of being a part of creation can be lacking. This induces a false sense of detachment, indifference or even disdain, where nothing is truly valued and nothing is appreciated. Life can quickly become dull and meaningless.

reactions

The base chakra relates to physical solidity and support, especially to the skeletal structure of the body and its flexibility. It is no use having a strong physical base if there is no flexibility. In order to survive any sort of stress, body and mind must be responsive. In an emergency, we must react quickly in an appropriate way, resisting or giving way as necessary. This instinctive feel for survival is the 'fight or flight' response of the adrenal glands just above the kidneys, which are responsible for preparing us for rapid action when faced with the threat of danger.

Like the adrenal glands, the base chakra has a relationship with the circulatory system and the blood supply. It also influences the skeletal muscles of the arms, legs and torso that allow us to move through the world. The base chakra is linked to the colour red and is responsible for maintaining the body's heat – the core temperature that allows chemical reactions to take place in the cells at the correct rate.

◁ Both the inability to sustain energy levels and the need for continual excitement or stimulation can indicate imbalance in the base chakra.

TO ENERGIZE THE BASE CHAKRA

Exercising the sense of touch, attending to practical matters, gentle movement and exercise can help to energize and re-connect us to the base chakra. Any of the following will help:

• A warm bath.
• Massage, aromatherapy or reflexology.
• Walking, running, jumping or stamping the feet improves the circulation, co-ordination and our link to the planet.
• Eating, especially high protein foods. Taking a good mineral supplement may also help. A shortage of zinc is one of the commonest causes of 'spaciness' and lack of mental focus.

▽ Any activity, such as bathing, that emphasizes physicality and stimulates the senses – especially smell – helps to balance the base chakra.

Imbalances in the base chakra can show up in many ways. Characteristic symptoms include a chronic lack of energy, with exhaustion following even slight exercise, problems with stiffness and painful movement, particularly in the hips, legs and feet. When poor physical co-ordination or poor circulation (a tendency to have cold hands and feet) is present, the base chakra is worth looking at.

The base chakra may also need healing and energizing when someone is uncomfortable with their body. This can lead to a sense of confusion or unreality and may show in a lack of drive or motivation and an aversion to getting involved in practicalities or physical exercise. Conversely, an imbalance in the base chakra can also cause excessive tension or excitability, with a continual need for stimulation.

Base chakra – seat of passion

The emotional responses that are associated with the base chakra express the need to ensure personal survival. They tend to be direct, explosive and strong, yet once satisfied, they will dissipate immediately. Young babies, in whom the base chakra is dominant, clearly demonstrate these qualities. They will express themselves forcefully and loudly whenever they are hungry, tired or uncomfortable, yet will fall asleep quickly once satisfied.

fear

Whenever there is a sense of loss of control or powerlessness, the base chakra energies and our survival instincts are activated. The fiery emotional states of anger, assertiveness and aggression all arise from one fundamental cause, and that is fear. Fear begins as soon as it seems that there is a loss of control, or a sense of being trapped. A dramatic response is still a biological necessity in some cases, but unfortunately as life has become more complicated, it is much less possible to feel that we are really in control of our own existence. Television, for example, presents us with events from all over the world over which we have no control, and yet we experience them emotionally and our bodies automatically

▽ **The innate survival instincts of the base chakra automatically activate whenever we feel threatened or powerless.**

respond as if we were actually involved. Our means for survival – food, water, heat, light and money – are all supplied to us by others. In these circumstances it is quite easy to become habitually fearful. This usually manifests itself as stress, which is an increasing inability to deal with changing situations in a flexible, creative way. Depending on the personality, stress and fear will show as either withdrawal – like a trapped animal hiding in a corner pretending not to be there – or aggression, in which case even those offering help will be perceived as a threat and attacked.

Remaining in a constant state of alert drains the body's energy and makes it more difficult to respond effectively when real danger presents itself. This can cause an emotional burn-out, which makes it impossible to become excited or motivated by anything.

▽ **The physicality and immediacy of passion easily bypasses the rational mind. It is energy that must be expressed immediately.**

releasing energies

There may be times when you feel the need to release an excess of base chakra emotional energy. There are several ways to do this. A simple and effective method, and a good way to begin, is to describe your strong feelings in writing, without judging them or censoring them. When you have finished writing your account, burn everything that you have written. This is the important element. The content of your writing is not important – it merely serves to let go of the excess energy.

When you are feeling the effects of withdrawal from emotional involvement, routine physical activities such as gardening, washing and cleaning can be helpful. Running, drumming, or dancing to music with a strong rhythm will keep the energy circulating and prevent a build-up.

It is a lot easier, however, to release an excess of base chakra energy, than it is to build it up if it is lacking. Poor motivation is one of the main features of insufficient energy in this chakra.

△ **Strong feelings initiated by the base chakra should not be held on to. Writing the feelings on a piece of paper and then symbolically burning them in a fire can help to release them.**

▽ **Channelling strong feelings into a simple, constructive activity, however mundane, helps to take the pressure off and regulates the safety valve of the base chakra.**

passion

Lust, physical passion and sexual excitement are complex emotions. They all involve many different chakras. But it is the motivation to ensure survival of the species that underlies immediate physical attraction, and this is associated with the base chakra. In this capacity the base chakra functions at many levels, promoting circulation, excitement, instinct and spontaneity and helping us to focus on the physical body in the present.

Imbalance within the base chakra can show as a build-up of strong emotions, which may then be released inappropriately or excessively. There can be a tendency to selfishness and a lack of concern for others, or a total denial of the emotions we are actually experiencing, especially anger. Lack of assertiveness can also indicate difficulties in this area.

Base chakra – the pioneer

The base chakra gives the energy and motivation needed to make good use of whatever resources are available. One of the main functions of the base chakra is to solidify, to make real. This includes the realization of dreams and the maintainance of energy levels within the body.

In order to survive, the human race learned to be very good at inventing and making new tools and creating new technologies. The base chakra is essential in the manifestation of any idea, dream or concept. Without its down-to-earth energy, it doesn't matter how wonderful our inspiration is or how useful a new invention may one day prove to be. The base chakra will find whatever is solid and viable in the most ephemeral concept and enable it to be made manifest and useful.

action

The desire to act, to move, to do, is an expression of the powerful energy of the base chakra. This energy is an absolute prerequisite for any new venture or project. Creativity, though, involves nearly every one of the main chakra centres in some way. Acting only by itself, the base chakra would be likely to 'make do' with the first thing it came up with and might well completely destroy it if it did not work right away.

Complete involvement in the practicality of making something new is a characteristic of this energy. The need is to see something coming into existence through personal skill

△ Whatever the drive of the base chakra may be, without sufficient food to sustain the physical body, nothing will be achieved.

▽ Surviving in dangerous situations puts our attention on physical skills, our senses and our feeling of being alive – all base chakra qualities.

and effort. As soon as it is there, taking its place in the real world, the job of the first chakra is done, and unless supported by other energies, the creator will become quickly distracted by another new project.

This short-lived burst of energy can be useful in an appropriate context. For example, people with the dynamic skills associated with the base chakra are happy to create possibilities but content to let others work on the fine details. They are not interested in keeping total control, so allow space for others to follow in their work.

going boldly...

The base chakra energy is the pioneer, always willing to go where no one has gone before and to do things that have never been done. In a balanced base chakra there is the energy, confidence, know-how and dexterity to survive and thrive in the moment-to-moment exploration of new territory. Exploring, mountain climbing, white-water rafting, and all other activities where people voluntarily put themselves in a completely self-reliant situation, engage with the survival instincts of the base chakra.

When base chakra energy is excessively dominating, however, only experiences that are life-threatening are enjoyed, and only the making of new things is important, not the uses to which they are put; 'doing' becomes the only comfortable state and 'being' is intolerably boring. Such states may arise from habit patterns that develop when there is actually a significant underlying lack of security. People with this problem feel the need to keep busy, which is often an attempt to disguise a sense of emptiness, a huge void that seems to threaten the existence of the individual.

The energy of the base chakra is one of concentration and gravity, so a feeling of vacuum, completely free from solidity and form, unable to be held or defined in any

▽ Base chakra energy initiates new projects but by itself will soon become distracted. We need other chakras to support and sustain our enthusiasm through completion.

SELF-PARENTING

This exercise helps to resolve some of the earliest memories and concepts we have around feelings of security and self-identity. It can help to release stresses held within the base chakra.
1 Settle yourself in a quiet, dimly lit room. In your imagination take yourself back to the moment of your conception. How would you like it to have been?
2 Move forward in time and see yourself as a baby in the womb, as a newborn child and as a young child. Imagine at each stage that you are happy, content, comfortable and as secure as you can be. Feel that sense of security throughout your body.
3 Sort out a daily routine that allows you more time to fulfil all your personal needs in every possible way. Try to follow that routine for a day, then a few days, then maybe a week. Allow the process to become a natural part of your routine, and feel the benefit of this self-parenting.

way at all, is completely alien to it. This feeling of emptiness often arises in situations where something established and apparently solid (a state the base chakra understands very well), becomes subject to change, death or decay. As change is the only constant in our lives, it is difficult for us to deal with the times when we feel our very foundations have been removed. Everyone will cope in different ways with such a situation, but it can be helpful to watch ourselves to ensure that our chakra energies, and the various activities they reflect, remain as evenly balanced as possible. Getting stuck in one chakra state will only lead to energy collapse sooner or later.

Base chakra imbalance at the mental level can show as obsessive focus on one thing to the exclusion of everything else, or else as a rigid and materialistic outlook that usually also masks deep insecurities about personal survival issues. People who are interested in only new and risky or dangerous ventures, or who show the opposite trait of being completely lacking in practicality, disintegrating into confusion when faced with practical projects or being unable to complete anything, might benefit from work with the base chakra.

Base chakra – the fortress

The spiritual purpose of the base chakra is the protection of individual integrity. The base holds together the fabric of the personality and is the very real foundation for every spiritual discipline. This energy centre is the place where the ladder to heaven rests. Unless that ground is completely solid in every respect, little else of true value will be accomplished.

anchor

The base chakra must be well balanced in order to anchor and make use of spiritual energy so that it can be of value to us here and now. The more someone works with spiritual growth and development, the more vital it becomes to anchor those energies. We are adrift in an ocean of different energies, physical, electromagnetic and subtle. Some are obvious to the senses, like those that create the weather. Others are more subtle, such as the electromagnetic fields that cover the planet from both natural and artificial sources. Each of these energy fields has the potential to disrupt the way we function if it bombards us with a

▽ Without the grounding influence of the base chakra our system would be constantly upset by the changing tides of energy around us.

THE WARRIOR

This yoga posture stabilizes the base chakra. You may be surprised at how much heat this static posture generates. Remember to breathe normally while you are doing it.

1 Loosen your clothes and take off your shoes and socks. Spread your feet apart, to make a triangle of equal sides with the ground.

2 Stretch your arms out to the sides, and rotate your left foot outwards. Bend your left knee, keeping the right leg straight. When you reach a position where you could be sitting on an imaginary chair – stop.
3 Hold the pose for as long as is comfortable, then return to standing.
4 Repeat to the right, holding the pose for the same length of time.

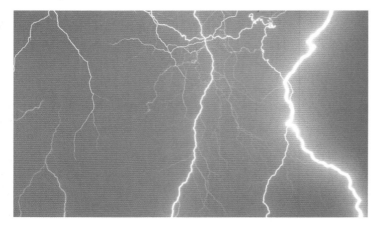

vibration that is stronger than our own. This is the process called entrainment, where an energy with a strong coherent pattern begins to make weaker, more disorganized energy fields vibrate at its own frequency.

Taking the analogy from electricity a little further: if we do not have an effective way of earthing outside energies, static will build up and begin to interfere with our own 'signal'. The base chakra is that lightning rod, that earth cable, which prevents unwanted energy signals from destroying our equilibrium.

One indication to look for that suggests a spiritual imbalance in the base chakra is an 'otherworldliness', a loss of awareness and

▽ The solid form and orderliness of the mineral kingdom reflects the nature of the base chakra. Dark-coloured crystals naturally ground and centre our own energies.

△ The purpose of meditation is to let go of all excess activity in the mind, emotions and body in order to experience the world as it is – not to escape from reality.

▽ Dancing and drumming have been used for millennia as a means to attain spiritual states. Energizing the base chakra, and all other chakras in turn, strengthens the body and spirit.

interest in the real world and in practical survival issues. There may also be a lack of discipline, an unfocused attitude, wishful thinking and fantasizing or a dissociation from the body and its requirements, often accompanied by a desire to escape physical incarnation. People with a weak base chakra may be easily swayed by their impressions, lack the ability to discriminate between viewpoints and belief systems, or receive psychic and clairvoyant messages over which they have little or no control. A lack of grounding can create hyperactivity, restlessness, the inability to settle, and very volatile emotions.

Grounding and earthing restores the natural flow of energy to and from the base chakra, and visualization is helpful. With your feet firmly on the ground, imagine tree roots extending down and out from where you are touching the ground. With each outbreath imagine the roots growing deeper and more firmly into the earth. With each inbreath, allow the sustaining energy of the Earth to flow through your whole body.

Sacral chakra – the pleasure principle

The sacral chakra is the second energy centre. It is located in the area below the navel and above the pubic bone, at the front of the pelvis. Physically this chakra is involved with the organs of the lower abdomen – the large intestine, the bladder and the reproductive organs.

Detoxification is one of the key functions of the sacral chakra, at every level, from the physical through to the spiritual.

▷ The sacral chakra is the reservoir of our life energy, from which energy, or chi, is chanelled or directed through the rest of the body.

▽ The sacral chakra, located in the area below the navel and above the pubic bone, is the second energy centre.

Traditionally this chakra is connected with the element of water and has its characteristics of flow, cleansing and movement. The symbol of the chakra is a white, blue or silver crescent, which is also a reminder of the moon's influence on all things watery, including the ebb and flow of the emotions.

So while the defining characteristic of the base chakra is the element of Earth, representing solidity, focus and the structure of the skeletal system, the sacral chakra represents the polar opposites of these: flow, flexibility and the emptiness or hollowness of the body's organs – bladder, intestine, womb and so on.

The whole pelvic region is shaped like a bowl, in which the energy focus of the sacral chakra lies. The pelvis is shaped to support the legs and the many different muscles that control their movement. Any strain or tension here can create a whole range of symptoms, from lower back pain, irregular or painful menstruation, constipation and sciatica to problems with fertility, impotence and fluid balance in the body.

Any disease state that features poor balance of fluids or flexibility will correspond to an imbalance within the second chakra. Water

▷ Belly-dancing is an ideal activity to balance the sacral energies. It strengthens the pelvic and abdominal muscles and it encourages flexibility.

△ The sacral chakra is associated with the energy of the moon and with the emotions and fluids of the body.

absorption is an important function of the large intestine, while control of the mineral and water balance in the blood is regulated by the kidneys. If the functions of these areas are impaired, the balance of chemicals in the body is upset, and it becomes more difficult to eliminate toxins and waste products, which effectively poison the body.

It is the job of the sacral chakra to keep things moving. Any rigidity of the joints, such as in arthritis and other similar conditions, can also reflect unbalanced energy at this centre.

balance and flow

The area of the sacral chakra within the pelvis is also our centre of gravity. It rules our sense of movement and balance, and gives grace and flow to our activity. It is the reservoir of what the Indians call prana and the Chinese call chi – the life-energy that infuses every living system, the subtle substance within the breath that is so important in the spiritual disciplines of the

△ The slow, graceful, physical movements of Tai Chi and Chi Kung stimulate the flow of chi, which is visualized as a subtle substance with a consistency and speed of flow similar to honey.

East and in the martial arts that developed among the spiritual elite of the Hindus, Buddhists and Taoists.

Today the West is familiar with the disciplined exercises of Tai Chi and Chi Kung. They have developed over thousands of years as an effective way to control and direct the flow of the subtle force of chi through the body and even beyond, into the environment. One of the main centres for gathering and distributing chi is known in Chinese as *tan tien*. It is equivalent, though not identical, to the sacral chakra. The same

place is called the *hara* in Japanese, the centre of the life-force. From this reservoir chi can be channelled and directed through the rest of the body to maintain health and give great amounts of strength and endurance, or to open up states of awareness.

It is only from a flow outwards from ourselves that we can begin to explore and experience the world that is not us. Remaining centred and solid within the security of the base chakra, our awareness can reach beyond the immediate, stretching out a curious hand to things just beyond our grasp. Movement and curiosity is required. The grace and balance of the sacral chakra's smooth flow of energy helps us succeed. Here we begin to experience the energy of the world around us.

WU CHI

One way of energizing and balancing the sacral chakra is to take up belly dancing. Another is to perform this standing posture exercise, called wu chi in Chinese. Begin by holding the posture for between two and five minutes, then increase the time gradually.
1 Stand with your feet apart, directly under your shoulders.
2 Let your hands hang loosely by your sides and allow your shoulders to drop.
3 Imagine your whole body is hanging by a thread attached to the top of your head, suspending you from the ceiling.
4 Allow yourself to relax, making sure your knees are not locked. Breathe normally.

Watch as you become aware of the tensions in your muscles and the internal chatter of your mind. Let them go.

Sacral chakra – feeling the need

The emotional level of the second chakra is reflected in its watery nature. Its activity is focused on flow, movement and exploration of the surroundings. Its motivation is enjoyment and pleasure and its reward is sensation – the invigoration of the senses.

The whole of life at the earliest stage of development revolves around feeling secure and well-fed. This is the level of the base chakra: making sure that survival is assured. Once these primary needs have been met, the priority is to explore the potential of the body through play, and to explore the surroundings using all the senses. This is where the sacral chakra comes in – any young animal playing is behaving under the influence of this chakra.

brain works

Experiments carried out to map activity in the brain show clearly that the first nerve pathways to be established directly after birth serve the parts of the brain where pleasure is registered. This helps the learning process of the infant, because it reinforces actions

△ Spontaneous enjoyment of experience, exploration of the senses and play are all characteristics of the sacral chakra, stimulating our ability to learn and develop as individuals.

that are more likely to be beneficial, rather than those that are more likely to cause damage, pain or suffering.

The parts of the brain concerned with registering pleasure – called the limbic system – also directly affect the hypothalamus. This small organ deep in the centre of the brain controls the hormone system and the activity of the autonomic nervous system – the involuntary processes that maintain balance in the heart rate, breathing and blood pressure.

enjoyment

Happiness and enjoyment are important factors in maintaining the smooth running of the individual. They have been built into our awareness to encourage us to stay in harmony with ourselves and the environment. The sacral chakra maintains

▽ In the animal world there is no distinction between playing and learning. Play leads to the development of skills for survival and a more successful life.

BADDHA KONASANA

Hatha yoga helps the flow of life energy and increases physical flexibility and resilience. This exercise, baddha konasana or the cobbler's pose, encourages energy flow in all levels of the sacral chakra.

1 Sit on the floor, bending your knees and keeping your back straight.
2 Turn the soles of your feet to face each other.
3 Place the fingers of both hands over your toes.
4 Allowing your knees to fall outwards, draw your feet in towards your body. Don't try to force your knees nearer the floor. The more you relax your pelvis, the more the muscles will allow the knees to fall.
5 Stay in this position for a few moments before relaxing.

this flow of communication between body and mind through sensation and emotion. In order to be most effective, the mind has to be aware of subtle changes in the feelings. Very often vague intuitions and 'gut' feelings are dismissed by the conscious mind because they are not precise enough. It is possible to educate the conscious mind to take notice of the flow of feelings and the energy fluctuations of the sacral centre, making us much more sensitive and responsive to what is going on around us.

Flowing in harmony with our own energy and with our surroundings requires a level of flexibility as well as the ability to change focus – to let go, when necessary, of things that are no longer useful or helpful to us. An imbalance in the sacral chakra often arises when for one reason or another we become fixated on something that we refuse to admit to ourselves is actually inappropriate or unrealistic.

Indications that the sacral chakra is out of balance can be emotional over-sensitivity or an unhealthy emotional dependency on someone else. Very often this includes intrusive behaviour and a failure to respect normal boundaries. At the opposite extreme there may be rigidity, with a lack of physical or emotional flexibility. Repression of feelings, a fear of sensuality, sex, pleasure or enjoyment, as well as guilt over feelings and desires, all indicate sacral imbalance that can result in frustration and bitterness.

▷ **Adults who display sacral chakra imbalances may well have experienced a lack of close physical contact as young children.**

Sacral chakra – the artist within

The sacral chakra is located right in the centre of the womb area. It is thus related to fertility, giving birth and all other aspects of creativity. Creativity at the sacral chakra level is to do with manipulation of the senses and the world. At the orange level of the second chakra the process is very personal. It is a spontaneous mechanism to keep energy moving, to avoid the build-up of stress. The complementary blue chakra, the throat, is also related to the creative process but as a means of external expression, a way of communicating.

the nature of stress

Stress is commonly understood to be the accumulation of difficult and negative circumstances. In fact it is any stimulus, good or bad, enjoyable or painful, that throws the body out of balance to such a degree that it is unable fully to return to its previous equilibrium. It is a widely held belief that creativity can be stimulated by stress, and that true art therefore requires suffering. This is really a misunderstanding of the processes that are controlled and directed by the sacral chakra.

The accumulation of physical stress in the muscles and organs of the body, and emotional and mental stress in the subtle

▽ The flow of the emotions is experienced like the tides of the sea, changing from hour to hour. Any activity, such as making music, can quickly alter emotional states.

△ It is the activity of a creative act that is important in stimulating life-energy, not the quality or permanence of the end product.

bodies and chakras, creates a breakdown in the natural movement and flow of life-energy. This rigidity, if allowed to build up unchecked, leads to atrophy and eventually to death. Old age can be seen simply as this process of accumulating stress. Indeed old age is a relative term – some people who have hard, unforgiving lives look old at forty, while others, who are flexible and happy despite the hardships they have endured, look radiant at eighty.

Stress initiates survival drives, which are first chakra functions. But the trouble with stress is that if it is not dissipated quickly by 'fight or flight' responses, a different approach is needed. The more creative, flexible energy needed to give the right response is provided by the second chakra.

△ **Creative activity explores the flow of mind, body and spirit as they focus on one object. Successful art communicates this life-energy whatever the technical skills of the creator.**

flowing energy

Life-energy is like a stream, it must keep moving. Once it stops moving, a stream is no longer a stream. Likewise, life-energy that is blocked stops being life-giving. The sacral chakra helps to ensure the supply of life-energy available to us by keeping the flow in motion. Where stress creates blocks and rigidity the sacral chakra creates opportunities for life-energy to move around them, much as a stream will divert its flow to move around a build-up of debris in its path. Creative activity is like this diverted stream of energy, restoring the quality of flow back into the systems of the body.

The sacral chakra often initiates creative activity as a way of finding new solutions to intractable problems. This is a sense-based process of feeling the way to solutions, rather than a conscious, rational assessment and analysis of the situation. The process can begin when stress levels are high enough to stop normal activity. There is an impasse and at that still, quiet moment, some small unconscious act, such as doodling, grabs all the attention and focuses the flow of life-energy into the creative process. Depression and despair may sometimes precede creativity, but once begun, the process of release is like an increased force of water, strong enough to wash the accumulated debris of stress aside, restoring a natural flow of life-energy.

Creativity is the natural state of life-energy and it restores life to a natural balance. Successful art, beautiful design and skilful craftsmanship are exhilarating and life-supporting because they embody this flow of life-energy. Creativity should never be seen as the domain of the expert and the specialist. We all have a sacral chakra, which is the womb of creativity, within us. If we let its energy flow naturally, everything we do will be an expression of the joyful creativity of living.

Sacral chakra – healing the wounds

The sacral chakra is the focus of our experience of pleasure and also the first place that experiences any kind of pain. Wherever trauma and pain may be in the body, they are registered in the second chakra. Pain is also held there if the trauma the pain creates is not released. Any shock to the system breaks the usual flow of our

▽ The effects of an accident or shock can last well beyond the actual event, colouring our lives for many years.

life. For example, the memory of an accident often gets stuck in the mind, where it is relived continually.

The sacral chakra is primarily affected for two reasons. First, the life-energy or chi is tightly gathered in this area of the body, so any threat to it causes turbulence and upset here. Second, it is the function of the sacral chakra to maintain the flow of life, which helps to remove the fragments of trauma locked within the different systems of the body.

EMOTIONAL STRESS RELEASE (ESR)

One of the most effective ways to release stress is to lightly touch the frontal eminences of the skull. These are two slight bumps above the outer edge of the eye at either side of the forehead. While stress is being released a slight irregular pulsing can often be felt at the eminences, which dies away once the process is complete.

1 Lightly hold the fingertips to the frontal eminences of the skull, or hold a hand across the forehead to catch both points easily.
2 Turning your attention to the stressful event will now automatically begin to release the accumulated tensions. It is not necessary to relive each event in detail, though often this occurs automatically. Strong feelings and emotions, as well as physical reactions, may surface while these points are being held.
3 As long as the process is allowed to complete itself, the body quickly and effectively releases the frozen memories once and for all.

▷ Stress becomes physically locked into the body as well as into the chakras. Intellectual understanding of a trauma alone is not always enough to remove it.

shock release

Emotional and mental shock can heal like broken bones, but scars may last for a long time, subtly affecting how we think and feel. Each event distorts or locks away energy that we need for our everyday lives. It takes a lot of psychic energy to separate memories of pain from our awareness and, like unwanted baggage, they load us down.

There are some very effective ways to help the sacral chakra release and let go of trauma and shock without the need to go through the pain of reliving the event. Counselling methods and psychological examination of trauma have been shown sometimes to increase, not decrease, stress levels. This is because the practical release of stress is a priority of the body, not simply an intellectual understanding of how the stress has been affecting behaviour. The sites, such as the sacral chakra, where the actual stress is located, need to be re-integrated into the present before the imbalances can be released effectively. One way to do this is to try the Emotional Stress Release exercise on the opposite page. It is important to remember that memories, particularly painful ones, tend to be stored with other memories that are in some way related. Releasing stress that initially appears to be caused by a minor event may be an opportunity for the body to let go of many other stresses that deal with a similar scenario or emotion.

An upset digestive system, particularly constipation, can indicate that stress and trauma are interfering with normal functioning. There may be an inability to become emotionally involved with life and to enjoy it. Emotional volatility and a tendency to aggressive behaviour or tearfulness at the slightest provocation are other signs of problems. Inability to let go of a stressful event, so that it preys on the mind, shows that this chakra is blocked, as does suffering from an increasing number of infections and illnesses.

CRYSTAL RELEASE
The sacral chakra can be supported in its release of stress by using a particular layout of crystals. You will need three clear quartz crystals, together with three moonstones or three rose quartz crystals.

1 With the three clear quartz crystals make a downward pointing triangle below the navel. If the crystals have points, these should point outwards.
2 Below these crystals and above the pubic bone, make an arc of the three remaining stones.

Chakras of relationship

The third and fourth chakras are at the solar plexus and the heart. They begin to integrate our energy with the environment and the people around us. Growth always involves expanding into new areas, so the skills of recognizing potential dangers and establishing a place of personal power are essential.

Solar plexus chakra – the organizer

The solar plexus, the third centre, is considered as a single chakra, but is, as the word 'plexus' suggests, a fusion of many different energies. Midway between the ribcage and the navel, it also corresponds to the lumbar vertebrae in the spine. The physical attributes of the solar plexus chakra fall into three main areas: the digestion, the nervous system and the immune system.

digestion

The process of digestion and assimilation of nutrients is vital to sustain life. The organs linked to the solar plexus are the stomach,

▽ The solar plexus chakra, below the ribcage, is the main organizing principle affecting all parts of the body and mind.

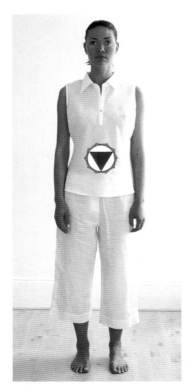

△ The solar plexus chakra is associated with the element of Fire, not only because it creates physical heat in the body, but also because it takes raw materials and transforms them.

▽ The solar plexus chakra is often referred to as the fusebox of the body. In this area are large concentrations of nerve tissue that, if disrupted, can affect the whole nervous system.

liver, gallbladder, pancreas, duodenum and small intestine. For digestion and the assimilation of nutrients to be successful, all these organs have to work in harmony. This involves a series of chemical reactions using a great many different catalysts. From the alkaline enzyme-rich saliva in the mouth, food moves to the acidity of the stomach. Here it is churned, thoroughly mixing the natural acids and enzymes. It then passes into the duodenum, where bile from the liver, via the gallbladder, begins to break down fats, and more enzymes from the pancreas begin to act on sugars and carbohydrates. As the mixture moves through the small intestine, the valuable nutrients from the food are absorbed through the wall of the intestine into the bloodstream. Failure to digest food efficiently means that nutrients are not absorbed.

immune system

The immune system works like a library or a computer. It stores and categorizes information about everything the body encounters. For instance, on meeting a virus, the body recognizes it as an enemy and activates the defence mechanisms to fight and overcome the infection. If the body later encounters the same virus again it has the information to prevent a serious invasion.

Problems with this identification process often show up when the body reacts to harmless or even beneficial substances as if they are dangerous. This is experienced as allergy or intolerance. The opposite malfunction happens when the body harbours an infection for a long time because it fails to recognize its presence and so neglects to fight it at all. Difficulties also occur when the body fails to recognize its own enzymes, hormones or neuro-transmitters, and sometimes there is an inability to recognize minerals and vitamins that should be absorbed by the small intestine. These problems surface as deficiencies but do not respond to increased intake because the problem is not lack, but a failure to recognize the substance.

The solar plexus chakra is put under great pressure by the way we live today. Its physical functions are strained by the types of food we eat, the pace of life and new toxins in our environment. It is not surprising that many of the diseases in our society today are a sign of some dysfunction in the solar plexus chakra.

ARDHA MATSEYANDRASANA
This exercise, the spinal twist, tones the whole of the solar plexus. The more upright you keep your spine, the easier it is to twist.

1 Kneel down on a blanket or thick mat, resting on your heels. Slide your buttocks to the right of your feet. Lift your left leg, so the left foot is across the right knee.

2 Shuffle your bottom around to get comfortable and to keep your spine straight. Bring your left arm round behind you, resting your fingers on the floor to steady yourself. Bring your right arm to rest on the outside of the left leg, the elbow bracing against the knee. Breathe in, then as you breathe out, lift your spine and twist round to look over your left shoulder. Breathe normally.

3 When you feel ready to release the pose, breathe in, then as you breathe out, unwind yourself. First bring your left arm back around to the front and follow its movement with the head, naturally straightening the spine. If you are unable to stretch into the full twist, simply hold the knee instead of bracing it with an elbow. Repeat on the other side, mirroring the steps.

Solar plexus chakra – sun of contentment

Use this visualization exercise to invite warmth and joy into your life. This is a good exercise to do if you have feelings of unease or fear that you want to dispel. Using the positive aspects and strength of the sun you will create a feeling of security and contentment.

1 Sit or lie down comfortably. Wrap a blanket around you if the day is cool. Breathe in, and as you breathe out, allow yourself to relax. Imagine a sphere of golden light beginning to form between your navel and the bottom of your ribcage. Imagine this sphere is also giving off a comfortable warmth. Allow the sphere to grow until it enfolds the whole of your body.
2 Stay still for a few minutes, allowing the light and warmth to fill every part of your body. Imagine the sphere shrinking back until it is the size of a tennis ball. Allow the small sphere to sink into your abdomen, before shrinking down to the size of a pea. Let the imagery dissolve. Bring your attention back to everyday awareness.

The solar plexus chakra is often identified with the element of Fire. Our emotional reaction to fire is two-fold. Fire gives warmth and comfort but brings fear and terror when it gets out of control. This echoes the emotional breadth of the solar plexus chakra.

△ **The unknown cannot be controlled because there is a lack of information. The mind becomes anxious and fearful.**

fear

The key negative emotion that spawns all others is fear. It can become an underlying emotion that drives other everyday emotional reactions. Fear arises in any situation where the outcome seems beyond the capacity of the mind to determine, and there is an inability simply to relax. The mind conjures up limitless scenarios and gets locked into self-defeating thought processes of 'what if…'

Fear can escalate into terror or subside into anxiety in any area of life. Issues

◁ **Threats and rules that restrict our natural exuberance easily block the solar plexus chakra.**

◁ When the solar plexus chakra is functioning well, we are able to accept happiness in our lives. We can feel and appreciate joy in the simplest of situations.

shame for this lack of compliance. Shame prevents us from working with the solar plexus chakra at the emotional level, and this drives us into interacting with the world primarily through our thoughts.

healing

In this area, healing can be approached in several ways. Allowing things to be as they are, rather than trying to control events, helps to remove fears. Expressing the Fire energy as anger helps to link the solar plexus with the sacral and base chakras.

People who experience a lot of anger often live so much in their minds that they do not realize how angry they are, especially with regard to authority figures who have dominated and disempowered them. Shame can often be recognized in internal conversations that replay critical comments from the past. Here the mental criticism, which effectively acts in the same way as a curse, needs to be neutralized by formulating an imaginary response from an adult standpoint.

concerning personal power are part of the solar plexus function. As children we were subject to the guidance of our parents, relatives and teachers, all of whom we related to and possibly still relate to, as figures of authority. If people in authority use their dominant position to force us into habit patterns that take our personal power from us, the solar plexus chakra becomes effectively blocked. Failure to accede to this dominance is often met by criticism and punishment. Subsequently we may feel

◁ The shame that might be felt from past humiliation by an authority figure can be neutralized in the present by visualizing the situation, changing the balance of power, and bringing the authority figure down to his or her proper size.

Solar plexus chakra – the librarian

Working at the mental level, the solar plexus chakra is one of the most powerful tools we have at our disposal to create our personal circumstances – our own heaven or hell. Sages and philosophers have known for thousands of years that personal belief systems, the thoughts by which we recognize and understand how the world appears to work, are of critical importance to our wellbeing.

recording

Like a librarian or custodian, this part of our 'body-mind' catalogues and files away experiences and information for reference and retrieval when it is required. To carry out this organizational task efficiently it is necessary to be able to identify things clearly and accurately, to label them correctly, to file them in the right place and to cross-index where necessary.

Failure to store information properly results in many difficulties. Confusion and fear often arise from false identification.

△ Memory has been shown to be a function of the whole brain (rather than specific areas). In order to retrieve memories, communication within the brain needs to be efficient.

Incorrect filing also creates confusion, learning problems and difficulties in retrieval (remembering). Inability to introduce cross-referencing severely limits the ability to integrate experiences.

If we are forced into certain learning situations before the solar plexus chakra, our personal librarian, is mature enough to cope, blocks occur around the issues involved and we develop negative belief systems about them. These beliefs will affect the way in which we interact with the world around us and create disharmony in that

◁ Concentration, analysis and effective study all rely on the balanced functioning of the solar plexus chakra.

MEMORY GAME

This game has many variations in different cultures. It exercises all aspects of the solar plexus chakra at the mental level – recognition, identification, categorization, recording and recall. This exercise can be repeated, preferably using different items. If you reach 25+ items you are doing very well. It is important that even if you can remember only five or so items, you do not get annoyed or disappointed with yourself. Practice improves scores. It is up to you how honest you are with yourself when doing this exercise.

1 Find around 30 small items and place them on a plain background. Cover the items with a cloth.

2 Collect a pen and paper. Uncover the items and look at them for not more than three minutes.

3 Cover the items with the cloth again. Write down as many items as you can remember.

relationship. Stresses build up and unless action is taken to correct the inaccurate beliefs, it usually results in physical, emotional and mental difficulties linked to the solar plexus chakra. If we are unable to identify events clearly, our capacity to judge, weigh up alternatives and make decisions becomes very limited.

◁ **The solar plexus chakra controls our ability to identify problems and find solutions to unlock our understanding.**

learning

In any learning situation, the information that needs to be learned has to be identified as such so that it can subsequently be catalogued correctly. Inability to learn or study may be the result of forced or inappropriate learning situations in early life. Stresses once created here will be remembered by the body-mind every time a similar situation arises. If the stress around the events can be released, new learning strategies can emerge.

Solar plexus chakra – know thyself

The solar plexus chakra at the spiritual level applies its energies to defining the boundaries of the self – the individual. The challenge at this level is to gain wisdom and insight into the true nature of the self beyond the everyday level of the persona.

It is not possible to define who you are unless you can also identify who and what you are not. Here the discrimination and judgement of the mental level of the solar plexus is brought to bear on the inner self. When you know who you are, you can start to understand your place in the world.

When we shine the clear light of understanding on ourselves, the first thing we tend to notice is faults and problems that have apparently been created in us by others. But as we look more closely, the need to blame others for the predicament in which we find ourselves recedes. We begin to realize that the only way forward is to transform the way we judge ourselves

△ It is necessary to turn our attention away from outer stimuli if we are to see ourselves clearly.

and others. A major sign of progress along the path to wisdom is accepting that the world owes you nothing and that you are no more important than anything else.

Solar plexus issues often arise from how we perceive ourselves in terms of our personal power. If, through experiences with overbearing authority figures, we have been led to believe that we are clumsy, stupid, worthless or bad, our whole relationship to the world will reflect this. We will feel powerless and prone to failure because of our perceived 'faults'. Similarly, if we come to believe that we are superior to other people, our actions will reflect this and there will be a tendency to ignore the wisdom of

◁ In nearly all spiritual philosophies the wisdom of the self has been compared to the light of the sun. The perfect clarity of the solar plexus chakra clearly illuminates everything for what it is.

others and forget our own shortcomings or failures. In both situations, current events or circumstances might be identical but the powerless focus on failure, while the powerful focus on success.

Looking with the spiritual discrimination of the solar plexus chakra, both of these viewpoints have been created by incomplete information. Our own interpretation of reality is coloured by other people's eyes, minds and emotions. It is the job of the solar plexus chakra to realize at a spiritual level that all such judgements are limited and ultimately false. Our view of ourselves and others is no more substantial than clothing or masks.

Solar plexus energy can best be employed as power to do something, but very often slides into power over others. This turns into a competitive race, where we try in all sorts of ways to be better than others – more wealthy, more intelligent, more happy, more spiritual. If the energies have been distorted by bad experiences, we become more hard-done-by, more lonely and so on.

Allowing the solar plexus an opportunity to shine with the clarity of the sun encourages a broader perspective where these false judgements can begin to be seen as the ephemeral shadows they really are.

▽ **Embrace and accept yourself in the same way as you love and appreciate your closest friends.**

MEDITATION WITHOUT FORM

This is one of the easiest, though some say also the hardest, ways of beginning to perceive the boundaries between your everyday self and the finer levels of your whole being. It is sometimes called meditation without form, and uses only the breath as a focus. Because you are always in the present during this exercise, if there is a sudden noise you should not be startled at all. But if you have disappeared into your thoughts or imaginings, away from the attention on your breath, you will find external noises quite disruptive. Begin by doing this for five minutes. As you become more practised, gradually extend the time to 20 minutes.

Sit in a comfortable position, upright but relaxed. Place your hands in your lap, the right resting on the left. Close your eyes partially, so that light still enters but no clear image can be seen. Leave your mouth slightly open and rest the tip of your tongue on the roof of your mouth, just behind your teeth. Turn your attention to the movement of your breath as it enters and leaves your body. Don't think about your breath, or try to control it, just keep your attention on it. When you become aware that your mind has wandered and you have been thinking about something else, gently bring your attention back to your breath and continue.

Heart chakra – embracing the world

The heart chakra is located near the centre of the breastbone or sternum. The physical organs and parts of the body linked to this chakra are characterized by their actions of expansion and contraction, drawing in and pushing away.

physical attributes

The heart, with its rhythmic expansion and contraction, is the powerful muscular pump that sends oxygenated blood to all parts of the body. By its movement, the diaphragm, the powerful muscle below the lungs, creates changes in pressure, allowing us to breathe in fresh air. As the diaphragm contracts, the

▽ The heart chakra is at the centre of the main chakras and is the balance point for the system.

△ The heart chakra governs our interactions as we reach out to touch and embrace other people.

outbreath expels carbon dioxide from the body. The lungs are composed of tree-like air ducts that bring air into contact with the bloodstream. The blood picks up oxygen from the air, releasing back into it carbon dioxide and other waste products as it returns from its journey through the body.

These processes of expansion, interchange and contraction are reflected in our relationship with the world. The heart chakra regulates our interaction, making sure that we become neither too involved nor too remote from the world around us. The relationship is in constant motion: if it stays stationary all balance is lost. Reaching out and physically touching helps us to gather information. As we gather information we respond and begin to relate.

The action of the arms can be one of enfolding, enclosing, embracing and absorption. Equally, the arms can defend, push away and protect. The degree to which we keep the physical balance between what

is outside us and our inner being is often reflected in the way we hold our upper torso and arms. Tension and rigidity suggest stasis and defensiveness. A relaxed stance and flowing movement not only shows ease with the world, it reduces the stress levels on the heart and lungs.

▽ Arms and hands are the executors of the heart chakra energy. They reach out to hold or ward off the world around us.

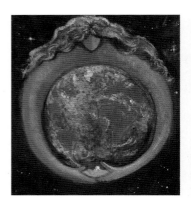

GOMUKHASANA

This exercise extends the muscles and cavities of the chest and stretches and energizes the shoulders and arms. If your hands do not meet, hold a piece of cane or wood 25–30cm (10–12in) to link your hands instead.

1 Kneel on a blanket or mat, sitting back on your heels. Stretch both arms out in front of you.

2 Raise your left arm over your head, bending it at the elbow so the left hand rests near the top of your back.
3 Sweep your right arm round to the right side, bending it at the elbow, sending the right hand up your back.
4 If your hands meet, lightly clasp your fingers, otherwise hold each end of the piece of wood.

5 When you have a grip on your hands, or the wood, take a breath in and bring your hands closer together, expanding your chest. Breathe normally. On an outbreath, loosen your grip then repeat, starting by raising your right hand above your head and mirroring the above stages.

Heart chakra   touching others

The art of balance is a theme that runs through all levels of the heart chakra. The element associated with this chakra is Air. Air flows from areas of high pressure towards areas of low pressure, always seeking a state of equilibrium. Likewise, the heart chakra continually strives to bring balance between external stimuli and internal emotions.

love

The experience of love is characterized by the flow of emotion. Falling in love is a wonderful, scary experience, but for every falling in love there is a falling out of love. Unless we accept this natural balancing mechanism, falling in love can become a fearful experience because of the inevitable grief and abandonment that accompanies falling out of love again. Understanding that ebb and flow happens from day to day, from moment to moment, eases any temporary sense of loss. Trying to hold on to any fluid emotional state like love will lead to an obsessive, possessive attachment reminiscent of an imbalanced sacral chakra response, or that of a four- to seven-year-old child.

△ **Keeping the balance between personal needs and the needs of others is the function of the heart chakra.**

acceptance

A balanced and coherent heart chakra is shown in the ability to accept ourselves, other people and all sorts of situations. Without a real self-acceptance there is no

▽ **The importance of unconditional love is never greater than in a parent-child relationship.**

way that we are able to tolerate the foibles and faults of others. When we feel comfortable in ourselves, with all our faults, we are less likely to be insecure or threatened by those who, through their own envy, jealousy or lack of self-worth, try to dominate or control everything and everyone around them.

relationships

Any relationship can be heaven or hell. In a balanced relationship, each person has autonomy, but both also share. In relationships that are unhealthy, love is conditional to the point of being a weapon used to coerce the other into behaving or responding as required. Phrases like 'Well, if you really loved me you would…' and 'I'm doing this because I think it's good for you and I love you…' make a relationship one-sided. Many of us experience this threatened withdrawal of love as small children, and until our heart chakras become truly balanced, we may continue to play out the same pattern on our own children, family and friends.

BALANCING A RELATIONSHIP

This visualization exercise can be helpful in sorting out a difficult relationship, or in finding solutions to problems in relationships where one partner shows an unhealthy dependence on the other. It encourages a personal sense of space and helps you to reach an acknowledgement of the qualities of the other person. You can repeat the exercise as often as you feel it is necessary.

1 Set aside some quiet time when you are unlikely to be disturbed. Sit in a comfortable position, in a chair or on the floor, with an empty cushion or chair placed near you. Close your eyes, breathing slowly and calmly, and settle yourself.

2 Once your breathing has slowed and you are feeling calm, start to visualize a cylinder of gold light shining all around you, reaching down into the ground and rising up above your head.

3 On the other cushion, or in the empty chair, visualize the person with whom you have a relationship that needs to be rebalanced.

4 As you visualize the person sitting near you, recognize the qualities in them that you feel are causing difficulties between you in your relationship. Recognize, also, all the qualities in them that you appreciate or admire.

5 Visualize a second cylinder of gold light surrounding the other person. In your mind's eye, visualize both of you sitting within your own separate cylinders of gold light. If you notice any stray threads of light connecting the two cylinders, allow them to dissolve. Become aware of the space between you and the other person. Slowly return to normal awareness.

Heart chakra – freedom to be

Most people are aware that their physical appearance and attributes are inherited through their genes from each parent. It is not so well recognized that we also inherit many of our thinking patterns in the same way.

inheritance

Dominant beliefs, especially negative ones, can be traced through several successive generations. If we remain tied to these beliefs we never discover who we are and independence is never really achieved.

Following the rules drawn up by someone else gives us guidelines and lists of what we 'should' or 'ought' to do in order to develop a sense of duty and responsibility. These rules may have been enforced in some way, to mould us into the person the maker of the rules had in mind. This process can create, for the most part, a very harmonious society in which to live.

In some work situations, especially those dealing with emergency services, following the rules becomes a survival issue. While everyday life does not have that sort of intensity, for some people 'following the rules' remains an absolute necessity. This type of thinking has a robotic quality, producing people whose interaction can only follow a set formula or etiquette.

values

As the heart chakra matures, the individual starts to examine the rules to see whether they are really valid. Repression and restriction becomes intolerable. Outright rebellion may seem to be the only way to break free of the suffocating pattern. Society as a whole does not deal kindly with people

◁ In modern urban society the individual is moulded to fit in with a required role. Personal freedom may be exchanged for rigid order.

who question the consensus: this stage of individualization can thus be a lonely journey.

The best outcome is the development of a personal set of values and ethics by which to live, which may be based on the old rules, but come from a fresh, up-to-date perspective with a personal relevance. It has been said by philosophers that there is no freedom without discipline. When a balanced state of individual self-discipline is achieved, self-acceptance and freedom become possible.

In many cultures, such as classical India and China, it was accepted that at some stage of life a removal from the rigidity of normal society was a natural phase of personal development. Usually this occurred in later life, when family responsibilities were no longer an issue. Individuals could concentrate on spiritual disciplines or remove themselves to remote spots to perfect skills of poetry or painting. In most cases, the rebellious can find alternative societies where they feel free from control, although every group imposes its own rules and taboos, which offer the kind of orderly balance the individual needs. This clearly demonstrates that restrictions are a burden only when they do not offer a balance to the unique heart chakra needs of each of us.

△ Expansion, growth and freedom are all pre-requisites for a healthy and mature heart chakra.

Whatever the rules and regulations of a society may be, those who are openly rebellious become primary targets for the criticism of the group. Today's behaviour censors are the tabloid press, who rely on the unusual behaviour of individuals to sustain their demand for interesting stories. At the same time, the media tend to take a tribal stance, rejecting new concepts and unique insights in favour of the establishment viewpoint. There are always, though, small groups and individuals on the edge of society who are prepared to explore new balances and create new patterns.

▽ Chains, restraints and restrictions are only recognized as such when the individual grows beyond the need for them. Before this point they offer security.

INDIVIDUAL OR INHERITED BELIEFS?

If you want or need to begin to de-programme yourself from values that are not yours, this exercise may help.

1 Take time to think about, then list on a sheet of paper, beliefs that begin with 'I should...' Add to your list over a period of a week or so, then don't look at it for a week. Look at the list – seeing if you can identify any of the statements with older family members, teachers or partners. If you do notice any links, ask yourself if you honestly believe the statement. Reflect on the relevance of the other statements you have made to your present life. Cross out those that no longer apply.

2 Copy out a list of the remaining statements, then leave them for another week. Repeat the self-questioning process. If there are any statements left

on the list, they may highlight key issues that need dealing with or healing. They could also show you some of your present key values.

3 A similar exercise focuses on your wishes. Make a list beginning 'I want...' Be completely honest and open with yourself. This has nothing to do with judging what is good or bad. Neither should you exclude things that seem to be unlikely, impossible or silly. Acknowledging your drives and ambitions, your daydreams and fantasies in this way can release many hidden levels of stress from your heart chakra and may allow your conscious awareness to move in a direction that is more self-fulfilling.

Heart chakra – following the heart

At a certain point in the development and maturing of the heart chakra there is an opportunity to see yourself and the rest of the world from a very different perspective. This new view of the world can present some discomfort if the inherent patterning has always been to look outside yourself for confirmation and verification of your own worth. The realization dawns that while you can care, love and share with others you cannot live their lives for them or live your life through them. It can also be a very lonely moment when you realize that others cannot live your life for you either. They can love you, advise you and commiserate with you, but in the end, everyone is responsible only for themselves. Everybody has their unique direction in life.

△ The heart chakra allows us to expand and grow in power while keeping harmony with the Earth and everything around us.

BALANCING THE INNER AND OUTER WORLDS

This exercise helps to balance your relationship with the world and can be extremely calming. Sit or lie down in a comfortable position.

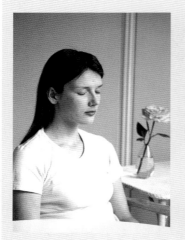

1 Breathe in then, as you breathe out, allow your body to relax. Visualize a flower giving off light at your heart chakra. Stay with that flower for a minute or two, feeling its energy and presence. In the centre of that flower, visualize the whole Earth.

Imagine the light of the flower filling the whole planet with incredible joy. Allow that joy and light to fill all of you too. Let that energy reach every single part of you, clearing away all negativity.

2 After a few minutes, bring your hands together over the heart chakra in the centre of your chest. Feel the energy under your hands and allow your hands to release that energy by slowly returning them to their original position lying in your lap.

Visualize the Earth at the centre of the flower at your heart chakra, melting into the flower and then the flower melting into your heart. Stay with this thought for a moment before slowly returning to normal awareness.

balance

If we are able to accommodate the paradoxical themes of the heart chakra, we can follow our own path while allowing others to follow theirs. The saying: 'If you love somebody, set them free' encapsulates the energy of a fully functional heart chakra. No matter how much you have shared with, taught, sacrificed for and loved someone, letting them be themselves is the greatest gift you can give. This releasing of the other person allows any possessiveness, misplaced sense of responsibility or dependence to disappear, and enables both of you to grow.

compassion

When you are able to achieve some sort of balance between yourself and everything outside yourself, the way opens for a special mix of compassion and caring. With this balance comes the understanding that, although the boundaries between the self and the world needed to be clear to get to this point, when you arrive there are no boundaries. This is not a sacrificial relationship with the world, but a complete openness and acceptance of it. In order to progress as a spiritual human being, avoiding

▷ At its spiritual level of function the heart chakra directs us along our path of life in a way that allows us to achieve our maximum potential.

the pitfalls of spiritual self-deception and egotism, it is necessary to arrive at a real awareness that, because all creation is connected, you cannot be truly free until everything else is too. The open acceptance of the world, and the awareness that the individual's spiritual development benefits everything, everywhere, is known as 'bodhicitta' or 'complete openness of mind'.

Bodhicitta has been fully explored in Buddhist traditions. It is found in the simple awareness of offering kindness to others at every possible opportunity. The Buddhist cosmology is huge, with millions of universes existing for millions of aeons. Within this ungraspable vastness of space and time, individuals are said to have incarnated numberless times. If this is the case then everyone we meet and every being we come across has, at one time or another, been our mother and has looked after, loved and cared for us to the best of their ability. In this context bodhicitta is simply acknowledging these past kindnesses.

▽ Equilibrium, or balance, is the key to the heart chakra energy. Without it there can be no way for us to adapt to constant change.

Chakras of communication

The upper three chakras are at the base of the throat, the centre of the forehead and just above the crown of the head. They are physically close together and regulate our communication with and understanding of the world. The throat chakra focuses on the expression of what we know and feel. The brow chakra brings clarity of perception and intuitive insight, and the crown chakra unites the individual to the greater universe.

Throat chakra – finding peace

Blue is the colour associated with the throat chakra. It is the colour of communication and information but is also the colour of peacefulness. The human nervous system is 'hard-wired' to respond to the blue of twilight by settling down, becoming quiet and preparing to rest during the hours of darkness. As the body becomes less active, so mental activity is also reduced. An observant detachment becomes more apparent. As physical objects become less visible, so too the mental functions become more imaginative, vague and dreamlike. Peace descends.

the easy flow of energy

With a balance of energies within the throat chakra, peace is a tangible experience, a familiar relaxed occurrence. Where the throat chakra is stressed or blocked in some way, peace may be longed-for, but difficult, if not impossible to achieve.

Wherever there is a concentration of inappropriate energy, pressure begins to build up. Whatever the cause of the build-up, an outward flow is the only means of restoring balance, with energy flowing from an area of high pressure to one of lower

pressure. This outward flow from the body is achieved through expression and communication, via the activity of the throat chakra. If the expression is blocked in some way, the energy will have to find release through one of the other major chakra functions, for example as aggressive, selfish behaviour via the base chakra or as escapism via the brow chakra.

Singing, chanting or playing a musical instrument, even banging on a drum, will help to restore balance to the throat chakra. Toning can also be useful. This is simply making extended vocal sounds out loud for as long as your breath allows. The sound and note are less important than the quality of the vibration created through your body. Toning can be effective at releasing physical and emotional tensions. Just allow whatever sound occurs to come up, and let it go.

the need to listen

Communication is not simply about personal expression. It is also necessary to listen to what is being expressed by others. Blocks or excess energy can often distract from the true meaning of what someone else is trying to communicate, for there is a

△ **A true sense of peace arises when there is equilibrium within the chakra system and an easy flow of energy through the body.**

▽ **Drumming quietens the mind while allowing excess energy to be dissipated harmlessly through the physical activity.**

tendency to react to each word or phrase as it is heard, rather than comprehending the meaning of the whole.

Without the appropriate outward flow of energy there can be too much involvement with what is being communicated – everything is taken as being relevant to, or critical of, oneself. A block at the throat centre creates a closed

circuit where nothing can escape. Problems also occur if individual expression has been stifled, often by overbearing discipline. When this happens the energy within the body must direct itself in one of two ways – upwards to become locked in a fantasy world of the imagination, or downwards to distort the base, sacral and solar plexus as excessive manipulation and dominance of others in overt or covert aggression.

RELEASING PHYSICAL AND EMOTIONAL TENSION

Use this exercise to release any block that you become aware of that can be traced back to some feelings that you have not expressed. Perhaps someone has made you feel hurt or angry, and instead of confronting those feelings you have suppressed them. Burning incense of some kind while you carry out this process will help to cleanse the emotional debris from your aura and surroundings. Pungent and sweet-smelling herbs were originally used in this way for purification and to drive away demons.

1 Write down what you wish to say to the person who has hurt or angered you. As you are doing this, let any anger you are feeling find its way on to the page, allowing the feelings to come. When you have finished do not read what you have written.

2 Take the piece of paper, fold it up, and burn it in the flame of a candle or on an open fire. Simply destroy it completely. If necessary, repeat the process until you sense that your equilibrium has been restored and you can feel peace returning.

creative expression

The resolution of such conditions is found in expressing the energy in an effective but safe manner. Any creative artistic occupation will work – as long as the focus is on the activity itself, rather than on the end product. Such activity is a release of excess energy – if a masterpiece of art is the end product this is a bonus, but it is not the intention. Not to be expressive simply because you believe that you 'can't paint' is just reinforcing the same repressive values that have probably caused the problem in the first place.

There are strategies to help you loosen artistic hang-ups that are well worth trying. One is to draw on pages from magazines or newspapers – a clean white piece of drawing paper can be intimidating. Draw with felt tip pens with broad tips. This prevents you from getting caught up with timid little lines. Alternatively, use very small pieces of paper and very fine pens – it is much easier to see your whole design and make an effective image. Set out to use all parts of the paper right up to the corners.

Throat chakra – getting the message

Language is the evolutionary leap that is often considered to have been the major factor in the success of our species. As a means of communicating complex concepts, planning the unknown future and sharing the experiences of the past, language has enabled us to begin living more in our minds and more in the past and the future than in the present moment. Language has given us the ability to understand what is happening to others around us. The growth of society and civilization are based on cooperation and shared dreams, which are communicated by language.

▽ **The throat chakra allows us to communicate how we feel and what we think. In the West it is associated with the colour blue.**

△ Every form of expression reveals the emotions and thoughts of the individual, for the acknowledgement of the group.

physical considerations

All the physical organs and structures of the throat have to do with letting energy move through – either inwards or outwards. The mouth, nose and throat are where we first come into contact with the air around us. Even though breathing is initiated in the solar plexus, we feel the air as it passes over the back of the palate and through the upper throat.

The mouth and oesophagus are our first contacts with food – in fact, vital digestive processes are carried out in the mouth. A great deal happens in this small area, and it all has to be carefully regulated – we are able to speak only on the outbreath as air passes over our vocal cords; we have to avoid breathing in at the same time as we swallow, or we choke.

Wrapped around the vital tubes carrying air and food – the trachea and the oesophagus – are the thyroid and parathyroid glands. These major endocrine glands regulate the body's metabolism, ensuring that enough energy is produced

◁ When our inner creativity fails to emerge in the way we want, a lack of energy at the throat chakra is often the cause.

from food for our needs. Lethargy and sluggishness result from an underactive thyroid and hyperactivity is due to an overactive thyroid.

voice

The voice allows us to express what we are feeling in the heart and mind. Expressing what is going on inside ourselves to those around us gives a shared understanding and a sense of belonging. Blocks in our ability to communicate may not cause an immediate problem, as they would with the physical organs of the throat, but the curtailment of personal expression is nonetheless deeply disturbing to the energy systems as a whole. In fact, lack of expression denies our existence, our individuality and our right to be heard.

Personal expression of ideas and thoughts, and the ability to communicate through spoken language, or the symbolic languages of writing, singing, performing or any of the other arts, help to maintain the healthy flow of energy through the throat chakra. The expression does not have to be perfect, unique or special in any way for it to be of benefit. Criticism and judgment of our expression are detrimental to the wellbeing of the chakra – indeed, if anything restricts the natural outward exuberant flow of expression, problems are likely to arise.

Indications of blocks in this area may be a stiff neck, throat infection or tension in the shoulders. Headaches or problems with swallowing or eating and metabolic disorders also point to underlying throat chakra problems. Some difficulties become obvious when frustration leads to shouting, or to its opposite: a complete withdrawal of communication.

The throat chakra is like a pressure valve. Its function is to allow the energy from the other chakra centres to express themselves so that other people can understand what is going on. If this ability is suppressed, either

USTRASANA

This exercise encourages good blood supply to the neck, keeping the energy moving through the chakra. It is a simplified version of the yoga pose ustrasana, the camel pose, which opens up the front of the body.

1 Sit on your heels on a blanket or mat, clasping your hands behind you.

2 Breathe in, then, as you breathe out, allow your head to drop backwards. At the same time, raise your arms a little behind you. Breathe normally.

3 When you are ready to release the posture, release your hands on an outbreath and bring yourself back to sitting upright.

4 Repeat this three or four times.

internally or because of outside influences, problems will inevitably arise. The chakra system works all the time as one continuous flow of energy, like cogs connected together in a machine. If one begins to seize up, all the other chakras will have their function impaired. For example, if there is a problem in a relationship, where feelings are not being acknowledged or talked about, there may be symptoms at the throat but the heart chakra will also be under strain. So if you find you are suffering from a recurrence of neck or throat problems it is always a good idea to take a look at your situation and see what restrictions might be blocking your ability to express yourself, whether they arise from others or whether you are putting unnecessary limitations on yourself.

Throat chakra – the teacher

Communication and sound are the keys to the throat chakra. Those who use these skills in their work are drawing on the energy of this centre. Through the throat we communicate how we feel inside – our emotional state – and how we think – our mental processes.

education

How effective and expressive communication is depends upon how we have been taught when still young. Many traditional forms of education pass knowledge from generation to generation through repetition and learning by rote. Very often, however, the content of the information can be misunderstood.

Many of us will be able to remember instances where hymns or prayers that were repeated regularly at home and school were misheard or just misinterpreted for many years, simply because the meaning of the words had never been explained. Communication by simple repetition has a tendency to break down very quickly, as the game known as Chinese whispers graphically illustrates.

If we, or those we talk to, are unable to understand the content of language – if we cannot 'take it to heart', true communication cannot take place. Problems with effective communication demonstrate that the chakra system has to work as an integrated whole. Without the input of the mind (the sixth and seventh chakras), and personal feelings (the heart), the throat chakra has nothing to work with.

▷ Learning by doing is often more effective than learning by rote because it actively involves a broader range of chakra energies, making knowledge personal.

△ Both teaching and learning use the energies of the throat chakra in the flow of communication.

teaching

The effective teacher is a person who feels excitement and interest and can express it to their students in a way that allows the knowledge to become their own. This requires an exploration of the views and opinions of others, with the possibility of dissent and disagreement. New information should be integrated with what is already known and believed, not simply asserted as inflexible dogma.

WHAT DO YOU BELIEVE?

This exercise is one way of looking at beliefs about yourself. Make a list of what you hold to be true beginning with 'I think that...' For example, 'I think that my feet are too big,' 'I think that I am ignored,' 'I think I talk too much,' 'I think nobody really listens to what I say,' and so on. Don't make excuses or try to rationalize or judge your statements. Very quickly, patterns will emerge that help to reveal core beliefs. Opposing views are often held simultaneously. These create internal tensions whatever viewpoint we adopt. Resolving them can free up enormous amounts of personal creativity. Discovering our inner patterns of belief reveals that we ourselves have been our teacher all along.

⊲ Communication is not simply an exchange of words. Over 90 per cent of meaning is transmitted by non-verbal signals. Modern forms of communication very often exclude these important clues.

experience and what we have been told by adults. As we mature new beliefs are categorized and grouped under the relevant core beliefs. By adulthood the original core beliefs may be completely obscured by their later, more sophisticated, accretions. Still, every experience is understood in terms of the belief systems we have built up for ourselves. What we are able to hear, what we are able to understand and what we are able to express and create, all depend upon the model that we have drawn up telling us how the world works.

The throat chakra is very much the mouthpiece of the other chakras. What it listens to, what it hears and how it responds are all flavoured by the patterns of stress found within each of the other six chakras. For instance, a series of blocks within the second, sacral chakra, which brings about our sense of playful creativity, may prevent real personal creativity from being expressed via the throat chakra – even though the individual may be a wonderful narrator of other people's material.

▽ We tend to notice things that interest us, and ignore the rest. We recognize our names being spoken by others even in noisy places.

Unfortunately, when we are young, we have a tendency to believe everything that we are told. Every scrap of information is gathered and memorized in the process of getting to know how the world works. Because their language skills are still forming, children are able to sense when a conflict of information is occurring, but usually cannot express it effectively, or else they are not given the opportunity to clarify what they have been taught.

absorption

Learning to explore alternative views, even taking up opposite viewpoints in a debate, is a useful way of developing attitudes of flexibility and tolerance. Without these skills there is the danger that whatever is communicated to us will be automatically believed. Personal belief systems gradually build up in complexity as we grow. However, the basic structure is laid down when we are very young and consists of core beliefs based on personal

Throat chakra – finding your voice

The throat is traditionally associated with the element of space, which is also called ether and, in the original Sanskrit texts, akasha. This fifth element was conceived as the original container, the vessel that held all the other elements.

sound

In the original Indian texts the first thing to be created, or to emerge out of the primal space, was the vibration we call sound. These waves of sound constituted the whole of creation – all matter, all thought, all energy are in reality the interplay of the sounds or songs of the Creator. The importance of sound and speech as a creative principle is very common among the peoples of the world. Creation myths often combine the moulding of creatures out of inanimate matter with the life-giving

▽ **Places of sacred significance have nearly always been chosen or constructed because of their special acoustic properties.**

△ Although mantras often have meaning their real value is in the quality of subtle sound they create within the body.

Chanting and using mantra meditation offer ways of releasing throat chakra problems and experiencing finer levels of speech. Mantras are powerful sequences of sound that enliven deep levels of energy in the body and mind. Traditionally, mantras are chosen by a teacher to be appropriate to the individual. It is important not to use 'any old sound' as a mantra, as this can have a disruptive effect on subtle levels. The primal sound in many traditions is 'AAAH' – the first vowel sound that is made with a completely relaxed throat. Taking a deep breath and simply chanting AAAH for as long as possible creates a clearing in the throat chakra. Begin loud and after a few repetitions, start to chant more softly, until the sound is simply a thought, then a silence in the mind.

▷ The soothing sound of storytelling trains the mind to understand many nuances of meaning and language.

addition of breath or the process of naming. Myths and stories show the magical and spiritual significance of knowing the right names for things.

truth

Where it is functioning at its highest level the throat chakra should be bringing out our own truth into the world. Truth is not just a matter of correct information. Neither does truth carry any moral weight, though it can be experienced as good or bad, comfortable or uncomfortable, depending on how it interacts with each person's beliefs about what is real. Each of us will dismiss as untrue those things that do not fall within our personal construction of how the universe works.

Speaking from a level of personal truth means that whatever is said carries the conviction of our whole being, sometimes referred to as will. Personal will or truth rarely emerges however, because we are all constrained by the values and concepts we have been taught by others. All our communications are filtered and distorted by the many energy blocks that have arisen from the stresses and traumas of the past. Only with the gradual removal of these stresses can a more honest and open relationship with the world emerge.

lies, damned lies...

Telling lies has a remarkable effect on the whole body. When a lie is told, conflict in the hemispheres of the brain releases stress hormones that create measurable changes in blood chemistry and skin resistance, and a dip in all the subtle energies of the meridians and subtle bodies. The throat chakra energies become strained and distorted if lying becomes habitual. Lying is

never successful, simply because the stress it causes cannot be totally disguised, but is communicated to the observer at subconscious levels, thereby arousing doubt and suspicion.

Fear, doubt and uncertainty all prevent honest, open communication. We can try to avoid telling lies, but until fear is removed completely all behaviour will be a compromise between what an individual really wants and what they perceive is required by others. By working to clear the throat chakra, these oppressive blocks to creativity and true expression of self can gradually be dissipated.

TIBETAN MANTRA

The best known mantra is probably OM. It consists of three sounds A-U-M, each of which expresses in seed form the creation of everything in the universe. AAAH is the most natural sound to emerge from the mouth. The O sound begins to shape and control this open flow of energy, symbolizing the creation of form. The M, actually a nasal hum closer to -NG, represents the continuity of the complex vibrations that make up the many levels of reality. The Tibetan mantra OM-AA-HUNG is a variation of this primal sound and can be used as a regular exercise to cleanse the

chakras, open the throat and quieten the mind. It can be done without accompanying visualization, though introducing the other elements adds significantly to the effect.

1 Take a good breath and sound an OM for as long as you can without straining, rhyming it with 'from'. At the same time visualize white light at the centre of the brow, or the Tibetan character for this sound.
2 Now take another deep breath and pronounce AA, rhyming it with 'car'. Continue for as long as you can. At the same time see red light at the centre of the throat or the character for this sound, coloured red.
3 On the third breath, sound HUNG, rhyming it with 'sung'. End the sound by humming with your mouth closed so that your skull bones vibrate. With this sound visualize a blue light at the heart or a blue Tibetan symbol for the sound. Repeat the sequence as many times as you like.

▽ The formal characters of the Tibetan alphabet spell out the primal sounds OM, AA, HUNG, encapsulating every aspect of creation.

Brow chakra – seeing the picture

The chakra located in the centre of the forehead is called ajña, meaning to perceive and to command. It is directly related to the senses of sight and hearing, although all three upper chakras – the throat, brow and crown – are physically close together and share many correspondences. Throat chakra influences extend to the mouth and jaw and up to the ears, while the brow has more links with the face, eyes, nose and forehead. The neck and base of the skull can be influenced by both brow and throat energies. Crown chakra energies relate to the cranium, the bones of the top of the head at and above the hairline.

▽ The brow chakra is the seat of understanding, from where we picture how the world is.

thoughts

Our everyday awareness is located in the area of the brow chakra, from where our higher sense functions scan the world around us. The consciousness of self, of the unique personality of the mind, is felt to be seated here, like a commander at his control post. We are very much in our heads – more than, say, in our heart or our solar plexus. The physical body belongs to us but we do not think of it as being 'us' in the same way.

We relate to our own thoughts, our interpretations and inner conversations, continually assessing the information that feeds in through the senses. We relate to others by focusing attention on the face – the eyes and the subtle changes of expression, feeling that the 'real person' is somewhere in there. This arises from the awareness that here at the brow chakra we

△ Perception is understanding how different parts come together to make a whole. It is the job of the brow chakra to interpret clearly.

begin to make sense of and interpret the world. The brow chakra is all about seeing, not just seeing with the eyes, but seeing with the mind – making sense of and understanding what is being perceived.

eyesight

We do not see what the eyes see. The eye focuses light through the lens and an upside-down image is thrown on to the retina at the back of the eye. However, only one tiny spot, the fovea, has a concentration of light-sensitive cells great enough to produce a complete focused image; the rest of the eye receives a vaguer, more blurred picture. Rapid movement of the eyes adds more

CLEAR SEEING

Seeing clearly depends on the coordination between the mind and the eyes. Confusion in understanding (seeing) arises when blocks in the brow chakra disturb the complex relationship between eye movements and nerve impulses as they travel to the centres of visual comprehension in the brain. Getting confused shows that stress is affecting coordination. Practice will re-open these pathways, increasing your ability to focus and understand the world around you. This simple exercise helps both the muscles controlling eye movement and the balance between the left and right hemispheres of the brain.

▽ Seeing is not simply a sense of perception. We use 'I see' to mean 'I understand'. Seeing relies on the flexibility of the mind as well as the sharpness of the eyes.

1 Sit in a relaxed position with an upright head. Gaze forwards with your eyes relaxed.
2 Turn your eyes upwards and as high as they will go, making sure your head does not move. Now slowly and attentively roll your eyes in a clockwise direction.
3 When you return to the top again, relax and gaze forward for a moment.
4 Now repeat the exercise, but this time move your eyes anticlockwise, in the opposite direction to before. Make sure your head remains still and that your eyes move as slowly and evenly as possible.
5 Repeat each cycle a couple of times unless you feel some strain. If you want to check your eye-brain coordination, do this exercise while you are saying a nursery rhyme or counting numbers.

of memories, the brain organizes the visual information so that we can understand and really 'see'. Perception is the art of creating order from potential chaos, from random impulses. Perception is the main function of the brow chakra.

Balancing this chakra can help physical problems with the eyes, but more than this, it will help remove confusion caused by an inability to distinguish important things from insignificant ones; in visual terms, the foreground from the background. Clear seeing, understanding and perspective are all mental skills that are needed to interpret visual data, as well as the mental pictures that are our thoughts, memories and ideas.

Seeing the picture allows us to move within the orderly, familiar patterns of life. Without the brow chakra making sense of information received by the brain, we would be paralysed by confusion and indecision.

▽ Pattern-making is essential for the mind to understand what it is being shown by the eyes. Whenever possible a pattern will be seen, even in a random display of colours.

information, scanning the field of vision to allow us to get a clearer set of images. When these images travel to the brain they are switched, so that information from the left eye travels to the right hemisphere of the brain and vice versa.

breaking the code

The brain interprets the flurry of electrical nerve impulses and fills in all the gaps itself. Recognizing familiar shapes and relationships between things, creating patterns that mean something from its store

Brow chakra – creative dreaming

The colour associated with the brow chakra is indigo – the deep blue of a midnight sky. It is the colour of deep silence and stillness, of resonant emptiness and solitude. The brow chakra has a certain degree of detachment from emotional concerns.

perspective

In order to see clearly, a distance must be maintained between subject and object. It is possible to recognize patterns only when the background, known as the field, is empty. In the same way, the emotions at the brow chakra have to be quiet in order to allow clear images to appear. Because the process of seeing involves so much 'filling in' by the brain, any strong emotional involvement can distort the picture we receive and our eyes can deceive us. If our emotional needs are too strong it is possible to become obsessed with the fine details of the pattern so that nothing else is seen – the 'big picture' is lost in the power of a single idea or dream. Silence and detachment allow the brow chakra to keep its perspective.

▽ Time and space are laws of physical reality that do not constrain the non-physical worlds of the mind and spirit. All things become possible.

detachment

Jumping to conclusions and making assumptions are signs that the brow chakra is becoming confused by too much emotional noise, blurring the clear distinction between 'I want' and 'I see'. Allowing the spaciousness of detached and passive watching increases the possibility that intuition – the flash of knowing that seems to come from nowhere – will arise in the mind. Receptivity and openness to new possibilities allow the necessary clarity in the brow for accurate perception.

Detachment is crucial to the functioning of the brow chakra at all levels, not just at the emotional level. Mental agility requires the ability to step back from the normal waking experiences of time and space. Where the throat chakra uses sound to communicate in language – a linear, time-based experience – the brow chakra uses light to carry messages in the form of visual symbols and pictures. The internal world of dreams, daydreams and the imagination is not limited by the rules of the physical universe. Anything can appear: the impossible alongside the mundane, the fantastic with the ordinary. As in dreams, the logic of time and matter can be ignored.

△ Making sense of things requires the perspective of distance to see the whole picture. Taking a rest from problems allows the ajña to see new patterns that may give solutions.

Transformations occur continually, changing scenes and context. Events can happen simultaneously or even run backwards in time. From the perspective of conscious awareness all this is confusing and difficult to understand. From the perspective of the mental functioning of the brow chakra this language of light is a straightforward communication of energy that directly affects the electrical impulses of the brain, and from there, the whole system.

The brow chakra, resting in its state of quiet observation, can build up, interpret and change the very nature of our reality. It is no wonder that its Sanskrit name, ajña, also means 'one who commands'. The new discipline of psychoneuro-immunology is a medical adaptation of the visualization techniques of yogis and mystics who, through experience, knew full well the power of the mind to alter every aspect of the body and the physical world by constructing meaningful images of light within their own minds.

MATSYASANA

Here are two versions of an exercise that can help to focus energy at the brow chakra. Try both versions and choose whichever is the most comfortable or effective for you.

The name for this posture, the fish, comes from Matsya, the name for the fish incarnation of Vishnu, the Hindu deity who is the source and maintainer of the universe and everything in it.

1 For the first version (left), begin by kneeling on a blanket or mat. Place the palms of your hands on the floor behind you, fingers pointing forwards, bending your elbows.

2 Lean back on to your elbows and breathe in. As you breathe out, let your head drop backwards and arch your back slightly. Breathe normally, focusing on your brow chakra.

3 For the second version (below), sit with your legs out in front of you and your feet together. Place the palms of your hands under your hips, bending your elbows behind you.

4 Lean back on to your elbows and breathe in. As you breathe out, lean backwards until you are supporting yourself on your arms. Allow your head to drop backwards and arch your back slightly. Breathe normally, again focusing on your brow chakra.

5 When you are ready to come out of this position, allow your elbows to slide away, lowering yourself to a lying position.

6 Roll on to your side and sit up.

Brow chakra – visions

In popular thought the brow chakra is considered to be synonymous with the 'third eye'. In traditional Indian texts the forehead has many interrelated smaller chakras, which extend upwards from the ajña between the eyebrows until they merge with the functions of the crown chakra. Each of these chakras deals with increasingly fine experiences of perception, clarity and realms of subtle energy where deities and other powerful spirits dwell. The sixth and seventh chakras enable consciousness to move beyond the physical universe. To the ardent materialist of the 21st century, reality is objective solidity. What happens in the mind, not being physical or measurable in any way, is illusory, ephemeral, subjective. In fact, normal reality is largely a mind-created construct that can only be experienced subjectively, within ourselves.

insight and intuition

Intuition is hard to define, but can be understood as a prompting from all the levels of awareness beyond the everyday conscious mind, which some would associate with the unconscious or subconscious mind. Intuition presents a whole picture, an overview and an understanding that goes beyond the simple explanation of its parts. The whole picture given us in a flash of intuition brings a sense of solidity, of usefulness to the mind. Giving ourselves space to notice and act on intuitive insight frees the energy of the brow chakra. Confidence in the subtle signals received from these areas of perception can develop into 'clear seeing' or clairvoyance.

clairvoyance

The clairvoyant experience is not necessarily only a visual one; it is 'clear seeing' in the sense of receiving clear, penetrating insight. The knowledge that accompanies the act of clairvoyance may include visual data, but these are not necessarily perceived in the same way that we see the everyday world. The information is more akin to dream imagery and memory. The attention travels, or moves beyond time and space, to visualize new information. For many people, it seems difficult to distinguish clairvoyance from imagination, and is usually referred to as 'only my imagination', as if it should be instantly discounted as an unsafe source of information. With experience and an increase in confidence the difference can be felt quite clearly – it is as though different mental muscles have come into play.

How we receive information depends very much on the way we naturally interpret our senses. Psychologists recognize three distinct types of response that we all possess, though we favour one over the others. A visual imagination will find it very easy to see thoughts in terms of pictures, in clear detail and full colour. A kinaesthetic imagination will interpret thoughts and images as feelings, either as moods or as sensations related to the body. An auditory imagination will interpret information as words, phrases or dialogue.

Recognizing which type we are makes it easier to identify the prompting of the brow chakra's intuition for what it is. For example, with a kinaesthetic mind it is no good expecting to see clear images. With a visual mind it is important to learn how the mind employs symbols, whereas with an auditory mind, thoughts pop into the head.

▽ The brow chakra has the ability to see beyond the obvious, accessing the realms of intuition and clairvoyance to gain insight.

PSYCHOMETRY

This exercise provides a way of receiving impressions about an object, its history and owners. It is best carried out with an open curiosity and a sense of fun. Don't worry about getting it right or wrong, just play with the possibilities. Practise with objects from many different people and places, and you will quickly develop your accuracy and the strength of your impressions.

1 Ask a friend for a piece of jewellery or a watch. If it is old and has had more than one owner, all the better. Sit comfortably and allow your breathing to settle, then turn your attention inwards and allow your senses to still.

2 Pick up the object, hold it in your hands and focus on it. Begin to process your thoughts, feelings and any sensations or imagery that come to you.

3 To deepen the process you might find it helpful to place the item against your brow chakra. After a minute or so put the object down. Turn your attention to yourself once again, allowing your breathing to settle. Turn your attention to the soles of your feet for a minute to ground your energy, then relate your impressions.

Crown chakra – the fountain head

The Sanskrit name for the crown chakra is sahasrara, meaning 'thousandfold'. This refers to the image of the thousand-petalled lotus which, in Hindu thought, represents the epitome of the human condition. The chakra is described as being positioned just above the head.

the pituitary gland

The gland most often associated with the crown chakra is the pituitary, though some texts do quote the relevant gland as being

▽ The crown chakra is the main co-ordinating centre of the body and ensures that the individual is also connected to universal sources of energy.

the pineal. The pituitary gland is located at the base of the brain. It has two sections, the anterior and posterior, which are each responsible for releasing particular hormones. The pituitary is often referred to as the 'master gland' because it affects so many other glands and body functions.

the brain

The brain is a most complex organ with four main sections and billions of nerves. One section of the brain, the cerebrum, is involved with sensation, reasoning, planning and problem-solving. The diencephalon contains the pineal gland, the thalamus and the hypothalamus, which are referred to collectively as the limbic system. This controls body temperature, water balance, appetite, heart rate, sleep patterns and emotions. The brain stem, midbrain, pons and medulla oblongata control breathing, heart rate and blood pressure. The cerebellum controls posture, balance and the co-ordination of the muscles that are associated with movement.

co-ordination

From the viewpoint of physical health, the crown chakra is mostly concerned with co-ordination. Co-ordination is needed at all levels. Individual cells within the pituitary gland and the diencephalon have to co-ordinate to ensure the smooth running of the bodily functions. The cerebellum is responsible for helping us to co-ordinate our muscles to achieve balance, posture and movement.

Co-ordination skills are learned at an early age – and reinforced by crawling on all fours. Research in the last 30 years has shown that children who do not crawl on all fours in infancy often experience co-ordination difficulties as they grow up. It has been found that returning to this early form of locomotion, even as an adult, can assist the cerebellum in gaining full muscle control. It has also been discovered that

ADHO MUKHA SVANASANA

The dog posture helps to balance the energy between the feet and the crown chakra.

1 Kneel on a non-slip surface on all-fours, making sure your knees are in a straight line under your hips. Make sure your hands are in a straight line under your shoulders and spread your fingers. Tuck your toes under.
2 Breathe in, lifting your pelvis and straightening your legs, keeping your head low.

3 Breathe naturally. As you stay in the posture, imagine your bottom is lifting upwards, but your heels are lowering to the floor, stretching your back.
4 When you decide to release the posture, breathe in, then as you breathe out, lower yourself back on to all-fours.
5 Slide yourself back until you are sitting on your heels, rest your forehead on the floor and relax for a few moments.

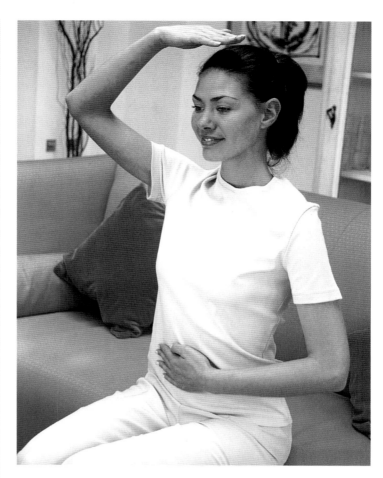

△ The well-known test of rubbing your stomach while tapping your head is a good example of body-mind co-ordination.

▽ Activities such as balancing and juggling require whole-brain co-ordination. Balance in life demands whole-chakra co-ordination.

many types of learning difficulties can be helped by exercises that utilize opposite parts of the body, confirming that brain co-ordination and function can be improved.

Co-ordination problems can occur on many levels throughout life. Physical difficulties like poor balance or clumsiness are quite obvious manifestations of the problem. Dyslexia often results from poor co-ordination between the brain hemispheres, as the eyes move across

a page of writing or scan down a text. On a less obvious level, co-ordination with the world as a whole is also a function of the crown chakra. Finding yourself at the right place at the right time, or just happening to meet the one person you were needing to speak to, having lucky coincidences and strange sequences of events that all work out very well, are signs that your crown chakra is feeding you good information.

Crown chakra – the illusion of detachment

The development of expanded awareness underpins the crown chakra at the emotional level. The opportunity to understand our individual role in the world does not present itself until our teenage years, when we start to move away from the family base.

Growing up in a balanced way, developing adults use the lessons from childhood to create a sense of unity and empathy with people around them. Service to others is often thought to be truly selfless, but there may be hidden motives. We often serve others so we can feel useful and needed, or to create an ideal world where we don't have to see people suffer. We may also see others as more worthy of being cared for than ourselves, diverting attention away from our own needs. Helping those less fortunate can sometimes suppress a sense of our individuality. The loss of personal identity can lead to feeling overwhelmed.

negative attachment

Many philosophies encourage us to free ourselves from emotional 'attachment' in order to achieve spiritual goals. However, the state of being 'non-attached' sometimes acts as a mask for a refusal to accept personal

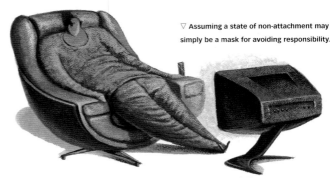

▽ Assuming a state of non-attachment may simply be a mask for avoiding responsibility.

▽ When there is a lack of awareness of personal needs, it is easy for the enthusiastic helper to be a martyr to idealism.

responsibility. The need to renounce or escape from the responsibility of the family, work or the world in general must be carefully examined for its real motive. Though a change in direction may seem to offer more personal freedom, it could be that working within the current situation could provide a better opportunity for growth. Being emotionally attached to something is sometimes bound up with a fearful unwillingness to allow that thing to change. This closes down other possibilities.

The crown chakra is concerned with openness, and when you get over-attached to a closed way of thinking or feeling, this will tend to prevent you from dealing with reality. The remedy is to be compassionate with yourself and consider all possibilities. Unless this open compassion is first directed towards yourself, allowing healing at the crown chakra, it is impossible to be truly compassionate.

reality and fantasy

With the upper chakras, particularly the brow and crown chakras, there are a lot of fine or subtle energies coming into play. Because we often feel restricted by the inflexibility of the three-dimensional world (things take time and effort to accomplish, plans go wrong, and so on), there can be a certain attractiveness in the ephemeral quality of these areas of consciousness. The lack of restrictions, the breadth of possibilities, the sense of freedom can work a powerful magic on those dissatisfied with the world of here and now.

For those not drawn to metaphysics and philosophy this might manifest as retreat into a fantasy world of imagination. In a dominant personality where the base chakra is still strong, this imbalance might become a dogmatic idealism or even a megalomania.

An interest in spirituality has the potential to open new awareness of thought and activity that can really help people to break out of old behaviour patterns and become more fulfilled. But equally it can trap us in a web of glamour filled with bright, shiny, amazing things that can never be grasped for long enough to integrate usefully into life. Balance is always achieved where all the chakras are able to perform efficiently. For example, when we are truly grounded, rooted in the secure energies of the base chakra, it will be possible to experience finer, less tangible qualities of reality without losing perspective.

OPENING UP

Sometimes it can be difficult to imagine how we could continue in life without someone or something. We may have become over-dependent on a person, a way of living or a belief. This exercise will help you to open your life to new possibilities.

1 Identify a person, situation or belief that you are overly or fearfully attached to.

2 Sit for a minute or two, allowing your thoughts and emotions to dwell on the issue.

3 Note down on a sheet of paper all the things you can think of that embody that attachment.

4 If it is a person: note their qualities, what they give you, what you feel you may lose if they go.

5 If it is a situation: note what it is you value about it, what status it gives you, why you need it.

6 If it is a belief, thought or feeling: note what will change if it is no longer with you, and try to include why it is that you fear this.

7 Look at what you have written. Try to discover the games you have been playing with yourself, or the stories you have been allowing yourself to believe. Sit with this for a few minutes, with your eyes away from your notes, then look again at what you have written.

8 Close your eyes and imagine all the illusions, untruths or problems you have discovered filling a large bubble in front of you.

9 When the bubble is full, imagine it floating slowly up into a cloudless sky and dispersing.

Crown chakra – thought

Thought processes associated with the crown chakra fall into two main categories: how we think the world operates and those thoughts linking us to the universal scheme of things. Our beliefs about the world, our role in it and what we expect from the world form the basis of a behavioural programme that affects all our chakras. We build up a store of beliefs from our experiences in the world. However, thoughts linking us to the wider universe tend to be less easy to identify, and often surface through dreams and meditation. What we expect, especially what we fear, has a knack of being drawn towards us in some way.

reactions

The way we interpret events and then react to them is the reason why our lives progress or falter in the way they do. For example, suppose you trap your fingers in a door. The possible reactions are:

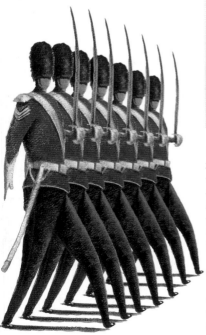

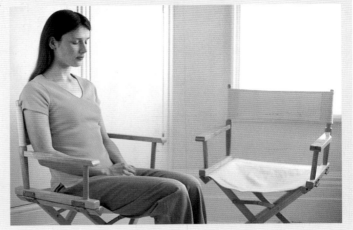

1 No reaction.
2 An exclamation followed by personal thoughts that you should have been more careful.
3 An exclamation followed by berating yourself for always being so stupid.
4 Slamming the door, blaming the person in front of you or behind you.
5 Hitting the person behind you because it was their fault.

◁ A society that makes no space for personal revelation runs the risk of becoming repressive and stagnant.

Each reaction to a stimulus reveals your programming concerning that stimulus, and at the same time reinforces that programming. Your reaction also determines how the world reacts back. In the case of the trapped fingers, options 4 and 5 would be likely to invite a negative riposte, escalating the situation further.

universal links

The crown chakra is our link to the universal sources of energy and information. In a natural maturing process the adolescent or young adult will begin to look for

△ **The desire to expand and grow is inherent in all chakras, from the base right up to the crown, where its connection to universal energy reminds us constantly that more is possible.**

answers to questions such as 'Why am I here?' that initiate the search for greater knowledge. Unfortunately this natural progression can be seriously hampered by family, social and religious backgrounds that do not accept individual exploration. In extreme cases, most traditions contain groups or factions whose fundamentalist, sexist or authoritarian practices instil

shame, fear and self-disgust into children who question the status quo. This repression effectively disconnects people from their personal links with spirituality of any type. Children who are experiencing these sorts of restrictions need to break through them or they will find it impossible to develop as individuals and reach their full potential. When the crown chakra is prevented from working normally it is unable to provide all the energy and information required by the other chakras.

A healthy crown chakra is finely balanced on all levels. The thoughts that come and go need to be allowed free passage. It is only when we try to hold on to thoughts, without allowing alternatives or the possibility of change, that disruption of the crown chakra happens.

◁ **Trying to control the thoughts of others is like trying to stop clouds moving across the sky. Holding on to another's way of thinking is as misguided.**

LITTLE YOGA NIDRA

This exercise, yoga sleep, combines the ability to visualize with the flow of information and energy throughout the body. Sit or lie in a comfortable position and relax for a few minutes, allowing your breathing to slow.

1 Take your attention down to your left big toe. Don't move it, but be aware of it as a focus for the mind.
2 Shift the focus in turn to your second, third, fourth and fifth toes. Then to the ball of the foot, instep, top of the foot and left heel.
3 Carry on to the lower leg, the back of the knee, the top of the knee, top of the thigh, back of the thigh and left buttock.
4 Take your attention down to your right big toe, second, third, fourth and fifth toes; the ball of the foot, instep, top of the foot and heel; lower leg, back of the knee, top of the knee, top of the thigh, back of the thigh and right buttock.
5 Take the attention to the left side of your back, the left side from hip to armpit and the left side of the chest. Then to the right side of your back, right side from hip to armpit, right side of the chest.
6 Take your attention to your left thumb. Then first finger, second, third and fourth; the palm of your hand, back of the hand, wrist, inside of the elbow, outside of the elbow, upper arm, left shoulder.
7 Then to your right thumb; first, second, third and fourth finger; the palm of your hand, back of the hand, wrist, inside of the elbow, outside of the elbow, upper arm and right shoulder.
8 On to your head and neck; left side of your face, right side of your face; left ear, right ear; left eye, right eye; mouth, inside the mouth.
9 At the end you should be feeling totally relaxed. You can repeat it if you are particularly tense or find it hard to relax.

Crown chakra – unity

△ With the crown chakra cleared of stresses, a sense of lightness, clarity and belonging flows through the whole chakra system.

▽ The series of poses, or asanas, that are undertaken during the practice of hatha yoga are designed to prepare the body for meditation.

The crown chakra focuses on what we experience as well as what we know or understand. If each level of each chakra has been integrated, the crown chakra represents illumination. Unless we truly understand what we see we are unable to apply our creative skills, fulfilling our visions of what is possible. The more we fulfil our visions, the more our consciousness expands, the more we understand what we see, and so on, in ever-increasing awareness.

yoga

Meditation is a key to the process of increasing awareness. In traditional Hindu philosophies, meditation is undertaken only when the body and mind have been harnessed towards that goal. This is the purpose of yoga, in particular raja yoga, also known as the eight-fold path. The steps or 'limbs' are sequential challenges or tasks:

1 Yama – 'general behaviour'. The student is expected to follow the disciplines that are said to be the foundation of an ethical society: ahimsa (non-violence), satya (speaking the truth), asteya (not envying or stealing), brahmacharya (not wasting

TRATAK

This is usually practised using a lighted candle as a focus, but you can use anything, like a flower or a stone. Although at first it may cause your eyes to run, it is used to improve eyesight. Place the object at eye level about an arm's length away from you.

Close your eyes and settle your breathing. Open your eyes and look steadily at the item. Try not to strain. After a minute, close your eyes. Visualize the item in your heart chakra or at the brow chakra. When the image fades, open your eyes and repeat.

resources), aparigraha (not hoarding what you don't need).

2 Niyama – 'observances'. The student should achieve the following: saucha (purity), santosha (contentment), tapas (effort), svadhyaya (spiritual study), isvara pranidhana (dedication of all activity to higher divine forces).

3 Asana – 'postures'. Physical exercises prepare the body for sitting in meditation.

4 Pranayama – 'breath control'. Breathing techniques control and redirect the life-force around the body.

5 Pratyahara – 'sense control'. This focuses on reaching an understanding of how the mind works so that unwanted tendencies can be weeded out.

6 Dharana – 'concentration'. This is the preparation of the mind for meditation.

7 Dhyana – 'meditation': the ultimate goal.

8 Samadhi – 'union': the fruit of all the preceding practices.

meditation

Although raja yoga may seem rigid and austere to Westerners, there is logic in it. When all the steps are followed, meditation comes more easily. If you simply decide you are going to meditate and sit down and expect your body, emotions and mind to comply, you will be very lucky if they do so for more than a few minutes, if that.

The mind is a wonderfully restless, inventive faculty and cannot be reined in without great understanding or cunning. Good meditation techniques offer the mind something to do to keep it occupied or active in a tight focus that enables us to experience ourselves in the gaps between thoughts. The more we experience the gap between the thoughts, the more relaxed our bodies become and the more clearly we can see how our thoughts shape our lives.

Keeping the balance

To be effective and long-lasting, chakra healing needs to keep in view a unified picture of the system. The chakras are dynamic energies that represent the whole person, so chakra healing must also deal with the whole person.

The dynamics of harmony

The chakra system is complex and interrelated – each chakra, both major and minor, can be thought of as a cog in a machine. A change in the movement of one will create changes throughout the whole structure. There will be an efficient flow of energy when all parts are locked together in their activity, working harmoniously together. If one chakra becomes damaged or has its normal range of activity restricted this inevitably puts strain on its closest neighbours, which will also begin to suffer.

A chakra that becomes unbalanced has become stuck at an inappropriate level of activity. It is either working with insufficient energy for its task, or it is working too hard. In either circumstance the other chakras will have to compensate by changing their levels of energy. This means that the system as a whole will be working at one level when it may be more appropriate for it to function at another.

overall balance

The chakra system, like the rest of the body, responds to the circumstances of its environment. In some circumstances a particular chakra will tend to take a larger role, but it should still operate in a balanced way within the normal working parameters of the system.

Different jobs and lifestyles need special areas of expertise, and the dynamics of the chakras need to adjust accordingly. For example, a singer will naturally need to have an especially active throat chakra to keep the voice healthy. The heart chakra, too, will need to have plenty of energy to foster a depth of feeling,

△ All parts of the chakra system respond to changes in every other part. Releasing stress from one area will help to relax the whole system, making everything run better.

empathy and personal involvement in the work. In such a person, an observer who was sensitive to energy fields would see a lot of activity at those two centres. Only if too much energy is focused in one area will problems start to show, beginning in

▷ False equilibrium is where a temporary stability has been achieved. However, even a slight change will bring about a breakdown in order. When this occurs in the chakra system, illness may develop.

◁ Crystals, with their brilliant colour and unique structures, are very effective in helping to bring balance to the chakra system.

those places where there are natural weaknesses as a result of past stresses or current overuse.

The chakra system will change gear with a change of activity. Meditation requires a different sort of energy from cooking the dinner; playing a musical instrument requires different skills from listening to an orchestra; escaping from a stressful situation uses different resources from gazing at a serene sunset. Problems arise when, through stress of one sort or another, the chakra system fails to change gear and becomes stuck in a single mode of functioning.

Throughout our lives, stresses of many sorts accumulate in all our systems, from physical to spiritual. These stresses can be like grains of sand or grit that create a little roughness in the workings of our chakra cogs, or they can be like a spanner that seriously throws the whole mechanism out of alignment.

considerations

In learning about the symptoms of chakra imbalance presented here and in other books, it is important not to become disheartened about your own state of energetic health. At one time or another most of us will experience extremes of under- and overactivity in all our chakras. It is more important to recognize the common tendencies that are repeated through our lives. Once the most prevalent states are known they can be worked on and necessary alterations can begin to be made.

A physical balancing technique can have a beneficial effect on an emotional chakra stress, and a mental visualization exercise can allow positive change to happen at a physical, everyday level. So use those techniques and exercises that you find most helpful and that fit most comfortably into your everyday life.

Many traditional systems of spiritual development take into account the differences between individuals and their lifestyles, providing different sorts of practices to suit their needs. Today we are lucky in having a wide range of chakra balancing techniques from all around the world. Even the most hectic lifestyle can accommodate sufficient practices to help to reduce the burden of stress that overloads the chakra system and will eventually lead to health problems. The only thing that is needed is for us to set aside a little time dedicated to our own repair. This is largely a process of developing a habit. At first, all sorts of

distractions may arise until the routine becomes a natural part of our day. Most balancing practices need a little effort and dedication in the beginning – not only to bring in a new routine, but also because we are beginning to make changes in our energy systems.

Correcting a false equilibrium requires skill and patience. Like a tightrope walker who has been working for years with a pole that has a large weight at one end and nothing on the other end, we adjust to the weight of stress we have accumulated in our lives in order to continue as best we can. Removing all the stress in one go may seem to be the best solution but, like the tightrope walker, we need to familiarize ourselves gradually with the new state of balance at each step. If not, the risk increases that we will feel less secure than we did when we had all the stress.

Like kicking an addictive habit, the biggest problem most of us face is that habitual patterns of behaviour feel comfortable and part of our true personality. Working with a balancing system that focuses on the different levels of body, mind and emotion can be helpful in maintaining an even development of chakra healing. Traditional methods like yoga, Tai Chi and Chi Kung all have outer, physical activities that release stress from the body. They also have mental techniques that involve meditative states, or visualizations that help to clarify the subtle energies of the mind and emotions. It is important to pay attention to all these different levels of practice. For example, it will be of limited value to have a body that is supple and toned if you are still emotionally insecure or stuck in some past trauma.

Contemporary techniques, such as crystal therapy, colour therapy and flower essences, can help to remove specific stresses in chakra centres as well as bringing the whole body into a better state of balance.

Maintaining harmony

The more our energy systems are brought into harmonious balance, the easier it is to maintain that balance. An old, worn engine is so full of leaks and random rattles it is hard to notice any new disturbing sounds of dysfunction. With a engine that runs smoothly the slightest drop in efficiency is noticed immediately and can be put right.

exploration

Until some of the stresses can be removed from the chakra system, every one of us will be so busy maintaining our false sense of equilibrium that there will be little spare energy for exploring individual potential. Learning to expand into life is what the evolution of the chakras from base to crown shows us. Getting stuck in any one area narrows our perspective on life. Rather than being able to explore the world with seven different lenses, each with its own special abilities to filter and magnify our experience, we can find ourselves with a single obsessive keyhole through which we squint in an eager attempt to find out what

▽ When all chakras are free of stress the individual also becomes free to move in whatever direction is of most benefit.

△ A balanced and sensitive chakra system will recognize any upset and be able to restore proper functioning automatically.

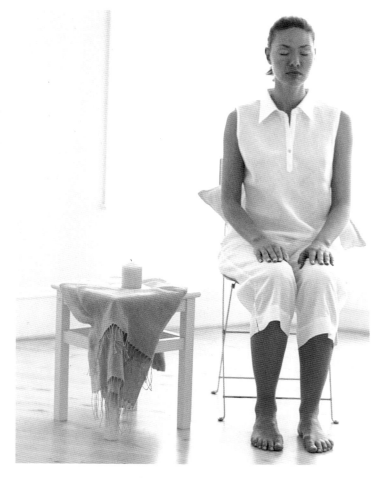

▷ Taking time to balance your chakras is giving time back to your life, so that you will be better able to achieve your goals.

our life has really been missing. In reality we have all the keys to all the doorways within us at all times. The chakra system is much more than a line of coloured spheres reflecting our bodies' other functions.

opening doorways

As the ancient yogis of India and Tibet discovered, clearing the chakras of the build-up of debris allows life to be entirely transformed – not by escapist fantasy but by the clear, honest experience of reality as satisfying and nourishing. In this state each chakra becomes a translucent doorway allowing a free flow of universal energies in and out of the body. False boundaries and a frustrating sense of separation dissolve because it was only the stress and imbalance that created them in the first place.

The chakra system always works in two apparently opposite directions. From the base chakra upwards there is an increasing experience of expansion, from the focus and solidity of physical matter, through experience of sensation, personal power, relationship with the rest of the world, communication, understanding and finally integration on all levels at the crown chakra.

Simultaneously there is a flow of energy towards the grounding solidity of physical reality, from the timeless and directionless unity of the crown chakra through the defining vision of the brow, the form-giving quality of naming, a stabilizing relationship between the self and the world, learning how to control one's power, exploring the senses and finally being able to mould and create the raw material of the world – the practical energy of the base chakra.

In the same way that the individual chakras reflect and balance one another,

▷ Once you are familiar with the sensation of balanced chakras it becomes easier to enjoy the new freedom it brings.

each relying on the others in equal measure, the two opposing tides are part of one process, where expansion into the spiritual realms can be effective only with a reciprocal exploration into the universe of matter.

Whether you consider yourself to be a spiritual or a pragmatic person, whether your goals in life are based on material success or spiritual fulfilment, whether you are a steel-worker or an aromatherapist, a teenager or an octagenarian, learning to heal and work with the chakras is one of the most effective routes to wellbeing.

Salute to the sun

The salute to the sun is a traditional sequence of exercises from hatha yoga that systematically activates the energies of each chakra. Practised regularly, it can help to energize each chakra and then keep them all in balance. Traditionally this sequence is practised as the sun rises.

1 Begin by deep breathing for two to five minutes.

▽ 2 Stand upright and bring your palms together in the traditional 'prayer' position at the centre of your chest. Breathe in and out. Become aware of the distribution of weight on each foot.

△ 3 On the next inbreath, stretch your arms up above your head and lean back slightly from your waist, looking up towards your hands.

YOGA EXPERTISE
Don't worry if when looking at the series of postures in the salute to the sun, you realize you cannot copy them exactly. Just do the best that you can, your chakras will still respond to the sequence, even if your yoga is not advanced.

△ 4 On the outbreath, straighten and bend forward from the hips with the intention of reaching the floor with your hands. (Don't worry if you have to bend your knees.) Place your hands on the floor, your fingertips in line with your toes.

△ 5 On the next inbreath, send your right leg back so that your knee touches the floor and your toes are tucked under. Look upwards. If you have to shuffle your hands and feet around for stability, that is fine.

▽ 6 On the outbreath, lower your head and send your left leg back behind you to join the right leg. Allow your bottom to lift upwards away from the floor. Let your head drop down between your arms. Breathe in.

◁ 7 On the next outbreath, lower yourself, bending your knees so they touch the floor. Continue lowering your chest to the floor, then your chin. (Your hips stay off the floor.)

◁ 8 On the next inbreath, lower your hips, flatten your toes and lift your head and chest up, straightening your arms. Look upwards.

▽ 9 On the next outbreath, tuck your toes back under, pressing on your hands. Lift your hips so they are the highest part of you off the floor, and lower your head.

△ 10 Breathing in (lifting your chin so your knee doesn't catch it), bring your right foot forwards between your hands. (You may have to shuffle your body around a bit to do this.) Look upwards.

▽ 11 Breathing out, bring your left foot up to join your left, creating a forward bend. Keep your head low.

12 The next inbreath takes you upright again, leaning back slightly, with your hands above your head, looking upwards.

△ 13 On the outbreath, lower your arms. Repeat, sending the left leg back first (in step 6). Gradually build up the number of rounds from two to four, then six, and so on. Try to coordinate your breathing as you go. It will eventually come naturally as the postures themselves create an ebbing and flowing of the breath.

Space Clearing

The principles of space clearing are based on the belief that all locations have a spirit of place. When acknowledged and cared for, this spirit can have a positive effect on the place and all those who occupy it. But environments can also be adversely affected by the build-up of negative vibrations. They therefore require regular clearing. Just as physical housework clears dust and debris from a home, so spiritual housework lifts the atmosphere of a place to a higher level of peace.

In early times it was recognized that the home was a very spiritual place. The Romans believed that each home had its resident *genius loci* – the individual deity of the place. The same idea occurs in ancient Chinese and Indian thought, and similar spiritual belief systems can be found all over the world and in all ages. In modern society, a growing awareness of the importance of sacred space is now rekindling this need to sanctify our homes and environments. Space clearing is an important factor in our rediscovery of the spiritual aspect of life.

This section explores different cultural approaches to space clearing and explains how we can keep our own environments clean and clear, and benefit from an atmosphere full of harmony, clarity and peace.

The ancient art of space clearing

Every human spirit requires peace and quiet, and home is the place, above all others, where we should be able to shut out the bustle and anxieties of the world. The spiritual integrity of the home was revered by our ancestors, and the rituals they observed to protect and maintain it hold valuable lessons for the modern world.

Spirit of place

It is one of the primal urges of animal life to seek out a location in which it can feel safe: a lair, a nest, a den, a shell, a tree or a cave. Human beings share that basic impulse with other animals, and we need to feel instinctively that we are secure.

We cannot be completely at ease in our surroundings unless our spiritual side is also comfortable. The human species may be technologically advanced, but within us there still resides a vestige of that mysterious 'sixth sense' that is possessed by all creatures. We can find many instances of its influence in the natural world. There are trees, seemingly indistinguishable from others, in which no birds will nest. There are corners of a house where no cat will linger to sleep. We humans, too, receive and react to this kind of subliminal input, and throughout history there have been those who have understood this and have recognized its importance to our wellbeing.

We choose our carpets because we like their colour or pattern, but the traditional designs from the Far East, Turkey and North Africa were woven to attract good fortune and domestic tranquillity to the places in which they were laid. This tradition has roots in even older cultures: the mosaic floors of the Romans and Greeks served the same purpose. We hang pictures on our walls because we like to look at them, but their origin also lies with the murals of ancient civilizations. For the Egyptians, Minoans, Greeks and Romans, wall paintings often served a spiritual purpose in placating and invoking local deities, who would thus be more inclined to favour the dwelling with their blessing. Further back still, this kind of spiritually enhancing decoration can be seen in the prehistoric cave paintings of France and Spain and their more recent equivalents executed by the Bushmen of Africa and the native Australians.

All these devices were originally intended to drive away bad vibrations or evil spirits and attract good, harmonious ones in their place. They were for clearing negativity and encouraging good vibrations. They were for space clearing.

psychology and intuition

As humankind grew more scientific in outlook, society tended to dismiss the ways of our forebears, but now there is a growing realization that we should not divorce ourselves from our ancient spiritual heritage. An appreciation of the power of the old ways is beginning to return.

All the traditional belief systems of the world include the principle of space clearing. The tribal witch doctor is conducting space clearing when he dresses

△ We need the comfort and security of a place where we feel at home, and instinctively surround ourselves with things we hold dear.

▷ When our home environment is balanced and harmonious, it is easier to relax and unwind there.

▷ **The simplest of altars – such as an arrangement of beautiful natural objects on a windowsill – can restore the spirit.**

in a mask and feathers and dances with rattles inside a hut. Whatever we may think of his particular method, it is a means to an end, and that end is to make the occupants of the dwelling feel good about their home because something magical has been done to drive away evil spirits. We may prefer to speak of negative vibrations rather than evil spirits, but the principle remains the same.

Psychology relates to the psyche, the deepest subconscious level of the mind. If we are not feeling comfortable at a subconscious level, we may not be able to put that feeling into words; we may not even realize that we are feeling ill at ease. Nevertheless, our ability to be happy and relaxed will be subtly impaired, and our whole outlook on life is liable to be adversely affected.

Our perception of the atmosphere of a space operates at a subconscious level. The positive changes felt by those who ask the witch doctor to make a house call are certainly psychological, but this does not mean the benefits are any less real.

creating positive space

Space clearing is the art of making a home or workplace feel good as an environment in which we can live at ease and go about our daily lives. Some people, thinking in purely material terms, may believe that if they spend enough money on a house they will automatically be happy there, but experience often shows this is not the case. Most of us have visited what seems like a 'perfect' residence that has been expensively decorated, only to feel somehow alienated and uncomfortable. Our psyche, or unconscious sixth sense, is at work again.

There is no doubt that some places feel cold or watchful while others, while they may not seem different in any obvious way, make us feel warm and welcome. Space clearing is the art of introducing the change from one condition to the other. It can be carried out wherever it is needed – in a

house, flat, room, office or even in a factory or workshop. It can be extended to the garden and to places we stay in temporarily when travelling, such as hotel rooms.

Today, we often hear of problems such as 'sick building syndrome' and 'geopathic stress'. These terms are used to describe the dysfunctional energy in a place that seems to have an adverse effect on the people who live or work there. Multinational companies are fully aware of the existence of these phenomena, and employ Feng Shui experts or architects cognizant with sacred geometry to correct the problem and restore the free flow of their businesses.

Even though techniques like space clearing may at times have been dismissed by the 'scientific' way of thought and pushed into the background of modern belief, our need for such traditions has never entirely gone away, and our lives and humanity have been impoverished whenever they are not acknowledged. Such things may be categorized by some people as superstitious magic and therefore not worthy of serious

▷ **Fresh flowers, plants and crystals not only bring interest and colour into an interior, but lift the atmosphere with their natural energy.**

consideration – but of how much value is a life that has no room for magic in it? It has often been said that it is impossible to draw a line between magic and psychology. Perhaps if we were to allow more magic into our lives, there would be less need for psychologists to heal our troubled minds.

The power of the spirits

As well as acknowledging the nameless spirits that sanctified and safeguarded a place, many traditions sought the protection and goodwill of the major deities. Symbols and depictions of gods and goddesses, and acts of devotion at the domestic altar, were a means of engaging in communication with the spiritual world. They honoured the powers that it was hoped would in turn confer blessings on the home and bring good fortune to its inhabitants. Some deities came to be particularly associated with the protection of the home, such as the Roman god Janus, who guarded the entrances, and the goddess Vesta, who presided over the hearth at the centre of domestic life.

Prayers are one method of focusing the thoughts in order to engage with the higher realm of the spirits, but there are other ways

▽ Prayer has been used in many cultures to engage with a higher realm of consciousness.

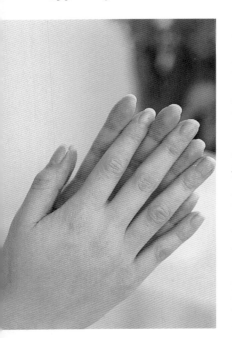

that this state of mind can be approached, such as meditation and the use of rituals and invocations. Specific scents and sounds can also serve to point the mind in a particular spiritual direction.

invoking the spirits

The higher, or astral, realms are usually described in terms that mirror human existence, because that is the only way in which we can comprehend them. It is natural that the energies of our lives should have been personified in the forms of gods and goddesses and various other spiritual entities, each of which embodies particular characteristics. In the ancient Greek pantheon, for instance, Aphrodite is recognized as the goddess of love, while Hermes is the patron of messages, healing and teaching.

Every astral entity has its own area of 'speciality', and we can put ourselves in tune with that particular energy by meditating upon the astral form that personifies it. By communing with these spiritual powers we can enhance the side of our own nature that corresponds to their individual energies. This is the basis of invoking the power of the spirits. By so doing, we allow the subconscious mind to achieve communion with astral forms.

Every culture has produced its own names and ideas for picturing these entities, sometimes with sub-cultural variations. As just one example, the Anglo-Saxon sky-god Tiw (from whose name we derive Tuesday – 'Tiw's day') can be identified with Tyr in Scandinavia, Tiwaz in northern Europe, Ziu in Germany and Dyaus in ancient India. The Sanskrit name Dyaus is related to the Aryan Djevs ('sky' or 'light') or Deivos, and to the Greek Zeus and the Roman Jove. Likewise, the spiritual embodiment of the love-energy appears in many pantheons, with many names other than Aphrodite or Venus, and is always represented by a female form. The great psychologist Carl Jung

△ Aphrodite, the Ancient Greek goddess of love, can be invoked if you are seeking aid with an issue concerning love or the emotions. She and the other ancient gods are aspects of archetypes that are, in a sense, patterns for self-change.

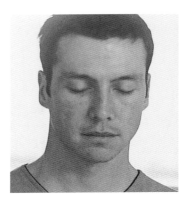

△ Everyone can benefit from taking a few moments to themselves to calm and focus their thoughts and feelings.

PROTECTIVE DEITIES

You can dedicate an altar to a protective deity such as those listed here, at any time when protection or blessings are required in your life.

Shiva, the Hindu Lord of the Cosmic Dance, and a powerful protective force for justice, healing and strength. When invoking Shiva, always light a candle to honour his presence. Serpents, elephants and the white bull are sacred to him. Use white candles on his altar.

Kali, the Hindu triple goddess and consort to Lord Shiva. She protects from all negative forces, and helps to reveal the truth. Marigolds are her sacred flower. Offerings to Kali of pleasing foods should be displayed on fresh green leaves. Use black candles on her altar.

Anubis, the ancient Egyptian jackal-headed deity and protector from psychic forces. Burn myrrh grains in a charcoal burner before a statue of Anubis or pictures of the jackal. Use indigo blue candles on his altar.

Innana, the Sumerian goddess of victory. She is highly venerated as the defender of peace, justice and the law. Lion and dog iconography can be placed on her altar, together with a wand strung with ribbons that is twirled when calling to her. Use red candles on her altar.

Hecate, the Greek goddess of the moon. She wards off evil and purifies and transforms negativity. A woven willow basket, fairy icons, dogs and frogs can be displayed. Use black candles on this altar.

Isis, the ancient Egyptian lunar goddess and protector of women. She brings healing and protection to the home. You can display a basket of figs, a small bowl of cow's milk, and hold a piece of carnelian or lapis lazuli while invoking her. Use turquoise blue candles in her honour.

called such deities archetypal beings. The power of the spirits is very real, not least because it has been reinforced by belief through the generations. By communing with them we enhance the side of our nature that corresponds with their energies.

▷ Creating time to meditate will allow your subconscious to commune with higher realms.

△ Lord Shiva, the Hindu creator deity, can be called upon whenever you are seeking transformation or clarity.

The folklore tradition

Many ancient space clearing ceremonies have persisted into the modern age as part of the folklore tradition. The spiritual beliefs and practices of our forebears gave rise to numerous local rituals that play an important part in the continuity of the community.

traditional forms of space clearing

'Beating the bounds' is an old custom whose original purpose was the spiritual protection of the community. The village boundary line was beaten with birch wands to ensure the safekeeping of the village and establish a magical barrier around it so that no evil spirit could enter. In later times, the ceremony also had a secondary purpose: to teach the young boys who accompanied the parish officers around the village to remember the position of the boundary, as a way of passing on knowledge and averting future disputes about land ownership.

In the Basque villages of the Pyrenees, ancient carnival rites have a similar purpose. The men of Ituren and Zubieta, for example, wearing dunces' caps and sheepskins with huge sheeps' bells tied on their backs, process from house to house ringing the bells to protect the inhabitants and their flocks from evil spirits.

A great many folklore traditions surround the Green Man, who embodies the vegetative energy of nature. He is the ancient legendary guardian of woodlands, forests and trees, who keeps out of his territory any threatening ogres or other evil spirits. Images of the Green Man, with his head emerging from foliage, have been found all over the world, but he is most closely associated with northern Europe. In England he is personified as 'Jack-in-the-Green', a leaf-draped character associated with traditional May Day revels, such as the chimney sweeps' festival still held in Rochester, Kent. His prancing about was held to ward off evil from every house he passed, and from the township in general.

In Scotland and northern England, the old Norse custom of 'first-footing' is still observed. A dark-haired man must be the first person to step across the threshold of a house immediately after midnight on the last day of the year. This is thought to bring luck to the household during the year

△ Wood from the birch tree was traditionally used in cleansing rituals, to expel evil spirits and to drive out the spirits of the old year.

▽ Garlic is well known to have a cleansing effect on the body, but in the old days it was also believed to drive out inner demons.

▽ The green, or 'wild', men of Europe signified the uncontrollable energy of nature, and their dances were often part of feasts and festivals.

through the gap between them in order to cleanse them of the influence of any evil spirits. (As a bonus, the process also got rid of cattle ticks.) The villagers would then throw a party and jump over the bonfires themselves to benefit from the magical cleansing process and bring good luck. The tradition of 'leaping the Beltane fires' has never entirely died out, and is still enacted by Wiccans and other pagans.

Throughout the world, the warmth and atmosphere of a friendly fire has always been recognized as a 'magical aura' of safety and protection from the powers of darkness. This may be why chimney sweeps and unglamorous lumps of coal have inherited their reputation as bringers of good luck.

A need to feel that some kind of spiritual energy safeguards the places we enter has always been present in the background of our society. Even though most people are unaware of the origins of the traditions they observe or participate in, the old customs thrive because they are still relevant to our spiritual life in the modern age.

▽ **Many pagan festivals were associated with light, as the bringer of life, and candles and other flames are still used in modern ritual.**

△ **The warmth of an open fire in winter conjures light, life and comfort from the cold. It is also a link with the fire festivals of the past.**

ahead, in other words, to clear its space of 'negative energies'. Very often, the first-footer brings with him a lump of coal, intended as a magical token to ensure that there will always be the warmth of a friendly fire in the home. The first-footer may also bring some bread and some salt, symbolizing a plentiful supply of food. He must not carry any weapons or sharp tools, and no one in the house must speak until the coal has been placed by the fire and the first-footer has poured a glass of whisky and toasted the head of the household.

clearing personal space

Another New Year folk tradition is wassailing, the giving of a salutation for good health and wellbeing with a cup of spiced ale, to clear away any evil spirits residing within a person's body. The term 'wassail' comes from the Anglo-Saxon *wæs hæl*, meaning 'be whole' or 'be well'. There is a story of this traditional personal space clearing toast being offered to Vortigern, last Roman king of Britain, in the sixth century.

The night of 30 April to 1 May constitutes the pagan festival of Beltane. This is a fire festival whose name is Gaelic for 'blaze-kindling'. It used to be the custom for the pagan priesthood to light two fires, and for the villagers' cattle to be driven

Wisdom for the modern age

The principles of keeping spaces clear remain the same today as they have always been. Where once the services of the witch doctor or tribal shaman were employed, it is now the Feng Shui consultant, the dowser, the earth healer or the psychic whom we consult. Some of the most modern and sophisticated companies employ space clearing professionals to alleviate or avoid problems in the workplace.

The Feng Shui practitioner might, for example, advise on an auspicious placement of the furniture, or place a Bagua mirror in a strategic position to deflect negativity.

The services of the modern dowser may reveal underground watercourses, electrical interference or areas of geopathic stress, and the dowser may suggest ways to divert the obtrusive energy around the building.

The psychic may point to restless energy fields or other psychic interference affecting the environment, and offer protective solutions. Experiments in the US and other parts of the world to clear environmental pollution using earth acupuncture and assistance from elemental spirits have proved to be very successful. It may be tempting to scoff at unseen forces, but if such methods

work, why not use them? Today, earth healers worldwide acknowledge and work with energy lines, just as Australian aborigines and other tribal cultures have done for thousands of years.

When considering why a space needs clearing, it is relevant to take into account unseen factors that can be the root cause of any problems the occupants are experiencing, such as geopathic stress or sick building syndrome, especially if the symptoms persist. The detection and correction of both conditions is best achieved by a professional dowser or architectural expert.

symptoms of geopathic stress

Geopathic stress is caused by disruption of the natural energy lines of the earth's grid system. These lines can be disturbed by any human activity, such as erecting buildings, damming rivers, or lowering water tables. Areas affected by geopathic stress can induce fatigue, depression, immune disorders,

◁ Traditional ways of using the land, such as these rice terraces carved from the hillsides, work in harmony with natural forces.

▽ When a modern metropolis is built without regard for the natural environment, it becomes a breeding ground for pollution and stress.

▷ Hectic lives in busy cities leave little time for the calm and quiet repose that is needed for health and wellbeing.

headaches, irritability, behavioural problems and insomnia. An environment affected by geopathic stress will affect all its occupants but not necessarily all in the same way. A general malaise hangs over the area, and its presence is often uncomfortably endured. These days dowsers are regularly called in to divert geopathic stress by using copper rods. Copper is a good conductor of energy, and by placing rods vertically in the earth the dowser can re-route the disturbed energy around an affected property.

sick building syndrome

This is another form of stress experienced in modern society. Its specific causes remain unconfirmed, but contributory factors seem to include external pollutants such as car fumes entering a poorly ventilated area, chemicals from indoor appliances and furniture, such as the fireproofing on upholstery and carpets, chemicals from office equipment such as photocopiers, and modern cleaning agents, as well as biological contamination from bacteria and moulds. Generally, lack of clean air, poor ventilation and the aggravating qualities of several chemical compounds when put together can lead to symptoms such as headaches, dry coughs, itchy skin, dizziness, poor concentration and fatigue.

The architecture of previous ages considered its surroundings and took a pride in its shape and form; our ancestors lived in homes made completely of natural materials. Modern building materials are treated with a cocktail of chemicals. Homes and workplaces are filled with fire-retardant chemicals, wall-insulation chemicals and cleaning fumes, and we also have to contend with external factors from the surrounding environment, such as emissions from factories, garages and agricultural farmland. Treatment for sick building syndrome is simple – it involves providing adequate, clean ventilation and removing the irritant factors as far as possible.

the modern world

In the past, our primary concerns would have been for the success of our crops, the welfare of our herds and our personal health and security. Today, in the developed world, our basic needs are largely catered for by the structures of society, so that our concerns now mainly focus upon success and achievement, prosperity and happiness. We live in a fast-paced consumer society, where more and more gadgets are provided for our use and entertainment, but it becomes increasingly difficult to find peace and quiet.

A century ago, most people were living far closer to nature. Even for those who lived in cities, travel was at a slower pace, often that of the horse or the bicycle, and everyone's day-to-day existence involved much more physical exercise and fresh air. Though life was undoubtedly more strenuous in many ways, many of the stresses we have to contend with in today's world were unknown.

As we fill our homes and workplaces with more and more modern technology, it is important that we do not become enslaved by it. We need to remain aware of the many different ways in which it can adversely affect the environment in which we live or work.

▽ Modern technology means that we can now travel the world with ease, but it also means increased noise and loss of green places.

Harmonious living

It is difficult to reach a state of inner peace if our material surroundings are in turmoil, filled with clutter and riotous colour. In our inner being there is often another kind of clutter – mental and spiritual. If we can learn to encourage harmony in our daily lives, we will have taken a big inner step away from the oppressive weight of riotous environments, which scream for attention and produce spiritual negativity.

The location of space

Where is space? The initial answer might be: "Space is all around us – everywhere." This, though, is not really true. The space that surrounds us is normally full of bits and pieces. Actually we tend to dislike space, although we may never have stopped to think about it. If there is a big space on a wall, we are likely to hang a picture there. If there is a large empty floor space, we put a rug on it. If there is an empty shelf available, we stand ornaments or books on it. An empty patch of garden can have a shrub planted in it. Most human beings are compulsive fillers of space.

The state of mind that produces this reflex action to 'put something there' has been brought about by the steady increase in materialistic consumerism. We have become indoctrinated into the belief that success – and therefore 'good' – equals possessions; that the greatest success equals the greatest number of possessions; and that failure – and therefore 'bad' – equals lack of possessions. This is a thought-pattern that has spread throughout the developed world.

▽ **The sensitive placement of objects in a room can create areas or oases of calm in which to relax and unwind.**

finding space

Eastern thought has supplied the opposite philosophy: success lies not in possessions or material wealth but in freedom from their grip. This is an idea diametrically opposed to the driving force of a capitalist consumer society. The philosophy of Zen Buddhism

△ **Uncluttered rooms decorated with simple themes of shape and colour can offer the senses both space and clarity.**

is reductionism, which has a weak echo in Western society in the saying (more usually applied to fashion) 'less is more'.

As an example of the difference between these two philosophical outlooks, compare a well-stocked flower garden with a Zen garden. Your own familiar garden may be filled with plants, a lawn, paths, seats, ornaments and a patio. A Zen garden, on the other hand, might consist of nothing more than a layer of gravel or beach shingle, with a single large boulder standing in the middle. Rather than filling the area with many objects and colours, the Zen idea is to draw attention to a defined space by virtue of the simple surfaces and textures contained within it. The beautiful flower garden encourages us to focus upon its contents: in contrast, in a Zen garden we are encouraged to become aware of the location of space.

LOOKING AT SPACE

This mental exercise helps to train the mind to become aware of space rather than the objects that fill it.

When you look in any direction, try to make yourself aware of the spaces between objects, rather than the objects themselves, as though what you were seeing was a picture on paper and you were able to use scissors to cut out the objects themselves, leaving only the spaces between them. This exercise can expand the perceptions and help you to escape from preoccupations with the material world.

△ The simplicity of the Zen garden leads the mind to concentrate on the space that is defined by it, rather than an accumulation of objects.

This is not just a design concept. Coming to terms with it involves a fundamental alteration, even a reversal, of an entrenched point of view. By developing our awareness of the importance of space, we can actually nurture and improve the space in our own homes, rather than trying to fill it with displays of possessions and material trophies. By so doing, we can actually become aware of the location of space, and begin to appreciate the space that really surrounds us and in which we live.

Gaining such an awareness of the location of space is an important step in learning how to evaluate its character, and

◁ A garden may be well cared-for and full of beautiful flowers, yet too cluttered and busy to inspire us with a sense of tranquillity.

in sensing the ebbing and flowing tensions of the subtle webs of energy that course through it. If we can extend our awareness, our subtle psychic 'feelers', into the spatial areas we inhabit and move within, we will be much better equipped to deal decisively and positively with any negative or oppressive vibrations (energies) we may find attempting to encroach upon us and undermine our emotional balance.

An awareness of space can help us to bring ourselves out of the habit of valuing possessions too highly. Preoccupation with the ownership of objects sets us at the centre of a cluttered world which limits us spiritually. To leave those limitations behind, we need to learn to value the release of such ties and anchors. In general, we too easily come to value objects for their own sake and not for what they represent. Once we can achieve freedom from the domination of material possessions, we can begin to set our spirit soaring.

The influence of colour

In any environment, colour can have a significant effect on the overall atmosphere. Hot colours will raise the energy levels of people in a room, and cool colours will calm and soothe. Confusion with colours can lead to confusion within human energy patterns. When you spend time in such a space, it can lead you to ask "Do I relax here or do I move about?" Therefore, when you are considering the atmosphere you wish to create in an interior, the first step is to decide whether you want the area to be a stimulating or a relaxing space.

Colours at the red/yellow end of the visible spectrum are stimulating, and colours at the blue/green end are soothing and relaxing. It becomes clear that to consider putting shades of red and yellow into a hyperactive child's bedroom would not have a calming effect upon his or her psyche. Conversely, if you have a lazy child who hates to get up in the mornings, a bright and vibrant colour scheme could be a very good choice. The same applies to any living

▽ A vibrantly coloured room may inspire you with the energy and confidence to face the day.

△ Water features bring the sounds of nature into a room and have a soothing effect.

or working space. Before you choose a colour for a room you should consider the characters of the people using it and the purpose or focus of the room. For example, a room where a lot of intellectual work needs to be done – such as a study or office – would benefit from having a yellow colour scheme. The bathroom, where you would wish to relax and unwind, could be decorated with colours from the blue/green end of the spectrum.

COLOUR EFFECTS
Within the broad division of the spectrum, each colour evokes specific responses.

STIMULATING COLOURS
Red: evokes confidence, power, strength and purpose.
Orange: invites brightness and joy, creativity and a positive attitude.
Sunshine yellow: encourages mental activity, stimulates thought, invigorates the nervous system.
Pink: as a blend of red and white, it holds the passions of red in check, encourages friendship, harmony in relationships and warm feelings.

SOOTHING COLOURS
All shades of blue: cooling and calming to the spirit and to over-emotional people, but can be unfeeling and cold if over-used.
Violet and mauve: warmer than blue because they contain a certain amount of red, these colours blend activity with rest and work well in living and dining areas.
Green: as the colour of nature, green is the harmonizer of the heart, helping us to be ourselves and to feel at peace with our surroundings.
Pastel colours: gentle on the eye and perfect for balancing any bright and colourful decorative objects.

◁ A blue interior can be very calming and soothing to the spirit. Splashes of orange and red prevent the overall effect becoming too cool.

include pink, mauve, red, yellow or orange. Moving water helps to encourage their activity and dynamism in expression. They would not be suited to cold blues.

colour and the elements

Each of the four traditional elements – Air, Fire, Water and Earth – has a colour associated with it that is balanced by a complementary colour. Air is represented by yellow, which is balanced by violet. Fire is represented by red, which is balanced by green. Water is represented by blue and balanced by orange, and Earth is represented by shades of green, balanced by shades of red. From this it becomes clear that a room can contain a complementary clash of colours that will still have the same ideological focus. For example, a fiery room can include orange and blue and still be a room that conjures activity and creativity.

When we want to use colour to good effect, a little research can go a long, long way to creating the desired balance at home or at work, so that our surroundings don't clash with who we are.

▽ Take time to consider what results you are trying to achieve in your rooms and spaces.

colour and Ayurveda

Ayurveda is the ancient Indian science of life. It acknowledges three basic personality types, or *doshas*: fiery, airy, and watery. Everyone is a mixture of the three types, but in most people one quality is dominant. If the dominant *dosha* becomes too strong it can lead to problems, so it needs to be brought back into balance.

In Ayurvedic terms a fiery personality (*pitta*) is a blend of water and fire. This active, creative and sometimes dominant personality benefits from the blue/green end of the spectrum. Someone of this type finds it hard to relax. Therefore indoor fountains, plant displays, natural furniture and an appropriate blue/green colour on the walls will help to calm and balance the fire. With too much stimulation, this personality will be unable to unwind and relax. A fiery personality who occupies a red room is likely to become a bad-tempered workaholic.

The airy personality (*vata*) benefits most from surroundings decorated in warm and earthy colours such as terracotta, sand yellow, creams and warm browns. These colours help to earth this particular personality type, which has a tendency to drift off and perhaps not achieve everything it sets out to do. Full of ideas, the airy personality often has several projects on the

go at the same time, never quite getting the time to finish them off. The airy personality benefits from an environment that features rocks and stone, natural earthy fabrics such as canvas and cotton, and objects that evoke safety and warmth, such as rugs and cushions, with gentle, subdued lighting. This personality would find it hard to live with the brighter yellows.

The watery personality (*kapha*) is a blend of water and earth. These people are emotional by nature, very sensitive but with a tendency to be inactive or insecure. Ideal colours for the watery personality type

A balanced interior

Human beings are governed and motivated in all things by their own psychology – the inner workings of the mind, and particularly the unconscious mind. Since each person's mind is unique and has been formed by different events, thoughts, experiences and genetic sequences, no two people have identical feelings, tastes or preferences. Therefore the ideal surroundings for one person may be considered jarring, tasteless, or lacking in harmony by another.

It is impossible to say that there is a single correct standard for everyone to adopt in order to ensure that a room, or their whole home, will be perfectly balanced for all those who live in it or visit it. There are, however, some general ideas and suggestions that individuals can adapt and adjust with intelligence and perception to suit their own unique needs.

These obvious but simple measures can affect us deeply at an unconscious level. When we spend time in rooms that have personal meaning, awareness of space and ease of access, we experience uplifted spirits, contentment, relaxation and the enhancement of inner tranquillity and peace. If we plan our interiors with sensitivity and care, we can create the states of mind we desire by the way we orient and theme our home or workspace.

placement and movement

Some guidelines for the planning process are fairly obvious and universal. For example, it is important not to have a lot of clutter or items of furniture placed too near the access points of a room. When you are planning the layout of any room, you need to concentrate on the room's function and how people are going to use the space. In the case of a bedroom or an office, this may be a fairly simple task, but your living rooms may need to fulfil a range of functions, with members of the family pursuing different activities in the same space.

You can enjoy finding the best-looking placements for decorations and furniture, but do not lose sight of the use to be made of them and the access that will be needed.

△ The careful placement of a few sensitively arranged items can provide a stunning focal point in a room.

◁ Choose furniture that fits harmoniously into its surroundings; a symmetrical arrangement can create a satisfying visual balance.

For example, a bookcase may look lovely beside the door, but it will not be such a good position if someone entering the room in a hurry throws the door open against a person who is looking for a book. Allow for the opening of cupboard doors and drawers, and don't place other pieces of furniture so close to them that they are difficult to use.

You should also visualize all the 'roads' in a room. Every room has routes within it that are frequently used. At its simplest, this may be the actual doorway into the room, as well as perhaps the route between a sofa and the television, or between the dining table and the kitchen. Plan around these routes, keeping them clear of anything that may impede direct progress.

▷ The routes people take when moving around your home should be kept clear and unobstructed by furniture. Easy access into and around the kitchen is especially important.

decorative themes

It can be effective to follow a particular theme in a room, or even within certain areas of a room. This is part of the art of successful interior design. Homes and offices are divided into specific areas precisely for this reason – offering a basic theme for each room, such as eating, relaxing or sleeping.

How rooms look should reflect their purpose. In general terms, the bedrooms should be calming and peaceful, the kitchen bright, warm and practical, the sitting room comfortable and relaxing. The use of colour is an obvious way to create a warm, welcoming atmosphere in a room, but other themes can be used to give a sense of unity to your decoration. A room might have an ethnic feel, for example, or be furnished with pieces from a particular period.

△ When placing decorative objects around the home, remain aware of thoroughfares so that you do not create obstructions and precious items remain safe.

comfort and proportion

Furniture should be in proportion to the size of the room so that it doesn't seem overcrowded. Even the most comfortable sofa will begin to look uninviting if it is at odds with the rest of the room. You also need to strike a comfortable midpoint between starkness and fussiness. In most cases, you will be furnishing rooms with items you already possess, but it is worth looking at all your furniture objectively to decide what you really want to keep and what would be better replaced.

Lighting can have a profound influence on the atmosphere of a space, creating excitement and drama or a sense of relaxation. Installing adaptable background and accent lighting means you can change the mood at the flick of a switch.

Avoid unnecessary and irritating clutter, and balance the contents of your rooms. By doing so the rooms' appearance is pleasing to the eye but also, equally importantly, to the soul, and you will be able to create harmonious interior spaces that generate feelings of spiritual comfort and inner wellbeing, whatever your personal style.

◁ To induce peaceful sleep, a bedroom needs to feel calm and balanced, uncluttered but also not too stark and minimalist.

Spatial harmony

The physical contents of an area are important contributors to our sense of peace and comfort, but the physical dimension works best when it forms the foundation for achieving the same conditions on a spiritual level. This is sometimes called the 'spatial' level because it provides space for the energies that contribute to our wellbeing. A simple space clearing ritual can be used to promote spiritual tranquillity, and effectively to de-tox the spiritual atmosphere of the room. This can lead us to feel supported and nourished by our living or working space, rather than overwhelmed by its clutter, whether this is on a spiritual or physical level.

a ritual for harmony

This ritual is designed to bring home the fact that there is far more to the cosmic whole than is normally experienced. It enables you, spiritually, to step outside yourself into a greater moment, gaining a wider perspective of the universe and your place within it. From the centre of yourself, the warmth and comfort of this broadened vision of life will spread out into the environment of the area you are in, calming negative vibrations and bringing in their place a feeling of great peace and tranquillity, clearing the space around you of all disruptive energies.

Just after the sun has set, or during the early evening, lay out a simple altar with two white candles, a cup or bowl of water, a small heap of salt in a saucer or bowl, a small green houseplant, and some lotus incense in a holder.

Light the candles and incense. If possible, play some quiet, relaxing music in the background. Kneel calmly facing the altar. Relax your body, mind and emotions, allowing the mystical atmosphere you are creating to envelope your senses.

Lower your head with your eyes closed while you take a few slow, deep breaths. Repeat the following:

I see flame. Flame is energy. Energy is vibration. There was fire and energy at the beginning of all things. This fire and energy were caused by me. Thus do I confirm my identity with creation.

Take a pinch of the salt and gently sprinkle it into the cup of water, then sprinkle a few drops of water from your fingertips over the altar. Next, pick up the plant carefully in both hands and contemplate it. Become aware of its natural beauty, colours and shape, and say:

This plant is energy. It is the latest generation in an unbroken chain from the beginning of all life. Its ancestors caused it to be here and now. These flames I see were not, but I caused them to be here and now. Yet were flames ordained also at

△ **Before beginning the ritual for harmony, light the candles and some lotus incense, and spend some time in meditation.**

the beginning. Thus was this living plant ordained, and thus was I, too, ordained to be here with them now at the joining together of our lines through eternity. So with all energy. So with all life.

Replace the plant carefully on the altar, considering how profound the plant's life is. Then repeat the following:

I see the sun and I do not question it. I see the stars and I do not question them. I see the seasons and I do not question them. Sunset and sunrise, I question them not, but behold they are beautiful even if no eye sees them.

ATMOSPHERES OF A SPACE

When we spend time in an area, we react to its atmosphere on a number of different levels, both consciously and unconsciously. Broadly speaking, this can be divided into four categories.

Physical atmosphere: the material level, which is tangible and solid. It includes the structure of the space, the furniture in it and all the solid, visible items.

Emotional atmosphere: the feeling level. It influences mood or sentiment, creating feelings of peace, inspiration or creativity through the use of colour, texture and shape. It can be described as the comfort factor.

Mental atmosphere: the formulative level of ideas, thought patterns and judgement. The use of colour, shape, sound and light can raise or lower mental activity. A simple example would be the use of bright or subdued lighting.

Spiritual atmosphere: the spatial level. It influences our state of being and gives meaning and depth to the other atmospheres of an environment, providing the space for particular energies to exist. The spiritual atmosphere around us provides a meaningful connection between the seen and unseen worlds.

△ Add a little salt to the bowl of water, then dip your fingertips into the water and sprinkle a few drops over the altar.

This ends the ritual. Stay for a few moments in quiet contemplation, aware of your thoughts, feelings and the calming spiritual vibrations produced by the ritual.

△ As you hold the plant in your hands, appreciate its unique beauty and sense its natural energy.

▽ Do not hurry through this ritual but spend some time during it to sit back and think about the words you are repeating, and sense the spiritual atmosphere you are creating.

Pause for a few moments to contemplate what you have said, then finish the ritual with the following words:

I have now seen myself, and I do not question it. I see myself in the light of a greater truth. I am a reflection in the eye of the universe. I am part of the Infinite throughout time from the first moment that ever was. [Here extend your arms towards the candles.] *May this light never be extinguished in my heart, but be with me through all times and all seasons. So shall it be.*

Inner space

As well as clearing the space around us, we need to learn ways to keep our inner environment clean and clear. In simple terms, we can view ourselves as having four layers: physical, emotional, mental and spiritual. In order to maintain a harmonious inner space, ideally we need to consider all four levels.

the inner you

Physically, your inner space will be influenced by your lifestyle and what you choose to eat and drink. You may like to consider changing things in your daily life that do not really serve you – or are actually harmful to you – such as too many late nights, poor eating habits, or any addictive patterns or over-indulgence in alcohol or drugs.

On a physical level, it is helpful to be more disciplined about transcending your 'bad' habits. A weak physical level can significantly affect your emotional, mental and spiritual health. On an emotional level, you should consider the effect your moods and emotions have on your environment.

Again, self-discipline and working to understand your emotional make-up will help to alleviate heated arguments, stress levels and heavy atmospheres. At this level, you need to consider 'relationship' – how you relate to the world and from what emotional perspective you see things. When you look closely at your emotional responses

△ Inner space is as important as the space around us. Regular relaxing yoga routines are very helpful to the inner state.

to life, you may realize that they are out-dated, linked to wounds from the past that have yet to heal.

On a mental level, it is normally a cluttered mind that suffers mental stress, anxiety, insomnia or depression. Albert Einstein said: "A clever mind is one that is trained to forget the trivial." It is advisable to consider physical exercise, which is known to reduce stress levels, or to begin practising a spiritual discipline such as yoga, Tai Chi or meditation. The benefits of meditation have been well documented: it allows us to relate to who we truly are without falling into the common traps of everyday life.

It is what we are within, rather than what we do, that is the important factor. It is the soul or spirit of the individual that colours life and identifies his or her relationship with the greater whole.

◁ Drinking lots of spring water rather than coffee or tea will increase energy levels and reduce fatigue.

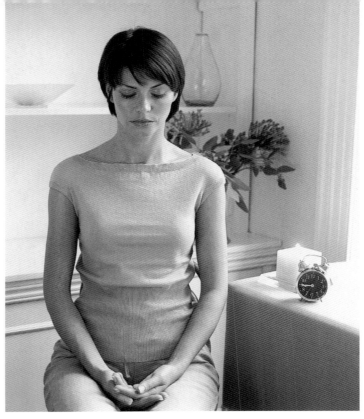

▷ Choose a chair for your meditation that allows you to sit comfortably but with your back straight. Place your feet flat on the floor and let your hands rest in your lap.

▽ Set an alarm clock or timer for the duration of your meditation so that you do not have to think about the time passing.

meditation for inner cleanliness

A period of meditation allows you the time and space to keep your inner world clean and clear, while at the same time creating space for spiritual harmony to filter down through the other layers. By spending time in quiet contemplation, you are creating an opportunity to simply be and so allow yourself the pause to catch up, or perhaps to unwind, without external stimulus or diversion. This enables you to centre and calm stressful states and thus bring about inner peace.

By meditating each day, you can subtly infuse your surroundings with balanced and peaceful vibrations, rather than the stress and anxiety of daily life. With regular meditation, you will feel revitalized physically, your mind will feel refreshed and your emotions calm. From here it is easier to step into each day with confidence and faith. Tasks become simpler to complete. It is as if meditation stretches time, and where before you may have felt the need to rush,

it is now possible to move at a pace free from stress and pressure.

Here is a simple daily meditation to keep you and your home, office or hotel room free from stress.

Set an alarm clock to ring after 10 minutes and place it beneath a cushion. Sit comfortably on a straight-backed chair with your feet flat on the floor, or sit cross-legged on the floor supported with pillows or cushions beneath you.

Imagine that your spine is being gently stretched upwards towards the heavens and at the same time downwards to the earth, and that the central point of balance is in your abdomen. Breathe fully, slowly and deeply, concentrating only upon your breathing. Breathe in 'Peace', and allow the breath to infuse your whole being. Breathe out 'Free from fear'. At first your thoughts may race, your concentration may wander,

▷ As you slowly open your eyes, imagine the sunrise coming out of your eyes and shining light on to a new day.

and you may feel restless. Simply continue to breathe and bring your mind back to the words on the rising and falling breaths. Gradually you will feel a calming influence as you maintain your focus on your breathing. Sit in contemplation until the alarm clock rings. On an outbreath, gently open your eyes and get up slowly.

The tools of space clearing

Tools are important to human beings – for whom the twin foundations of knowledge and the use of tools have been the basis of success as a species – and, like all skills, space clearing has its special implements. Whether you choose to follow a particular magical tradition such as Wicca, or take a more general approach, there are many things that can help to enhance your rituals and spiritual actions.

Scents and aromas

In the world of sensation, scents and fragrances play a very important part in controlling our feelings and responses. Smell stimulates a response by association, sometimes triggering clear and detailed memories of past experiences that we had long forgotten.

Foul or acrid fumes repel us, whereas sweet or fragrant aromas tend to draw us closer to their source. This is the basis for the choice of the different scents and incenses used during particular space clearing rituals. Just as they attract or repel us, some scents attract negative vibrations and others drive them away.

In the human world, our natural reaction to unpleasant smells is to try to get away from them, but in the spirit world, negative vibrations are attracted by dirt, dust, debris, carrion and uncleanliness, because they have the opportunity to 'feed' off the presence of energy that is being held there. This is the reason why cleanliness is considered so important as a way to keep spaces clear of old or stale vibrations.

▽ The sweet scent of the jasmine plant can help to keep the atmosphere positively charged once a space has been cleared.

repelling negativity

In situations where a strongly negative atmosphere is experienced and serious space clearing is needed, the ideal aromas to drive away negativity are hot, spicy, vibrant and dynamic. These fiery scents include asafoetida, fumitory, pepper, garlic and chilli. Asafoetida, in particular, smells so foul when it is being burnt that the natural human response is a particularly averse one. This has a psychic effect on the person performing the space clearing of pushing all negativity away with a force of repulsion as strong as the smell itself.

The same principle applies to the use of fumitory – a herb used to expel negative vibrations of a lesser nature. The dried herb is sprinkled on to hot charcoal and fumigates the room with a smell that we would not consider particularly pleasant. However, it serves the purpose of clearing the room of psychic debris before it is filled with any positive input or charge. Both asafoetida and fumitory can be used to clean a space in situations where you need to 'start

△ Scented flowers used as decoration in the home send subtle messages to the brain as well as stimulating the senses.

▽ Hot, spicy aromas such as garlic, pepper and chilli are associated with the fire element and are all strongly protective.

PSYCHIC ATMOSPHERES

You can perform a simple test using a lighted candle to see if the psychic atmosphere of an area is clear. All you need for this is a candle and holder, matches and an absence of draughts.

Fit the candle securely into its holder and stand it on a table that is out of any draughts. Light the candle and sit quietly and calmly by the table, but far enough away so that your breath does not disturb the flame. In a well-balanced room, the candle flame should burn gently with a small golden yellow flame, flickering only now and then with the natural movement of air through the room. If the candle flame sputters, burns blue, behaves erratically, jumps rapidly or sparks, you have confirmation that the psychic atmosphere is charged and would benefit from a space clearing.

△ **Sprinkle some dried fumitory on burning charcoal to repel negative vibrations from a room, ready for a fresh beginning.**

again', perhaps when you are taking over a new office or moving into a new home. They can also be useful when gentler routines have not seemed to work for any length of time.

Once a psychically clean room has been established in this way, it is advisable to maintain the standard by making the space less attractive to negative energies – keeping clutter to a minimum, having a regular cleaning routine, and ensuring that life energy in the environment is positively charged by introducing healthy plants, dust-free carpets, fresh air, light and comfort. In this way, the space will serve you, rather than those things you are trying to avoid.

aromatic influences

Here is a quick guide to scents and aromas that will repel negativity, attract harmony and protection, or balance an environment. All the fragrances can be obtained in the form of aromatherapy oils, incense sticks, gums and resins or loose herbs. Use whichever form you prefer.

Aromatherapy oils should be added to water in an aromatherapy burner, gums and resins should be burned on hot charcoal in a charcoal burner, and loose herbs can also be sprinkled over hot charcoal. The dried leaves of some herbs can simply be lit and left to smoulder in a suitable container, but you will need to experiment with the different herbs to discover which leaves ignite well on their own, and which benefit from the extra heat of charcoal.

Once a clearing has been established, a choice of balancing or harmonizing fragrances can be used to help maintain the clarity of the space and ensure a pleasant atmosphere for the occupants of the room. This acts to keep the space positively charged until it is felt that another clearing may be necessary.

These scents attract harmony and protection in any environment where they are burnt: frankincense, myrrh, lotus, rose and geranium.

These scents repel negative vibrations and can be used when a room needs clearing: cypress, juniper, fumitory, and sage.

These scents encourage and enhance feelings of peace and calm: bayberry, gardenia, magnolia and rose.

Essences and remedies

Since the pioneering work of Dr Edward Bach in the 1930s, there has been a strong and steady increase in the use of vibrational remedies for a variety of physical, mental and emotional complaints. Bach developed a method of harnessing the natural energies of flowers by floating the blooms in pure water and leaving them for a certain time in sunlight, which draws the healing essence from the flower into the water.

From the humble beginnings of the 28 original Bach flower remedies, there are now thousands of essences from all around the world, covering a wide range of sources, from ocean to crystal, animal to tree. Each essence has its own particular qualities that are channelled into pure water and then preserved in alcohol. Vibrational essences act on the 'subtle anatomy', or the body's life force, in a very similar way to homeopathic remedies. At this level, the essences work to influence and heal imbalances in energy patterns.

remedies to cleanse the body

Just as rooms and environments can be affected by undue negativity, so can the physical body. At times when stress seems overwhelming, emotions are running high, or perhaps deep fatigue from too many demands is hindering clarity and peace, any of the following remedies will be helpful in cleansing negativity.

A SPACE CLEARING ROOM SPRITZER
The following recipe can be made up and stored in a spray bottle. Spritz it around a room to clear negativity, emotional memories, mental stresses or psychic unrest.

The mixture is quick and simple to make and offers a convenient, quick-fix solution for clearing an atmosphere when time is short, such as cleansing between clients when you are at work, for example.

3 drops pine oil (purifies and refines energy)
3 drops rose geranium oil (atmospheric harmonizer)
3 drops cypress oil (closes astral doors)
5 drops lavender oil (mental cleanser and harmonizer)
7 drops myrrh oil (for consecration and protection)
7 drops crab apple flower essence (general cleanser)
1 tsp vodka
distilled water

Clean out a spritzer bottle with warm, salted water, rinse and allow to dry. Measure the aromatherapy oils and the flower essence into the bottle. Add the vodka, which preserves the mixture and allows the oils to blend more cohesively with the water. Top up the bottle with distilled water. Seal and shake gently to blend. Spray around yourself and your working or living area whenever you feel that the spirits need lifting or clearing.

△ Spritzing an area with water to which you have added a few drops of essential oils or flower essences can be a quick and easy way to lighten and clear an atmosphere.

White yarrow: works to strengthen the aura and acts as a shield against negative environmental influences.

Angelica: an all-round auric strengthener and protector, bringing the ability to cope with challenges or difficulties that could otherwise affect performance.

Crab apple: cleanses the body and soul of unnecessary or outdated vibrations.

Olive: an energy reviver that is helpful at times when you feel overworked, overwhelmed or just tired.

Vanilla: acts like a psychic shield, allowing you to maintain control of your environmental atmospheres without being affected by them.

Lotus: a spiritual harmonizer.

When you are making up a remedy mix, the order of application offers a map for the consciousness – an energy path for the psyche to follow. Adding the last essence encourages the energy to aim for spiritual harmony and peace.

▷ Honeysuckle flower essence is helpful when you are dwelling too much on past experiences and feel unable to move forward.

a cleansing mix

A mixture of the cleansing remedies can be taken when you feel you need an energetic protector and pick-me-up. Like all vibrational remedies, this mixture works by flooding out negative feelings. If you have been repressing your emotions, some unexpected feelings may be stirred up, but the remedy is safe and has no side effects.

Either place 7 drops of the mixture directly on your tongue, or mix 7 drops in spring water and sip it throughout the day. (If you are dropping it straight on to your tongue, don't allow the dropper actually to touch the tongue, to avoid the possibility of bacteria entering the remedy bottle.) While taking the mixture, avoid drinks containing caffeine, because it interferes with the remedy's healing path in the body.

YOU WILL NEED
spring water
vodka
7 drops crab apple flower essence
7 drops olive flower essence
7 drops white yarrow flower essence
7 drops angelica flower essence
7 drops vanilla flower essence
1 drop lotus flower essence

Rinse out an essence bottle with spring water. Fill the bottle one third full with vodka and then add the six flower essences in the order listed. Top up the mixture with spring water and shake gently to infuse the essences. Label the bottle 'Cleansing Mix' and add the date it was made.

This essence can be kept for three months and should be stored in a cool, dark environment when not in use. If it becomes cloudy during this time, discard it and make up a fresh mix.

▷ To ensure inner balance, you can sip a cleansing mix of flower essences whenever you feel that stresses are rising in you.

Smoke and fire

Fire is intimately linked with light, and candlelight is often used during peace vigils and meditations to symbolize the spirit of remembrance and peace. Apart from its historical link as a symbol of light and hope, fire has also long been an instrument of purification. The ancient Celtic fire festivals, such as the winter festival of Yule, involved fires or beacons, not only to represent the light of life, but also to assist the community in driving away unwanted influences. A new log was kindled from the previous year's log, which had been extinguished, preserved and re-lit to ensure continuity and blessing from one year to the next.

In modern times, fire is used mainly as a source of warmth and not so much for its powers of cleansing and purifying, although there are several ways in which fire can be used in space clearing.

▽ The lighting of red candles in a room invokes the positive energy of Fire, the element of purification and transformation.

candles

The simplest way to represent the Fire element in the home or office is with candles or lanterns, and one of the simplest fire rituals is to make an affirmation as you light a candle. This could be something like "May there be peace in this place", or "By the power of Fire, this room is filled with brightness and strength", or perhaps you might like to say "With this flame to protect me, no harm may enter here." The affirmation can be about anything or anyone you would like to call on to fill your environment. Your intent will be carried symbolically by the burning candle for as long as it remains alight.

When you are working with a black candle, light it and let it burn for up to one hour (but do not leave it unattended during this time) before extinguishing it and removing it from the room to be buried or discarded respectfully in the earth. You should then replace the black candle with a white one, allowing that to burn for

△ The symbolic act of burning away negativity serves to mirror that occurring in our lives.

REMOVING NEGATIVITY

A candle can be used to remove negativity by utilizing the flame to burn it away. This can be done by writing down those things you wish to release from the environment (such as the energy left in the room after a heated argument) and letting the written message be consumed by the candle flame. Once the paper has been lit, drop it into a fireproof container and let it burn to ashes completely. You can then scatter the ashes outside in the wind, as you visualize the negativity being blown away.

▷ Sprinkle some sacred herbs on to an open fire to conjure a mystical atmosphere.

another hour. As you light the white candle, affirm your call for peaceful vibrations to prevail in the place.

open fires

If you have an open fire, or a garden where a fire can be lit, you may like to build a stronger relationship with the purifying abilities of the Fire element by having that intention when you light the fire. Instead of simply laying a fire for warmth, add a handful of purifying herbs, with offerings to the Fire spirits such as a handful of peppercorns or a few sprinklings of tobacco. Add your intention that, as the fire burns, it will provide protection, and call for the spirits to be ever watchful to drive away negative influences from your home or land. The smoke from the burning herbs will infuse the environment with a protective haze. The open fire is no longer a place of winter practicality, but becomes a magical cauldron in which to gaze and observe the spirits as they dance away the dark.

▽ Laying flowers at the base of a candle can act as a focus for what you wish to call on or change.

colours, flowers and herbs

When you are working with Fire affirmations, certain candle colours will complement your particular requirements, and the following list offers a basic guide to colour correspondences.

To enhance an affirmation further, you can also surround the base of your candle with flowers or herbs chosen to complement and strengthen the focus of your ritual.

Red is for power, strength and protection, and is the colour of Fire; surround a red candle with carnations.

Black absorbs negativity and draws away psychic intrusion; surround a black candle with rue or sage leaves.

Green promotes harmony and emotional balance; surround the base of the candle with roses.

Light blue is for healing vibrations and peace; surround a blue candle with white jasmine flowers.

Pink represents love, romance, happiness and felicity; surround the base of a pink candle with pansies.

Yellow promotes change, new beginnings, wisdom and understanding; surround a yellow candle with lavender.

Orange is for healthy atmospheres, positivity and creativity; surround an orange candle with cloves.

White is for purity, balance and all general ritual work; surround the candle base with white lilies or camellias.

Music and sound

Sound is a form of vibration, which is at the root of our existence. Albert Einstein asserted that living things are not solid matter but a dance of atoms in space, and when we look closely at our physical nature, this is indeed the case. All matter vibrates, emitting waves of energy, and within a certain range of frequencies we respond to these vibrations as sound.

Sound can be used for protection, clearing or harmonizing, depending on the level and tone of the sounds used. Loud, shocking noises, such as fireworks or drums, for example, have long been used by many different cultures to drive out evil spirits. Conversely the gentle, almost inaudible, sound of a mother's heartbeat is capable of soothing a baby to sleep.

Our response to sound is largely determined by the associations we make with a particular noise. Sounds of nature can be either stirring or soothing, as can music.

▽ A gentle, repetitive sound such as a chime can be used to induce a feeling of peace in an environment that needs calming.

For thousands of years the power of sound has been encapsulated in the use of voiced mantras and chants by many traditions throughout the world. Repetition of the 'Aum' mantra, for example, can be used to harmonize an environment. It is a simple, safe and effective method. A variety of sacred mantras and chants can be sung or played, either to clear a space or to fill it with a particular vibration after a space clearing has been done.

△ Rhythmic sounds, especially in the form of drumming, are used in shamanic ritual to summon the assistance of the spirit world.

noise pollution

If you consider for a moment the myriad modern day sounds humans emit, which ride over and above the hum of earth's organic life, it is not surprising that noise pollution is now a well-established problem. Traffic, machinery, appliances, loud music

▷ Tibetan singing bowls can produce a variety of sound vibrations that touch the body with resonance.

and voices can all contribute to noise pollution. Many of us will have experienced a craving for peace and quiet as a result.

As we tune into the more subtle sounds of the earth, and simplify our lives, we have to acknowledge this orchestra of noise more seriously as a major contributor to stress and distress at home and work. We all need to consider how much we ourselves contribute to noise pollution, and take steps to naturalize and neutralize our part in it. By consciously filling our environment with more harmonious sounds and music, we can bring a depth and meaning to our world way beyond mere entertainment value. If you are looking for ways to naturalize the sounds around you, it is well worth exploring what is now produced by the New Age music industry. The sounds of nature and her creatures, such as whale song, waterfalls, or waves on the shore, are often found in the background of what is known as 'ambient' music.

the powers of sound

Sound, music and the voice can all be used very effectively for space clearing. Fast or loud music and sounds will increase energy in an environment, whereas quiet, slow, rhythmic sounds will induce a sense of peace and tranquillity.

A drum, when played loudly and with authority, will help to expel negative energies, and when played rhythmically it will harmonize and raise the Earth element. Wind instruments, the didgeridoo, cymbals, tingshaws (Tibetan bells) and gongs can help to alleviate stress, mental chatter and frenzied atmospheres. Sacred instruments such as the bamboo flute, sitar or aeolian harp can also balance Air atmospheres. Crystal singing bowls can be utilized to balance the Water element, along with water features such as fountains, fish tanks and watery music. These are ideal for harmonizing emotions and for removing emotional conflict from living and working areas.

A MANTRA TO LORD SHIVA

The following mantra to the Hindu deity Shiva is a powerful way to clear an environment of any unnecessary vibrations, especially those that are blocking you personally, or stifling spiritual peace or understanding. Always burn a candle when performing this chant.

1 Sit in front of the candle and any representations you may have of Lord Shiva, such as a statue. Chant "Om namah Shivaya" (pronounced 'Om narmar Shiv-eye-yah') rhythmically for at least ten minutes.

2 If you have a set of rosary beads, you can perform the chant the traditional 108 times, moving one bead round with each repetition. For particularly difficult problems you can chant this mantra over a period of 40 days. The mantra can also be used as part of a regular spiritual practice, which will strengthen its influence upon you and your surroundings.

Crystals and pendulums

Because we are all subtly influenced by our environment and will be affected by it at a subconscious level, we may need help to reveal to our conscious minds what we are sensing subconsciously.

Crystals, as part of the earth's structure, emit energy waves at natural frequencies in harmony with our own biological make-up, and for this reason they can help to balance and harmonize our inner and outer environments. In fact, some parts of the human body are actually crystalline structures, including our teeth.

In dowsing, a pendulum acts in relation to our energetic impulses, revealing positive or negative responses to questioning, and we can use this technique to reveal the cause of a sense of disharmony.

▽ The amethyst is part of the quartz family of crystals and is safe and reliable for daily use in counteracting electromagnetic emissions.

using crystals

As children of the earth we need to acknowledge that we function best when we are in harmony with nature, and all kinds of crystals can play a significant part in maintaining that harmony.

Crystal clusters are excellent at keeping communal spaces clear. Their many points direct and charge energy positively, and placing a crystal cluster in a negatively charged room will clear it quite quickly. To clear negativity, use a smoky quartz cluster, to alleviate stress, use an amethyst cluster, and for harmonizing and emotional cleansing, a clear quartz cluster. If the problem is excess energy, crystals that will ground it effectively include smoky quartz, obsidian, hematite, chrysocolla, yellow fluorite, onyx and turquoise.

Modern electrical appliances give out electromagnetic energy at frequencies way beyond nature's own. To give an example,

△ Many crystals, including turquoise, quartz and obsidian, have beneficial protective and harmonizing qualities.

the earth's electromagnetic field functions between 1 and 30Hz. Human brainwaves range from 5–30Hz. Electrical appliances are much higher than natural frequencies, and range from 35–100Hz. We may be subjected to these high frequencies for a considerable length of time if we have to work with electrical equipment such as computers; placing crystals around them will help to counteract any harmful effects.

Rainbow crystals (those that have rainbow colours within them) placed on a sunny windowsill can work to bring the colours of joy to a depressed room. They also work well where moods need lightening. Rainbow colours are most commonly found in clear quartz crystals. Twin crystals are attached to each other but have two separate terminations at one end. They can be used to heal relationships and underlying relationship difficulties.

You can wear or carry any of the crystals suggested here by scaling down the size to smaller stones or single points.

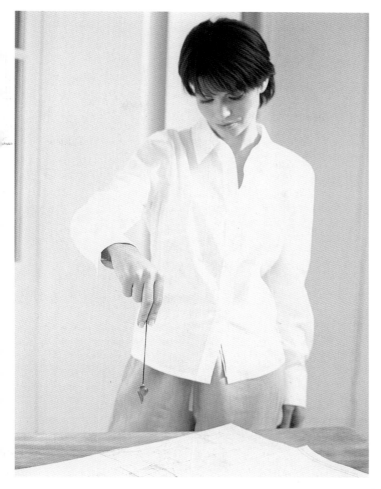

◁ You can dowse using a pendulum to find out which areas of your home or office may be out of balance.

289

the tools of space clearing

indicate 'yes' and 'no'), to give it some kind of momentum to work with. To avoid concerns that you are influencing the outcome, after asking a question, empty your mind of everything except the words "I wonder what the answer will be?" and wait for the pendulum to respond.

To use a pendulum as an assessment tool for space clearing, draw a scaled-down floor plan of your chosen building, writing which room is which on your sketch. Hold a pendulum in your right hand. Place your left index finger on one area of the sketch and ask the pendulum "Is this room energetically balanced?" When you receive an answer, make a note of it. If the answer is 'yes', move on to the next room. If it is 'no', go on to ask a series of simple questions to discover what may be causing the problem, such as "Is this room emotionally charged?" or "Is it affected by electrical emissions?" and so on, until you find what is affecting the area.

HOLDING A PENDULUM

Hold the chain between the thumb, index and middle fingers, leaving about 15cm/6in above the pendulum free. Hold the chain with the fingers pointing downwards so the pendulum can swing freely.

dowsing

A simple dowsing technique can help you to discover if there are any areas of your home or workplace that are energetically unbalanced. Once any imbalances have been uncovered, you can correct them using whichever space clearing exercise seems most appropriate.

Before you begin, you need to discover which pendulum swing indicates a 'yes' and which indicates a 'no'. The simplest way to find out is to ask a question such as "Is my name [*state your real name*]?" and wait to see what movement the pendulum makes. You will then know which swing means a 'yes'. To discover a 'no' swing, ask the pendulum "Is my name [*state a false name*]?" and wait to see the movement. Once you have

established your 'yes' and 'no' swings, you can start asking questions. If at any time the pendulum behaves in a different way to your yes/no swings, it usually indicates that you need to re-phrase your question. A common error is to ask a question with more than one possible answer, such as "Is this room balanced or not?" It is important to ask questions of the pendulum that require a straight 'yes' or 'no' answer. If you reduce the question to "Is this room balanced?" the pendulum will be able to give a definitive answer.

Another common problem when working with a pendulum is complete lack of movement. To facilitate a response, dowsers may swing the pendulum to and fro (avoiding the particular movements that

Magical implements

Just about anything can be used as a magical implement, and throughout the history of magic, just about everything has been. However, over time certain tools have become paramount and in general they are associated with the four elements – Air, Fire, Water and Earth – together with a fifth, the Quintessence or Spirit, which unites the other four.

The magical symbol of the pentagram, the five-pointed interlocking star, represents this concept, bringing together the five elements that are necessary to sustain life: each of the four lower points of the figure represents one of the physical elements, while the topmost point represents Spirit. The pentagram is often traced during rituals and symbolizes protection and wholeness.

magic and the elements

Each of the physical elements has its own magical tool. The sword is associated with Air, the wand with Fire, the cup or chalice with Water and the pentacle with Earth. The athame (pronounced 'ath-ay-me') is a general-purpose tool, which is used as a psychic pointer.

There has been some controversy amongst occultists regarding the correct tools to use to represent the elements of Air and Fire. Many magicians use the wand for Fire and the sword (or dagger) for Air, as

△ Shamans decorate their magical items with power objects such as feathers and claws.

▽ The traditional altar tools of the Wiccan practitioner are the chalice or cup, athame (knife), wand (stick) and pentacle (salver).

▷ The tools you use in magical ritual can be as simple as an ordinary black-handled kitchen knife and a glass bowl. The important thing is to use what feels right to you.

this is how they are depicted in packs of Tarot cards originating from the 19th-century occult Order of the Golden Dawn. Others believe that this was a blind intended to confuse the uninitiated and, instead, prefer to use the wand for Air and the sword or knife for Fire. But in magic, the only thing to avoid is worrying about it. The basic rule is to find the way that feels right for you and stick to it.

In the ancient past, magicians tended to be educated scholars and practised ceremonial 'high magic'. As they were high-born they were permitted to carry swords and therefore used them as implements for their magic. Witches, on the other hand, originated from the village wise-person. They were very often followers of the old pre-Christian fertility religion called Wicca and were usually advocates of 'low magic'. Witches did not have access to the ceremonial regalia of high magic and instead developed their tools from ordinary household objects such as bowls, platters and kitchen knives. They were usually well-versed in herbal lore.

The magical implement that is appropriate to any particular ritual depends

THE HAND AS A MAGICAL IMPLEMENT

At times when it is not advisable or possible to use a blade in a ritual, you can substitute the fingers of your hand as a pointer, imagining that they are like the blade. The hand can be held in a symbolic position, in which the first finger represents Isis, the female, and the middle finger represents Osiris, the male. The thumb is positioned between these two fingers, and the posture thus invokes the protection of the god and goddess over their child, Horus.

on the nature of the ritual, or 'working'. Emotional matters are governed by the Water element, competitive matters by Fire, mental matters by Air and worldly matters such as finance and success by Earth. This is a very generalized picture, however. Another use of the Earth element, for instance, is in calming energies and dispelling hostile psychic vibrations, as well as for self-defence against occult attack. The idea behind this – as with electricity – is to run excess and unwanted energies to earth. Thus, the Earth element is regularly used in space clearing.

assembling the tools

A sword is probably the most difficult and expensive item to obtain, but like all the other implements can be purchased from occult suppliers. You can easily make the other magical implements yourself, using a little imagination.

The pentacle originated as a platter or salver. It can be made of any material, but is usually a round flat piece of metal or wood: a wooden breadboard or coaster is very suitable, and you can paint a pentagram on it yourself. An ordinary black-handled kitchen knife can be used as an athame, and any glass bowl or stemmed glass from your kitchen can serve as a chalice. Much folklore is associated with the magic wand: according to tradition, it had to be cut in one slash on

the last stroke of midnight. This is not really necessary, but it is a way of showing respect and gratitude for anything that you take from nature, and this is important.

▽ The Fire element can be quickly represented by a lit candle, and the act of lighting it takes on a symbolic meaning of its own.

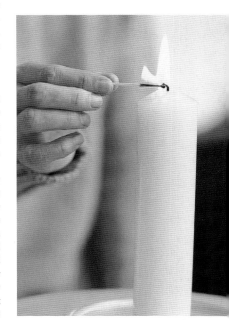

Space clearing rituals

A ritual is an act repeated in a formalized manner to give it greater meaning and focus our concentration upon it, and ritualistic behaviour of various kinds helps to give structure and pattern to our lives. The application of rituals for space clearing greatly enhances our energy and determination, helping us to bring abstract knowledge into physical play to accomplish stronger results.

Preparing for ritual

One of the ways ritual magic works is through what is known as psychodrama, in which a physical enactment – involving sight, sound and the other senses – produces a corresponding change of consciousness, especially in the subconscious mind. This is the primal area of the mind – the basic and ancient root of the human consciousness. As the psychologist Carl Jung showed, it recognizes and communicates in symbols only, not in logical linguistics. Within it are stored not only our personal memories but also our racial memories, reaching back through thousands of years, which come up to the surface layers of our mind in the form of instinct. Some experts believe that we retain not just racial but species memories – that our deeper minds may contain the memories of our pre-human ancestors.

The subconscious reacts to enacted behaviour just as it reacts to real situations occurring spontaneously, so it can help if you treat a ritual like a theatrical production, learning your part as though it were in a play. Instead of standing self-consciously mumbling the words under your breath, this approach can encourage you to be bold with your movements and loud and confident in your declaration of the words.

purifying and cleansing the area

Any proper magical ritual, including space clearing, needs to be 'written on a clean slate'. If there are psychic impurities or negative energies present when the ritual is carried out, they can intrude and interfere, contaminating the result and sometimes changing it completely. As a modern analogy, we might think of such impure energy as a kind of 'occult computer virus'. A purifying and cleansing routine acts like an anti-virus programme. There are two areas that can benefit: the environment in which you intend to perform a space clearing, and yourself.

Every culture has its own purifying and cleansing methods, from the Christian 'bell, book and candle' to the pagan 'rites of passage', and there are a great many to choose from. The simplest method is burning a suitable incense and carrying it round the area, calming your mind and projecting that calmness out into the room with the smoke wafting from the incense.

A slightly more intricate version, practised by occultists, is called the Rose Cross ritual. The lighted incense is carried around the room in a pattern, travelling from corner to corner, in a cross shape, then circling the middle of the cross. The shape resembles a cross with a rose in its centre, which is the symbol of the Rosicrucian Brotherhood, an occult order dating from before 1614.

▽ It is important to approach an area you are preparing for space clearing in a dignified and respectful manner.

▷ Keep a bowl of sand ready for when you want to extinguish the smudge stick.

smudging

The most popular purifying and cleansing technique is probably smudging, a shamanic method which has enjoyed a widespread revival in recent years. This method has several advantages. Its shamanic origin means it lends itself to just about any magical path without causing contention, so it can be used as a prologue to any kind of space clearing ritual. It is very simple but extremely effective and because it needs a little more input from you, it encourages magical thought and activity while you are putting together the basic tools for the ceremony: a smudge stick and a smudge fan.

The smudge stick is simply a bundle of dried herbs, usually including sage. The fan should be made of feathers, a single feather can also be used. The purpose of the fan is to waft the smoke all over the area, over the walls, floor and ceiling and round the doors, windows and any other openings into the room, such as the fireplace. The nature of the herbs and the intention of the person who gathered and tied them, together with the action of the fan, drives away any negative energies lingering in an area.

▽ As you fan the smoke, strengthen the action by visualizing the herbs' cleansing qualities.

MAKING A SMUDGE STICK

It is very rewarding to grow and dry your own herbs, thus ensuring that their magical qualities are tended during all stages of growth, and that you honour the spirits of the herbs when cutting them. The three suggested here (three is a magical number) are all for purification. The best variety of sage to use is American white sage or mountain sage (*Salvia apiana*). All the herbs must be completely dry.

YOU WILL NEED
dried sage stalks
dried lavender flower stalks
dried thyme stalks
natural twine

Gather all the dried herb stalks together and arrange them in an intertwined bundle. Bind the stalks loosely with twine and trim the ends to neaten the bundle. Light one end, extinguish the flame, and let the smoke rise to fill the area.

For any ritual cleansing work, preparing yourself is a very important prerequisite. There is a saying that 'cleanliness is next to godliness', and it is an esoteric belief that harmful negative energies – or evil influences – will fasten on to any dirt on the body of an individual commencing a ritual. (This applies equally to the clothing you are wearing, so fresh, clean clothes are also recommended.) Apart from this consideration, relaxing in a hot bath, especially one made fragrant with herbs, before a space clearing ritual serves to put the conscious and unconscious parts of the mind in closer touch with one another.

While you are bathing, imagine that you are cleansing away all impurities from your body and soul and, as the water runs out of the bath, visualize all those impurities draining away from you. You may like to anoint yourself with rose geranium essential oil diluted in some sweet almond oil.

△ Bathing ensures that all impurities are removed from the physical body prior to a space clearing ritual.

Alternatively, scent some almond oil with one or two leaves harvested from a *Pelargonium graveolens* plant you have bought to help with your magical and ritual preparations, thus ensuring a regular supply of the natural herb. Always harvest leaves with respect and care for your plant.

Another preparation often used, in religious activity as well as in magic, is fasting. This is a valid technique, as it helps to separate the mind from its material bonds by encouraging a semi-trancelike state. However, it is not an essential preparation for space clearing. You may like to consider a purifying diet instead, but check with your GP first as to whether this is advisable. If you feel that this is appropriate, you should begin the diet five days before you plan to carry out your ritual.

◁ You can anoint your body with rosewater or an oil blend containing rose geranium essential oil before performing a cleansing ritual.

▷ Preparation of your body and mind before you begin any ritual carries the same importance as the ritual itself.

mental and psychic preparation

It is important to be in the right frame of mind when undertaking any ritual work, so mental and psychic preparation is also recommended. For space clearing purposes, the correct frame of mind is relaxed, confident, at peace with yourself, calm, positive and assured.

After you have bathed, or made other physical preparations, a period of meditation immediately preceding the start of a ritual will help to achieve calm and composure. Space clearing is a spiritual process that can be quite draining, and its success will depend on your mental preparation and state of mind. Meditation can be accompanied by some quiet, spiritually inspiring music and burning a suitable incense, which should not be too thick or heavily scented: a light fragrance is best for the preparation before a ritual, leaving the heavier aromas for the ritual itself, in cases where they are considered to be necessary.

A banishing ritual can be performed after the meditation period. This will prepare the working area for the main ritual to come, and it will also put your mind into a receptive state for ritual work.

There are a great many things that can disturb the harmony of nearby energies: for example, a serious argument that took place the previous day between the couple living next door could have left 'heaving' psychic vibrations, like a sea with a rough swell where there ought to be smooth water. Such vibrations can weaken the result of a space clearing ritual, or even make it completely ineffective.

A banishing ritual is like pouring oil on troubled waters, to smooth psychic shockwaves. Such troubled vibrations can spread out over a surprisingly large distance, and they need to be eliminated before space clearing can be properly undertaken, so adequate preparation is an important part of the ritual itself.

HERBAL BATH MIX

All the ingredients for this mix are easily available to buy, or they can be grown in a herb garden or window-box. They are all associated with purification and cleansing. Use fresh herbs if possible.

YOU WILL NEED

2 tsp organic oats
small square of cotton muslin
7 basil leaves
3 bay leaves
3 sprigs oregano
1 sprig tarragon
pinch of rock or sea salt
thread to secure

Pile the herbs in the centre of the muslin square, then add the oats. Top with the rock or sea salt, pick up the corners of the muslin and tie with thread. Hang the sachet from the bath tap so that the water is infused with the essence of the mixture.

Magical circles

Magic evolved through the ages into two broad types, referred to as 'low magic' and 'high magic'. These terms are very generalized and the two often merge seamlessly together. Low magic was practised by the simple and poor: peasants who had no access to education, riches or reading and writing. This is the kind of magic that originated with the tribal shaman, or the wise woman mixing her herbs in a steaming cauldron. High magic grew out of it and became the province of the rich, the nobility and the educated.

As an example of the essential difference between high and low magic, a kitchen knife was often used as a 'psychic pointer' in low magic, and this evolved into the athame, the ritual pointing knife used by witches. In contrast, the upper classes were permitted to carry swords, which were usually forbidden to the peasantry, and therefore in high magic a ritual sword is frequently used as a pointer instead of the athame. The magical implements used today no longer have any association of this kind with class structure. Today's witches use swords freely, and ritual magicians use herbs and athames.

◁ A handful of sacred herbs can be put into a heatproof container and burnt to raise bright vibrations in a room.

△ A visual magic circle can be created by forming a ring on the floor with night lights or small candles.

casting a circle

In both high and low magic, a magic circle is considered indispensable. The idea, greatly simplified, is that this creates what might be called a protective 'energy field' around the place of working, through which no hostile or negative astral forces can penetrate. (Although it is seen with the eyes as a circle on the ground, the mind should perceive it as a sphere.) Casting a magic circle is an important part of witchcraft, or Wicca, which follows the traditions of the 'low' magic of the ordinary people.

In casting a magic circle, great importance is attached to astral beings called the Guardians of the Watchtowers. The 'watchtowers' are the four compass points and the four elements of Air, Fire, Water and Earth to which they are linked (Air corresponds with east, Fire with south, Water with west and Earth with north). The Guardians of the Watchtowers protect those who invoke their aid and ensure the security of the circle. In low magic, especially in Wicca, complex rituals and magical regalia are not normally used.

a simple space clearing

This can be used anywhere as a space clearing procedure, and is a short and simple ritual. But in spite of its simplicity, it is a powerful piece of low magic. As with any magical or mystical activity, you should prepare yourself beforehand. Make sure you

▽ Drawing a magic circle around yourself using an athame, or ceremonial knife, follows a tradition that is many centuries old.

choose a time when you will not be interrupted. A short period of meditation is recommended to calm the mind and spirit, and to eliminate all disruptive thoughts from daily life intruding on the ritual.

The first part of the spell involves casting a magic circle. For this, if you do not have an athame you can use an ordinary kitchen knife as a pointer, preferably one with either a black or a natural wood handle, or you can use your hand.

performing the ritual

Having meditated, stand facing north. Slowly raise the knife or your hand to point in that direction, then turn to the right to face east, imagining that you are drawing a line of pure light in the air as you move. Then turn again to face south, then west, then north again until the circle is complete. As you do this, repeat the following circle-opening invocation, saying each line as you face the appropriate point of the compass:

I call the Guardians of the North, protect this
place from earthly wrath.
I call the Guardians of the East to calm the airs
and bring me peace.
I call the Guardians of the South, protect me from
the fire's red mouth.
I call the Guardians of the West to lay the stormy
seas to rest.

When you have completed the circle, remain facing north, relax and say:

Let blessings be upon this place,
and let my Circle clear this space
of spirits wicked, cruel or fell,
so that I in peace may dwell.

Imagine the circle you have cast is spreading out through the universe like the ripples in a pool, bringing tranquillity and peace to its centre, which is you and your space.

▽ Ripples in water, moving outwards, will eventually be still and calm, like the space you have just cleared.

A zodiac ritual

This space clearing ritual draws on your astrological sign to personalize it and give it power. Use the chart of sun signs to select the correct corresponding tools and materials, and insert the name of your sign where appropriate in the wording.

All astral or psychic energies are intimately connected with zodiacal influences, but while virtually everyone has heard of the zodiac, fewer actually know its definition. While the earth makes its annual orbit of the sun, from earth we perceive this movement as if the sun is travelling along an imaginary line across the sky, called the ecliptic. The zodiac is the name given by astrologers to the band of 12 constellations that appear along the ecliptic through the year. During each 30-day period of the year, the sun appears to rise against the background of one of these groups of stars, and that constellation is said to be the sun sign of anyone born in that period.

The zodiac space clearing ritual has 12 variations which all use the same ritual framework, and there are two ways to choose the appropriate zodiac sign to include in it. You can either choose your own birth sign (or that of anyone you may be helping) or select whichever sign covers the date on which you are to perform the

△ **This variation of the zodiac ritual uses turquoise, benzoin and the chalice to fit with the sign Scorpio.**

ritual (you can check this in the horoscope section of a newspaper if you are unfamiliar with all the zodiac dates).

preparation

Set up the altar so that you will face east when standing in front of it. You will need an altar cloth, an incense burner, a small heap of salt in a container, and the four magical implements: wand, pentacle, sword/athame and cup/chalice (all four should be present, even if only one is to be used in the ritual). Place the tool corresponding to the chosen zodiac sign near the front of the altar. The cup or chalice should contain a small amount of water, whether or not you will be using it.

the ritual

Light the incense and the candles. Pick up the cup or chalice and sprinkle a pinch of salt in the water, saying: "Thus do I cleanse and purify thee, oh spirit of Water, that thou mayest aid me." If you are not using the cup further, replace it on the altar.

Take up the appropriate magical tool and hold it out towards the east, at arm's length. State in a commanding voice:

By the ancient magic of [zodiac sign] I call now upon the spirits of time and space to assist me in cleansing this place of all impurities. By this [name of tool], the symbol of the authority over

SUN SIGNS AND CORRESPONDING TOOLS

SIGN	INCENSE	MAGICAL TOOL	CANDLE COLOUR
Aries	Dragon's blood, lily	Wand	Scarlet
Taurus	Storax, mallow	Pentacle	Red, orange
Gemini	Orchid, wormwood	Sword/athame	Orange
Cancer	Lotus	Cup/chalice	Amber
Leo	Sunflower, olibanum	Wand	Yellow
Virgo	Lily, sandalwood	Pentacle	Yellow-green
Libra	Aloe, galbanum	Sword/athame	Emerald green
Scorpio	Benzoin	Cup/chalice	Turquoise
Sagittarius	Lignum aloes	Wand	Blue
Capricorn	Hemp, musk	Pentacle	Indigo, black
Aquarius	Galbanum	Sword/athame	Violet
Pisces	Opium, ambergris	Cup/chalice	Crimson

again, repeating the action for the fourth and last time.

Replace the magical tool on the altar and cross your wrists over your breast, fists clenched, right wrist outermost (in what is called the 'Osiris risen' position). In a very firm and commanding voice, say this:

Let no creature of any sphere now malign this place. Let all malignity depart hence, and all good enter herein. Let no disturbing influence or visitation descend upon this protected place.

Take up the cup once more, whether it was the main magical tool or not. In a dignified manner, carry it round the perimeter of the area you are clearing. As you go, sprinkle occasional drops of water with your fingertips. This forms a magical circle of protection around the area that hostile astral forces cannot penetrate.

End the ritual by returning to the altar, turning your back to it and announcing to the world: "Go ye in peace!"

▽ **When sprinkling your water in an area imagine it is holy water charged with light and blessings.**

△ **Be clear and authoritative when speaking the words of a zodiac ritual, believe in what you say.**

the occult powers of [zodiac sign], *I command that all that is hostile, of negative intent or malicious of form or mind, depart hence. Depart, I say, and return not, for the forces of* [zodiac sign] *stand now guard upon this place of enchantment. Thus is my will! Thus is my command! Thus is my power!*

Turn to the right so that you are facing south, thrust the magical tool forward in that direction and bark out loudly the word "AVAUNT!" (meaning 'depart'). Turn to the right again to face west, again thrust the magical tool forward and say again, "AVAUNT!" Turn to the north and repeat the action, and finally return to face east

A shamanic ritual

NATIVE AMERICAN SACRED HERBS

For thousands of years, the indigenous people of North America have maintained a very close relationship with the plant kingdom. They use many herbs for healing, protection and blessings, but their four most sacred herbs for purification and protection are sweetgrass, sage, cedar and tobacco.

Sweetgrass is traditionally used for self-blessing, for keeping evil spirits away from the home and to purify tools and equipment, because its sweet smell calls up the good spirits. It is plaited into a braid, then the end is lit and the smoke wafted over magical tools or around the room.

Sage is a powerful cleanser and purifier, and native Americans have been known to sit on sage leaves in sweat lodges, thus physically linking

into its purifying abilities. The leaves can also be used for smudging, either loose or in smudge sticks. The most effective types are white or mountain sage and desert sage.

Cedar is an evergreen tree also known as the Tree of Life; it is a very powerful psychic and spiritual cleanser. Smudging with cedar is advised when conditions are particularly difficult or obstructive, as its powers deal with the more 'problematic' energies. It can be obtained loose and dried, to be sprinkled on hot charcoal when required.

Tobacco is used for offerings to the Great Spirit and to the elemental and natural powers of creation. Tobacco is also cast into the sweat lodge fire as an offering to the fire spirits, and is sometimes given to elders and medicine men as a mark of respect.

The word 'shaman' comes from the Tungusic dialect of the Ural-Altaic tribes of Siberia, but it is now used to describe individuals of many traditions throughout the world that commune with the natural and supernatural world.

The shaman employs sacred herbs, drums and chants to summon the assistance of the spirit world, in order to cleanse a person, situation or environment of any perceived negative or stale influences.

the ritual

The shamanic ritual outlined here calls upon the powers of the drum, of sacred herbs, and of the *inyan* (the stone people of the native Americans) to cleanse and purify an area.

YOU WILL NEED
loose dried sage
smudge bowl or shell
black or dark feather
large stone chosen for
　its individuality
tobacco
drum

▽ **Begin the ritual by smudging yourself and the large stone with smoke from the smouldering sage. Use a feather to fan the smoke.**

▷ Beat the drum while moving in a spiral around the room, towards the centre.

Place the sage in the smudge bowl and light it. Use the feather to fan the smoke around yourself and over the large stone.

Take a pinch of tobacco and stand in the centre of the area you are clearing. Facing north, say "Great Spirit, I honour you, and humbly seek your presence within this grandfather rock." Place the pinch of tobacco at the central point of the room. Pick up the large stone and, holding it to your heart, ask it to help you to clear the environment by absorbing any stray energies. Set the stone in the centre of the room on top of the tobacco, saying, "Mitake oyasin" ("For we are all related").

Take another pinch of tobacco and, still facing north, hold out your hand in that direction. Call with feeling and respect, "Buffalo." Place the tobacco on the floor to the north. Take another pinch of tobacco, face the east and call: "Hawk." Place the tobacco on the floor to the east. Repeat the gesture for the south, saying, "Coyote," and for the west, saying, "Bear."

Turn to face north again and now say, "Guardians of the four winds, I – your brother/sister – do call your presence here."

▽ Hold the grandfather rock to your heart and ask it to help you in your task.

Stand the smudge bowl on the stone so that the smoke coils up through the room.

Take up the drum and, beginning at the edge of the area, walk clockwise in a spiral until you reach the centre, drumming the atmosphere towards the stone. Drum over the stone into the herbs, visualizing the stray energies coiling away in the smoke. Thank the Great Spirit, grandfather rock, and the four guardians for their help. Repeat "Mitake oyasin" and remove the smudge bowl from the stone. Take the stone outside to rest on the earth in order to discharge any remaining energy into the ground.

▷ As the smoke coils through the room, sit for a moment and visualize the cleansing process.

A ritual in the Zen style

Zen is a philosophy of Chinese origin, adopted by the Japanese in the 12th century, that has its own unique identity within the wider practice of Buddhism. The name is derived from the Chinese word *ch'an* which, in turn, originates from the Sanskrit *dhyana*, meaning "meditation". The essential concept of Zen is that a true state of perfection – nirvana – is attained only when all is reduced (or expanded) to nothing. It cannot be reached while the surface of life ripples with emotion, desire, concern, ambition, curiosity or selfishness.

A number of "koans" (exercises in paradox) originate from Zen teachings and give an indication of what needs to be accomplished by the mind of the acolyte who seeks nirvana. Perhaps the most famous of these questions is "What is the sound of one hand clapping?" If everything is reduced (or elevated) to its ultimate state of non-being, perfection has been reached. Zen rituals, therefore, tend toward simplicity, quiet, stillness and deep inner reflection to

△ Zen epitomizes simplicity, and rituals in the Zen style are likewise always simple.

▽ A room decorated and furnished in accordance with the philosophy of Zen will always reflect spaciousness and composure.

create an atmosphere of intense and almost solid peace; they are ideal for dispelling any form of psychic disharmony or negative energy in space clearing.

Because this ritual comes from the eastern rather than the western tradition, it is not necessary to precede it with a banishing ritual, though this can be done if you feel it is appropriate.

PRONUNCIATION

'Aum' (or 'Om') is spoken after taking as deep a breath as possible. It begins with the sound 'Ahh', moving into 'Om' (like the first syllable of 'omelette') and continuing the 'mm' for as long as the out-breath lasts. This word is held to symbolize all the sounds in the universe.

▷ A clear mind is the perfected state of Zen.
Meditation is an ideal practice to help you move
towards such a state.

preparation

Arrange for as much silence and stillness as
the surroundings permit. If possible, use a
gong to mark the beginning and end of the
ritual: otherwise, find something else that
will produce a similar clear, simple sound,
such as a stone to bang gently on a small
block of wood. You will also need a low
table or altar covered with a plain black
cloth and a few sticks of sandalwood incense
in a suitable container.

Set up the altar as close as possible to the
exact centre of the area you wish to include
in the space clearing, so that you can sit or
kneel before it facing east.

the ritual

Light the incense. Kneel on a cushion or sit
on a straight-backed chair before the altar,
or adopt the lotus position if you prefer.
When you are settled, perform the fourfold
breath to still your thoughts: to do this,

▽ A simple sound, such as the striking of a gong
or chime, is used to mark the beginning and
ending of a Zen ritual.

breathe in to an unhurried count of four,
hold your breath for a count of four, breathe
out for a count of four and hold your breath
again for a count of four, then take the next
breath and repeat the sequence. Continue
to practise the fourfold breath for a few
minutes, until you feel a state of great calm
begin to unfold.

When you feel sufficiently calm and at
ease with your surroundings, gently sound
the gong once. As the sound fades, begin to
chant the single word 'Aum' as slowly as
possible. Keep your head bowed towards the
altar. Repeat the chant ten to 12 times,
taking care throughout to avoid any feeling
of 'hurrying things along'.

Once you have reached the end the
chanting, take two or three more fourfold
breaths, then slowly bow towards the east,
with your hands held at your chest in an

attitude of prayer. In this position, repeat a
single long 'Aum'. Your mind should now
be clear enough to concentrate your
thoughts. Close your eyes and make your
mental image as sharp as you can, aiming
for a reality equivalent to having your eyes
open. This may take a little practice before
you undertake the ritual itself. Visualize a
circular ripple of light in the centre of your
abdomen, slowly spreading out horizontally,
like the ripples from a stone tossed into a
pool filmed in slow motion. As this circle
of light reaches the horizon, it continues
out into the universe and to infinity.
Continue to observe this visualization for
several minutes.

To end the ritual, stand up, place your
hands in the prayer position at your chest
as before and bow deeply from the waist.
Sound the gong once more to close.

An angelic space clearing

The concept of angelic beings is familiar in the Judaeo–Christian tradition, in which these high and pure spiritual entities act as messengers, protectors and guides to humans. Some angels, such as Gabriel, are mentioned in the Bible, but in fact they predate the Biblical period, originating in earlier cultures such as those of Sumer, Babylon and Ur (in modern Iraq). Angelic invocation formed the basis of many ancient occult practices, and individual angels were traditionally associated with various entities, such as the seven ancient planets, specific days of the week, certain colours, incenses, symbols and powers. There are stories of angels being seen on battlefields or by individuals in danger, whose lives were saved by the angelic beings.

If you are attracted to this kind of spiritual conception, you may well draw the strongest benefit from performing an angelic

THE ATTRIBUTES OF ANGELS

Traditional correspondences exist for each angelic presence, and this list will help you to call upon the assistance of the most appropriate angel for your needs. In your ritual, utilize the appropriate symbols for the angel you choose.

ANGEL/CHARACTER	HELPFUL FOR	DAY	COLOUR	SYMBOL	INCENSE
Michael Angel of the sun, guardian and protector	Summon to encourage success, or with issues involving the maintenance of stamina or physical health	Sunday	orange/gold	six-pointed star	olibanum
Gabriel Angel of the moon, protector of women and children	Summon for fertility, healing, psychic abilities and all issues concerning harmony in the home	Monday	pale blue	nine-pointed star	myrrh, jasmine
Samael Angel of Mars, protector and guardian, guide to men	Summon to protect against violence, to dispel negative opposition and to obtain justice in your life	Tuesday	red	five-pointed star	tobacco, dragon's blood
Raphael Angel of Mercury	Summon to protect during times of change, upheaval or travel and for issues of mental stress.	Wednesday	yellow	eight-pointed star	galbanum, storax
Sachiel Angel of Jupiter	Summon when you are seeking justice, or protection of your financial situation or status	Thursday	purple	square	cedar
Anael Angel of Venus	Summon when conflict involves relatives or friends, where emotional harmony or love may be lacking	Friday	green	seven-pointed (or mystic) star	rose, red sandalwood
Cassiel Angel of Saturn	Summon in cases involving the protection of property, land or possessions, to clear obstacles such as chronic health conditions, or in situations where you feel blocked by another's actions	Saturday	indigo or black	straight line	myrrh

▽ To end the ritual, extinguish the candles with respect and give thanks to the energies that will respond to your call.

space clearing. When an angelic presence is invited into the place you wish to be cleared, it will leave a lingering protective power and the strong influence of its own characteristics, which will make the place feel calm, tranquil and thoroughly cleared of all hostile or negative influences.

an angelic altar

When you have decided which angel is most appropriate for your needs, you can set up an altar to your chosen protector. This is done very simply by assembling two candles in the colour that corresponds to your angel, and the correct incense, perhaps with an image or symbol to focus your thoughts. Place a candle on each side of the incense container and write in appropriately coloured ink the name of the angel you wish to call upon, drawing the symbol of that angel above the name.

Light the candles and the incense and sit before the altar for about 15 minutes each day, asking for assistance and/or intervention on your behalf in dealing with the situation or energy you are trying to clear. Repeat your request three times and then sit quietly in contemplation of your angel and the help you will receive. Extinguish the candles with respect and give thanks to the energies that will respond to your call.

△ Each angel has an association with a particular colour and fragrance: use the appropriate candles and incense on the altar.

▽ Light the incense and leave it to smoulder while you spend about 15 minutes each day in contemplation of your chosen angelic power.

A druid space clearing

We know very little about the Druids of old, because they were members of a culture that kept no written records. The knowledge we have comes almost entirely from a few books written by the Romans, who were responsible for exterminating the Druids ruthlessly. The typical Druid seems to have been an athletic warrior who possessed remarkable knowledge. From childhood, he would have committed to memory the wisdom, culture and history of the Celts, all of which was transmitted orally.

The Druids were the priesthood of the Gaulish tribes, also known as the Celts, who populated west and central Europe in the pre-Roman era. Later invaders, such as the Anglo Saxons (who reached Britain from Germany after the Romans had abandoned the islands), pushed the Celts into the most remote areas of Europe, including Scotland, Cornwall, Wales, Brittany and the Basque region of northern Spain.

The Druids regarded oak trees and mistletoe as sacred: when we 'kiss under the mistletoe' at Christmas, we are actually enacting part of an ancient pagan fertility rite. They also practised human sacrifice (often by burning their victims in groups inside wooden cages shaped like giant human figures), which was the Romans' declared reason for stamping them out. However, it is more likely that the Druids were destroyed because they were the intellectual leaders of Celtic society, and were capable of organizing resistance against Roman rule.

The modern order of Druids was invented in the 18th century, probably as a rival to Freemasonry, and has no direct

△ Druidic rituals were often performed in groves of oaks, the most venerated of trees and sacred in ancient times to the sky-gods.

▽ Today we are more often surrounded by buildings than the wonders of nature, but we can still express our respect for the natural world.

GOD OF THE EARTH
'Father Dis' was worshipped by the Druids as the god of the earth. The Romans equated Dis with their god Pluto and the Greek god Hades, the rulers of the underworld.

△ Having set twigs and boughs around the space to be cleared, arrange the candles and incense around the room and light them.

produce an aura of calm about yourself. When you feel calm, approach the east of the area. Stand and draw a deep breath. Without shouting, use the breath to declaim authoritatively: "There is peace!" Now approach the south, take another deep breath and again use it to declaim: "There is peace!" Repeat in exactly the same way to the west, and finally to the north.

Returning to face the east, adopt the occult salute of Dis, by crossing the forearms at the level of the forehead, with clenched fists. In this position, take another deep breath and state levelly and quietly: "I have peace! Let peace prevail!" Lower the arms and visualize the atmosphere of peace spreading like a white mist throughout the area. Gather up the twigs and burn them ceremonially outside or on an open fire indoors. If fire poses a problem, you can bury the twigs, preferably beneath an oak tree. In this case, let the oak tree know what you are burying and why.

connection with the Celtic priesthood. Some writers have suggested that Druidism and Wicca share a common origin in the remote past, and there seem to be some grounds for this. Wicca is known to be a combination of the native lunar-based agricultural tradition with the sun-worship brought by the migrating Beaker people of the Bronze Age, around 1500 BC. Thus Wicca observes four lunar festivals (known as the major Sabbats) and four solar festivals (the lesser Sabbats). It is possible that Druidism in Roman Gaul was descended from the sun-worshipping aspect of the Beaker folk, before their beliefs merged with the native religion.

This space clearing ritual is based on the romantic Druid idyll constructed in the modern period, rather than on the accounts of Roman historians, who accorded only a few lines to ancient Druidic practices, which were evidently not pleasant.

preparation

You will need to gather several twigs of oak leaves from the ground (they should not be picked from the tree). In winter you can use bare oak twigs. A few sprigs of mistletoe can be added if available, but be aware that the white berries are poisonous. Select an 'Earth' incense such as sage, pine or patchouli, and candles in Earth colours: black, brown, olive-green, mustard-yellow or white. No altar is used in this ritual.

the ritual

Set the twigs and leaves around the space to be cleared. Arrange the incense and candles carefully here and there around the area and light them.

Stand for several moments, breathing in slowly and deeply, with your eyes closed, to

▽ Stand quietly in the centre of the area, breathing deeply, to calm yourself before beginning the ritual.

Hedgewitch rituals

The term 'hedgewitch' describes a magical practitioner who works alone and very much according to individual style and belief. In days of old, the hedgewitch would have been called upon regularly to assist in house blessings and clearings, in the protection of property and personal possessions, and also to act as an oracle to discover the reasons behind any problems and hindrances. Traditionally, he or she would have lived on the edge of the community, surrounded by hedgerows and perhaps also concealed behind the garden hedge around the house.

Living in harmony with nature, hedgewitches use their knowledge of herbs,

▽ Hedgewitches have a very close link to the spirit world, and to elementals like the fairies.

flowers, roots and leaves to make up concoctions for such purposes as healing, protection or fertility. A hedgewitch is able to keep one foot in the material world and the other in the world of spirit, and this is what the hedge represents: the veil between the worlds. The hedgewitch might use any of the following for space clearing.

spirits of place

Everything in the world is made up of energy and this includes the energy that makes up the blueprint for the home and place of work. For the purposes of communicating with them, the various energies around us can be called spirits of place. By communing regularly with the spirits of place, the hedgewitch can discover what is causing particular problems to arise.

fairies and elementals

A hedgewitch believes strongly in the elemental energies that inhabit gardens, plants and other natural objects. These entities are a vital part of the energetic life force system, and together are known as elementals because they are related to the four elements, and each shares the characteristics of the element to which it is related. They are called sylphs (those that are related to the Air element), salamanders (those that are related to Fire), undines (related to Water) and gnomes (related to Earth). Fairies and dryads are nature spirits and the hedgewitch will work with both elementals and nature spirits when seeking causes of inbalance.

Creating an elemental area will provide these helpful spirits with a space to be close to you and will be somewhere you can connect with them at times when you need their assistance. At first you may not believe in them, but once you have made an elemental space and asked for their assistance, you will find that something will happen that will definitely shift your belief towards their existence.

△ Obsidian, onyx, flint and other dark stones are frequently used by hedgewitches for their rituals and charms.

dark crystals and stones

Any dark stone can be programmed to draw in negative vibrations from its local environment. Placing dark stones in a problem area can help to cleanse it before it is filled with symbols and objects of warmth and light.

Flint is commonly found throughout most of the world and this stone is a powerful protector against psychic or negative intrusions.

sharp objects

To give protection against negative influences, place needles, pins, thorns, prickles, or any other sharp objects in a jar, then fill it with a mixture of protective herbs. The jar should then be sealed and left in the area that seems to be causing problems. It can also be placed under the bed for protection at night. Putting rusty iron nails around your property, facing away

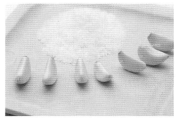

▽ Garlic has powerful cleansing properties on both the physical and energetic levels.

from the walls, is another traditional means of protection, and will guard against any kind of opposition.

a horseshoe

An iron horseshoe should be displayed with its horns facing to the left in the shape of a crescent moon. Iron is the metal of Mars – the planet of power, strength and courage. A horseshoe placed in this way displays the properties of Mars and moon goddesses.

spells, charms and amulets

Charms such as runic symbols, or those made specifically for an individual, can be used for protection, as well as natural amulets

▽ Hedgewitches display a horseshoe on its side, with its horns facing left like the crescent moon, to invoke the power of moon goddesses.

△ Hedgewitches will often grow and harvest their own herbs, for use both in rituals and charms and for healing.

like oak leaves, onion and nettle. A protection spell is one of the skills sought from a hedgewitch.

herbs and spices

The hedgewitch frequently uses herbs and spices in her work and those commonly used in space clearing include the following:

Angelica: an all-round protective plant.
Asafoetida: removes all negativity, but smells acrid, so is used only in severe cases.
Cactus: all spiny plants and tree branches offer protection. Prickly plants or stems in the home or workplace will deflect negativity from the surrounding area.
Fumitory: to expel negative thought forms.
Garlic: the strong smell and taste of garlic deters negativity. Cloves of peeled garlic can be strung over door frames, or placed in strategic positions and replaced once a week with fresh cloves.
Rowan: all parts of the rowan tree have magical protective properties. String the leaves and berries into a garland and place them around whatever you wish to gain protection for, keeping it out of reach of small children or babies.
Yarrow: a powerful psychic protector.
Salt: central to many of the hedgewitch's practices, salt is one of the sacred items for all magical practitioners. It is a crystal and its cleansing powers mean that it is held in great respect.

A HEDGEWITCH SALT CLEANSING
This ritual can be performed once a week to keep your home or workplace clear and clean. Sweep up any old salt and take it outside your property boundary before repeating the ritual.

Begin at the doorway and move clockwise around the room. Take a pinch of undyed natural sea or rock salt and sprinkle it in the first corner saying as you do so, "Clean and clear this corner [or window, or fireplace] be, from all that is not good for me." Repeat in all four corners, around the door frames, windows, and fireplace, in the same way.

▽ Salt is absorptive and has been used for centuries as a cleanser.

Space clearing for life

Wherever we are, we become aware of an atmosphere that we perceive through our deepest senses. The atmosphere of each place is subtly different from any other and can profoundly influence our mood. If you dislike the appearance of a room, you can change it, and the same is true of its atmosphere. Space clearing can make a room feel the way you want it to.

To dispel a negative atmosphere

The 'atmosphere' of a place can be experienced by those in it as good or bad, but what exactly is it? In occult terms, an atmosphere is a 'thought-form' of a certain type. Just as living creatures may have tiny parasites living on them, the psyche has its own form of parasites that attach themselves to it, and these are referred to by occultists as thought-forms.

Thought-forms can be extremely valuable when a magician deliberately creates them, and they form a major part of magic. Unfortunately, the unco-ordinated and primal regions of the mind (the regions responsible, amongst other things, for our dreams) are just as capable of generating a subconscious thought-form as the controlled regions are of deliberately producing a conscious one.

On the subliminal unconscious level, the mind is very susceptible to the psychic vibrations inherent in a place, or produced by people who have been there before, or even by people living nearby and not actually in the place itself. Such vibrations are received by the subconscious mind, rather like a radio set receiving broadcast messages, and a thought-form is created that reflects the nature of the broadcast – it may be happy, sad, gloomy, cheerful, spooky, holy, welcoming, resentful and so on. In our upper, conscious mind we are not aware of how this information – this feeling – arrived inside us, but we recognize it and describe it as the 'atmosphere' of a place.

Any kind of good, positive atmosphere is welcome and wholesome, but we sometimes need to cure a negative, unwholesome one. This can be achieved in two ways. We can generate a sufficient quantity of positive psychic vibrations and literally blast them into the affected area, like a kind-of 'psychic fly-spray', to change the nature of the vibrations emitted (like changing the broadcast signal). This is the process called exorcism, and it requires tremendous psychic strength and control: it is not recommended unless you are an expert. Also, in nearly every case it is unnecessary, like using a sledgehammer to crack a walnut.

The second way is generally much more useful, helpful and simpler: to continue the broadcast analogy, we can re-tune the receiver so that it picks up a better signal – and the 'receiver', of course, is ourselves. In other words, we endeavour to change our own state of mind so that the unwelcome vibrations are no longer received. This process helps us to become stronger, more psychically capable, and less vulnerable to negative influences.

Rituals that produce changes inside ourselves – changes of consciousness – need to be approached with care and sensitivity, and they work best when they are kept short and simple, unless you are a fully trained and proficient occultist.

◁ **As you light your central candle, visualize the flame protecting you and your space.**

▷ **The fourfold breath is used to calm and centre yourself before the ritual.**

the ritual

You will need a selection of white candles and tea lights, including one large white candle, and a rattle such as the one described right. Distribute the candles about the floor of the room and light them. Use as many or as few as you feel is appropriate.

Sit on a cushion in the centre of the room. Light the large white candle and place it on the floor directly in front of you. Spend several minutes performing the fourfold breath (breathe in for a count of four, hold for four, breathe out for four, hold for four before taking the next breath). Then pick up your rattle in your right hand and repeat the following in a deep and warning tone:

Pay attention (shake rattle)
Snake is here (shake rattle)
It is true
Snake is coming (shake rattle)
So beware adversary – snake is ready to strike.
(shake rattle loudly)

Then repeat the following chant:

Life is love; love is life; let there be an end to strife.
Let the good replace all bad; let love release all spirits sad.

Let my will reveal the power, starting at this present hour,
To enhance the energy, so that I possess the key,
To allow all ills to go, and to let the goodness flow,
Into this place where I now kneel, let love begin all things to heal.

Repeat the chant several times. Visualize all negativity departing from you at great speed, as you chase it away and re-claim what is rightfully yours.

▽ **All kinds of noise will chase away negativity, but the noise of your rattle has the added potency of the power of the rattlesnake.**

MAKING A RATTLE

Rattles can conjure the ominous sounds of the rattlesnake as it warns of its presence by shaking its tail. The rattle when used in ceremony can either summon the energy of snake to protect, or can warn intrusive energies that they should step back and withdraw. You will need an empty aluminium drinks can, some paper, and a handful of dried long grain rice. Remove the ring pull completely, empty the contents, wash and thoroughly dry the aluminium can. Place the can on the paper and draw round the circular base to form a circle the same size. Cut out the circle. Pour the rice grains in through the ring-pull hole. Place the paper circle over the top of the can to cover the ring pull hole and glue in place. Decorate your can as you feel drawn to do. When it is completed, pass your rattle through the smoke of burning sage, calling for the powers of the rattlesnake to enter your shamanic rattle and for snake to help you.

Dedicate your rattle to Sosho (the snake) and to the spirit of life before using it.

Sometimes the atmosphere of a space needs to be changed if its function is to be altered. For example, if a former bedroom, which has acquired a relaxed atmosphere over the years, is changed into a sitting room, psychically sensitive people may feel drowsy when they spend time in the room. If the planning department of a company moves out of an office and the accounts department moves in, employers may wonder why the accounting staff now seem to be spending so much time in earnest discussion. The atmospheres in these spaces are not particularly negative – they are just misplaced echoes of former thought-forms, each with a residual power of subliminal

◁ **These objects will help change the masculine atmosphere of a home office – symbolized by a pen – to the gentler atmosphere of a little girl's bedroom – symbolized by the little pink bag.**

persuasion, that need to be overwritten by a more appropriate one.

Transmuting one positive atmosphere into another can be done with a ritual in which you begin by focusing on the old atmosphere, and then swing your focus to the new atmosphere, whatever it may be. This could also be described as stamping a new psychic impression upon a place.

YOU WILL NEED
4 small tumbled rose quartz crystals
altar
white candle
2 or 3 candles in a colour that reflects the new usage of the space
small token of the original use of the space
black cloth large enough to cover or contain the token
rose geranium essential oil and burner
small token of the new atmosphere

CANDLE COLOURS

Use this list to help you choose candles in the most appropriate colour, which will represent the new function of the room and enhance the atmosphere you are seeking to create.

Red: active areas, energy, dynamism.
Orange: creative areas, socializing, a supportive ambience.
Yellow: thought, the mind, offices and places of study and learning.
Green: areas of relaxation, harmony, balance, calm.
Blue: peace, calm, relaxation.
Violet: warmth and relaxation. A combination of blue and pink, it is ideal for areas where both liveliness and rest are required, such as a dining room.
Pink: inspiration, happiness, positivity.
Purple: depth, reflection, authority, contemplation, for areas requiring stillness, depth and meaning, such as a meditation room.
Silver: magic, dreams, the feminine, for changing a very masculine room into a more feminine one.

Gold: prosperity, abundance, the masculine, for changing a feminine room into a more masculine one.
Brown: grounding, practicality, commitment, for an atmosphere that requires stability and reliable energy. Ideal when changing a mentally oriented space to a more practical one, such as a kitchen or utility room.

the ritual

Set up an altar in the middle of the room using appropriate colours to reflect the change you are making. Put the white candle in the centre of the altar with the three coloured candles arranged in a triangle around it. Put everything you are going to use in the ritual on the altar for a few moments, then take the rose quartz crystals and put them in each corner of the room.

Take the object you have chosen to represent the old atmosphere, and place it in the western quarter of the room. Take the object that is representing the new atmosphere of the room and place it in the eastern quarter. Light all the candles. Start the ritual at the east side of the altar, facing west. Take a few deep, calming breaths and say the following:

△ As you clap your hands, visualize the sounds driving away the old atmosphere of work, business and stressful activity.

△ After removing the old object, bring in the new one and place it in a central position in the room as a focus point for the new energies.

CLAPPING HANDS

Like any loud and sudden noise, clapping the hands serves to alert and charge the atmosphere. It has the effect of startling a room's energies into an awakened and expectant state.

Go! Depart! Begone ye hence! Avaunt I say, this is my will!
Be ended, finished, changed, transposed,
Leave no disturbing echoes still!

Clap your hands loudly, then take the cloth over to the object in the west and cover it. Return to the altar, but this time stand at the west side facing east, in the opposite direction to the earlier part of the ritual. Say the following:

Now welcome be, now welcome stay, now welcome is for evermore!
Be started, newborn, fresh, unfurled,
And bring thy presence to the fore!

Go to the object in the east that represents the new atmosphere and bring it reverentially to the altar to place it there. Sit beside the altar and leave the item there for several minutes while you meditate on it. As you do so, absorb the new atmosphere that is emerging in the room and reflect it back at the object.

When you feel this is complete and the atmosphere has been altered, close the ritual by extinguishing the candles. Dismantle the altar and remove the object that represented the old atmosphere from the room. Leave the object that represents the new atmosphere in a prominent position on a windowsill or shelf.

To make a place feel special

When we expect visitors and spend time preparing for their stay, our aim is to make our home feel especially welcoming. If we are holding a dinner party, we take great care both to prepare good food and to provide a jovial atmosphere. It is important to us to provide for our guests' physical comfort, and we are also concerned about doing the equivalent on a psychic level.

There are two key words that relate to making a place feel special, both materially and magically, and these are 'pride' and 'respect'. Without one, we will not feel the other. When both these elements are brought into play, our place – whatever and wherever it may be – will begin to fill with that special atmosphere of sparkle and excitement.

YOU WILL NEED

altar and orange altar cloth
2 orange or gold candles
frankincense incense and charcoal
*   burner or essential oil and burner*
wand
additional orange candles for dark
*   areas*
rosewater in small bowl

the ritual

Position the altar so that you will face east when standing before it. Arrange the cloth and the two candles in holders upon it, together with the incense or essential oil burner and the wand. Place the additional candles randomly around the room in the shadowy areas that light does not normally illuminate, and where the candle glow will enhance the richness of the room's appearance. The aim is to achieve a depth of perspective in the room, so try to arrange the candles in a non-linear way. Try to avoid having any two candles at a similar distance from the altar.

Light all the candles, then stand in front of the altar and bow your head. Take several deep and calming breaths. Use the wand to

'draw' a solar hexagram in the air in front of you above the altar. The hexagram, a six-pointed star (identical to the 'Star of David') is associated with the zodiac, the planets and the sun. At its centre, 'draw' the symbol of the sun: a small circle with a dot in the middle. As you do this, visualize the outline appearing as a line of brilliant golden light. Then in a commanding voice, say:

Let none undo the spell I cast,
For it is well and three times good;
This place is special now at last,
Be it now full understood!

△ **Candles randomly arranged in this ritual brighten every corner.**

▽ **The solar hexagram is a six-rayed star with a representation of the sun in the centre.**

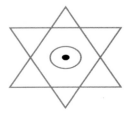

▷ When drawing the hexagram visualize its lines as brilliant golden light.

CREATING AN ENTRANCE

In magical terms, the doorway or entrance to a space is symbolic of a new beginning or a journey of discovery and change. It is therefore an ideal setting to affirm the new atmosphere you are calling in, by using decorations to make the place feel special as you enter.

Bead curtains add a sense of mystery and magic.
Foliage, such as rosemary, ivy and laurel, garlanded around a door frame invites protection, fun and harmony into the room.
Flowers and herbs invite connections with the natural world and convey a sense of ease and relaxation.
Fairy lights strung around the doorway create a sense of light and warmth, and invite the fairies into your space.
Images and charms hung over the door attract specific qualities: angels invite blessings, protective deities offer strength and coins invite prosperous exchanges.

Now pick up the bowl of rosewater and, as you walk clockwise around the edge of the room, dip your fingers in the water and then brush your hand over the walls and floor areas. As you do so, say, "Blessed be this boundary". Where there are areas of the room that might be damaged by the rosewater, pass your hand over the walls a little distance away. It is helpful to visualize that the blessing water is creating a sphere of happiness and peace, as you mark out the boundary of the room.

To close the ritual, extinguish all the candles, starting with the furthest away from the altar and ending with the nearest. Give thanks and discard any remaining rosewater into the earth.

▷ As you distribute rosewater around the room concentrate on what you are doing and visualize a sphere of happiness being created.

To give a sense of belonging

To generate a sense of belonging in a space, we need to start off by feeling special there, and then begin to form a bond with it. A space clearing ritual performed with this intent first needs to produce a subtle change of consciousness. Then, at a second level, it needs to establish an aura of association connecting us with the place.

As you develop your awareness of the energy in a room you will be able to sense any imbalance that creates a disturbing or unsatisfactory atmosphere. Such imbalance can be defined in terms of the four elements, and you can consider ways in which you could bring each element into the space, by introducing them in ways that are relevant to you personally. First it is necessary to find which element is required, and each imbalance will tend to manifest within you in a distinct way as you spend time in the room.

▽ A bedroom may have everything it needs to be serene and peaceful, but you might still feel that its atmosphere is lacking something.

sensing the need

Calm and centre yourself before entering the room, then go in and sit down in the centre of the floor, or on the most important piece of furniture, such as a bed in a bedroom, or the sofa in a sitting room. Make your body into a complete circuit by putting both feet flat on the floor or surface, with one hand resting on each knee. After about three minutes, turn your hands palm upwards on your knees and begin to sense the area, also taking into account how you normally feel when you are in the room for any length of time. An imbalance between the elements may be indicated by any of the following feelings:

Crowded – compulsive, mentally intense: too much Air.

Forgetful – unable to remember or recall information, absent-minded: too little Air.

Explosive – having difficulty in keeping one's temper, or a compulsion to outdo everyone: too much Fire.

Disempowered – overly meek and submissive: too little Fire.

▷ To be able to sense the need of a room, you will want to be calm, relaxed and receptive.

ELEMENTAL BULBS

Once the needs of your environment have been established, you can balance or summon the relevant element into your room by installing a painted and patterned light bulb.

Air: violet circles on a yellow background.

Fire: red flames on a green background.

Water: blue bands on an orange background.

Earth: citrine and russet brown diamonds.

Overwhelmed – being or feeling too emotional: too much Water.

Insensitive – being unfeeling, callous, hurtful or cold: too little Water.

Dull – reluctant to change anything: too much Earth.

Restless – desiring to change things continuously for no reason: too little Earth.

elemental lighting

Install the appropriate elemental light bulb in the room, preferably in the central light fitting, and light some incense of the appropriate fragrance. Breathe deeply, calming the mind. Absorb the atmosphere and the character produced by the colours from the light falling upon the walls of the room. Then repeat one of the following statements, according to the element:

From Air I arise, in Air I live, in Air my kin, to Air I shall return.

From Fire I leap, in Fire I triumph, in Fire my kindred, to Fire I shall return.

From Water I spring, in Water I form, in Water my kingdom, to Water I shall return.

From Earth I come, in Earth I dwell, on Earth my people, to Earth I shall return.

Meditate upon bonding spiritually with your chosen element. Visualize, as appropriate, clouds for Air, gentle flames for Fire, rivulets for Water or roots for Earth stemming from you and twining about the entire area. This will give you a strong feeling of connecting with and belonging intimately to the place, as you become more and more comfortable with the atmosphere you are creating around you with your

ritual. Once you feel that the balance and connection you are seeking in the area have been achieved, remove the bulb and return the lighting in the room to normal.

▽ Let your hands 'feel' and sense the area you are intending to balance and clear.

Space clearing for a new beginning

In order to facilitate a new beginning for ourselves, we must first create the space to enable it to materialize in our lives. For this reason, the acknowledgement of endings is highly significant. Our lives follow cycles that are continually changing, evolving and shifting from moment to moment, and nothing in the physical realm remains permanently the same.

In modern society, we have come to fear or abhor most endings, seeing them as associated with failure or as the loss of something we value or want to keep. However, change is not only inevitable but good, and when we are able to let go of things that do not really serve us, or of an experience that has run its course, our lives can open up in very positive ways.

So to attract a new beginning, we must first close the door on that which is ending. This could be a work contract, a relationship, a house move or perhaps grown-up children leaving home; whatever the situation, it is important to create an ending that honours the change, while remaining positive about it. The ceremony can be as simple or elaborate as you wish. The simplest way to honour an ending is to voice the fact in your life and world, and give thanks for what you have experienced as you indicate your intention to let it go and move on to a new beginning.

moving

If you are moving house, cleaning and clearing out naturally become paramount in the process of moving on. After the physical clearing and cleansing has been finished, an ideal way to acknowledge the act spiritually is to sweep the house symbolically with a bundle of birch twigs or a birch broom, imagining each area being purified as you do so. In ancient times, brushwood from the birch tree was used to sweep out the spirits of the old year, preparing the way for the beginning of the new one. Let the house know of your

SYMBOLS OF NEW BEGINNINGS

These are many ways in which you can call for a new beginning, once you have recognized and acknowledged an ending in your life.

• A pair of lodestones placed as a pair in a central area of a room will call for the attraction of a lover.
• If you see shooting stars and comets together in the sky, wishing upon them calls the Sky Father's protection and blessing for any wishes you make.
• The cowrie shell is sacred to the Goddess and empowers wishes for love, friendship and family. Decorate a small pouch with cowrie shells and drop your written wish inside.
• A bowl of seeds (such as sesame, sunflower or pumpkin) with a wish tucked into them, placed on an altar or on the kitchen windowsill, will encourage the growth of whatever you have called for.
• A birch broom propped up beside a doorway will encourage the old to depart and the new to arrive, and will also provide protection for the home.

• Written symbols, such as Beth from the Druidic tree alphabet, or the Greek letter Alpha, will encourage new beginnings. Write them in places of significance, such as over a written wish or trace them in the air in a space where new beginnings are being called for.
• Write a wish on a piece of paper, fold or roll it and place the paper within the cone of a white lily flower, this bloom is sacred to Ostara, the goddess of birth and new life.
• When you are seeking new work or prosperity opportunities, turn silver coins in your pocket on the first night of a new moon to invite growth in your finances.

▷ In Celtic lore, the birch is associated with January, the month dedicated to Janus, the Roman god of new beginnings. Therefore, sweeping with birch twigs symbolizes your call for a new beginning.

△ Sprinkle blessed, or sun charged, water around a room for a new beginning into it. As you do so, focus your mind on what you are doing.

▽ Rosemary is traditionally associated with remembrance and is helpful for rituals that deal with releasing grievances or loss.

intentions in performing this act, and thank it for having been your home. You can also use the birch broom to sweep the new house you are moving into, as a first step to claiming it as your new home. Here it will have the effect of sweeping away the atmosphere created by the previous occupants, creating space for your own spiritual energy.

To prepare your new home for the beginning of your life there, bless it by walking around all the rooms and sprinkling them as you go with drops of water that you have charged with the energy of the sun. This will add vitality and vigour to your new environment.

relationships

At the beginning of a relationship, we want to spend all available time with our new partner. If a parting becomes inevitable, so does our attention to the relationship, which can sometimes end with total silence, resentment and disregard or, conversely, with trauma, abuse and blame. If possible, try to remember the love you once shared, honour each other's differences and accept that your time together has had some value in your lives. If you can achieve this, you will be closing the relationship cycle with love, which will set up the vibration for love to meet your new beginning. It is a question in all cases of starting as you mean to go on.

Space clearing your office

If you have a private office where you can ensure that no one will disturb you, any of the rituals described in this book can be performed in it: you can simply perform one that you find relevant to your needs. However, most people do not have such privacy at work, which can make it awkward to conduct any kind of overt ritual, so an alternative system of conducting a space clearing needs to be employed.

At its purest and most powerful level, magic needs no special equipment or physical actions, including speech; the entire ritual, including all scents, colours and tools, can be imagined through creative visualization. In order to achieve the full-blown magical results of an occult master by this technique, it is necessary to develop and train the mind and willpower so that anything created in the imagination becomes indistinguishable from absolute reality in all respects. However, only a shadow of this ability is required in order to accomplish a practical and effective office space clearing.

preparation

Try to choose a time for the space clearing when you are unlikely to be disturbed. Even though outwardly you will not be doing anything that would raise any eyebrows among your colleagues, you will be better able to concentrate if you are alone.

Before the day you have planned to perform the ritual, obtain a small notepad to form a scrapbook that lends itself to the concept of a silent, mental space clearing. You will also need to collect a number of appropriate images to represent your working environment. These could be taken from magazines and catalogues. Your tools for this ritual will be nothing more complicated than scissors, glue and paper.

the ritual

Cut out the pictures you have collected and use them to assemble a collage, or compound image of the office, by arranging and sticking them together. Remember that it does not need to look like your own office, nor does it need to be artistic or to

△ As offices are usually crowded and busy places, space clearing at work oftens needs to be a private, mental exercise.

scale, or to have perfect perspective. You are simply aiming for a surreal general impression of an office environment, not an accurate reconstruction.

Everyone is familiar with the ancient voodoo practice of sticking pins into a doll that represents someone you don't like. This follows the principle of sympathetic magic: the idea is that the doll and the target become inextricably linked, so that whatever happens to one will transfer itself to the other by association. Though this practice is definitely immoral, sympathetic magic can be employed in a similar way to space clear the office.

Just as the doll is only a rough image of a real person, your office collage need only be an approximation of your actual office.

◁ Create a scrapbook of images that represent your working environment, and use this as a focus for your thoughts.

▷ If a co-worker is causing problems, take a cactus to work and place it between you and the offending party to create a symbolic barrier.

PROTECTION STRATEGIES

Here are some other simple ways to keep your office psychically protected and clear:

• Display some plants and flowers that have protective qualities, such as fern, yarrow and geranium. Put them in waiting rooms and reception areas to reduce any invasive effects upon your space of the energy of visitors.

• Place smoky quartz crystals in the four corners of your office. Cleanse them once a month by soaking them for eight hours in salted spring water. Rinse them thoroughly and before replacing them hold them in your hands while affirming their abilities to continue absorbing stray energies from your office for the month to come.

You can make one collage, or as many versions as you like, until you find an image that you resonate well with. All you now need to do is look at the image you have assembled and, as you concentrate on it, visualize that you are projecting a space clearing energy into the office. This exercise should be repeated several times for maximum effect.

guarding against negativity

There are other things you can do to space clear your office and repel negativity, such as keeping the area clean and free of clutter, just as you would your home. To protect yourself from negativity coming from another worker in your office, take in a cactus and put it between yourself and the offending party.

If when you are at work you feel a sudden vulnerability, try using your mind to project an image of a guardian figure at your office door. This should be someone you feel safe and happy with, who will keep stray energies (or human nuisances) from entering the office. But it is important never to visualize such a guardian as actually taking the offensive against other people, no matter how much they may annoy you. It is a guardian only, not a hostile spirit.

Space clearing on the move

Like space clearing in an office, space clearing 'on the move' can be awkward if people who are unsympathetic to spiritual rituals are likely to be present or to arrive on the scene unexpectedly. You may find yourself in a variety of temporary situations where some psychic negativity may make its presence felt and need to be dealt with for your comfort and peace of mind. These could include hotel rooms, holiday accommodation, cars and caravans, as well as public transport: in short, anywhere that you enter for a limited period but cannot conveniently leave if you encounter a negative energy field. While you would probably not become aware of anything negative during a short journey on a bus or in a taxi, a longer journey by air, sea or rail might benefit from space clearing.

A handy ritual based on certain elements of Wicca can fulfil the need for a space

△ Your hotel room might be charming to look at but could have a lingering atmosphere from previous guests that you want to dispel.

clearing whenever you are on the move. It is unobtrusive and very simple, and can easily be performed in a hotel room or even in a crowded train compartment or a car

▽ Ships' cabins can seem cramped and impersonal. Use your space clearing skills to claim the space as your own.

(providing you are not the driver) because everything is carried out in the mind, rather than physically.

The ritual can be done purely as a mental exercise, but an important magical technique that can help greatly when you are doing a mind-working is to visualize yourself actually performing it as a full ritual. This usually takes only a little practice. Try to imagine a 'ghost image' of yourself stepping out of your real body, like a double exposure in a film. Visualize your image standing up and saying and doing the things that the physical you is only thinking. The use of this magical double, or doppelganger, is actually an occult method dating back many centuries. In ancient times people believed that a powerful magus was able to send out such a doppelganger that could actually be seen by others who took it for the real person. Such a self-projection was sometimes called a 'fetch'.

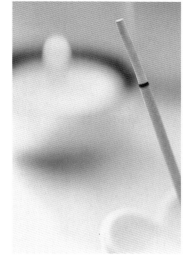

▷ **Try using frankincense or lotus joss sticks, which you can easily include in your luggage, to bless your temporary home.**

the ritual

This is a quick and easy method of conducting a space clearing in crowded or cramped conditions. Throughout the ritual, repeat this chant continually in the background of your thoughts:

Echo echo Azarak! Echo echo Zomelak!
Echo echo Babalon! Echo echo Zebulon!

While doing this, imagine a ball of bright blue glowing fire (like the blue part of a hot flame) starting at the centre of your chest and expanding at about the speed at which a party balloon is inflated, until it has filled the whole area with its glow. (If you are visualizing a doppelganger, the glow should emanate from its chest.) This blue ball is begun again and again, repeating its expansion in waves or pulses. As you proceed, the 'balloon' of light expands faster each time, until you can do it in time with the chant, so that eventually each three-word phrase covers an expanding blue pulse. Continue this for a few minutes, then stop and relax.

a portable space clearing kit

If you are regularly on the move, it may be a good idea to assemble a portable space clearing kit, to help bring you peace of mind wherever you may be. Include the tools you feel happiest working with, but a good list of items to include would be:

small sage smudge stick
frankincense incense sticks
matches
packets of dried herbs such as rosemary, marjoram and dill seeds
salt

△ **Salt spread on a mirror or other reflective surface can help to absorb negativity sensed in a room and reflect it away into the light.**

The smudge stick and frankincense sticks can be used to 'clear the air', and the dried herbs can be sprinkled lightly around the edges of a room to act as a circle of protection if you are occupying a place that makes you feel disturbed or restless. A small handful of salt in each corner can be utilized when the room itself feels in need of cleansing or balancing.

◁ **You can make up your own portable space clearing kit quite easily, to ensure happy and successful trips.**

▽ **Remember that charcoal gets very hot, so take a heatproof container in your kit, and check there are no smoke alarms in your room.**

rituals

space clearing for life

The purpose of doing regular daily rituals is not so much to provide a space clearing for a specific room, but to enhance and empower yourself, so that you will have a stronger and more stable foundation. This will help you radiate an aura of authority wherever you go. This practice can also be described as 'self charging'.

an early morning ritual

The following ritual is a simplified adaptation of an ancient magical technique called 'invoking by pentagram', by which various energies can be summoned for a multitude of purposes. In this case, you are summoning a fresh charge of personal psychic energy to strengthen your being, calm all atmospheres you may enter and encourage you to appreciate the joy of a new day.

Light your chosen incense or essential oil. Stand facing a window, towards the east (during warm weather this ritual can also be performed outside facing the sun). Take some slow, deep breaths.

When you are calm, make the sign of the pentagram on your body. To do this, touch the fingertips of your right hand to your

▽ As you touch your forehead to begin the pentagram, say clearly and firmly, "I am Spirit!"

forehead and say, "I am Spirit!" Touch the fingertips to your left hip, saying: "I am Earth!" Touch your right shoulder, saying: "I am Water!" Then touch your left shoulder, saying: "I am Air!" Touch your right hip, saying: "I am Fire!" Finally, touch your forehead again to complete the figure of the pentagram, saying: "Thus I seal my affirmation." Inhale the fragrance of the incense or oil for a few moments before beginning the new day.

△ Choose an incense depending on the qualities you feel you may need to call on during the day.

WAKE-UP HERBS
For protection and purification: frankincense, juniper
For physical energy and success: cinnamon, carnation, cloves
De-stressers: bergamot, cedar.

a bedtime ritual

To end the day, you can use this specially modified version of a much more elaborate ritual known as the Middle Pillar Exercise. This ritual has its origins in the teachings of the cabbala, an immensely powerful Hebrew magical system that may be more than 3,500 years old.

Before you begin the ritual, calm and centre yourself. Stand facing west – the direction of the setting sun – and for a few moments relate to the sun setting on the horizon, whether it is actually still daylight or already dark.

Imagine a beam of brilliant white light shining down on you from an infinite height. As it touches your head, it transforms your entire body into light-filled glass, like a clear bottle of human shape. As the light courses down through your body, it changes hue, moving through all the colours of the rainbow. As these colours flow down, imagine any dark areas of your body being cleansed by the rainbow light pushing the blackness down and out through the soles of your feet. As it flows out of your feet,

▽ Placing an amethyst under your pillow will help you to achieve a deep and untroubled sleep.

imagine that it is forming a pool or puddle of black mire, and that this pool is then draining away into nothingness, leaving you clean and filled with brilliant, opalescent, rainbow hues.

To add to the effectiveness of the ritual and enhance your ability to sleep, place an amethyst or clear quartz crystal under your pillow before you settle down to sleep.

△ After you have finished your bedtime ritual relax with a cup of dreaming herb tea and allow the tensions of the day to disperse.

A DREAMING TEA MIX

Mix the following herbs to make up a dreaming tea, which can help you to recall your dreams and have a restful night's sleep. (It is not advisable to drink this tea if you are pregnant.)

1 heaped tsp jasmine flowers
1 heaped tsp chamomile flowers
2 sprigs fresh marjoram
a large cup or mug of boiled
*   spring water*

Place all the herbs in a jug and pour over the boiled spring water. Leave to infuse for five minutes, then strain into a cup and sweeten with honey if desired. Sip this relaxing tea about half an hour before you go to sleep.

As we go about our daily lives, we can pick up energy from our journeys, from those we meet and interact with, from our own feelings, thoughts and emotions and from the environment. The level of demand on our energy will determine how often a clearing may be necessary to counteract the effects of negative energy. For someone who is working with people in a caring capacity, such as a therapist, for example, whose clients may be ill, depressed, or temporarily unbalanced in some way, it will sometimes be necessary to clear at least three times a day, if possible, or after seeing each client. For someone whose existence is more solitary, the need for clearing diminishes proportionally.

The same applies to objects: if they are in regular use a daily cleansing routine could be advisable, but if they are used in less specific ways about once a month would be sufficient. For example, if you are working with a protective crystal during an ongoing dispute with a neighbour, this would be considered 'regular' usage and a daily cleansing of the crystal would be appropriate. If you work from home or in a small office and simply wish to use crystals to help keep your working environment

▽ Objects such as crystals and ritual implements may need daily or monthly cleansing, depending upon how often they are used.

spiritually clean and clear when no particular issue or problem is evident, then cleansing them once a month will probably be sufficient.

There are a variety of ways in which people and possessions can be cleared of negative vibrations. Some of these have been described on previous pages, such as the use of smoke and fire or herbs and aromas. Outlined here are some specific methods that you can use to cleanse yourself or objects around you: simply choose the technique that best suits your circumstances or requirements.

clapping

Creating loud sounds has been a traditional way of space clearing for centuries. You can use this method when there is very little time available and you wish to clear an object such as a crystal, a piece of jewellery or a seating area. Stand in a commanding position, breathe deeply and centre yourself, then clap your hands firmly a few times around and over the object, imagining as you do so that the energies are being commanded to leave and chased away. You may like to make a positive affirmation after clapping, such as, "Be clear, be bright and filled with light."

absorbing

This clearing is ideal when you have been working hard and feel drained or ungrounded, or for an object that has been put to hard use. It can also be useful when life needs to be slowed down a little. Sprinkle some salt on the floor or in a container and stand on it with bare feet, or place the object on top in the centre, for five minutes. During this time visualize all impurities being absorbed into the salt. When the time is up, brush the salt carefully from the soles of your feet (or from the object) sweep it up and discard it in running water. Rinse the salt from your hands and feet and/or the object.

△ When cleansing an object by clapping over it, you should be authoritative and commanding with your gestures.

▽ Laying your bare feet upon rock salt is a good way to ensure that negative vibrations are drawn away from you. Rinse your feet well afterwards.

△ Laying crystals on your body and relaxing for a few minutes will replenish your energy levels.

crystal cleansing

You can use crystals to clear both objects and people, and this method is most suitable when there is more time available for cleansing. Space clearing yourself will take approximately half an hour, while for objects the ideal time would be overnight or for approximately eight hours. When you are using crystals for cleansing purposes, it is important that they themselves are clean and clear before you use them.

Lie down in a comfortable position and place a smoky quartz crystal beneath your feet with the pointed end facing towards you. Place a clear quartz crystal above your head with the pointed end facing towards you. Place a rose quartz crystal on your chest. Lie quietly for as long as you feel the crystals are having an effect upon you, which should take about 25 minutes. Remove the crystals in reverse order and bury them in the earth for about eight hours before unearthing them and rinsing

them clean. If you do not have a garden, the crystals can be buried in a pot of earth on a windowsill.

To cleanse an object, place it in a dark coloured cloth with a smoky quartz crystal or other black or dark stone such as obsidian. Wrap them up together completely and leave undisturbed overnight. Next morning, remove the object and bury the working crystal in the earth as before.

smudging

Purification using the smoke of smouldering herbs such as sage, thyme and rosemary, is a traditional space clearing method employed by Native Americans. The fragrant smoke has a cleansing effect on the environment, but it is also very useful when you need to clear negativity from a person or object.

You can buy smudge sticks for this purpose, or grow your own herbs and tie the stalks into firm bundles. Simply light the stick, extinguish the flame, and waft the smoke around the object or person to be cleansed. Loose, dried herbs can be burnt and the smoke used in the same way.

▽ For cleansing with smoke, use a feather and a smudge stick to waft the sweet-smelling herbal smoke around you or an object.

Altars and Shrines

An altar is a meeting point, where the divine reaches down to touch the everyday world and where we can concentrate our intentions and desires for spiritual growth. When you visualize an altar, you may imagine a monumental table in a lofty, echoing building, covered with a sumptuous cloth and with ritual objects formally arranged on it. Or perhaps you see an ancient monolith, open to the sky, potent with the memory of mysterious sacrifices and pagan rites. Altars like these are awesome and remote, approached only by priests and forbidden to ordinary worshippers. A different kind of altar – a simple shrine where you need no intermediary to help you reach the world of spirit – is the subject of this section. When you create a personal altar you place yourself at the very centre of your own sacred space, bringing the divine right into your life.

The domestic altar is a constant reminder of the search for spiritual fulfilment, anchored in the context of daily life. It can be a focus for prayer, a shrine to honour those you love, a place where you choose to meditate, or somewhere to spend a few minutes in quiet contemplation. The act of creating sacred space is a way of inviting spirit into your home and your life. An altar will grow, change and develop as you do: take it with you on your spiritual journey.

Altars through life

A sacred space brings positive energy into your home and life. Your altar and the precious objects you place on it, whether specially made for the purpose, or something that has significance in your life, will help to focus that energy.

A personal altar

It is in times of solitude and quiet reflection that we find the space we need to centre and renew ourselves, and to gain patience and wisdom to deal with all that life throws at us. We need time to see beyond the mundane and the everyday, to find a way of viewing life as a connected whole, and to feel integrated with that whole: to achieve a sense of spirit.

Creating a personal altar is a way of inviting spirit into your home. The sacred space it occupies is available to you all the time, whenever you need an interval of repose to nourish your soul and restore your sense of the sacred. As you use your altar for prayer or meditation you energize it, and its influence widens, flowing out through and around you, to sanctify your home and everyone in it. An altar can be a physical expression of your deepest attachments and longings; by giving them form you bring them into your daily life and empower yourself to achieve what you desire.

△ We instinctively bestow significance and importance on items of remembrance, and make out of them tiny, temporary shrines.

instinctive altars

Most of us display an instinctive need to enshrine what is precious to us. If you look around your home you can probably already find an altar you have created unconsciously – perhaps several. The lovely sea shells you collected during last summer's holiday, the family photographs upon the mantelpiece, the candles and flowers in the centre of the table: we all make such arrangements with love and care, and they inspire us with feelings of harmony and beauty.

Young children naturally make altars of their favourite toys. They will often arrange their most special things so that they can look at them as they go to sleep and find them still there when they wake in the morning. If a child is sick or upset, arranging some pretty things on her bedside table will help to cheer her up. Children have a wonderful ability to invest all kinds of objects with magic. A child will turn a handful of toffee wrappers into jewel-

△ A simple altar for a child that is a collection of their favourite things, will encourage them to build a magical relationship with their spirit.

coloured windows, transforming his familiar surroundings. Fragments of translucent, sea-worn glass, with their delicate colours and subtle texture, are valued as rare marine gemstones. Leaf skeletons or unusual feathers picked up in the park are mysterious treasures – the fresh vision of children can teach us to see such things as they really are: small miracles of natural form.

As children grow up they need to establish their separate identity and personal space. The teenager's room is a shrine to growing individualism (which may mean that it's a mess). Friendships might be celebrated by a whole wall full of photographs, reinforcing the good feeling of being a member of a supportive group. Another wall might be devoted to posters of pop stars, but there may still be a shelf somewhere

with just a few flowers and a single candle, and you can add items as they become significant. It will evolve as you use it and your relationship with it grows closer and stronger, until all its various elements mirror the many facets of your personality.

practical considerations

Any flat surface can become an altar when it is hallowed by intent. It needs to be somewhere quiet, where no one will bump into it as they pass and where you will be able to stand, sit or kneel before it comfortably. But if it suits you, the surface could be a shelf, a windowsill with a tranquil view beyond, the top of a chest, even the top of the refrigerator.

Traditionally, altars have been made from natural materials, often wood. If you choose to make a shrine on an old piece of furniture, it will hold the resonance of its past use, while a new piece could be the foundation of an altar for new beginnings. Prepare the space the altar will occupy by removing clutter from the surrounding area and cleaning everything until it sparkles.

337

altars through life

dedicated to some much-loved toys, whose missing eyes and worn fur show how much emotion was invested in them – a little altar to the childhood that is being left behind.

creating an altar with intent

The altar is a work of intuition and imagination. As you play around with ideas for it, handling and thinking about the objects you are placing on it, you will be feeding into it your own energy and creativity, making it more deeply personal. You will know instinctively when it is right. Allow your

creativity to flow freely, straight from your spirit. The intention behind what you place on an altar, and what it represents, is more important than its physical reality.

Your altar can be for you alone, or to share with others. A family altar can work for cohesiveness, like the traditional ancestral altars of the East. A couple could share in the creation of an altar to promote a deeper commitment to one another.

Let your altar grow freely, moving things around, or setting up a new altar whenever you wish. It can begin very simply, perhaps

△ A bowl of floating candles, lit to create a welcoming atmosphere for visitors, is one of the simplest altars.

Altars through the home

Most people have one room that feels special, where the sense of positive energy is most complete. It could be the living room, the kitchen, or a welcoming entrance hall. Traditionally, the hearth is regarded as the centre of the home and is really a prototype altar. But if you want an altar to be very personal to you, you may prefer to have it in a more private place.

Feng Shui can help you position your altar effectively, using the directional chart called the Bagua to find areas that represent the various aspects of your life. An altar in the wisdom and experience area could benefit your spiritual life, while an altar dedicated to love would be most effective in the relationships area. The Bagua can also be imposed on a room to determine the best placement for an altar, or on the altar itself to help you arrange objects on it.

All the different activities that we pursue create distinct types of energy in each room. This is why it can be very difficult to get to sleep in a room that has been full of lively conversation, for instance, or to concentrate on a piece of analytical work in the kitchen. Every altar will be influenced by the energy of its surroundings. You can use this power to create a life-enhancing altar

◁ This simple bedroom altar to Gaia, the goddess of dreams, includes lilies to invoke calm.

△ A bedroom altar reminds us as we wake that the spirit of the sacred is always with us.

in any room by drawing on the intrinsic energy of the space, and there is no reason why you shouldn't have several small altars around the house, wherever you feel they are needed.

the bedroom

Most of us want our bedroom to be a sanctuary where we can be wholly ourselves. It is where we take our secrets and prayers, joy and grief. A bedroom altar acts as a focus for these, and for daily rituals to help you greet the day and prepare for night.

For peaceful rest, place sleep crystals on your altar: amethysts, a piece of jade or obsidian. The scent of lavender or jasmine will help you sleep. Honour the earth deity and goddess of dreams, Gaia, with barley grains or laurel, or include an image of Nephthys, who sheltered the sleeping pharaohs beneath her protective wings.

At bedtime, set a bowl of water scented with jasmine oil near your bed and place your sleep crystals in it. On willow leaves – to help your wishes come true – write what you wish to come to you in sleep.

▷ **Our working environment, like any other, benefits from a spiritual atmosphere. An office altar dedicated to Thoth encourages inspiration.**

THE FOUR DIRECTIONS

Ancient traditions honour the four directions of the compass, and attribute specific qualities to each one. The custom is preserved in the architecture of Christian churches and Buddhist temples, where the altar always stands in the east. By placing an altar in a particular direction, you can harness its particular qualities.

EAST: new beginning and rebirth.
SOUTH: motivation, creativity and growth.
WEST: healing and transformation.
NORTH: looking within.

There is, however, a Buddhist saying, 'Where faces the yogi, there is the east of the yogi': in other words, 'the east within' – your own state of mind – is more important than geographical direction.

the study or office

An altar in the workplace will generate positive energy to help you concentrate. Wisdom and inspiration are personified by Thoth, the scribe of the Egyptian gods who wrote down the wisdom of the universe.

Yellow candles assist communication and learning. Helpful crystals include emerald, to give insight, azurite, for clarity, and hematite, to aid reasoning and memory.

the hallway

The Roman god Janus is a traditional protective deity, and could stand on a shrine by the door, or it could house a guardian animal such as a dog, lion or tiger. Sacred objects at the entrance help to sanctify the whole of your home, and you will carry blessings with you as you leave.

the kitchen

At the hub of the house, the kitchen is a potent place. The energy of the earth – in the form of food – is transformed by the magical process of cooking, which demands creativity and concentration. An altar for

◁ **A kitchen altar can incorporate any kind of food, although traditionally it would have included grains, honey and spices.**

hospitality could be dedicated to Hestia, goddess of the hearth and home, or to Demeter, goddess of abundance and unconditional love. Leave offerings of rice, grains, fruit or honey for the nature spirits and light the altar candles each time you prepare a meal. A shrine behind the sink would engage your attention as you work there. You could hang herbs and flowers, chilli and garlic around the window like a garland, or decorate the sill with evergreens.

the living room

To promote harmony between your family and friends, set up an altar to the four elements on the mantelpiece. This could combine salt for earth, a red candle for fire, sea shells for water and feathers for air.

Green is the colour of harmonious relationships. To create a prayer bowl, place a clear quartz cluster in a green bowl filled with spring water and invite members of the family to write down their prayers for others and tuck them under the bowl.

Collecting natural offerings

We are part of the natural world, even if urban living makes us feel removed from it. We rely on nature for food and sustenance, and have a responsibility as its caretakers. Placing natural objects on an altar helps to reinforce its connection with earth energies, and underlines our commitment to preserving the natural world.

Nearly everyone has at some time brought home a beautiful stone or sea shell as a souvenir of a precious day, or because it came from a place that made us feel happy, somewhere we felt a sense of spiritual peace. The resonance of that experience clings to the object for ever. In school, the tradition of maintaining a nature table encourages children to share their unusual and beautiful natural finds with others. This kind of display also involves a kind of reverence for the wonders of the earth, and can become a visual calendar, recording the cycle of the seasons.

Reverence for nature of course precludes stealing from it: if you are moved by a beautiful natural environment, the last thing you want to do is disturb it. Rather than cutting flowers or trees, you may prefer to take only things that have fallen. Leave an offering to signify your appreciation of the gift. This could be a traditional offering, such as

tobacco – which is considered a sacred herb by Native Americans – or salt, sacred to the Celts. Or express your gratitude in a simple action, such as clearing away litter.

flowers and trees

Plants are great healers, both physically and spiritually. If you respond particularly strongly to a flower or tree, keep it or an image of it on your altar. Trees are powerful emblems of nature, and each has its special attributes and symbolism.

According to legend, the birth of Gautama Buddha was greeted with birdsong and showers of sweet tea and fragrant flowers, and this is why fresh flowers are placed on Buddhist altars. Flowers are a universal symbol of youth and gentleness, and an appreciation of their beauty has helped civilizations to flourish artistically since

△ **Driftwood carried by the oceans conveys the blessings of the Goddess and can be placed on an altar dedicated to emotional healing.**

▽ **Flowers are filled with grace and beauty, and can remind us of our own innate qualities of innocence and purity.**

▽ **Fossils represent the ancestors and past life memory. Placing a fossil on an altar will aid memory and help us find our roots.**

▷ Pebbles and stones represent the earth element. Their presence on an altar can help to stabilize stress-filled atmospheres.

TREE ASSOCIATIONS

APPLE: youth, beauty, innocence.
ASH: the world tree, purification and cleansing.
BAY: guardian of the house, protection against illness.
BEECH: stability, flow of energy, protector of knowledge.
DOGWOOD: charm and finesse.
HAWTHORN: marriage, fertility, protection of children.
HAZEL: wisdom and fertility, used to divine water.
OAK: wisdom, strength and endurance.
ROWAN: protection against evil.
WILLOW: love and regeneration, lunar and feminine rhythms.
YEW: immortality, transformation and inner wisdom.

ancient times. Their brief lives encapsulate the cycle of birth, life and return to the earth to nurture the next generation. A single flower is an expression of natural but fleeting perfection. Gazing into it, you can find peace and serenity that you can take into yourself.

herbs

The use of herbs – for healing, spiritual cleansing and magic – has a long history. Many are tried and tested remedies, and almost every plant is useful in some way.

Herbs are used as talismans in magic: St John's wort, for example, is hung over windows and doors on Midsummer's Day to

cleanse and protect the house. They can be placed on an altar to represent particular qualities. Basil, for example, is said to protect from pain, and sage is a purifying herb.

fruits, nuts and grains

At harvest time, it is traditional to bring offerings of nuts, fruit and grain to the altar to give thanks for the abundance of nature. The fruits brought for blessing contain within them the seeds of next year's crop, so this ritual of thanksgiving also includes a prayer for fertility in the future.

stones and sea shells

A stone belongs to the earth and brings grounding energy to the altar. It conveys the character of the place where it originated: the moving river bed, the windswept seashore or the eternal mountains. Rocks

and stones also carry the resonance of millions of years of history, and fossils remind us even more vividly of the antiquity of earth's life story, of which we are a part.

Emblems of the sea, shells are associated with its fluid, feminine energy. They signify water, the element of the emotions. They also have traditional links with regeneration, baptism and prosperity.

feathers

Representing the element of air, feathers symbolize the connection between earth and heaven, and therefore between humanity and the creator. Their complex structures and natural beauty make them valuable objects for contemplation during meditation.

▽ Feathers represent birds, who are honoured as a link between earth and heaven.

Objects of beauty

While you are assembling your altar, it will help you to decide on the form it is to take if you constantly keep in mind your purpose and intention: that you are honouring the spiritual centre of your life and providing a focus for it. All the elements you bring to the altar, such as candles, incense, pictures and objects that are important to you, are tools to help you to this end. Make your altar beautiful, so that each time you see it, it lifts your heart.

sacred images

Deities from any religion may have a personal symbolism for you, whether or not you are an adherent of any faith. A statue of the Buddha in meditation could help with your own meditation and prayer, for example, while a picture or statue of St Francis of Assisi may have special meaning if you have a deep affinity with animals.

In the Christian church, the symbolic power of imagery is seen in the icon, a visual expression of faith. The Byzantine artists of the early Church developed a characteristic style for the painting of these holy pictures, using a language of symbols to transmit the tenets of Christianity to worshippers who could not read the scriptures for themselves. Because God had appeared on earth in human form, it was felt that the image of the human Christ could be por-

▽ Statues of female or male figures will honour the archetype you wish to represent.

trayed to help the faithful understand the nature and intention of God.

Icons can be anything from small paintings on wood panels or paper, to large frescoes. Their nature is defined not by their size but by their sacred subject matter and the traditional style and symbolism used to depict its essence. They are recognized universally as objects of great beauty and power. In the West, they tend to be regarded as symbols of faith, comparable with a cruci-

△ Creating an altar with objects of personal meaning can reinforce spiritual connections.

fix or a stained glass window. In the mystical tradition of the Orthodox church, however, they are precious objects of prayer, veneration and contemplation.

If you wish to bring the blessings of the Goddess into your life, dedicate your altar to her by enshrining her image. This might be a reproduction of a fertility figure, or a

▷ Angels are believed to provide protection and guidance. An angelic altar brings loving support during times of sadness and loss.

ANIMAL SYMBOLISM

Images of animals can be used on the altar to symbolize an aspect of your character or to help you focus on a quality you desire.

BEAR: receptive female energy, earth wisdom, introspection.
BISON: wisdom of the elders.
CAT: independence, intuition.
DEER: security and protection.
DOG or WOLF: loyalty, family.
DOLPHIN: understanding.
EAGLE: divine and earthly power.
FROG: cleansing, emotional healing.
HARE: quickness of thought.
HERON: self-reliance.
HORSE: freedom, power.
LION: strength.
LIZARD: illusions, letting go.
OWL: magic, wisdom.
RABBIT: fertility.
ROBIN: new beginnings.
TURTLE: endurance, experience, knowledge.

counsellors and guardians

If you call on a guardian angel for spiritual support, you can place a picture or figurine of a beautiful angel on your altar to focus your prayer. Photographs of loved ones who have died will remind you that they are still part of your life; pictures that show them full of happiness and vitality help you to remember your whole relationship with them, not just the fact that you have lost them. Seek their wisdom and advice as you remember them.

In the shamanic tradition, everyone has a spirit ally in the form of an animal. Your guardian animal could be one that you particularly identify with, or you may want to call upon an animal spirit whose energy can help you in a time of need. Placing an image on your altar will deepen your connection with your animal ally. Your prayers might be inspired by a picture of a soaring bird: birds are traditionally seen as spiritual messengers, flying between earth and heaven.

gemstones and crystals

Crystals – points of sparkling light created in the darkness of the earth – are potent emblems of spiritual illumination, purity and durability. The ancient Greeks considered all quartz crystals to be fragments that had fallen from the perfect crystal of truth that resided on Mount Olympus. As well as being objects of great beauty, crystals and

△ The points of a crystal help to direct energy. They can also help to channel healing thoughts.

gemstones are storehouses of powerful energies, and magical powers of healing and protection have been ascribed to them. Each crystal is believed to have a distinct spiritual nature and to exert a specific influence on the human spirit; each has its own associations and symbolism. Place crystals to which you feel drawn on your altar to endow it with their special power.

△ A crystal's structure can serve to align and harmonize the physical and mental worlds.

statue or painting of one of the many aspects of the Goddess worshipped by ancient cultures, such as Isis the compassionate mother of the Egyptians, Athene the Greek goddess of wisdom and craft, or Diana, the moon deity who lights up the darkness within. By invoking the Goddess and seeking her ancient wisdom you will find an aspect of her in yourself. Bringing her into the heart of the home in this way upholds a tradition that has been practised throughout history.

Objects of symbolic value

Everyone has a collection of treasures that represent memories of close relationships and happy times, and such things have a place on a home altar. They probably already have their own special places, either on display like little shrines where we see them each day, or nestling secretly and safely where we can always find them when we feel the need to touch them and remember. A private arrangement of this kind can be a good place to start exploring a relationship with a personal altar.

A lock of hair, a baby's first shoes, or a trinket from a wedding cake are traditional mementos that many people keep all their lives. Other items are precious because they were gifts: they carry the memory of the giver, as well as the positive energy associated with the act of giving. Placing objects of symbolic value on an altar sets them in a new context that makes us see them afresh. It acknowledges the importance of all that they represent.

seasonal symbols

Altars can change with the seasons, celebrating the coming of spring with fresh flowers and seeds, or ushering in the Christmas festivities with garlands of evergreens. Special seasonal items could be arranged on an altar in honour of the traditional festivals of the Celtic eightfold year. For city dwellers, especially, seasonal altars reaffirm a connection with nature.

△ Tiny items of personal significance can be kept safe on your altar in a pretty bag.

abstract symbols

Symbols predate writing as a means of conveying ideas. Ancient symbols were carved, painted, stitched and worked in metal for magical purposes, to ward off evil or to invoke gods. Some signs, identified as archetypes, appear to be universally understood. A symbol gains its significance from the emotional and spiritual weight it carries. Like music and art, symbolism is a language of the emotions.

Some of the most compelling symbols are the simplest, such as the circle that represents the cycle of life, death and rebirth. The spiral, too, stands for the cycle of existence, but its outward motion also symbolizes growth and the energy of the vortex. In Celtic symbolism, the triple spiral stands for the three stages of life personified by the Triple Goddess: maiden, mother and crone.

The cross is the emblem of Christianity, and also represents the four cardinal directions. In pre-Columbian America the cross was a fertility symbol related to the four rain-bearing winds. The *ankh*, a cross with a loop forming the top arm, was an ancient Egyptian symbol of immortality.

The pentacle, or five-pointed star, is an ancient symbol of harmony and mystic power. When used magically it is inscribed on a disc. It is a female symbol related to the earth element.

Ancient graphic symbols such as these can bring their energy and associations to your altar. By painting or carving them yourself, you will enhance your connection with them: it is worth learning new craft skills to achieve this.

▽ **Altars can provide a focus for poignant memories and remind us of the good in our lives.**

RUNES AND THEIR MEANINGS

ᚠ FEOH: spiritual richness.

ᚢ UR: strength in a time of change.

ᚦ THORN: contemplation before action.

ᚫ ANSUR: messages and new opportunities.

ᚱ RAD: the wheel of life, a journey or quest.

ᚲ KEN: enlightenment and inspiration.

ᚷ GEOFU: a spiritual gift, love and partnership.

ᚹ WYNN: success and achievement.

ᚺ HAGALL: strength to face a challenge.

ᚾ NIED: need.

ᛁ IS: standstill, preparation before moving on.

ᛃ JARA: harvest, reward for past effort.

ᛇ EOH: transformation.

ᛈ PEORTH: choice, taking charge.

ᛉ ELHAZ: protection within.

ᛋ SIGEL: good fortune.

ᛏ TYR: dedication, perseverance.

ᛒ BEORC: new beginnings.

ᛖ EHWAZ: progress.

ᛗ MANN: destiny.

ᛚ LAGU: attunement to creation.

ᛜ ING: the inner spark.

ᛞ DAEG: the light.

ᛟ OTHEL: focus and freedom.

runes

The runes are a sacred writing system of northern Europe, which, according to legend, appeared to the god Odin during a shamanic initiation rite. They were his gift of knowledge to humanity, and they are empowered with ancient wisdom. Runes can be used as guides for meditation and divination, as protective talismans and in wishing ceremonies.

portable altars

Some people like to know that their personal altar is completely private to them. If you feel this way, you could arrange a beautiful small shrine inside a cupboard or box. A small wooden box makes a lovely altar, because you can lay out all your sacred things on the flat lid. It is also portable, so you can take it with you when travelling – especially useful if you are making a difficult trip and need spiritual support. Alternatively, when you leave home you could carry with you a crystal that you have programmed at your home altar (see *Rites and Ritual* at the end of this chapter).

△ A portable altar kit can be an excellent idea if you are often on the move, and wish to carry the essence of your home with you.

△ Runes are used for spiritual guidance, and can also add a symbolic message to an altar.

Candles and incense

Candles embody the positive symbolism of light as spiritual illumination, and the fragile candle flame is a powerful emblem of the individual soul, especially in a time of darkness and distress. Other lights, such as oil lamps and lanterns, can have a similar reassuring significance, and a perpetual flame on an altar stands for the constant presence of the divine.

Watching a lighted candle can be an aid to meditation and, like the candle flame, the fragrance of incense helps to focus the senses and calm chattering thoughts. Incense smoke has a symbolic status on the altar as an offering and is also used in ritual purification. It is an integral element of worship in many traditions.

altar candles

The lighting of candles is a simple ceremonial act that initiates and hallows ritual. It acts as an announcement of the intention to worship. In the Catholic church, a prescribed number of candles must be lit before

each mass, the number varying depending on the solemnity of the service. It is common practice to light a candle and leave it to burn out before the shrine of a saint as an act of devotion, symbolizing both prayer and sacrifice. Candles are also used to mark rites of passage, from baptism to funerals. Placed around a coffin, their light is believed to protect the dead from evil during the vulnerable time of transition.

The Christian use of altar candles was adopted from older traditions, and candles have been significant in religion and magic since the earliest times. The ancient Egyptians, who practised dream incubation, would sit in a cave staring at a candle flame until they saw a deity in it. When they went to sleep the deity would answer their question.

The feast of Candlemas at the beginning of February was grafted on to the pagan fire festival Imbolc. A traditional feature was the blessing of all the candles that were to be used in the church for the rest of the year.

△ **Candle-gazing can increase concentration, and can be helpful when focus is required.**

Candlemas is a time of purification and dedication, and is a good time to clean and rededicate an altar.

△ **Resins produce impressive clouds of fragrant smoke, infusing the environment with scent.**

△ **White candles represent purity and simplicity and can be used for any ceremony or ritual.**

COLOUR ASSOCIATIONS FOR CANDLES

WHITE: spiritual enlightenment, healing, peace and purity; can be substituted for any other colour for ritual use.
YELLOW: intelligence, communication, concentration, movement.
ORANGE: attraction, stimulation, strength, luck.
GOLD: understanding, confidence, prosperity, cosmic influences; honours solar deities.
PINK: harmony, nurturing, family, affection.
RED: energy, life, courage, passion.
VIOLET or PURPLE: spirituality, inner harmony, wisdom.
INDIGO: cleansing, meditation.
BLUE: wisdom, inspiration, truth, healing; honours lunar deities.
GREEN: love, nature, renewal, abundance.
BROWN: home, wealth, stability, older family members.
SILVER or GREY: secrets, compromise.
BLACK: conclusions; banishes guilt, regret and negativity.

magic and ritual

Traditional candle magic often involves writing the name of something you wish for on a piece of paper and then burning the paper in the candle flame, so that the wish is carried away in the smoke. In another candle charm, a symbol of the wish is engraved in the wax. As the candle burns down, the melted wax dripping down its

side may form an image to indicate how your wish might come true.

For ritual use, candles can be empowered by 'dressing' or anointing them with oil, to cleanse them of energies and influences from the past. The oil is wiped from the middle of the candle to the ends if the ritual aims to send energy out, or from the ends to the middle if the intention is to achieve or attract something.

In pagan tradition, the candle flame represents the element of fire, associated with life, creative energy and passion. Blowing candles out is said to be an affront to fire, and will have the effect of blowing away your intent or desire. It is best to let the candle burn down completely, although this is not always possible. Tibetan Buddhists consider that in blowing out a candle they are blowing away the breath of life, so pinch out the flame instead. For the same reason, incense sticks should be waved rather than blown before the altar.

incense

The burning of incense on the altar is a gentle form of offering, with its associations of purity and sweetness. It clears the sacred space of invasive thoughts and images, giving a feeling of peace and serenity. It allows your spirit to soar above the mundane.

Combustible incense, in the form of joss-sticks and cones, is readily available.

◁ Incense comes in many forms, from cones to loose herbs and resins. All the different scents have particular associations and symbolism.

Alternatively, mixtures of fragrant resins, herbs and spices can be bought or prepared at home for burning on a charcoal block. For this you will need an incense burner, preferably with a stand or feet to protect the altar. Line the burner with a layer of sand to stabilize it and insulate it further. Concentrate on your intent as you light the incense, so that it is charged with your positive thoughts and the scented smoke drifts upwards carrying your prayers with it.

There may be times when you prefer to scent your altar with more delicate fragrances than incense. You can use essential oils in an aromatherapy burner, natural pot pourri mixtures or scented flowers.

INCENSE ASSOCIATIONS

COPAL: for honouring the gods, cleansing, and to bless love.
FRANGIPANI: for the blessing of friendship and love.
FRANKINCENSE: for cleansing and blessing, banishing bad influences and enhancing insight.
HONEYSUCKLE: for healing and psychic power.
JASMINE: for increasing sensitivity and to bless meditation.
LOTUS: for clearing the mind.
MUSK: for courage and vitality.
MYRRH: for purifying and cleansing of negative thoughts.
PATCHOULI: for grounding, fertility, protection and prosperity.
PINE: for strength and reversal of negative energies.
ROSE: for emotional healing and the expression of feelings.
SANDALWOOD: for protection, healing, and granting of wishes.
VANILLA: for rejuvenation, love and mental concentration.
WHITE SAGE: for purifying and cleansing sacred space.

Rites and ritual

Setting up an altar at home is one step on your spiritual path, but the journey continues. Although your journey is an inward one, a sacred place serves as a reminder of the way. Each time you use it in personal ceremonies and rituals you strengthen the positive energy it holds for you.

If you share the altar with your partner or family, the occasions on which you come together for worship and ritual help to reinforce the bonds between you. Or you may think of your altar as a private and personal space, somewhere you can go when you are angry or upset to be quiet and restore your calm and inner strength. Use it to nourish your soul and help you unwind at the end of a tiring day. At difficult times of transition, use it as a support, and at times of peace, go to the altar to give thanks.

preparation

To prepare for your ceremonies, you should purify your sacred space by cleaning the room and clearing away clutter, and cleanse yourself so that you feel refreshed and energized. See that the altar is clean and free of dust, the flowers are fresh and candles new.

△ Sage gets its name from *saga*, meaning 'wise woman', and burning it summons protection.

Burn some incense or white sage to clear away any negative energy from the area.

If you include crystals on your altar, cleanse them to clear past vibrations so that they become personal to you. You can do this in various ways: smoke is a gentle cleanser, or they can be placed in sunlight or moonlight, or washed in rain or spring water.

It is a good idea to devise a formal beginning for your time before the altar: light a candle or some incense to quieten your thoughts and prepare you to concentrate all your energy on the subject of your meditation or prayer. Focusing on deep, relaxed breathing helps to still your mind.

▽ Singing bowls can produce a variety of sound vibrations that touch the body with resonance.

▽ Calming the mind with meditation helps to cope with stress, and builds inner strength.

◁ An offering of salt made to an earth goddess such as Gaia helps to build a close relationship with the earth.

▽ Mark the beginning or end of a ritual by ringing a bell or some chimes.

349

altars through life

daily ritual

Greeting the morning with a small ritual is a positive way to start a new day, and doing this before an altar sanctifies the act. If you practise yoga, for instance, you can perform your salutations to the sun in your sacred space. The ritual will strengthen your spiritual bond with creation while the movements invigorate your body.

Remember that you can change the format of your worship freely, as your needs and ideas change: you are not just an observer, as in a formal religious ritual. You might wish to read a text that inspires you, or recite a poem that helps you express your emotions. Singing, striking a singing bowl, playing a musical instrument or listening to music could form part of your ritual.

prayer and meditation

If you are accustomed to saying daily prayers, or spending a particular period of time in meditation, your altar can become the focus of these regular practices. Prayer and meditation are complementary routes to spiritual development. As a request for help or guidance, or thanksgiving, prayer is active, while meditation is a passive exercise

in contemplation, quietening the mind to increase its receptivity and allow the subconscious to surface.

Using an affirmation can help to focus your meditation. Create a thought that feels right to you: it needn't describe your present reality, but the reality you dream of. The affirmation is a way to make your dream real. Repeat the positive thought again and again, silently or aloud, to allow it to sink into your unconscious mind.

programming a crystal

You can use the energy of your affirmation to programme a crystal on your altar (choose one that has properties appropriate to your particular goal, such as rose quartz for love or citrine for abundance). Hold the crystal in both hands and gaze into it as you concentrate on your wish. Breathe deeply and each time you inhale repeat the affirmation and picture what you want. As you exhale, project your desire into the crystal. You can also write your wish on a piece of paper and leave it under the crystal.

If you are travelling, or when you go to work each day, keep the programmed crystal near you by carrying it in a small bag.

offerings

As part of your ceremony, place an offering on your altar as an expression of gratitude for the blessings of your life. Leaving a gift for another person on the altar for a while before you give it will endow it with positive energy and reinforce its value as a token of love. Adopt a way of closing your ceremony that you can repeat each time. Play a piece of music, say a farewell prayer, a thank you, or simply "amen", to give you a feeling of completion.

△ A prayer can be as simple as a few moments of silent communion with the spirit.

Altars of the elements

The ideas that follow for establishing your personal altar are based on using the Four Elements as a starting point. By doing this you have a framework in which to express symbolism and communicate wishes and desires.

The element of air

Air is the element of life and breath – when we cease to breathe, life ends. Speediest and most ethereal of the elements, it rules the east, the direction of the sunrise. Because it is associated with the new day and with the freshness of the new year, air symbolizes new beginnings, enterprise, infancy and the generative energy of the seed. It is creative, focused, aware.

In the form of wind, air may be a gentle, cooling breeze or it may have the destructive force of a hurricane. Its energy is projective. Because air is the element of the four winds, it governs movement and is associated with travel, freedom and new discoveries. It is also the element of thought and ideas – the fresh, moving force of the open mind, of intellect and the imagination.

△ The air element corresponds with the east, the direction of the rising sun, and with the morning.

▽ The fresh, fast-moving element of air helps us to disperse the clouds of ignorance and doubt.

▽ Creatures of the air, birds symbolize the connection between earth and heaven.

▷ Use incense and yellow flowers and candles on your altar to symbolize the qualities of air.

Those in whom air is the dominant element are rational and analytical.

In daily life the areas governed by air include workplaces, offices, meeting rooms, schools and libraries, as well as places concerned with travel, such as railway stations and airports. It presides over the eastern quarter of a room or building. In the natural world, air's places are mountain tops, windy plains and clear or cloudy skies.

The power of the mind can include psychic ability, and air governs the arts of divination and visualization. It enhances positive thinking, allowing the mind to expand into wider realms, and to connect personal experience with the universal.

gods of the air

Deities associated with air are Shu, Thoth, Hermes and Mercury. Shu was the Egyptian god of the air who, with his consort Tefnut (the goddess of moisture), created the earth and sky. The Egyptian moon god Thoth was the sacred scribe of Osiris. As the god of wisdom, he was endowed with secret knowledge. It was said that his book of magic contained spells that would give the user power over all the gods, and that between them his books contained all the wisdom of the world. He eventually became associated with the Greek god Hermes, the messenger of the Olympian gods, who could travel as fast as thought.

Hermes was versatile and changeable, eloquent and inventive, the personification of consciousness. His quick wits and slippery character made him the patron of thieves and merchants as well as travellers. His Roman equivalent was Mercury, whose cult spread widely among the Celtic and Germanic peoples of the Roman Empire. The latter identified him with Wotan or Odin, the god of speech, breath, wind, storm and magic. Mercury gave us the word 'mercurial' to describe a volatile, lively, quicksilver character. Invoke these deities to bless an altar with the energy of air.

THE ATHAME

Wiccans use this ritual knife to draw circles, control elemental spirits and direct energy during ceremonies. It has a dark handle and a double edge. It is seldom used for actual cutting, and would never be used as a weapon. It represents the masculine force on the altar.

AIR CORRESPONDENCES

DIRECTION: east.
SEASON: spring.
TIME: dawn.
MOON PHASE: new.
PLANETS: sun, Mercury, Uranus.
GENDER: masculine.
COLOURS: yellow and violet.
SENSES: hearing and smell.
MAGICAL TOOLS: wand, athame, sword.
INSTRUMENTS: wind instruments.
CREATURES: birds, winged insects.
NATURAL SYMBOLS: feathers, incense smoke, fragrant flowers.
TREES: elder, eucalyptus.
HERBS: comfrey, lavender, mint.
INCENSE: sandalwood, lemon.
MINERALS: mercury, aventurine, topaz.
SIGNS: Gemini, Libra, Aquarius.
ARCHANGEL: Raphael.

An altar for new beginnings

The most challenging times in life are those of transition. At moments when we are breaking with old customs and habits, or taking on new responsibilities, we need a boost to our self-confidence to stop us feeling uncertain, isolated or afraid. The established routines of our everyday lives have to be abandoned, and we may doubt our ability to meet a new challenge. We need to feel supported.

In traditional societies, the moment of setting out on a new chapter in life is invariably marked by some form of ritual that offers this kind of spiritual support, but in modern times many of the old ceremonies have been curtailed or lost. Others that do survive – such as weddings – have become so commercialized that their spiritual value can be hard to hold on to.

A simple ceremony at your altar will help you focus your thoughts and find the resolution to make a bold leap into the new. If you have just fallen in love you could be entering a new relationship that will be central to your whole future. If you are expecting a child the focus of your life is about to change radically. If you are moving house or starting a new job, you will be embarking on a series of new encounters and opportunities to shape your future.

△ The yellow triangle and violet circle both symbolize the air element.

◁ For new beginnings, such as the dawn of spring, yellow and violet flowers are ideal as they are the colours associated with a fresh start.

Sometimes the impetus towards a fresh start has to arise from sadder circumstances, such as divorce, children growing up and leaving home, or moving to a new area, away from people you love. At such times, the transition is one from grief and loss to healing and moving forward. The creative act of setting up an altar can be part of the process of transformation.

Invoke the element of air to inspire you with confidence and hope for a new beginning. Set your altar in the easterly quarter of a room, so that when you stand before it you are facing east, the direction of the sunrise. If possible, arrange it under a window so that it is bathed in the morning sunshine. Place a bell on the altar.

To symbolize new growth and natural energy you could add a vase of flowers: choose violet and yellow flowers, the colours of the air element, to help you focus your intent. Burn incense containing rosemary to clarify your thoughts. White candles represent new beginnings and clear vision.

◁ The number three is associated with manifestations – ringing your bell three times will help to call new realities into your life.

AN INCENSE MIXTURE FOR FOCUS

Incense is a tool of the air element, and will help to clarify your thoughts.

2 parts dried rosemary
1 part dried thyme
1 part lemongrass
Few drops rosemary essential oil

Pound all the dry ingredients together using a pestle and mortar, then add the essential oil. Mix the oil in well with your fingertips. Burn a few pinches of incense on the altar, using a charcoal block.

ritual for a new start

The time of the waxing moon is the period between the new and the full moon, when the half moon can be seen in the sky during the first part of the night. This is the

▽ Burn a pinch or two of incense in the morning to cleanse your mind for the day ahead.

time of new beginnings, and during this period you can perform a simple ritual to help you approach the next part of your life with confidence. As you meditate before your altar, focus on your hopes and wishes for the future. Write these down on a piece of yellow paper cut into a triangle, and lay the triangle on a larger violet or blue circlet of paper or cloth on the altar.

Place the bell on top of the piece of paper. Each morning of the period of the waxing moon – as near sunrise as possible – come to the altar and ring the bell three times as you visualize your hopes and wishes being realized and achieved.

THE SEASON OF NEW BEGINNINGS

The pagan festival of Ostara is celebrated at the Vernal Equinox, around 21 March in the northern hemisphere and 23 September in the southern hemisphere, when day and night are of equal length and the sun begins its ascendancy: a time of balance and regeneration. Ostara signals the return of spring and is a festival of new life and fertility. This is the time to plant seeds and initiate new plans. An altar to celebrate Ostara could be decorated with spring flowers and herbs: celandine, daffodil, primroses, violets, sage, tansy and thyme. Yellow and green candles represent clear focus, optimism and new growth.

An altar for meditation

Creating a personal altar in a garden is a rewarding way to acknowledge our connection with nature, and provides a tranquil space for quiet thought and meditation. It can be a breathing space, both literally and metaphorically, where the freshness of the breeze, the scent of leaves and flowers and the sound of birds inspire us with a sense of gratitude and awareness.

Meditation is a way of focusing the mind, stilling the endless mental chatter that distracts us from concentrated thought. It is not a way of escaping from the reality of our everyday responsibilities. It increases awareness and enables us to live fully in each moment with contentment and serenity.

According to Zen Buddhism, the practice of gardening is itself an active form of meditation. The size of the garden is not important: the message of Zen is that the large can be experienced in the small, and

▽ Taking a little time with your designs helps the mind become relaxed and centred.

△ The patterns you create in your miniature Zen garden will contain potent messages to and from your subconscious, and will help to integrate your inner and outer worlds.

the meaning of the whole world can be seen in a grain of sand. The garden is the universe in microcosm. The concept can be adapted to your own garden, where you can fashion a serene space for meditation with stones, gravel and moss, inspired by the temple gardens of Japan.

gardens of contemplation

Respect for nature and a sense of connectedness with natural cycles are basic tenets of Zen Buddhist thought. Zen arrived in Japan from China in the 11th century, and its emphasis on contemplation and tranquillity found a natural counterpart in the Japanese love of simplicity. Buddhist monks applied the concepts of Zen to their daily lives, and designed their living quarters and gardens in accordance with them, producing simple, peaceful spaces for meditation in perfect accord with nature.

Zen gardens are often conceived as miniature re-creations of natural scenes, such as mountains and forests. Composed of simple elements such as moss, leaves, stones and water, they are timeless havens of silent contemplation. Paths meander, and a stream may be crossed by a zig-zagging 'eightfold' bridge, forcing the visitor to move slowly and appreciate each vista.

In a 'dry' garden, a natural scene is re-created without water. The rocks are arranged with artful judgement to appear as if naturally strewn in beds of pale gravel, which is carefully raked. The elements of such a garden are symbolic: the stones represent the great age of the universe, and the swirling patterns in the gravel imitate the river flowing around them. Some stones lie hidden or partly buried in the gravel, so that the eye is led down beneath the surface, just as in meditation Buddhists look within themselves to seek enlightenment.

Symbols also abound in the plants that grow in Japanese gardens, and these ideas can be used to enhance the significance of elements in your own outdoor sacred space. Evergreen pines, for example, stand for longevity, and the fleeting, delicate plum blossom that appears in the cold of early spring is a symbol of courage.

FORM AND EMPTINESS

The serenity of a Zen garden has an almost hypnotic effect, and you can use its combination of form and emptiness as a starting point for a meditation. When you have worked on your Zen garden, and created a pattern that springs from your inner consciousness, sit back and contemplate it. Empty your mind of its clutter and confusion and absorb the simplicity and peace of the natural forms in front of you.

a miniature zen garden

You can create a garden on a miniature scale, following the ideas of Zen, on a wooden platter or tray. The process of creating and working in the garden itself becomes a form of meditation, helping to soothe the mind and reduce stress.

Fill the tray with sand or fine gravel, and arrange some groups of beautiful pebbles in it. The stones you use could be found anywhere: in the street, in the park, on the beach. Once you begin to look at them properly you will be amazed at their beauty and form. Gazing on the stones you choose for your garden – all of them millions of years old – may prompt you to see your life in a new perspective.

You may decide to make your garden entirely with sand and pebbles. This art of gardening is called *bonseki* in Japan, and is the 'dry' equivalent of bonsai. Or you can add fresh flowers or small plants to represent living natural forms. Use a stick or a small rake to create spirals and circles in the sand around the stones and plants. These patterns can be smoothed away and redrawn whenever you come to the garden: they evoke the fluidity of the present moment and the impermanence of human life.

Try to dedicate a few moments a day to contemplation. Even if your time for meditation is short, the garden can become a small oasis of peace and quiet where you can find some spiritual freedom.

An altar for motivation

We are all motivated by many different things: physical and emotional drives, the need to survive, self-satisfaction and pleasure, our values, interests and ambitions, rewards, fears and established habits. Often the different influences that press upon us oppose each other in confusing and defeating ways. It's very easy to spend too much time and energy on activities that seem urgent but aren't really important. Instead we need to concentrate on the issues that may not seem so urgent, but are actually much more important to us, such as clarifying what we want our lives to be, fostering good relationships with others, and preserving our health by exercising, eating properly and getting enough rest.

Motivation comes with feeling capable, self-directed and hopeful, and challenging and positive goals are motivating in themselves. Pinning your hopes on impossible dreams, on the other hand, simply becomes frustrating: deep down you know you will not succeed, so you build in the idea of failure before you begin.

It's important to set goals that are achievable but that stretch your capabilities: this is a fine balance and needs careful thought –

◁ Choose incense ingredients that mirror and magnify your intent or goal.

△ Orange or yellow flowers on your motivation altar will inspire creative thinking.

about what you really want to do, and about yourself. You have to listen to your inner voice, and face honestly how you are feeling about a situation: sometimes an apparent lack of motivation conceals anxiety about beginning a difficult task. Once you acknowledge that you are fearful it is easier to face up to your fear and see the problem objectively. Break a seemingly impossible task down into tiny steps and do the first one – once you've started, the next step ceases to feel so momentous.

Lack of motivation can often stem from simple fatigue. If you're feeling frantic, don't be afraid to take a break. Stand back from

your situation and re-organize it. However busy you are, make time for exercise, proper meals and sleep. Don't wear yourself out meeting other people's expectations if they are unreasonable.

moving forward

Making an altar invites change into your life. It is a positive statement that you intend to focus your inner resources and move forward. With most of the things that we find difficult, the hardest part of all is beginning: the creation of an altar is an act of faith that gets you started and underlines the seriousness of your endeavours. The altar is a

◁ When you are setting your goals, include only those that you can realistically expect to meet.

INCENSE FOR MOTIVATION

2 parts cinnamon
2 parts frankincense grains
1 part nutmeg
1 part allspice
1 part ginseng
1 part juniper berries
Few drops frankincense essential oil

Pound all the dry ingredients with a pestle and mortar, then add the essential oil. Burn a few grains at a time on a charcoal block.

tangible expression of your intent to set aside time to evaluate your dreams and wishes. As a place where you can contemplate your life, it will help you to set worthwhile goals and to achieve them.

As air is the element of the intellect and the imagination, of dreams and ideas, its influence is important in an altar dedicated to motivation. When you feel sluggish and unable to get going, visualize a fresh breeze blowing away the cobwebs of your mind, bringing clear thought and inspiration. Add a little fire to your altar, too, to inspire you with drive and creativity. Fire is the element of change and helps to break old habits.

Your altar for motivation should sparkle with energy and light. Place it in a sunny window so that when you come to it in the morning the freshness and beauty of the new day greet you and fill you with optimism. If possible, use the windowsill as the altar, and on fine days open the window to let in the morning air.

Choose a beautiful, shimmering piece of fabric, such as a length of organza shot with gold, to use as an altar cloth, and decorate the altar with yellow and orange flowers. Yellow candles will help you to concentrate single-mindedly on your goals. Include an incense burner on which you can sprinkle a few grains each morning. Your altar ritual can include reviewing the achievements of the previous day and writing out your list of goals for the forthcoming day.

A TIMETABLE FOR ACHIEVEMENT

Planning your day effectively helps you to stay in control, which increases motivation. It also helps you to decide on priorities. Get into the habit of making weekly and daily schedules that are based on realistic goals, rather than a wish list that is impossible to achieve. Set clear starting and stopping times for work sessions, with proper breaks. Include plenty of time for rest and recreation, and allow some flexibility for unforeseen demands.

The element of fire

Fire is both creative and destructive. It can cleanse and purify, but it consumes: it is the only one of the four elements that cannot exist without feeding on something else. It creates warm, welcoming homes and cooks our food, but it is dangerous and can get out of control. It has the power to transform everything it touches.

Fire rules the south, the direction of the sun's fiercest heat (in the northern hemi-

▽ Fire can be dangerous and destructive, but it may burn away obstacles to new growth.

sphere), and it is related to motivation, creativity and passion. Its energy is quick-acting, forceful and positive and its power can be frightening. It symbolizes the inner child, the spirit within and the creative spark. Because it is the element of the passions, it gives courage and strength to fight for faith and quality of life. Those in whom it is dominant are passionate and intense. Fire consumes obstacles to faith and trust, and banishes negativity.

Areas governed by fire are kitchens, fire-places and boiler rooms, gyms and athletics

△ The turbulent, uncontrollable energy of lava illustrates fire's governance over the passions.

fields, and creative spaces such as studios and playrooms. Fire presides over the southern quarter of a room or building. In the nat-ural world, its places are deserts, hot springs and volcanoes.

Fire governs the sense of sight, it also inspires the need to offer and accept the power of touch. It is the element of physi-cal challenge, sensation and sexual energy. It celebrates life.

FIRE METAL
One of the fire metals, iron, is found on earth in its pure form only in meteorites. It is present in our blood, and is essential for physical energy and clear thinking. Wearing it as a talisman is said to increase physical strength. In some cultures, an iron talisman is worn as protec-tion against evil or negative energy: for this reason Sikhs wear an iron or steel bangle called a *kara* on their right wrist at all times.

▷ The lighting of a candle on the altar is a simple act that initiates ceremony as well as honouring the element of fire.

gods and goddesses of fire

Some of the deities associated with fire are Re, Sekhmet, Apollo and Lugh.

Re was worshipped by the ancient Egyptians as their pre-eminent solar deity. As a creator god, he brought order out of chaos – from his tears, the first human beings were formed. He was born each morning and journeyed across the sky in his solar boat, entering the underworld each night to do battle with the cosmic serpent, Apep. 'Son of Re' was one of the titles bestowed on the pharaoh. Re's daughter was the sun goddess Sekhmet, 'the Powerful One', who was usually portrayed with the head of a lioness. Re sent Sekhmet as his 'Eye', the terrible burning power of the sun, to punish the wickedness of humankind, but at the last moment saved his creation from total destruction by diverting Sekhmet's frenzied rage. Sekhmet was the terrifying aspect of Hathor, the goddess of joy and maternal love.

In Greek mythology, the sun was guided across the sky by Apollo, who also represents light, truth and clarity. He was the god of medicine and of music, and was the patron of the nine Muses, the embodiments of the creative imagination. The Celtic sky-god Lugh was a deity of the sun and the weather, and his spear is sometimes seen as a fork of lightning. As the god of skills and arts, he could be honoured by an offering of a creative work. The pagan summer festival of Lughnasadh, celebrated at the beginning of the harvest, is held in his name. Invoke these deities to bless an altar with the energy of fire.

▽ The lion is a universal symbol of strength and courage. Medieval alchemists also used it to represent transformation through fire.

FIRE CORRESPONDENCES

DIRECTION: south.
SEASON: summer.
TIME: midday.
MOON PHASE: first quarter.
PLANETS: Mars, Pluto.
GENDER: masculine.
COLOURS: red and orange.
SENSE: sight.
MAGICAL TOOLS: candles, lanterns, solar icons, wand.
INSTRUMENTS: stringed instruments.
CREATURES: dragon, snake, lion, ram, phoenix.
NATURAL SYMBOLS: flame, lava.
TREES: oak, hawthorn.
HERBS: basil, bay, garlic, hyssop, juniper, rosemary, rue.
INCENSE: frankincense, cinnamon, basil.
MINERALS: brass, gold, iron, fire opal, garnet, hematite, red jasper, sardonyx, flint.
SIGNS: Aries, Leo, Sagittarius.
ARCHANGEL: Michael.

An altar for creativity

Assembling a personal altar is a wonderful act of self-expression, and is in itself a creative act. Dedicating the altar to creativity recognizes and honours your powers of invention and originality. It is a very positive way to affirm your own talent. If you dream of a creative endeavour but have not dared to pursue it for fear that you will fail, bringing your dreams to your altar can help to dispel your inhibitions.

The spirit of creation flows through every one of us. We may describe it as divine inspiration, chi, life-force or quintessence, but it is the energy that we put into everything we create – whether that thing is a sculpture, a letter or a meal. No narrow definitions apply here: creativity should not be confined to writing, painting or other 'artistic' pursuits. It is important for everything we do to be approached creatively, giving spiritual value to even the most mundane tasks.

inspiration

To inspire literally means to 'breathe into', and the ancient Greek poets, whose word it is, would invoke one of the nine Muses to inspire them. They saw themselves as channels through which the divine voice could be heard. As a focus of positive energy,

△ The creative altar should be filled with colours of the rainbow, inviting variety, vibrancy and colour into your own world as a result.

▽ Focus your creative altar by adding elements that symbolize your own artistic endeavour in your chosen field.

◁ Displaying items associated with babies may help someone who is eager to conceive.

▽ If you are expecting a baby, give expression to your hopes and dreams for your child at the altar.

the altar is a place to tune into the creative spirit and call on it to inspire us.

In addition to inspiration, the creative process demands hard work, discipline, judgement and the courage to make mistakes and learn from them. At the altar we can find the motivation to acquire the skills

IMBOLC: THE LIGHT OF INSPIRATION

The festival of the return of light is at the beginning of February, and honours the Celtic triple goddess Brigid, a fire deity, celebrating her union with the god of light. It is a time of inspiration and creativity, when rituals are performed to bless new love, fertility, and the planning of new projects. Imbolc is predominantly a female festival, and Brigid blesses women's self-expression and creativity.

At this season, the goddess is honoured in her maiden aspect as the patron of inspiration and poetry. By tradition, if a white cloth is left outside overnight at Imbolc, the goddess will bless it with inspiration.

we need to express ourselves. In our own sacred space we can leave behind the limits of self-consciousness, so that our open minds attract fresh ideas like magnets, faster than they can be expressed. It is in this state of intuitive awareness – a form of meditation – that creativity flows.

creating the altar

Make your altar a thing of shimmering beauty to awaken your senses and fill you with the joy of creation. Dress it with a rainbow of colour and let its flamboyance give you the confidence to express yourself in other ways as you have here. The objects you choose to put on it can reflect whichever creative opportunities you want to explore, such as brushes and paints for artistic endeavour, or pens and paper if you are searching for the courage to express yourself in writing. Use this special place to try out your dreams, and bring your own creations to beautify your altar.

an altar for fertility

The most profound act of creation is that of new life itself. If you are trying to have a baby, the energy of your creativity altar can be devoted to your desire to conceive. Some

of the world's most ancient altars were erected for this purpose, celebrating the fertility of the earth and of women with the element of fire, the spark of life.

If this is the special purpose of your altar, include on it objects that speak of abundance and new growth, such as seeds and flowers, and add some beautiful images of parenthood and babies. You could also include a figure of the great Goddess to ally yourself with her fertile power.

THE FULL MOON

When the moon is full, its energy is opposed to that of the sun as they are on opposite sides of the earth, and the moon rises as the sun sets. The time of the full moon is therefore a period of high potency. It is the best time for rituals at the altar to encourage fertility, passion and abundance. In ancient times, women would rise before dawn on the day of the full moon and go into the fields. There they would wash themselves in the morning dew, asking the moon to bless them with children.

An altar for positive outcomes

It has long been acknowledged that if you have a clear idea of what you want you are far more likely to achieve it. Thought is a form of energy, and positive thinking contributes energetically to the fulfilment of your desire. Just as an artist has an idea that leads to the creation of a work of art, ideas are the first step to creating your future.

You should begin by thinking clearly about what you want. This is an effective way to make things happen, rather than simply allowing them to happen to you. Ideas, thoughts and wishes are running through our minds all day, but often we hardly give our-selves the chance to hold on to them before they disappear. Voicing such thoughts in a conscious way harnesses their energy to help us work towards their successful fulfilment.

When you are facing a challenging situation it is easy to focus on all the difficulties that might arise and to become preoccupied with the chance of failure. While it's impor-tant to have a realistic idea of what you are facing, the negative energy created by worry and fear can be paralysing. You may spend more time identifying all that could go wrong than in constructing a detailed and positive image of the outcome you want. A daily ceremony at your altar helps to focus your energy on what you want to happen.

The life-affirming qualities of an altar ded-icated to the element of fire will support you and give you the courage to achieve success. Place on your altar images that symbolize courage and strength, such as a lion, a pic-ture of a great oak tree or an object made of its wood. An image of the Archangel Michael would invoke his aid: he is the angel of fire and prince of the sun, who assists in matters of achievement and ambition.

▽ Use orange candles and images of strength and power on an altar to ensure success.

▽ Invoke the aid of the Archangel Michael on your fire altar by lighting a candle in front of his image. The image of a lion is also a potent one for a fire altar.

HERBS AND SPICES FOR SUCCESS

BASIL: gives protection, repels negativity and brings wealth. Leaves carried in the pocket bring luck in gambling, scattered on a shop floor they bring business success.

BERGAMOT: attracts success and prosperity. Rubbing the oil on money before it is spent will ensure the return of riches; the leaves in a purse attract money.

CINNAMON: draws money, protection and success.

CLOVE: banishes any hostile or negative forces and helps to gain whatever is sought.

VERVAIN: attracts money, protection; transforms enemies into friends.

△ When burning a wish it is vital to ensure that the paper is completely burnt to ashes.

TURQUOISE: THE LUCKY STONE

A popular amulet, turquoise has many protective qualities. It is said to guard its owner against ill-health and poverty, and to guarantee success in any field. The Aztecs tied turquoises to their weapons to make them more effective in battle. It attracts new friends, brings joy and increases beauty. As a gift, it bestows wealth and happiness on the receiver.

a ceremony for success

Use an orange candle for your ritual, because orange is the colour of ambition, goals and success. It has the power to draw good things to it and to change luck. Anoint the candle with oil to charge it with your personal vibrations and make the ceremony more effective. Using a few drops of bergamot essential oil, wipe the candle from the base to the middle and then from the wick to the middle – concentrate on your desire as you do this so that it is transmitted to the candle, and hold the candle so that you make the strokes towards your body, expressing drawing success towards you.

Place the candle in the centre of the altar. Arrange basil leaves around its base like the rays of the sun, and use cloves to make a spiral pattern around the candle, symbolizing growth and energy. (Knocking anything over on the altar might make you feel less confident of success, so avoid this mischance by arranging everything carefully.)

As you stand before the altar and light the candle, focus all your thoughts on achieving the result you desire. You can also write down your wish on a piece of paper, fold it twice and leave it under the candle. Or burn the paper in the candle flame so that the wish is carried away on the smoke, all the time thinking clearly about what you want. Empowered by your magical efforts, you can follow them up with practical strategies to achieve the right outcome.

An altar to the sun

The sun is a central symbol of creative energy, and has been an object of worship since the earliest times. The ancients recognized that without the sun, there would be no life. It is the giver of light, heat and fire: as light, it symbolizes knowledge and truth, and as heat and fire it stands for vitality and passion. In Celtic belief, fire was thought to have been brought to earth from the sun by a sacred bird – a swallow, swift or wren.

The sun provides the rhythmic structure of life on earth. It governs the seasons' annual cycle and controls our biological rhythms as we wake and sleep each day. We are creatures of the light. Even in the modern world where we can switch on artificial light and heat whenever we need it, we still

▽ Use herbs and spices that reflect and evoke heat on your solar altar.

△ Gold is the colour and metal of the male in its purest form and is offered to all sun deities.

suffer both physically and mentally if we are deprived of natural daylight for any length of time. When we talk of having a place in the sun, we are describing an enviable position where we can develop and grow, just as plants flourish in the sunlight.

deities of the sun

In most traditions, the sun is associated with the male principle, though in archaic times it was perceived as an aspect of the great mother goddess. One example of a surviving female sun deity is the beautiful sun goddess of Shintoism, Amaterasu-o-mi-kami, ruler of the high plains of heaven, who wove the fabric of the universe in her sacred weaving hall. The Arunta people of Australia recount the myth of the sun woman Yhi. Germanic and Norse tribes revered Sunna, and the Celtic sun goddess

◁ Light a gold candle on your sun altar first thing in the morning, as part of your ritual for greeting the day, and to honour whichever sun god you have chosen as your focus.

CATS IN THE SUN

The Egyptian goddess Bastet, the daughter of Re, was first worshipped as a solar deity who represented the sun's life-giving warmth. After about 1000 BC she was portrayed with the head of a cat, perhaps because of that animal's fondness for basking in sunshine. Bastet was generally a benevolent and protective goddess of love and fertility, and cats were venerated in her name.

The whole cat family is identified with the sun and the element of fire. Michael, the angel of the sun, can be called upon if a cat is in need of help. If you have a cat, you may notice it responding to the energy of your altar, and sleeping there.

Sul was adopted by the Romans, who dedicated altars over the sacred spring at Bath to Sulis Minerva.

In patriarchal societies, the sun became a male deity. Re, the Egyptian sun god, was revered as the creator of the world, whose tears engendered humanity. The Egyptians believed that Re would one day tire of his creation and return the world to chaos; therefore he had to be placated by their worship to safeguard the future of the cosmos. But they also looked to him for fatherly protection, and his regular daily progress across the sky was evidence of the celestial order that kept them safe.

The rayed sun-disc is an important symbol in many religions, and is related to the wheel of existence. For Zoroastrians, the winged sun-disc is the manifestation of Ahura Mazda, the supreme embodiment of light and goodness. In Christian imagery, a halo of golden rays surrounds the heads of the blessed, and Jesus is described as the 'light of the world'. In the Roman Empire, Jesus inherited the role of Mithras, god of light and emblem of invincible resurrection.

solar symbols

An altar dedicated to the blessings of light and the fiery energy of the sun needs to stand in the southern quarter of a room. Dress it with the colours of sunlight: a sparkling golden cloth, orange and yellow flowers and citrus fruits. Sunday is the day of the sun, and the ideal time for a special ritual is on this day, at noon, when the sun is at its zenith. Kneel in front of your altar, raise your arms in a salute to the sun at the height of its cycle and draw in its energy and power. This is a time for vigour and self-reliance, and for fostering creative energy.

On every day of the week, light a gold or orange candle each morning to represent the light of the divine presence, and make offerings of saffron, turmeric and rosemary. You may choose to call on the power of a sun deity: Apollo for creativity and harmony, or Vishnu, the protector of the world. Or ask for the intercession of the Archangel Michael, the prince of the sun.

▷ To invoke the power of the sun into yourself is to draw in the light of life.

The element of water

Water is the element of love and the emotions, because it is as fluid as our feelings. It rules friendship and marriage. It also relates to the subconscious mind, constantly shifting and active beneath the surface, and this element therefore governs intuition. It influences sleep and dreaming, as we sink down into the swirling depths of the subconscious to discover our deepest desires.

The moon tugs at the oceans of the world to create the tides, which follow her

▽ The moon is the ruler of the water element, creating the tides and influencing human moods.

ever-changing cycle. She exerts the same pull on the fluids in our bodies, affecting our emotions, menstrual cycles and health. Thus the ebb and flow of water is mirrored in the cycles of our own lives.

The energy of water is feminine and receptive. It rules the west, the direction of the setting sun. Water is an element of purification and healing: this can take the form of healing counsel leading to emotional release, sweeping away stale feelings and inducing us to face the truth about ourselves. People dominated by water are sensitive and spiritual. It is cleansing and essential to life, and our own lives begin in water. The element is thus symbolized by the womb and is related to fertility.

Areas of the home ruled by water are the bathroom and the kitchen sink. Because it presides over friendship and relationships, it also governs the living room, the arena of social interaction. In its cleansing and healing role water is also the element of medical rooms and hospitals. In the natural world its places are seas, lakes, rivers, marshes, pools, wells and rain-drenched lands.

△ Water may be cleansing and soothing, but it also possesses frightening, unstoppable power.

▽ Though fluid and changeable, water has the power to overcome obstacles in its path. Over time it carves its way through the hardest rock.

Neptune, the Roman god of the sea, was revered by seafarers whom he generally protected, but they feared his temper: his mood could change in an instant, giving rise to perilous ocean storms. Venus, the archetype of love and beauty, was said to have been created from the foam of the sea, and to have been carried on a sea shell to Cyprus. As she stepped from the sea, drops of water that fell from her body turned into pearls at her feet. The goddess had the power to calm the sea and ensure safe voyages, just as she could bring balance and harmony to human instincts and emotions.

Epona was a Celtic horse goddess worshipped during the period of the Roman Empire. She was portrayed carrying fruit or corn to show her connection with fertility and the earth's abundance. She was also a goddess of water and healing, and was the presiding deity of healing springs.

Invoke these deities to bless an altar with the energy of water.

▽ The dolphin is an animal of the water element, and symbolizes understanding and awareness.

WATER CORRESPONDENCES

DIRECTION: west.
SEASON: autumn.
TIME: dusk.
MOON PHASE: full.
PLANETS: moon, Neptune, Venus.
GENDER: feminine.
COLOURS: blue and orange.
SENSE: taste.
MAGICAL TOOLS: chalice, cauldron, mirror.
INSTRUMENTS: cymbals and bells.
CREATURES: cat, frog, turtle, dolphin, whale, otter, seal, fish.
NATURAL SYMBOLS: shells, water, river plants, watercress.
TREES: willow, alder, ash.
HERBS: chamomile, hops, lemon balm, orris, seaweeds, yarrow.
INCENSE: jasmine, rose.
MINERALS: silver, copper, amethyst, aquamarine, turquoise, tourmaline, opal, jade, pearl, sapphire, moonstone.
SIGNS: Cancer, Scorpio, Pisces.
ARCHANGEL: Gabriel.

gods and goddesses of water

Deities associated with water are Tiamat, Venus, Neptune and Epona. Tiamat represents chaos and the raw energy of the salt ocean. In Mesopotamian mythology, she was the primeval mother whose waters mingled with the fresh water of Apsu to initiate the creation of the gods.

An altar for healing

The home altar can be a source of healing for physical, emotional or spiritual problems. If you are in need of healing, call on the divine spirit to help you focus healing energies on yourself. Seek the wisdom to listen to your body and work in harmony with it to restore it to wholeness. If another person who is dear to you is suffering in some way, ask for help on their behalf.

Enlist the aid of the cleansing energy of water by setting an altar for healing in the west, and stand facing west to make your offerings or to say prayers. Make the altar a vision of pure watery beauty, fresh with the colour blue and decorated with flowers such as jasmine, lilies, lotus, iris or poppies, or with water-smoothed pebbles, shells, seaweed or watercress. Choose sandalwood incense, which is associated with purification and healing, or the cool, cleansing scents of camphor or eucalyptus.

If someone is receiving treatment in hospital, a small altar can be very comforting. You can simply arrange a blue shawl or scarf on a windowsill or side table, where it can be seen easily from the bed. Place on it images of wholeness and health, perhaps with some beautiful white flowers or other natural forms that speak of the vibrancy of the world that waits outside to be enjoyed.

A healing ceremony will be most effective during the time of a waning moon – particularly in the four days following the full moon. This is the time when things can be cast away or released, including grief and anger. To perform a healing ceremony on behalf of someone who is ill, light two blue candles on the altar and present a bowl of clear spring water as an offering.

Ask for the healing help of Archangel Gabriel, or Ceridwen, the white goddess of the Celts, or appeal to the compassion of

△ **Write the names of people to whom you wish to send healing on the petals of white flowers.**

▽ **Set up a healing altar by someone's bedside to offer solace and beauty when spirits are low.**

HEALING STONES

AMBER: relieves depression.

AMETHYST: protects against weakness
of the immune system, calms fear and
defeats insomnia.

AVENTURINE: soothes the emotions
and promotes balance and well being.

BLOODSTONE: calms in threatening
situations; detoxifies the blood.

CARNELIAN: increases physical energy
and power.

CHRYSOCOLLA: assists in the release
of grief, worry and pain.

CHRYSOPRASE: helps to relieve tension and stress.

CLEAR QUARTZ: a powerful talisman
for healing, known in many cultures
as the 'all-healer'. It guards against
loss of vitality and strength and draws
out pain, raises self-esteem, balances
emotions and increases insight.

GARNET: protects against depression;
boosts sexuality and fertility.

HEMATITE: protects against negativity, may be helpful for jet lag.

JET: dispels irrational fear and guards
against illness.

LABRADORITE: heals co-dependence
and instils courage and clarity.

LODESTONE/MAGNETITE: balances the
body, relieves the pain of arthritis.

MALACHITE: releases trauma, relieves
depression, acts against negativity.

ROSE QUARTZ: comforts and heals,
enhances cardiovascular health.

TOURMALINE: relieves stress.

Kuanyin, the Buddhist goddess of mercy.
Using a silver pen, write the name of the
person and their ailment on white paper
or white flower petals, and float them on
the water. Place a clear quartz crystal in the
water, and hold a second crystal in your
hands while voicing your prayer, so that it
transmits the healing power. Visualize the
ailment being lifted out of the sufferer and
give thanks for their recovery.

THE GODDESS OF COMPASSION

Chinese worshippers flock to the
shrines of Kuanyin to seek her favour,
because they believe she can cure
almost every sickness and alleviate
every distress. Her image stands on
many family altars in the East.

Kuanyin's name means 'One who
sees and hears the cries of the whole
world'. She carries a vial containing
the dew of compassion, and cures the
seriously ill by sprinkling a few drops
on their heads. While the birthdays
of the gods are usually celebrated
with firecrackers to ward off evil, there
are no explosions for Kuanyin
because she is so pure that no evil
would dare approach her.

◁ Place a quartz crystal in a bowl of water and
hold another while you are sending your prayers:
the crystal will transmit the healing.

The moon presides over the deep mysteries of our inner world, and is especially the guardian of women. As the appearance of the moon changes from crescent, full and waning to dark, it exerts its gravitational force on the waters of the earth, creating the tides and affecting the pattern of the weather. We, who are creatures of water, are also subject to its sway. The moon has always been an object of wonder.

In the moon's periodic growth and decay, the ancients saw an echo of the seasonal patterns of their lives. As it seemed to be reborn each month, the moon was widely believed to be the abode of human souls awaiting rebirth. But while the sun, rising each morning without fail, represented the stability of the cosmos, the moon appeared changeable and dangerous. It ruled the weather and could raise floods and storms,

PHASES OF MOON MAGIC
NEW/CRESCENT MOON (days 1–2): new opportunities, health and personal growth.

1st quarter
WAXING PHASE (days 1–7, active time, days 3–7): expansion, development and motivation; associated with Artemis.

2nd quarter
HALF TO FULL MOON (days 8–14, active time, days 12–14): fertility, abundance, illumination; associated with Isis, Selene, Arianrhod.

3rd quarter
WANING PHASE (days 15–21, active time, days 15–18): release, insight, wisdom, healing; associated with Hecate, Angel Gabriel.

4th quarter
DARK PHASE (days 22–29/30): meditation and preparation, time of no action; associated with Hecate, Cybele, Ceridwen.

△ Use lunar gemstones, clear crystals and lunar images to dedicate your altar to the moon.

but it also brought life-giving rain: it was both creative and destructive, and lunar deities shared this duality. The Mayan goddess Ixchel, for instance, was a vengeful goddess of storms, but also a protector of women in childbirth.

phases of the moon

Each phase of the moon's cycle came to be personified distinctly, as aspects of the 'triple goddess' or 'great mother' – maiden, mother and crone (or wise elder). The Greeks, for example, worshipped Artemis as the new moon, Selene as the full moon and Hecate as the waning and dark moon. These archetypal figures have appeared in the pantheons

▷ Blue and orange are the colours of the water element, ruled by the moon.

▷ Your lunar altar will help you to connect with the energy of moon deities, as you light a candle in their honour.

LUNAR GODDESSES

ARIANRHOD: the Celtic mother goddess and keeper of the silver wheel of stars, symbolizing time and fate.

ARTEMIS: the Greek goddess of the waxing moon and of wild places, defender of women; invoked by women in childbirth. Her Roman equivalent is Diana.

CERIDWEN: the Welsh mother, moon and grain goddess whose cauldron contains a potion for the gifts of inspiration and knowledge.

SELENE: the Greek goddess of the full moon, who rides in a chariot pulled by two white horses and presides over magic. Her Roman equivalent is Luna.

HECATE: the powerful three-headed Greek goddess of the waning moon, who rules magic, sorcery, death and the underworld.

ISIS: the Egyptian mother goddess, who governs magic, fertility and regeneration.

SOPHIA: the female representation of the holy spirit who stands for divine knowledge and wisdom.

CYBELE: the Phrygian dark moon goddess who governs nature, wild beasts and dark magic.

of many cultures, as their characteristics have been adapted and absorbed.

Although the Gregorian calendar is based on solar time, older calendars are calculated according to lunar cycles, and the moon determines the dates of many major religious festivals. The lunar cycle is celebrated by pagans at ceremonies known as 'full moon esbats', which celebrate the Goddess in all her forms.

lunar ceremonies

The full moon is the time for ceremonies to 'draw down the moon', connecting with the energy of the deity to empower wishes and ask for blessings for others. Write your wishes for them with a silver pen and burn them in a candle flame.

Setting up an altar to the full moon can help with emotional balance, bringing peace and harmony in your relationships. Decorate the altar with a light blue cloth and images of the moon or her deities. Use silver or light blue candles, jasmine, lilies or water-loving flowers, and burn jasmine or sandalwood incense. Moonstones, pearls, aquamarine and clear crystals are all associated with the moon, and will help to focus lunar energy on your altar.

TOTEM ANIMALS OF THE MOON

BEAR: sacred to Diana, goddess of the new moon, and connected with dreams, meditation and intuition.

CAT: associated with the night and the lunar goddess Artemis, it represents the mystery of the moon.

COW: sacred to Isis, who is crowned with her horns; milk is considered to be one of the gifts of the moon.

FROG: brings cleansing rain and is also a lunar fertility symbol.

HARE: represents the cycles of the moon and is associated with fertility. Indian and Chinese myths tell of the 'hare in the moon' and Eostre, the Anglo-Saxon goddess of fertility, was depicted with the head of a hare.

OWL: considered to be a harbinger of death, it is associated with the wisdom of Hecate, goddess of the dark moon. Its hooting is most often heard when the moon is full during the winter months.

WOLF: bays at the full moon, and stands for the psychic aspects of moon wisdom.

The element of earth

Earth is the element of all physical and material things, and its energy is grounding. It is our nurturing mother, and is related to health and prosperity. It is the densest of all the elements, whether it is represented by hard rock or fertile, moist soil, and it stands for stability. It is the solid foundation over which the other elements move.

People in whom the earth element is dominant are home-loving, dependable and loyal, and happiest when surrounded by their family. Earth's energy is receptive. It teaches patience and self-sufficiency, and helps us to recognize and accept our own characters – both their limitations and their potential. It shows us how to take responsibility for our lives and our destiny. Its symbol is the wise elder.

Earth's season is winter and its direction is north, where in the winter darkness the shifting, moving waters are frozen into immobility. In the natural environment, earth's place is a cave, the primal symbol of

△ The immobility of ice represents the earth element, whose season is winter.

▽ Earth is the stable foundation under our feet, but it can also be massive and awe-inspiring.

shelter. The cave's womb-like image makes it a symbol of birth and rebirth, where oracles speak and enlightenment is achieved. Forests, valleys and fields are other places of the earth element. In the home, earth governs areas of physical needs – the dining room and loo – and practical tasks: the workshop, greenhouse and garden. It is the element of buildings and their construction, and presides over financial institutions.

Earth is the element of ceremony and ritual, through which we regain our connection with the spiritual wisdom of nature. It shows us the way home.

earth gods and goddesses

Some of the deities associated with earth are Gaia, Pan and the Horned God. Gaia is the ancient Greek earth goddess whose name has been given in modern times to the life force of the earth. The daughter of Chaos, she gave birth to Uranus, the sky, and Pontus, the sea. Gaia's union with Uranus produced

EARTH CORRESPONDENCES

DIRECTION: north.
SEASON: winter.
TIME: midnight.
MOON PHASE: dark.
PLANETS: Earth, Saturn.
GENDER: Feminine.
COLOURS: citrine, brown, black,
olive green, sometimes white.
SENSE: touch.
MAGICAL TOOL: pentacle.
INSTRUMENTS: percussion.
CREATURES: ox, dog, wolf, goat,
stag.
NATURAL SYMBOLS: fossils, stones,
grains and seeds, salt, earth.
TREES: cypress, pine.
HERBS: pennyroyal, lovage, sage.
INCENSE: myrrh, patchouli.
MINERALS: lead, emerald,
aventurine, pyrites, coal, onyx.
SIGNS: Taurus, Virgo, Capricorn.
ARCHANGEL: Auriel.

▽ The wolf is a creature of the earth element,
and represents loyalty and family ties.

the Titans, or giants, including Cronos
(Time), the father of Zeus. Gaia was the
pre-eminent prophetess, the first deity of the
great oracle at Delphi. Even the other gods
and immortals were subject to her law. The
Greeks worshipped her as the giver of life
and the giver of dreams, and the nourisher
of plants and children.

In Greek mythology Pan was a shepherd,
and his name is believed to be derived from
a word meaning 'pasture'. He was easy-
going, lazy, sensual and unpredictable, and
represents the spirit of untamed nature. He
was usually said to be the son of Hermes,
and was portrayed with the hind legs and
horns of a goat (one of the first animals to
be domesticated). Pan was a very ancient

△ Earth's energy is fertile and abundant, seen in
the growth of all living things.

god of wild things, and his importance gradually increased until he came to be
worshipped as the 'Great God', and father
of all living things.

The pagan Horned God, who is related
to the Celtic fertility deity Cernunnos, represents sexuality and vitality. He is the
consort of the Triple Goddess. Like Pan, he
is represented as half-man, half-animal. As
lord of the woods he is the hunter, but he
is also identified with the hunted or sacrificial animal.

Invoke these deities to bless an altar with
the energy of earth.

THE PENTACLE

This five-pointed star may be created
from clay, wood, wax or metal. It is a
protective symbol of positive power
(represented by a circle which often
encloses it). The five points represent
air, fire, water, earth and spirit.

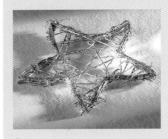

An altar for abundance

The laden altar of the harvest festival is a traditional manifestation of abundance. Corn, bread, fruits and vegetables are brought to the altar as offerings – to give thanks for the bounty of nature – but the mass of produce also acts as a visual re-assurance to members of the community: a reminder of both natural abundance and of their own abilities to harness earth's energy when they grow their food. The sight is an enriching one, expanding hearts and minds: it helps everyone to concentrate on all the good things they have, putting aside thoughts of what they lack.

Dedicating an altar to abundance is about tuning in to the blessings of life, shifting emphasis away from personal limitations and all that we lack, and opening ourselves to new and prosperous possibilities. Prosperity is not only a matter of material possessions, but an attitude of mind that includes spiritual and emotional riches. The altar can be

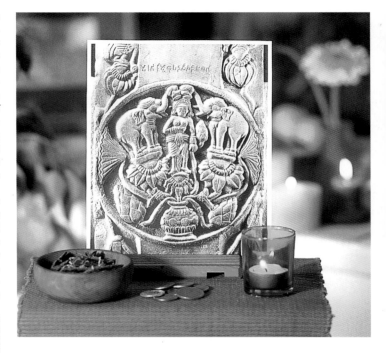

△ An altar of abundance dedicated to Lakshmi should reflect earth colours and scents.

a manifestation of that attitude and also a focus for meditations that build up inner abundance – the greatest wealth of all.

Use warm earthy colours such as russet, deep yellow, rich browns and olive greens. Add spicy scents to warm your soul and attract prosperity, such as patchouli, star anise, clove and cinnamon – or make up some prosperity incense mix. Make an offering of some silver coins. Think of all the things that already enrich your life and represent them on the altar to create a positive reminder of your spiritual wealth, and to express your gratitude. The more thankful you are, the more you will find greater abundance being drawn into your life.

the goddess of prosperity

An appropriate deity for this altar would be the Hindu goddess Lakshmi, who is the personification of abundance, wealth and

harmony. Deepavali, which is the third day of Diwali, the festival of lights, is dedicated to her worship: lamps are lit inside every home to welcome her and fireworks are exploded in her honour.

Lakshmi is portrayed as a beautiful woman seated on a sacred lotus throne. With two of her four hands she offers blessings of love and joy, while gold coins fall from the other two into the ocean of life. She is a symbol of everything that is fortunate, and it is the nature of good fortune that it is distributed randomly. But the elephant-headed god Ganesha, the lord of obstacles, helps to clear the path of anything that stands in the way of good fortune, therefore his presence on the altar can also help to bring abundance into your home.

INCENSE FOR PROSPERITY

1 part cassia bark or cinnamon
1 part grated nutmeg
1 part finely grated orange rind
1 part star anise
Few drops orange essential oil
2 parts frankincense grains

Pound the first four ingredients using a pestle and mortar, bind with the oil and mix in the frankincense grains. Burn on a charcoal block.

◁ One of the best ways to find abundance is to have gratitude for everything you receive.

CHAI SHEN, THE GOD OF WEALTH

Chinese families have for generations set up an altar outside their homes on the eve of the Lunar New Year to receive the blessings of Chai Shen, the god of wealth, for the coming year. The god arrives from a different direction each year and this must be carefully calculated in case the altar is wrongly placed and welcomes the god of evil instead.

All the family members say prayers and make offerings that symbolize abundance and good fortune, including sweets, fruit and wine. Everyone writes their wishes for the year on red paper, which is burned with offerings of incense. Last year's portrait of Chai Shen is burnt and firecrackers are set off. After the ceremony, the god's portrait is carried inside to watch over the household for the next year.

▽ Be careful what level of prosperity you wish for – greed will not be rewarded.

a prosperity box

To focus on what you want to bring into your life, choose a box to be your 'prosperity box'. Using black ink, write a list of what you wish for. Then write another list using energy-enhancing orange ink: this list should contain all the things you are prepared to do in order to achieve your desires. Fold the pieces of paper and place both lists in the prosperity box, together with a handful of prosperity incense, a few silver coins and a small piece of jade to attract prosperity. Keep the box on your altar. When you receive a gift, leave that too on the altar for a while and always remember to give thanks for what you have, to sustain the flow of abundant energy.

▷ Prosperity boxes can also be filled with wishes for others and with offerings to the wish-granting powers you are calling upon.

An altar for exploring wisdom

The inner journey is a quest for understanding and insight. Regardless of how much is known or learnt, no information can be of true benefit until we have understood how to make the best use of it, and this ability is defined as wisdom. It is an alignment of thought, feeling and experience, and it is only in the light of life experiences that we acquire it.

Wisdom is represented in the person of the sage, or wise elder – someone who has lived long enough to gain experience. If a child or young person seems wise, it is said that they are 'old before their time'. Yet we accrue wisdom throughout life, gaining insight through periods of reflection in solitude and with other people, when experience can be pooled and we can benefit from the learning processes, achievements and errors of others. With wisdom, we can apply knowledge to make sound decisions.

A vast body of traditional 'wisdom literature' has been handed down by ancient sages who spent their lives pondering the eternal truths of life and humanity's place

▽ **Sage placed in a shell increases a connection with the Goddess, to whom shells are sacred.**

in the universe. In the Judaeo-Christian tradition, for example, these revered texts include many books making up the Bible, Islam is embodied in the Koran, as revealed to the Prophet Muhammed. Hindu wisdom is set out in the Upanishads and the Bhagavadgita, while Buddhists study the Sutras to learn the teachings of Gautama Buddha, and Taoists find wisdom in the *Tao Teh Ching* and the *I Ching*. Classical texts of wisdom include the works of Aristotle and Plato.

Aristotle defined two aspects of wisdom. The first concerns the meaning of life – the 'big picture' – which can be sought through meditation and spiritual practices. The second is a more practical kind of wisdom

△ **Juno Lucina, the light-bearer, is an ideal deity to invoke for wisdom and illumination.**

SOPHIA

In the Hellenistic, Jewish and early Christian traditions, Sophia (the Greek word for 'wisdom') was acknowledged as the female aspect of the divine, and the eternal mother of all. According to the Gnostics, Sophia was born from silence before the beginning of creation. Her greatest shrine was the church of Hagia Sophia, built in Constantinople during the 6th century.

▷ Touch each sage leaf to the candle flame and then drop it into a heatproof bowl to burn and release its sanctifying smoke.

which might almost be described as common sense: the ability to look at things afresh to find ways around everyday problems. In both respects, our exploration of wisdom can lead to a greater perception and acceptance of the connectedness of all things, and an awareness that this wholeness or integrity – the order of the cosmos – includes ourselves. By learning detachment from the individual and particular, we rise above the concept of a separate self to reach a higher level of consciousness that is at one with the universe.

Wisdom can lead us along the right course in our individual lives, but even more important is its role in the wider world, where only the integrating vision of true wisdom can move society towards a more equitable state.

an altar to the Goddess

In the iconography of the Triple Goddess, the third manifestation of the deity is the crone, or wise elder. Her wisdom stems from long experience and she is associated with old age, the closing of the year and the evening of the day, when thoughts turn inwards to memories of the past and visions of the future. She is personified as Hecate

or Cybele, deities of the waning and dark moon, which is the time when insights can be gained. In the darkness of the winter night, the images of the mind's eye lead towards enlightenment.

To evoke the wisdom of the Goddess, dress an altar in purple, the priestly colour of inspiration and spiritual strength. An inspirational figure for its centrepiece could be the Goddess herself, or an image of a wise man or woman whose vision you particularly respect. A figure of an animal that represents an aspect of earth's wisdom could act as an ally in your quest for insight. Focus your thoughts with an amethyst, which brings spiritual peace and good judgement, and aids meditation.

Burn white sage in your ceremony at the altar. Sacred to the Romans, sage was also

used in Native American shamanic rites to cleanse and sanctify, and is known as 'grandfather sage' because it represents wisdom. It clears the head and promotes insight. Hold each sage leaf in the flame of a violet candle before dropping it into a shell or bowl to burn, and let its cleansing smoke awaken your wisdom.

◁ Think of the wisest grandparent figure you can imagine when you burn sage, and allow its fragrance to permeate your mind.

ANIMAL TOTEMS

BEAR: going within to find wisdom.
CAT: intuition.
JAGUAR: focused power.
OWL: inner wisdom, vision, the unconscious.
RAVEN: mystery, secrets, memory and thought.
TORTOISE: ancient wisdom, experience, endurance.
WHITE BUFFALO: generosity, selflessness, spirituality.

Feng Shui

The human race has reached a stage where it is capable of the most amazing feats on the one hand and the most amazing follies on the other. We have the capacity to cure hereditary diseases while the foetus is still in the womb, but we also let genetically engineered organisms loose into the environment in the most dangerous form of warfare humankind has ever known. We send people into space to collect information never dreamed of half a century ago, yet at the same time we allow the planet we inhabit to become increasingly at risk from our pollution, and less able to sustain the life forms we depend on for our own survival. These anomalies of modern life are becoming more and more destructive, and less easy to understand or explain away. More and more people are turning to different approaches to living, in order to attempt to redress the balance. Feng Shui offers us the opportunity to achieve health, happiness and prosperity by living in harmony with our environment, and taking control of our own space so that it becomes more balanced. This section of the book provides an insight into how we can interpret Feng Shui principles to create nurturing and life-enhancing spaces, and begin the process of establishing our own spiritual home.

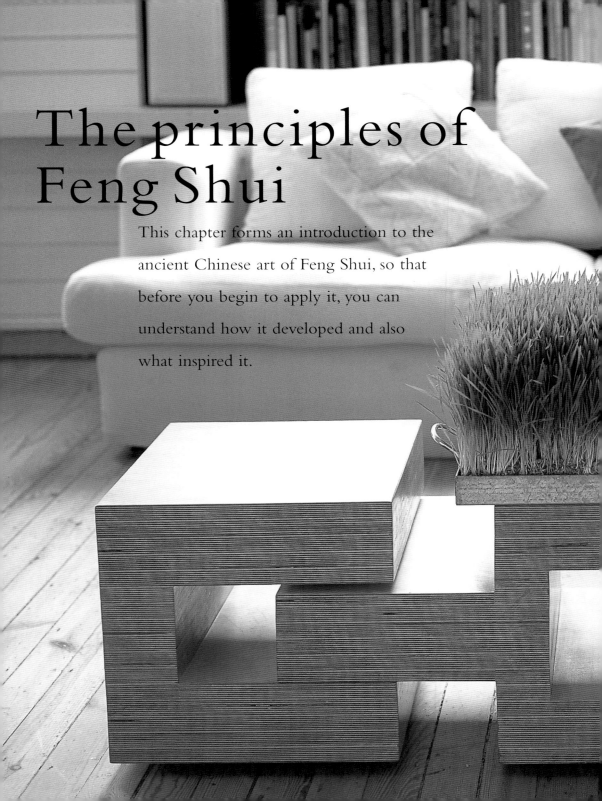

The principles of Feng Shui

This chapter forms an introduction to the
ancient Chinese art of Feng Shui, so that
before you begin to apply it, you can
understand how it developed and also
what inspired it.

What is Feng Shui?

The Chinese have a saying, 'First, luck; second, destiny; third, Feng Shui; fourth, virtues; fifth, education': although Feng Shui can be a powerful force in shaping our lives, it is not a cure for all ills. Luck plays a major role, and personality, or karma, is almost as important. What we do with our lives and how we behave towards others will play a part, and education gives us the tools to make sense of the world. Feng Shui is just one part of the complete package.

△ In China the dragon is a symbol of good fortune. Its presence is felt in landforms and watercourses, such as hills and rivers.

△ The Dragon Hills which protect Hong Kong are believed to be responsible for its prosperity.

▷ Much of the symbolic imagery that is integral to Feng Shui is taken from landscapes such as this, in Guilin, southern China.

The single factor which sets Feng Shui apart from other philosophical systems is that it has the capacity for change built into it. Most systems evolved from similar principles; understanding the natural world played a major role and natural phenomena were believed to be imbued with a spirit or deity, recognition of which would give people some benefit in their lives. Where these systems became established as religions, the deities were worshipped, but Feng Shui has remained a philosophy and can be used in any culture and alongside any belief system.

Feng Shui uses formulae which determine the rising and falling energy in a given time span of an individual or a house. Other formulae indicate a person's best location within a home or office, and can suggest the best placing of beds and desks. Many Chinese people consult astrologers annually to further refine this, so that every activity within the year can be pinpointed accurately and undertaken at an auspicious time. This advice can be

as precise as the best time to conceive or even when to wash your hair.

The philosophy of Feng Shui is embraced by people who are aware of the impact their surroundings have on them and who feel the need to take action to improve their lives. Using Feng Shui correctly, however, is a skill and its principles cannot be instantly applied, or adapted simply to suit the circumstances of a place or an individual.

▽ **Our surroundings affect us. Fresh air, natural products and a healthy environment enhance our mental and physical wellbeing.**

Feng Shui enables us to position ourselves within our environment to our best advantage. The positioning of our houses and offices as well as their internal design affects each of us positively or negatively. Feng Shui helps us to determine the most favourable positions for us and the layouts, colours and designs which will support us. In the garden we can determine the best locations for the different activities we intend to pursue there, but we also have to take account of the plants in the garden and their needs, which are equally important if the environment is to thrive.

△ **Water energy plays a significant role in Feng Shui. Here a fountain brings life to an office courtyard.**

The following chapters provide information on those aspects of this complex and fascinating subject that can be utilized by everyone in their own space. When we introduce Feng Shui into our lives we can only benefit, even where we only touch the surface. As we become more aware of our surroundings, and actively begin to change those factors with which we feel uncomfortable, we begin to gain a deeper insight into ourselves and our part in the wider picture.

▽ **The T'ung Shui almanac, produced for centuries, details the best times to move house, change jobs or even bathe.**

Approaches to Feng Shui

Feng Shui is about interpreting environments. Practitioners use a number of different approaches to connect with the energy or 'feel' of a place, and fine-tune it to make it work for those living or working there. Provided the principles are understood, the different approaches will be effective. More often than not, practitioners use a mixture of methods to create the effects they want.

the environmental approach

In ancient times, people lived by their knowledge of local conditions, handed down through the generations. Their needs were basic: food, water and shelter. Observation would tell them from which direction the prevailing winds were coming and they would build their homes in protective sites. They needed water in order to grow and transport their crops so rivers were important, and the direction of the flow and the orientation of the banks would determine the type of crops which could be grown. This branch of Feng Shui is known as the Form or Landform School and was the earliest approach to the subject.

▽ The Form School regards this as the ideal spot on which to build. The Black Tortoise hill at the rear offers support while the White Tiger and Green Dragon give protection from the wind, with the all-powerful dragon slightly higher than the Tiger. The Red Phoenix marks the front boundary, and the river irrigates the site as well as enabling crops to be transported for trade.

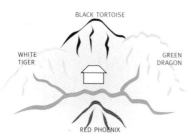

BLACK TORTOISE

WHITE TIGER

GREEN DRAGON

RED PHOENIX

△ These 'Karst' limestone hills in China symbolically protect an area of rich agricultural land.

▷ A luo pan or compass, used by geomancers in ancient China. Much of the information it records is regularly used by Feng Shui consultants.

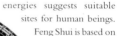

the compass approach

In ancient China, geomancers investigated earth formations and watercourses while astronomers charted the skies. Those who understood the power of the information they possessed recorded their knowledge on an instrument called a luo pan, or compass. The luo pan illustrates not only direction, but also investigates the energy of each direction, depending on the landform or heavenly body to be found there. Interpreting these

energies suggests suitable sites for human beings. Feng Shui is based on the *I Ching*, a philosophical book which interprets the energies of the universe. Its 64 images from the yearly nature cycle form the outer ring of the luo pan. With the wisdom of ancient sages added to it over the centuries, the *I Ching* offers us a means to connect to the natural flow of the universe. Its built-in time factor allows us to connect to it in different ways at different times in our lives.

the intuitive approach

Ancient texts illustrate every shape of mountain and watercourse. The names illustrate concepts significant to the Chinese psyche. 'Tiger in Waiting' suggests a negative place, where residents will never be able to relax, whereas 'Baby Dragon Looking at its Mother' indicates a much more restful environment.

The ancient text of the *Water Dragon Classic* provides more information on the best places to build, showing flow direction and position within the tributaries, with the names again indicating the type of environment. The sensibilities of people living and working on the land were finely tuned and their knowledge of the natural world endowed them with an instinct for suitable sites to grow crops.

▷ Mournatin sites (1 & 2) and river sites (3 & 4); the dots represent buildings. All except for 'Tiger in Waiting' are auspicious positions to build a new home.

▽ This prime site is protected by mountains, with healthy watercourses.

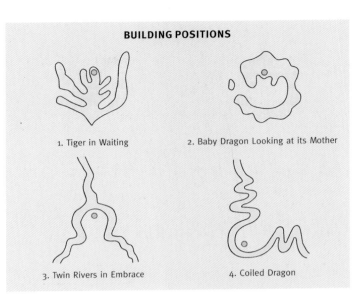

BUILDING POSITIONS

1. Tiger in Waiting

2. Baby Dragon Looking at its Mother

3. Twin Rivers in Embrace

4. Coiled Dragon

The theories of Feng Shui

Ancient peoples regarded the heavens, the earth and themselves as part of one system. This holistic view of life persists in many cultures, where health and medicine, food and lifestyle, and the route to salvation are all interconnected in one ecological system.

the Way

The Tao, or the Way, the philosophy of which underlies Feng Shui, shows how to order our lives to live in harmony with ourselves, each other and the natural world. We can use Feng Shui to help us work towards achieving this.

▽ 'The Dragon Breathing on the Lake' – the lake is a powerful Chinese image, that symbolizes a light-reflective surface harbouring a dark and deep interior.

yin and yang

Positive and negative forces act together in order to create energy – in electricity, for instance. Yin and yang represent these two forces which are in constant movement, each attempting to gain dominance. Where one achieves dominance, an imbalance occurs, so when one

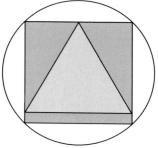

force becomes too strong its influence subsides and the other takes over. Still water, for example, is yin; a raging torrent is yang. Imagine a slow-moving yin river. When it hits rocks and descends, turbulence occurs, it speeds up and becomes yang. When it flows into a lake, it slows down and becomes yin once more. Yin and yang are opposing but interdependent concepts – without the idea of cold we would not be able to describe heat. At their extremes they change into each

△ The Tai Chi symbol illustrates the concept of yin and yang, the opposite yet interdependent forces that drive the world.

◁ Circle, Square, Triangle – signifying Heaven, Earth, human beings – the universal cosmological symbol.

YIN	YANG
Moon	Sun
Winter	Summer
Dark	Light
Feminine	Masculine
Interior	Exterior
Low	High
Stillness	Movement
Passive	Active
Odd numbers	Even numbers
Earth	Heaven
Cold	Heat
Soft	Hard
Valleys	Hills
Still water	Mountains
Gardens	Houses
Sleep	Wakefulness

other; ice can burn and sunstroke sufferers shiver. The aim is to achieve a balance between them. There are examples throughout the book of how we can achieve this in our own environments. Some of the more common associations are listed left.

chi

The concept of chi is unknown in Western philosophy but figures repeatedly in the philosophies of the East. It is the life force of all animate things, the quality of environments, the power of the sun, the moon and weather systems, and the driving force in human beings. The movements in Tai Chi, widely practised in China, encourage chi to move through the body. Acupuncture needles are used to unblock its flow when stuck. Chinese herbal medicine uses the special energetic qualities of herbs to correct chi when it becomes unbalanced. Meditation helps to establish a healthy mind: every brush stroke of the Chinese artist or sweep of the calligrapher's pen is the result of trained mental processes and the

▽ An acupuncturist at work. The needles unblock the energy channels and enable chi to flow round the body.

△ Chinese people practising Tai Chi. The exercises are designed to aid the flow of chi in the body.

correct breathing techniques, which ensure that each carefully composed painting or document is infused with chi.

The purpose of Feng Shui is to create environments in which chi flows smoothly to achieve physical and mental health. Where chi flows gently through a house, the occupants will be positive and will have an easy passage through life. Where chi moves sluggishly or becomes stuck, then the chances are that problems will occur in the day-to-day life or long-term prospects of those living there.

Where chi flows smoothly in the garden, the plants will be healthy and the wildlife there will flourish. Animals, birds, insects and the myriad of unseen micro-organisms that live there will regulate themselves and create a balanced and supportive environment. Where chi cannot flow unimpeded and becomes sluggish or stuck, an area may become dank or there may be an imbalance which creates, say, a plague of aphids.

In an office where chi flows freely, employees will be happy and supportive, projects will be completed on time and stress levels will be low. Where the chi is stuck, there will be disharmony and the business will not flourish.

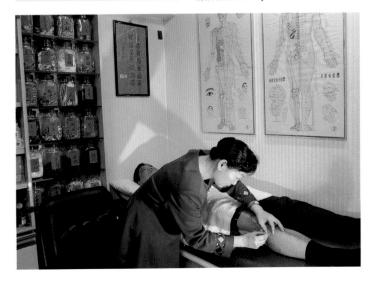

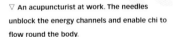

Five types of energy

Some of the latest scientific theories enable us to make sense of the ancient formulae on which Feng Shui is based. It is accepted that everything in the universe vibrates. All our senses and everything we encounter are attuned to certain frequencies, which react with us in a positive or negative way. We are all familiar with sound waves, which bring us radio, and electromagnetic waves, which bring us television. Colours, shapes, food, weather conditions – everything in our lives affects us on a vibrational level for good or ill and, in turn, we react in various yet predictable ways, depending on our individual traits.

The concept of elements exists throughout the world. The Chinese recognize five which arise out of the interplay of yin and yang and represent different manifestations of chi. They represent a classification system for everything in the universe, including people, as seen in the Relationships of the Five Elements table.

Ideally, there should be a balance of all the elements. Where one dominates or is lacking, then difficulties occur. Interpreting and balancing the elements plays a major part in the practice of Feng Shui. The elements move in a predetermined way, illustrated as a cycle in which they all support each other. A useful way of remembering this is by looking at the cycle in the following way. Water enables Wood to grow, Wood enables Fire to burn resulting in ashes or Earth, in which forms Metal, which in liquid form resembles Water. Another cycle indicates how the five elements

control each other and can be memorized as follows: Water extinguishes Fire, and in turn is soaked up by the Earth, which is depleted of energy by Wood in the form of trees, which can be destroyed by Metal tools.

The 'Relationships of the Five Elements' table shown below introduces another aspect – how in supporting a different element, an element can itself be weakened. The applications of each of the five elements, and the ways they relate to each other, are illustrated throughout this book.

△ Storms are nature's way of restoring a balance. They replenish negative ions in the atmosphere, which improves air quality.

▽ The heavenly bodies are essential to our lives and their movements lie at the heart of Feng Shui theory.

THE RELATIONSHIPS OF THE FIVE ELEMENTS

Element	Helped by	Harmed by	Weakened by	Weakens
Wood	Water	Metal	Fire	Earth
Fire	Wood	Water	Earth	Metal
Earth	Fire	Wood	Metal	Water
Metal	Earth	Fire	Water	Wood
Water	Metal	Earth	Wood	Fire

THE FIVE ELEMENTS

ELEMENT	CHARACTERISTICS	PERSONALITIES	ASSOCIATIONS
WOOD	Symbolizes spring, growth and plant life. In its yin form, it is supple and pliable, in its yang form as sturdy as an oak. Positively used, it is a walking stick; negatively used, a spear. Bamboo is cherished in China for its ability to sway in the wind yet be used as scaffolding. Viewed as a tree, Wood energy is expansive, nurturing and versatile.	Wood people are public-spirited and energetic. Ideas people, their outgoing personalities win them support. They visualize rather than committing themselves to plans. *Positively* – they are artistic and undertake tasks with enthusiasm. *Negatively* – they become impatient and angry and often fail to finish the tasks they have begun.	Trees and plants Wooden furniture Paper Green Columns Decking Landscape pictures
FIRE 	Symbolizes summer, fire and heat. It can bring light, warmth and happiness or it can erupt, explode and destroy with great violence. Positively, it stands for honour and fairness. Negatively, it stands for aggression and war.	Fire people are leaders and crave action. They inspire others to follow, often into trouble, as they dislike rules and fail to see consequences. *Positively* – they are innovative, humorous and passionate people. *Negatively* – they are impatient, exploit others and have little thought for their feelings.	Sun symbols Candles, lights and lamps Triangles Red Man-made materials Sun or fire pictures
EARTH 	Symbolizes the nurturing environment that enables seeds to grow, which all living things emanate from and return to. It nurtures, supports and interacts with each of the other elements. Positively, it denotes fairness, wisdom and instinct. Negatively, it can smother or represent the nervous anticipation of non-existent problems.	Earth people are supportive and loyal. Practical and persevering, they are a tower of strength in a crisis. They do not rush anything, but their support is enduring. Patient and steady, they possess inner strength. *Positively* – earth people are loyal, dependable and patient. *Negatively* – they are obsessional and prone to nit-picking.	Clay, brick and terracotta Cement and stone Squares Yellow, orange and brown
METAL	Symbolizes autumn and strength. Its nature represents solidity and the ability to contain objects. On the other hand, metal is also a conductor. Positively, it represents communication, brilliant ideas and justice. Negatively, it can suggest destruction, danger and sadness. Metal can be a beautiful and precious commodity, or the blade of a weapon.	Metal people are dogmatic and resolute. They pursue their ambitious aims single-mindedly. Good organizers, they are independent and happy in their own company. Faith in their own abilities inclines them towards inflexibility although they thrive on change. They are serious and do not accept help easily. *Positively* – they are strong, intuitive and interesting people. *Negatively* – they are inflexible, melancholic and serious.	All metals Round shapes Domes Metal objects Door furniture and doorsteps Kitchenware White, grey, silver and gold Coins Clocks
WATER	Symbolizes winter and water itself, gentle rain or a storm. It suggests the inner self, art and beauty. It touches everything. Positively, it nurtures and supports with understanding. Negatively, it can wear down and exhaust. Associated with the emotions, it can suggest fear, nervousness and stress.	Water people communicate well. They are diplomatic and persuasive. Sensitive to the moods of others, they will lend an ear. They are intuitive and make excellent negotiators. Flexible and adaptable, they view things holistically. *Positively* – water people are artistic, sociable and sympathetic. *Negatively* – water people are fickle and intrusive.	Rivers, streams and lakes Blue and black Mirrors and glass Meandering patterns Fountains and ponds Fish tanks Water pictures

Chinese astrology

An analysis of an environment using a luo pan compass looks at the energetic qualities of the various compass points. The Earthly Branches on the compass represent 12 of these points and also correspond to the 12 animals which relate to Chinese astrology. We often find ourselves in situations at home, or at work, when we canot understand how another person can view the same situation so differently from us, or can make us feel uncomfortable, or find different things irritating or amusing. Looking at the animals enables us to explore these differences by allowing us an insight into the make-up of our natures and personalities.

With this knowledge, we can come to know ourselves better and to accept the personalities of others. At home, it may encourage us to think twice, for instance, before launching into a tirade on tidiness or punctuality. It also has an important use in the workplace in keeping warring factions apart and ensuring a harmonious balance between productive output and socializing.

the cycles

The Chinese calendar is based on the cycle of the moon, which determines that each month is approximately 29½ days long, beginning with a new moon. The years progress in cycles of 12 and it is helpful to appreciate the subtleties of Chinese symbology since each year is represented by an animal and the characteristics of each animal and its way of life are used to identify different types of people. Cultural differences are apt to get in the way if we attempt this identification ourselves; whereas Westerners would describe the Rat's character, for example, as sly and crafty, the Chinese respect its quick mind and native cunning.

◁ In the Chinese calendar each year is represented by an animal and each animal is governed by an element.

Each animal is governed by an element which determines its intrinsic nature. The cycle of 12 is repeated five times to form a larger cycle of 60 years and in each of these cycles, the animals are ascribed an element with either a yin or yang characteristic, which determines their characters. Thus in 60 years, no two animals are the same. We begin by investigating the basic animal characteristics.

THE NATURE OF THE ANIMALS

Rat	Water
Ox	Earth
Tiger	Wood
Rabbit	Wood
Dragon	Earth
Snake	Fire
Horse	Fire
Goat	Earth
Monkey	Metal
Rooster	Metal
Dog	Earth
Pig	Water

If we do not get on with someone, it may be that the animals associated with us in the Chinese calendar are not compatible. Alternatively, it may be that the elements that represent the time of our birth are not in harmony with the elements of the other person.

finding your animal

The Chinese year does not begin on 1st January but on a date which corresponds with the second new moon after the winter equinox, so it varies from year to year. Thus someone born on 25th January 1960 according to the Western calendar would actually be born in 1959 according to the Chinese calendar. The 'Chinese Animals Table' opposite gives the exact dates when each year begins and ends, as well as its ruling animal and element. Their outer characteristics are identified by the element of the year they were born, as shown in 'The Nature of the Animals' box (left). The ways in which the elements affect an animal's personality are described in 'The Five Elements' table.

animal cycles

One of the 12 animals represents each lunar month, each with its own element governing its intrinsic nature. Over 60 years, the Five Elements cycle spins so that each animal can be Wood, Fire, Earth, Metal or Water, which determines its character.

In a full analysis by an experienced Feng Shui consultant, each of us will have a collection of eight elements that together make up not only our character, but also our destiny.

CHINESE ANIMALS TABLE

Year	Year Begins	Year Ends	Animal	Element	Year	Year Begins	Year Ends	Animal	Element
1920	20 February 1920	7 February 1921	Monkey	Metal +	1967	9 February 1967	29 January 1968	Goat	Fire –
1921	8 February 1921	27 January 1922	Rooster	Metal –	1968	30 January 1968	16 February 1969	Monkey	Earth +
1922	28 January 1922	15 February 1923	Dog	Water +	1969	17 February 1969	5 February 1970	Rooster	Earth –
1923	16 February 1923	4 February 1924	Pig	Water –	1970	6 February 1970	26 January 1971	Dog	Metal +
1924	5 February 1924	24 January 1925	Rat	Wood +	1971	27 January 1971	15 February 1972	Pig	Metal –
1925	25 January 1925	12 February 1926	Ox	Wood –	1972	16 February 1972	2 February 1973	Rat	Water +
1926	13 February 1926	1 February 1927	Tiger	Fire +	1973	3 February 1973	22 January 1974	Ox	Water –
1927	2 February 1927	22 January 1928	Rabbit	Fire –	1974	23 January 1974	10 February 1975	Tiger	Wood +
1928	23 January 1928	9 February 1929	Dragon	Earth +	1975	11 February 1975	30 January 1976	Rabbit	Wood –
1929	10 February 1929	29 January 1930	Snake	Earth –	1976	31 January 1976	17 February 1977	Dragon	Fire +
1930	30 January 1930	16 February 1931	Horse	Metal +	1977	18 February 1977	6 February 1978	Snake	Fire –
1931	17 February 1931	5 February 1932	Goat	Metal –	1978	7 February 1978	27 January 1979	Horse	Earth +
1932	6 February 1932	25 January 1933	Monkey	Water +	1979	28 January 1979	15 February 1980	Goat	Earth –
1933	26 January 1933	13 February 1934	Rooster	Water –	1980	16 February 1980	4 February 1981	Monkey	Metal +
1934	14 February 1934	3 February 1935	Dog	Wood +	1981	5 February 1981	24 January 1982	Rooster	Metal –
1935	4 February 1935	23 January 1936	Pig	Wood –	1982	25 January 1982	12 February 1983	Dog	Water +
1936	24 January 1936	10 February 1937	Rat	Fire +	1983	13 February 1983	1 February 1984	Pig	Water –
1937	11 February 1937	30 January 1938	Ox	Fire –	1984	2 February 1984	19 February 1985	Rat	Wood +
1938	31 January 1938	18 February 1939	Tiger	Earth +	1985	20 February 1985	8 February 1986	Ox	Wood –
1939	19 February 1939	7 February 1940	Rabbit	Earth –	1986	9 February 1986	28 January 1987	Tiger	Fire +
1940	8 February 1940	26 January 1941	Dragon	Metal +	1987	29 January 1987	16 February 1988	Rabbit	Fire –
1941	27 January 1941	14 February 1942	Snake	Metal –	1988	17 February 1988	5 February 1989	Dragon	Earth +
1942	15 February 1942	4 February 1943	Horse	Water –	1989	6 February 1989	26 January 1990	Snake	Earth –
1943	5 February 1943	24 January 1944	Goat	Water –	1990	27 January 1990	14 February 1991	Horse	Metal +
1944	25 January 1944	12 February 1945	Monkey	Wood +	1991	15 February 1991	3 February 1992	Goat	Metal –
1945	13 February 1945	1 February 1946	Rooster	Wood –	1992	4 February 1992	22 January 1993	Monkey	Water +
1946	2 February 1946	21 January 1947	Dog	Fire +	1993	23 January 1993	9 February 1994	Rooster	Water –
1947	22 January 1947	9 February 1948	Pig	Fire –	1994	10 February 1994	30 January 1995	Dog	Wood +
1948	10 February 1948	28 January 1949	Rat	Earth +	1995	31 January 1995	18 February 1996	Pig	Wood –
1949	29 January 1949	16 February 1950	Ox	Earth –	1996	19 February 1996	6 February 1997	Rat	Fire +
1950	17 February 1950	5 February 1951	Tiger	Metal +	1997	7 February 1997	27 January 1998	Ox	Fire –
1951	6 February 1951	26 January 1952	Rabbit	Metal –	1998	28 January 1998	15 February 1999	Tiger	Earth +
1952	27 January 1952	13 February 1953	Dragon	Water +	1999	16 February 1999	4 February 2000	Rabbit	Earth –
1953	14 February 1953	2 February 1954	Snake	Water –	2000	5 February 2000	23 January 2001	Dragon	Metal +
1954	3 February 1954	23 January 1955	Horse	Wood +	2001	24 January 2001	11 February 2002	Snake	Metal –
1955	24 January 1955	11 February 1956	Goat	Wood –	2002	12 February 2002	31 January 2003	Horse	Water +
1956	12 February 1956	30 January 1957	Monkey	Fire +	2003	1 February 2003	21 January 2004	Goat	Water –
1957	31 January 1957	17 February 1958	Rooster	Fire –	2004	22 January 2004	8 February 2005	Monkey	Wood +
1958	18 February 1958	7 February 1959	Dog	Earth +	2005	9 February 2005	28 January 2006	Rooster	Wood –
1959	8 February 1959	27 January 1960	Pig	Earth –	2006	29 January 2006	17 February 2007	Dog	Fire +
1960	28 January 1960	14 February 1961	Rat	Metal +	2007	18 February 2007	6 February 2008	Pig	Fire –
1961	15 February 1961	4 February 1962	Ox	Metal –	2008	7 February 2008	25 January 2009	Rat	Earth +
1962	5 February 1962	24 January 1963	Tiger	Water +	2009	26 January 2009	13 February 2010	Ox	Earth –
1963	25 January 1963	12 February 1964	Rabbit	Water –	2010	14 February 2010	2 February 2011	Tiger	Metal +
1964	13 February 1964	1 February 1965	Dragon	Wood +	2011	3 February 2011	22 January 2012	Rabbit	Metal –
1965	2 February 1965	20 January 1966	Snake	Wood –	2012	23 January 2012	9 February 2013	Dragon	Water +
1966	21 January 1966	8 February 1967	Horse	Fire +	2013	10 February 2013	30 January 2014	Snake	Water –

The animal signs

Using characteristics that are perceived to be an inherent part of the natures of the 12 animals, Chinese astrology attributes certain aspects of these to the characteristics and behaviour of people born at specific times. This system operates in much the same way as Western astrology.

the rat

An opportunist with an eye for a bargain, Rats tend to collect and hoard, but are unwilling to pay too much for anything. They are devoted to their families, particularly their children.

On the surface, Rats are sociable and gregarious yet underneath they can be miserly and petty. Quick-witted and passionate, they are capable of deep emotions despite their cool exteriors. Their nervous energy and ambition may lead them to attempt more tasks than they are able to complete successfully.

Rats will stand by their friends as long as they receive their support in return. However, they are not above using information given to them in confidence in order to advance their own cause.

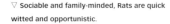

▽ **Sociable and family-minded, Rats are quick witted and opportunistic.**

△ **Dynamic and generous, Tigers are warm-hearted unless they are crossed.**

▽ **Dependable and loyal, the Ox displays endless patience until pushed too far.**

the ox

Invariably solid and dependable, the Ox is an excellent organizer. Oxen are systematic in their approach to every task they undertake. They are not easily influenced by others' ideas. Loyalty is part of their make-up, but if crossed or deceived they will never forget. Oxen do not appear to be imaginative though they are capable of good ideas. Although not demonstrative or the most exciting people romantically, they are entirely dependable and make devoted parents. They are people of few words but fine understated gestures. Oxen are renowned for their patience, but it has its limits – once roused, their temper is a sight to behold.

the tiger

Dynamic and impulsive Tigers live life to the full. Tigers often leap into projects without planning, but their natural exuberance will carry them through successfully unless boredom creeps in and they do not complete the task. Tigers do not like failure and need to be admired. If their spirits fall, they require a patient ear to listen until they bounce back again. They like excitement in relationships and static situations leave them cold. Tigers are egotistic. They can be generous and warm, but sometimes show their claws.

the rabbit

A born diplomat, Rabbits cannot bear conflict. They can be evasive and often say what they think someone wishes to hear rather than start a discussion. This is not to say they give in easily: the docile cover hides a strong will and self-assurance. It is difficult to gauge what Rabbits are thinking and they often appear to be daydreaming, while in reality they may be planning their next strategy. The calmest of the signs, Rabbits are social creatures up to the point when their space is invaded. Good communication skills mean they enjoy the company of others and are good counsellors. They prefer to keep away from the limelight and enjoy the finer things of life.

△ **Powerful leaders, Dragons prefer to follow their own path in life.**

△ **Good counsellors and communicators, Rabbits also need their own space.**

the dragon

Natural pioneers, Dragons launch straight into projects or conversations. They often fail to notice others trying to keep up (or plotting behind their backs). Authority figures, they will make their own laws and hate restrictions. They prefer to get on with a job themselves and are good at motivating others into action.

They are always available to help others, but their pride makes it difficult for them to accept help in return. Although always at the centre of things, they tend to be loners and are prone to stress when life becomes difficult. Hard-working and generous, Dragons are trustworthy and are loyal friends. They enjoy excitement and new situations. When upset, they can be explosive, but all is soon forgotten.

the snake

Although a connoisseur of the good things in life, Snakes are also inward-looking and self-reliant. Snakes tend to keep their own counsel and dislike relying on others. They can be ruthless in pursuing their goals. Though very kind and generous, Snakes can be demanding in relationships. They find it hard to forgive and will never forget a slight. Never under-estimate the patience of a snake, who will wait in the wings until the time is right to strike. They are elegant and sophisticated and although they are good at making money, they never spend it on trifles. Only the best is good enough for them. Very intuitive, Snakes can sense the motives of others and sum up situations accurately. If crossed, they can bite with a deadly accuracy. Snakes exude mystery and ooze charm. They can also be deeply passionate.

▽ **Mysterious and passionate, Snakes have endless patience.**

△ Active and excitable, the Horse's nervous energy often runs away with them.

The horse

Ever-active, the Horse will work tirelessly until a project is completed, but only if the deadline is their own. Horses have lightning minds and can sum up people and situations in an instant, sometimes too quickly, and they will move on before seeing the whole picture. Capable of undertaking several tasks at once, Horses are constantly on the move and fond of exercise. They may exhaust themselves physically and mentally. Horses are ambitious and confident in their own abilities. They are not interested in the opinions of others and are adept at side-stepping issues. They can be impatient and have explosive tempers although they rarely bear grudges.

The goat

Goats are emotional and compassionate. Peace-lovers, Goats always behave correctly and they are extremely accommodating to others. They tend to be shy and vulnerable to criticism. They worry a lot and appear to be easily put upon, but when they feel strongly about something they will dig their heels in and sulk until they achieve their objectives. Goats are generally popular and are usually well cared for by others. They appreciate the finer things in life and are usually lucky. They find it difficult to deal with difficulties and deprivation. Ardent romantics, Goats can obtain their own way by wearing their partners down and turning every occasion to their advantage. They will do anything to avoid conflict and hate making decisions.

▽ Peace-loving Goats are kind and popular, they hate conflict and will try to avoid it.

The monkey

Monkeys are intelligent and capable of using their wits to solve problems. Monkeys often wriggle out of difficult situations and are not above trickery if it will further their own ends. Monkeys tend to be oblivious of other people and of the effect their own actions may have on them. In spite of this, they are usually popular and are able to motivate others by their sheer enthusiasm for new projects. Monkeys are constantly on the look out for new challenges and their innovative approach and excellent memories generally make them successful. They are full of energy and are always active. They have little sympathy for those who are unable to keep up with them, but will soon forget any difficulties.

▽ Energetic Monkeys use their intelligence to push their own ideas forward.

accumulating wealth for themselves. They like to spend time relaxing. Dogs take time to get to know people but have a tendency to pigeon-hole them. When they want something badly they can be persistent. If roused they can be obstinate and occasionally they lash out, although their temper is usually short-lived. Some Dogs can be rather nervous and they may be prone to pessimism.

△ **The flamboyant Rooster can be easily won over by flattery and admiration.**

the rooster

Highly sociable creatures, Roosters shine in situations where they are able to be the centre of attention. If a Rooster is present, everyone will be aware of the fact because no Rooster can ever take a back seat at a social gathering. They are dignified, confident and extremely strong-willed, yet they may have a negative streak. They excel in arguments and debates. Incapable of underhandedness, Roosters lay all their cards on the table and do not spare others' feelings in their quest to do the right thing. They never weary of getting to the bottom of a problem and are perfectionists in all that they do. Roosters can usually be won over by flattery. Full of energy, Roosters are brave, but they hate criticism and can be puritanical in their approach to life.

the dog

Dogs are entirely dependable and have an inherent sense of justice. Intelligent, Dogs are loyal to their friends and they always listen to others, although they can be critical. In a crisis, Dogs always help and will never betray a friend. They can be hard workers, but are not all that interested in

▽ **Dogs are loyal and hard-working, but enjoy relaxing too.**

△ **Peace-loving Pigs are sociable and popular and are able to organize others well.**

the pig

The Pig is everybody's friend. Honest and generous, Pigs are always available to bail others out of difficulties. Pigs love the social scene and are popular. They rarely argue and if they do fly off the handle, they bear no grudges afterwards. They abhor conflict and very often will not notice when others are attempting to upset them. They prefer to think well of people. Over-indulgence is their greatest weakness and Pigs will spend heavily in pursuit of pleasure. They always share with their friends and trust that, in return, their friends will make allowances for their own little weaknesses. Great organizers, Pigs like to have a cause and will often rally others to it as well.

Compatibility of signs

The saying, 'You can choose your friends but not your family', is often heard from those who do not have harmonious family relationships, and we all find that we are drawn more to some people than to others. Chinese astrology uses the year, month, day and time of birth (each of which is represented by an animal and the yin or yang attributes of its accompanying element) to analyse characters and predict fortunes.

Analyses of relationships depend upon the interaction of the elements on each person's chart. We can gain some insight

▽ We are drawn to people for a variety of reasons. Compatibility of animal signs and elements can certainly help.

into our own characters and those of our family and colleagues by using the 'Chinese Animals Table' and then looking at the associated elements with their yang (+) (positive characteristics) or yin (−) (negative characteristics) in 'The Five Elements' table.

△ We function well at work when we are compatible with our colleagues. The man on the right looks uncomfortable.

▽ This table shows which of our family, friends and colleagues we relate to best according to Chinese astrology.

COMPATIBILITY TABLE

	RAT	OX	TIGER	RABBIT	DRAGON	SNAKE	HORSE	GOAT	MONKEY	ROOSTER	DOG	PIG
RAT	+	=	+	−	*	=	−	−	*	−	+	+
OX	=	+	−	=	+	*	−	−	+	*	−	+
TIGER	+	−	+	−	+	−	*	+	−	=	*	=
RABBIT	+	+	−	+	=	+	−	*	−	−	=	*
DRAGON	*	−	+	=	−	+	−	+	*	+	−	=
SNAKE	+	*	−	+	=	+	−	=	−	*	+	−
HORSE	−	−	*	−	=	+	−	=	+	+	*	+
GOAT	−	−	=	*	+	+	=	+	+	−	−	*
MONKEY	*	+	−	−	*	−	−	+	=	+	+	=
ROOSTER	−	*	+	−	−	*	+	−	−	+	+	+
DOG	+	−	*	=	−	+	*	−	+	−	=	+
PIG	=	+	=	*	+	−	−	*	−	+	+	+

KEY: * Excellent = Good + Workable − Difficult

The animal years

As we have seen, each year is ruled by an animal and its character is said to denote the energetic quality of the year.

The animal which rules each year and the date of the Chinese New Year for around a hundred-year period are shown on the 'Chinese Animals Table'. For ease of reference, 1999–2010 are shown below. Our fortunes in each year are indicated by whether or not we are compatible with the animal ruling that year, which can be checked by referring back to the 'Compatibility Table'.

1999	Rabbit	2005	Rooster
2000	Dragon	2006	Dog
2001	Snake	2007	Pig
2002	Horse	2008	Rat
2003	Goat	2009	Ox
2004	Monkey	2010	Tiger

year of the rabbit

A respite from the past year and a breather before the next, rest is indicated here. This is a time for negotiations and settlements, but not for new ventures. Women's and family concerns are considered important.

year of the dragon

The time for new business ventures and projects. Euphoric and unpredictable, this is the year for wild schemes and risks. Dragon babies are considered lucky.

year of the snake

Peace returns and allows time to reflect. Care should be taken in business matters as treachery and underhand dealings are indicated. Money is made and communication is good. A fertile year, in which morality becomes an issue.

year of the horse

An energetic and volatile year in which money will be spent and borrowed. Some impulsive behaviour will bring rewards, while some will fail. A year for marriage and divorce.

year of the goat

A quiet year in which family matters are to the fore. A year for consolidating and for diplomatic negotiations, rather than launching new projects.

year of the monkey

An unpredictable year when nothing goes according to plan. Only the quick-witted will prosper. New ideas abound and communication will flourish.

year of the rooster

A year for making feelings known and letting grievances out. This may cause disharmony in families so tact is required.

year of the dog

Worthy causes abound – human and animal rights and environmental issues are in the public eye. Security should be

▽ **Family relationships are usually harmonious if the animal signs are compatible and the elements do not clash.**

checked, by governments and at home. A year for marriage and the family.

year of the pig

The last year of the cycle and unfinished business should be concluded. Optimism abounds and the pursuit of leisure is indicated. Family concerns will go well.

year of the rat

This is a lucky year, a good time to start a new venture. The rewards will not come without hard work, but with careful planning they will arrive.

year of the ox

Harvest is the symbol for this year so we will reap what we have sown. Decisions should be made now and contracts signed. This is a conservative year so grand or outrageous schemes are not considered appropriate.

year of the tiger

Sudden conflicts and crises arise in this year and will have an impact for some time. The year for grand schemes for the courageous, but underhand activities may suffer from repercussions.

The Bagua and the magic square

The compass directions and their associations are fundamental to the practice of Feng Shui. Astronomical and geomantic calculations and the place of human beings within them are plotted on a luo pan, an instrument so powerful that it has been likened to a computer. The luo pan can indicate, to those who know how to interpret it, which illness someone in a certain location might be suffering from, or the fortunes of a person living in a certain room in a house.

This vast amount of information has been reduced to a shorthand form incorporated in a 'Magic Square'. In cultures worldwide, this was used as a talisman. Many formulae based on the magic square are used to discover whether a place is auspicious, in itself and for the people living there, and the simplest of these are introduced in this book. The diagram on the right shows how the energies repre-

sented by the Magic Square always move in a fixed pattern. These patterns are repeated over time and can indicate the fortunes of a person or building in a certain year.

the bagua

The information contained in the luo pan is condensed into the Magic Square, which forms the basis of the Bagua, or Pa Kua, a tool we can use to investigate our homes and offices. The Bagua below holds some of the images which describe the energies of the eight directions and the central position. The Bagua represents the journey of life, the Tao, and we can use it to create comfortable living, working and leisure spaces.

When applying Feng Shui principles to your house, garden or office you will need a tracing of the Bagua with the colours, compass points and directions all added on.

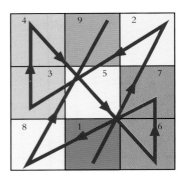

△ **The Magic Square: the 'magic' lies in the fact that every line adds up to 15. Magic squares exist all over the world. In ancient cultures, such symbols were a source of power to their initiates. In Hebrew culture, the pattern formed by the movement of energies is known as the seal of Saturn and is used in Western magic. In Islamic cultures, intricate patterns are based on complex magic squares.**

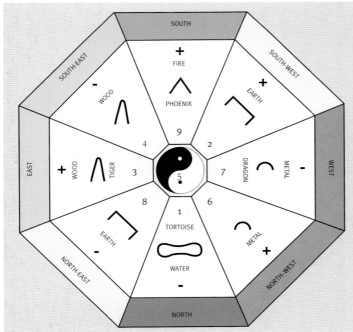

THE BAGUA, OR PA KUA

This shows the energies associated with the eight directions. The outer bar shows the colours and directions associated with the five elements. The symbols indicate the yin (-) or yang (+) quality of the element associated with each direction. Also shown are the shapes associated with each element. The four symbolic animals which represent the energy of each of the four cardinal directions – north, south, east, west – are indicated, and the numbers of the Magic Square are shown in their associated directions. We take on the characteristics of a number and the energies associated with it, which shape we are, where we feel comfortable, and our fortunes. The Chinese compass is always drawn facing south but this does not affect the actual magnetic north-south directions.

Finding your magic number

To complete the picture, it is necessary to discover how human beings fit into the scheme. Each person is allocated a 'magic' number that enables them to position themselves to their best advantage. Before finding our number from the tables opposite, we must check the date of the Chinese New Year from the 'Chinese Animals Table'. The previous year is used if our birthday falls before the start of the new year.

▽ Each of the magic numbers represents a particular type of energy suggested by the annual nature cycle. Find your number on the table and discover your energy below.

ENERGY OF NUMBERS

1. Water. Winter. Independent. Intuitive
2. Earth. Late Summer. Methodical.
3. Thunder. Spring. Progressive
4. Wind. Late Spring. Adaptable.
5. Earth. Central Force. Assertive.
6. Heaven. Late Autumn. Unyielding.
7. Lake. Autumn. Flexible. Nervous.
8. Mountain. Late Winter. Obstinate. Energetic.
9. Fire. Summer. Impulsive. Clever.

USING THE MAGIC NUMBERS

Some Feng Shui consultants use only the male, or yang, numbers in their calculations, some use both male and female, or yin, numbers. Others regard the yin (female) numbers as depicting the inner self, while the yang (male) numbers represent the image a person presents to the world. Modern men and women, with more interchangeable roles, tend to have both yin and yang characteristics, rather than the traditional gender stereotypes.

east-west directions

People tend to fare better in some directions than in others. They fall into two groups, the east group or the west group. Those who fall into the east group should live in a house facing an east group direction, those in the west group a west group direction. If this is not possible, your bed and/or your chair should face an appropriate direction.

▽ Once you have found your magic number, you can identify which group you are in, east or west, which directions suit you, and whether your house is compatible.

GROUP	NUMBERS	DIRECTIONS
East	1, 3, 4, 9	N, E, SE, S
West	2, 5, 6, 7, 8	SW, NW, W, NE, CENTRE

THE MAGIC NUMBERS

YEAR	M	F	YEAR	M	F	YEAR	M	F	YEAR	M	F
1920	8	7	1952	3	3	1984	7	8	2002	7	8
1921	7	8	1953	2	4	1985	6	9	2003	6	9
1922	6	9	1954	1	5	1986	5	1	2004	5	1
1923	5	1	1955	9	6	1987	4	2	2005	4	2
1924	4	2	1956	8	7	1988	3	3	2006	3	3
1925	3	3	1957	7	8	1989	2	4	2007	2	4
1926	2	4	1958	6	9	1990	1	5	2008	1	5
1927	1	5	1959	5	1	1991	9	6	2009	9	6
1928	9	6	1960	4	2	1992	8	7	2010	8	7
1929	8	7	1961	3	3	1993	7	8	2011	7	8
1930	7	8	1962	2	4	1994	6	9	2012	6	9
1931	6	9	1963	1	5	1995	5	1	2013	5	1
1932	5	1	1964	9	6	1996	4	2	2014	4	2
1933	4	2	1965	8	7	1997	3	3	2015	3	3
1934	3	3	1966	7	8	1998	2	4	2016	2	4
1935	2	4	1967	6	9	1999	1	5	2017	1	5
1936	1	5	1968	5	1	2000	9	6	2018	9	6
1937	9	6	1969	4	2	2001	8	7	2019	8	7
1938	8	7	1970	3	3						
1939	7	8	1971	2	4						
1940	6	9	1972	1	5						
1941	5	1	1973	9	6						
1942	4	2	1974	8	7						
1943	3	3	1975	7	8						
1944	2	4	1976	6	9						
1945	1	5	1977	5	1						
1946	9	6	1978	4	2						
1947	8	7	1979	3	3						
1948	7	8	1980	2	4						
1949	6	9	1981	1	5						
1950	5	1	1982	9	6						
1951	4	2	1983	8	7						

Key: M = male F = female

▽ A Feng Shui expert studies the luo pan.

Perception and the symbolic Bagua

Much of the skill in undertaking a Feng Shui survey of our immediate environment is in reading the signals there. If we are healthy and happy, this may prove to be a comparatively easy process. If we are not, our perception may be coloured by our emotional or physical state and we may not be able to see things clearly.

The Chinese phrase 'First, luck; second, destiny; third, Feng Shui; fourth, virtues; fifth, education' is worth repeating, as it shows that to some extent our fortunes and personalities are out of our hands. If we embrace Feng Shui, think and act positively, and make use of the knowledge the universe has to offer, then we can begin to take charge of the parts of our lives that we can control and make the best of them, without struggling against the things we can't change.

Part of the process of Feng Shui is to awaken our senses and sensibilities to our environment. Among other things, each of the Five Elements governs different senses, and our aim is to create a balanced environment in which all our senses are satisfied and none is allowed to predominate over the rest to create an imbalance.

We can heighten our perception of the world if we introduce ourselves to different experiences. Take an objective look at your weekly routine and decide on a new experience or activity which will add something different to your life.

a magical template

When Feng Shui began to take off in the West several years ago, the workings of the compass were known only to a handful of scholars. Those early days were distinguished by the creation of, and endless discussions on, the workings of the Bagua. It was used then, as it is now, by the Tibetan Black Hat practitioners, as a magical template that is aligned with a front door, the entrance to a room, the front of a desk or even a face.

This template is then used to supply information which can enable us to understand our energy and make corrections to create balance and harmony. Some Chinese practitioners have since

A HEALTHY LIFESTYLE AND A HEALTHY MIND

Stuck energy in our homes is often a reflection of our lifestyle and state of mind. A healthy daily regime will make us receptive to the powers of Feng Shui. Ideally, we should take time out each day to meditate – or just to escape from stress. Often a short walk, gardening or a few minutes sitting quietly will help us to relax. Chi Kung and Tai Chi are part of the same system. Their exercise programmes help to keep the energy channels in the body unblocked, while also releasing the mind.

Eating a healthy balanced diet of food-stuffs, produced without chemical interference, is another way of ensuring that harmful energies, or toxins, do not upset our bodily balance.

If we do become ill, acupuncture and acupressure and Chinese herbal medicine can balance the energies in our bodies and help to keep us fit.

◁ Meditation (left), hiking in the mountains (bottom left) or a daily session of Tai Chi (bottom right) will all benefit our mental energy and help to heighten perceptions.

the symbolic bagua

Throughout this chapter we will see how various images are connected to each of the eight points of the Magic Square or the Bagua, which is based on it. The symbolic Bagua uses the energies of each direction to relate to the journey of life. The journey begins at the entrance to our home – the mouth of chi – and moves in a predetermined way through the home until it reaches its conclusion. By focusing on an aspect of our lives which we want to stimulate or change, we can use the energies of the universe and make them work for us. Psychologically, focusing on an area enables us to create the circumstances to bring about change.

So far, a traditional compass approach has been used, but the diagram to the left allows us to use either approach. From now on readers should feel free to connect with the Bagua as they wish, and through it to the intangible forces which make this such a fascinating subject. Most people who have used Feng Shui have experienced changes in their circumstances. These often correspond to the actual energy around a relationship or situation rather than our desires. The results will ultimately serve our best interests, but the outcome is often unexpected.

sought to use the Bagua alongside the compass method. They place it over the plan of a home so that it is positioned with the Career area in the north, irrespective of where the front door lies.

Other traditional Chinese approaches concentrate on interpreting the energies indicated by the Five Elements and by the rings of the luo pan. Such is the 'magic' of Feng Shui that, in the right hands, all approaches appear to work.

Newcomers to Feng Shui may find it difficult to connect to a compass. Hopefully, they will use either method to experience for themselves the magic of the early days of discovery, and will be drawn deeper into this amazing philosophy, gaining an insight into its power.

△ Mountains afford protection to the rear and sides of this village, while a lake in front accumulates chi – the perfect situation – all that remains is to arrange the inside of the house to echo and maintain the supportive external environment.

▽ The Three Gates Bagua. This may be entered through 'Career' (back), 'Knowledge' (bottom left) or 'Helpful People' (bottom right). The compass Bagua with associated colours is shown inside to help you balance the elements of your home.

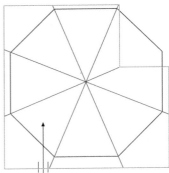

△ The Three Gates Bagua is flexible. If a home has an irregular shape, the corresponding area of the Bagua is also considered to be missing. In this house, the front entrance is in the 'Knowledge' area and the 'Relationships' part of the house is missing.

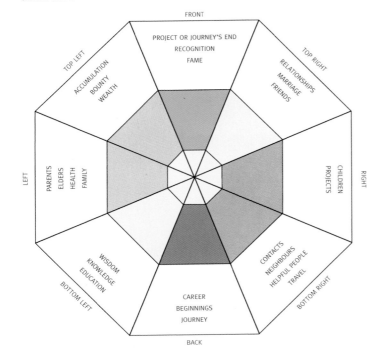

FRONT

PROJECT OR JOURNEY'S END
RECOGNITION
FAME

TOP LEFT

ACCUMULATION
BOUNTY
WEALTH

TOP RIGHT

RELATIONSHIPS
MARRIAGE
FRIENDS

LEFT

PARENTS
ELDERS
HEALTH
FAMILY

RIGHT

CHILDREN
PROJECTS

WISDOM
KNOWLEDGE
EDUCATION

BOTTOM LEFT

CAREER
BEGINNINGS
JOURNEY

CONTACTS
NEIGHBOURS
HELPFUL PEOPLE
TRAVEL

BOTTOM RIGHT

BACK

Feng Shui in the modern world

Modern lifestyles are far removed from those of our ancestors. For them, charting the progress of the moon and sun, and interpreting the different weather conditions and other activities occurring in the natural world in relation to the movement of the stars and planets, was vital.

▽ A village in Chad in which ancient skills and lifestyles remain unaffected by the technological development in the West.

△ Night-time in Mexico City. The 23 million inhabitants are denied a view of the stars because of neon lighting and pollution.

▷ The rice harvest in traditional regions of China has used many of the same processes for the past thousand years.

These peoples depended on the land to provide them with the means to survive. The modern city-dweller may never see food growing naturally and may not even be able to view the night sky because of pollution and neon lighting. However, we still depend on the natural world for our wellbeing. We can be at the mercy of hurricanes, or bask on sun-drenched beaches; mountains may erupt, or provide sustenance for livestock; human beings are able to pollute the air and contaminate the land, while at the same time create sanctuaries for wildlife species.

Ancient peoples regarded the heavens, the earth and themselves as part of one system. This holistic view of life has persisted in many cultures, where health and medicine, food and lifestyle are all interconnected.

In the West, scientific development has created different disciplines which have advanced in isolation from each other. Through recent changes in health and food production, we are now seeking to correct the imbalances caused by this approach. The Tao, or the Way, the philosophy which underlies Feng Shui, shows how it is possible to order our lives to exist in harmony with each other and the natural world. We can use Feng Shui to help us work towards achieving this.

The traditional concept of Gaia, the Greek earth goddess, was used by James Lovelock and Lynne Margulis in the 1970s to encourage us to perceive the world as a biosphere in which each constituent part has a role to play. In order to understand Feng Shui we need to expand this concept of ecosystems further to include human beings and the impact of

△ In 1948 science writer Fred Hoyle predicted: "Once a photograph of the Earth taken from the outside world is available ... a new idea as powerful as any other in history will be let loose." The environmental awareness movement began during the same period that human beings landed on the moon.

WORKING WITH THE NATURAL WORLD

A good example of working with the natural world is provided by an apparently admirable scheme to plant 300 oak forests in Britain. But in the natural world oak trees grow singly and not in rows in large groups, and recent research has indicated that where many oaks grow together there is a higher incidence of Lyme disease, a debilitating illness which attacks the nervous system. The reason for this is that mice and deer feed on acorns and also carry the ticks which transmit the disease. Thus, where there are many oaks, there is also a high incidence of Lyme disease. Mixed planting, which mirrors the natural world, would be preferable.

In order to save money, one forest was planted with Polish oak trees that came into bud two weeks later than the native trees. This meant there were no caterpillars feeding on the buds to provide food for newly-hatched fledglings. These mistakes might have been avoided if Tao principles had been applied.

▽ Native trees act as the Tortoise, Dragon, Tiger formation to protect these buildings.

the cosmos, and to expand our awareness so that we can predict the consequences of our actions.

As we investigate the ideas behind Feng Shui and consider practical ways of introducing them into our lives, we also need to shift our perception. Feng Shui in the modern world incorporates intuition. Maori warriors navigate hundreds of miles by the feel of a place and by observing signs. The Inuit language incorporates many words to describe the complexities of different types of snow. Similarly, we can heighten our awareness of our environment by adopting the principles of Feng Shui.

Until recently navigators used the stars to steer by, and in some parts of the world those who work with the land still use the stars to determine planting times for their crops. These people recognize patterns in the interrelationship between different parts of the natural world, noticing which plants are in flower or when birds return from migration and comparing them to the weather. Many customs are firmly based in natural wisdom.

The outside world

The primary consideration when beginning to
understand Feng Shui is to assess the world
around us, to take stock of the energies and
influences that surround our living spaces.

Choosing a location

Whether we own our own home or apartment or apartment or live in rented accommodation, we can use the principles which follow to create a living space in which we feel comfortable. If we are on the verge of moving, or are in the fortunate position of having acquired a piece of land to design and build our own home upon, there are some important considerations to make. You will probably already have a location in mind, but within the area there will be choices you can make which will affect your well-being in your new home.

When choosing a property we normally investigate the immediate environment. We use certain criteria to judge it according to our individual requirements – the appearance of neighbouring properties, proximity to schools, efficient transport for travel to work, green spaces, sports facilities and so on.

Some moves are dictated by new jobs in different areas, some when people give up their hectic urban lifestyles and relocate to rural areas. Many older people retire to the coast. Young people leaving home for the first time might be attracted by the hurly-burly of city living.

▽ Living on a remote farm will suit some people perfectly, but not others.

△ The modern city of Durban in South Africa is full of young energy.

▷ A seaside location is very attractive in summer but can be inhospitable in winter.

The decline of heavy industry in many countries has seen a rise in the regeneration of dockland and riverside areas with large warehouses being developed as spacious apartments for these new city dwellers. Whatever the reason for the move, few people remain where they were born, or retain the extended support networks which prevailed only a generation or two ago. Our choice of home as a nurturing space is therefore important. With a little foresight and a knowledge of Feng Shui principles, we can select prime positions for our homes.

think before you move

There are certain things to consider when selecting an area to which to move before we even consider choosing a house. Ideally we should know the area well. An idyllic bay in summer may be cold and windswept in winter, and a woodland glade at the end of an unmade track may be inaccessible after heavy winter snows. Although it's impossible to see the house in all seasons you can at least try to visualize how it will be.

Neighbours can prove to be a problem. They may resent a new house which spoils

ASSESSING A LOCATION

NATURAL PHENOMENA	IMMEDIATE ENVIRONMENT	POSITIVE ASPECTS	NEGATIVE ASPECTS
Wind direction	Proposed road developments	Local amenities	Factories
Sun direction	Proposed building developments	Trees	Petrol stations
Rainfall	Land use plans	Street lighting	All-night cafés
Flood areas	Previous land use	Good street maintenance	Pubs and discos
Geological faults	Tree preservation orders	Good schools	Police stations
Soil type	Local architecture	Community spirit	Fire stations
Height above sea level	Neighbours, predecessors	Local shops	Airports
		Clubs and classes	Cemeteries and crematoriums
		Playgroups and nurseries	Motorways and highways
			Electricity sub-stations and pylons

◁ **This sheltered village is a delightful location to return home to after a day in the bustling city.**

▷ **High-rise flats in Hong Kong – financially the sky is the limit and young people are attracted there, but few of them stay to put down roots.**

a view, or may erect screens that maintain their privacy but deprive you of light. It is important to determine the ownership of boundaries. Previous owners are another consideration. Perhaps earlier occupants have tipped chemicals just where you want to grow strawberries, or you may learn that all the previous owners got divorced or mysteriously contracted a similar illness while living in the house. Feng Shui may be able to offer an explanation for any of these negative aspects.

▽ **Pavement cafés are part of metropolitan life in many cities around the world.**

The modern world has problems that did not exist in the ancient world and these must be taken into consideration when we apply Feng Shui today. It is no use selecting a site with the classic Tortoise, Dragon, Tiger formation if the Tortoise is an electricity pylon, which may be linked to childhood leukemia, the Dragon is a chemical factory leaking its waste into the river, and the Tiger is a poorly managed petrol station. In modern times we have to apply the formulae to contemporary life and the ancient sages were wise enough to allow us the leeway to do this by building in formulae for change.

Our environment makes a psychological impact on us: whatever we see, hear or smell will make an impression and have an affect. We also have to look at ourselves and what type of people we are in order to understand our needs in terms of living spaces. There is no point moving to a remote country area if you enjoy street life and love shopping because you will never feel comfortable. Someone whose astro-

logical sign is the Rabbit who retires to the seaside will, at best, be tired and drained and, at worst, become ill. With a new insight into our own natures and increased awareness of the effect our environment has on us, we can use Feng Shui principles to find harmonious spaces.

When you are ready to sell your home and move on, Feng Shui can help to speed up this often lengthy and stressful process. The tip below combines the energy of the Five Elements to give a powerful boost to the progress of the sale.

FENG SHUI TIP FOR SPEEDING UP A HOUSE SALE

If you are having problems, take a red envelope and place in it:

A piece of metal from the kitchen
Some earth from the garden
Some wood from a skirting board

Seal the envelope and throw it into a fast-moving river.

Unseen energies

Before finally deciding on a location, it is wise to check if there are any underground water sources, geological faults or major other earth disturbances. These all create unseen energies which could affect your wellbeing.

geopathic stress

The word 'geopathic' comes from the Greek *geo*, meaning 'Earth', and *pathos*, meaning 'disease'. It covers naturally occurring phenomena that cause problems for us and our homes. The Earth and living organisms vibrate at complementary frequencies, which are negatively affected by geopathic faults. Dowsers are able to detect these problems, which a property surveyor may miss.

underground streams

Just as water erodes rocks on the coastline, underground streams have had the same effect underground, beneath the Earth's surface. This process alters the electromagnetic frequency of the Earth so that it is out of our frequency range. Fast-moving or polluted underground water produces the same effect.

Underground streams produce energy spirals, the effects of which are felt inside

△ If trees lean for no obvious reason, they may be situated on a geopathic stress line.

any buildings directly overhead. Where a clockwise spiral meets an anti-clockwise spiral, ill health may be experienced by people situated above them. Where spirals meet other forces, such as leys, the problems are accentuated.

leys

Leys, or ley lines, are a network of energy lines running across the land. Some think that our distant ancestors may have built their churches and standing stones on these lines, performing a kind of 'acupuncture of the Earth' as they tapped into its energy. It is believed the leys also provided routes for travellers.

△ Underground water creates magical places, but it is not desirable near a house as it can undermine the foundations.

◁ Stone circles are extremely powerful places. They harness the Earth's energies and respond to those of the Cosmos.

△ The Chinese believe that quarrying damages the Dragon – the spirit of a place.

△ Nearby railway lines can cause land disturbance and create instability.

earth is covered by a series of force lines which are activated by the interaction of the Earth's magnetic field and the gravitational pull of the sun and moon. It is thought that these lines shift as a result of their interaction with the movement of charged particles trapped in the atmosphere as the sun blasts the Earth with radiation. The point where these lines cross may adversely affect the human body.

human activity

It is also possible for human beings to disturb the Earth's energies. Quarries, tunnels, mines, polluted water and railways have all been found to contribute negative effects. Before erecting or buying a house, check for any mining or tunnelling that may have taken place in the area.

radon

We are exposed to radiation throughout our lives, mainly from the sun. Exposure over long periods to higher than normal levels may make us ill. Leukemia and birth defects have been linked to exposure to radon, which occurs naturally in uranium in the Earth. As the uranium breaks down, it forms radioactive ions which attach themselves to air particles that become trapped inside houses. Some regions in the world have recorded dreadfully high

levels of radioactivity, in excess of those recorded after the Chernobyl disaster. Pockets of high incidence have been found in Sweden and the US as well as in Derbyshire and Cornwall in Great Britain. Local authorities are aware of the problem and assistance is available to eradicate it from buildings.

earth grids

Two German doctors, Hartmann and Curry, have advanced the theory that the

STRESS INDICATORS
Leaning trees
Cankers on tree trunks
Elder trees
Illness shortly after moving
Uneasy atmosphere
Tunnelling activity
Cold, damp rooms

CLEARING THE ENERGIES

If there is no apparent reason for feeling unwell for a long period of time, then geopathic stress is a possible cause. Experienced dowsers are able to detect Earth energies and, in some instances, divert negative energies, albeit often only on a temporary basis. Many people can detect water with rods or pendulums, but experience is needed to deal with Earth energies and protection is needed to minimize ill effects. It is best, if possible, to move away from such energies, and it may be a question of simply moving a bed 60cm–1m (2–3ft). The effect of clearing energies can be dramatic, and the work should be done slowly.

△ Dowsing rods are part of a Feng Shui consultant's tools. Metal coat hangers also work for dowsing.

△ Dowsing rods cross when they detect underground water. They are used to locate landmines and to find pipes.

The urban environment

Urban environments are very diverse. Living in an apartment above a shop in a city centre throbbing with night-life is quite different to the tranquillity of a house in a leafy suburb or the vast buildings in a re-developed docklands area.

city and town centres

The centres of large cities, where clubs and restaurants are open through the night, are full of yang energy and lifestyles will reflect this. City centres attract younger people with no roots, who can move about freely. Homes in the inner cities tend to be apartments, and inside we should aim for some yin energy – muted colours, natural flooring and a large plant or two to create a quiet haven.

Smaller town centres, particularly where there are shopping precincts, tend to close down at night and the atmosphere is yin and rather spooky. If you live here, make sure you have plenty of lights on the perimeter of your property and bright colours inside to prevent feeling closed in.

parks and spaces

These green oases are somehow apart from the bustling city centre. Homes are usually expensive and sought after, since they

△ An enticing night scene in Villefranche, Côte d'Azur, France. Summer in the city can be invigorating and exciting.

provide tranquil spaces and fresh air while still connected to the life of the city. People residing here will have more stable lifestyles as they have the yin-yang balance. Their

▽ Suburban living at its best in Sag Harbor, New York; well kept, clean, wide streets, mature trees and no parked cars.

homes should reflect this with a mixture of stimulating shapes, colours and materials, plus restful spaces.

urban renewal

The energy of reclaimed industrial areas in inner cities is interesting. The yang energy of the large converted warehouses contrasts with the daytime yin energy when the occupants, usually business executives, are at work in large, highly charged, corporations. At weekends this changes as café life and leisure activities take over. Old dockland areas for example, are usually on main traffic routes, so on weekdays there is often stuck energy. Large trees should be planted to help cope with the pollution, and also to bring yin energy into the area. Rooms in converted industrial buildings tend to be huge and it is difficult to ground the energy. Cosy yin spaces need to be created within to offer support.

suburbs

The energy in the suburbs is mainly yin, with little nightlife. People tend to hide and become insular in suburbs, and often a yang balance is required. Imaginative use of colour is often all that is required to raise the energy of suburban homes.

roads

It is roads that conduct chi through an environment, and transport patterns can affect the nature of a neighbourhood. Living close to urban highways is an obvious health risk, but so too is living on narrow suburban 'rat runs'. Chi travels fast on straight urban roads and thus residents will not relax easily. In the US, where suburban roads are built on a grid system, large gardens compensate and help to maintain a balance. Check the transport patterns before purchasing a new home and visit at different times of the day. Well-designed cul-de-sacs have excellent chi, but those where car movement has not been well planned create stuck energy and danger for children playing there.

The visual impact of a flyover in a residential area can be devastating. The fast-moving traffic conducts chi away from the area and will greatly affect the fortunes of those living at eye level or underneath the flyover.

railways

The effect of a railway is similar to a motorway in that trains carry chi away from an area, particularly if they are at the end of the garden. Trains also create slight unease in the subconscious expectation of their arrival. Underground trains are destabilizing if they pass immediately below houses. If systems are old and poorly maintained the Chinese saying 'Angry Dragons waiting to erupt' applies.

▽ Parks and green areas are a very important part of city life. This park, overlooking the city, is located in Adelaide, Australia.

Roads conduct chi. Steadily moving traffic on curving roads near our homes is beneficial. Fast traffic and roads pointing at us are not.

THE CURVING ROAD The road gently curves and appears to 'hug' this house. This is a very auspicious Feng Shui position for a dwelling.

THE BENDING ROAD House B is in an inauspicious position. Traffic from both directions may break suddenly at the bend and could hit the house. At night, car beams will illuminate the rooms. There will always be a negative air of expectancy here. Convex mirrors on the outer bend would deflect and deplete the energy of the auspicious house A. Instead, a better solution would be to have traffic-calming measures in place.

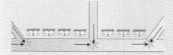

THE FAST ROAD This creates a visual and psychological barrier. Waist-high shrubs and plants on the boundary of the garden and plants on the windowsill inside the houses will slow down the chi. Those living at the junction of such roads are likely to be jumpy. Screeching brakes and even crashes are common at such points.

THE DEAD-END ROAD The house facing the entrance is at risk since the chi seems to hurtle towards it, as at a T-junction. Deflection is needed, and a hedge would help, or a porch with the door at the side. Mirrors are often used to return the harmful influence back on itself. If the path to the door faces the road, it would be better to move and curve it. The effect is the same where a bridge points at a house. Residents will feel exhausted in such a location.

THE KNIFE The road appears to cut into the apartments like a knife. The constant flow past the window will leave residents tetchy. A mirror outside will symbolically deflect the problem. Coloured glass in the windows facing the road would block the unattractive view whilst allowing light in.

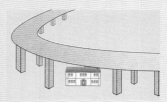

THE FLYOVER Residents here will feel overwhelmed. Lights on the corners of the house will symbolically lift the flyover, but this is not a good house to live in. Residents will feel oppressed and have no energy.

Rural locations

The energies found in the countryside are quite different to those of urban areas, but just as powerful. By carefully positioning our homes within the natural features of the landscape we can draw on their protection to nourish us.

country living

A sheltered position contained by trees or hills is ideal, especially in remote areas where protection from the elements is very important in winter. The classical arrangement of the four animals is the perfect site but if there are no woods or mountains where you wish to live, large trees and buildings can also act as protectors. Road access is vital in rural areas but, as in towns, it is preferable not to live close to major roads or through routes.

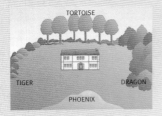

BENEFICIAL LOCATIONS

A tree belt behind acts as the Tortoise, and hedges represent the Dragon and Tiger. The Dragon is higher to keep the unpredictable Tiger in its place. A small hill in the foreground acts as the Phoenix.

A stream feeding a healthy pond is auspicious. Shrubs hide the water's exit from the property.

△ This lovely Mediterranean-style house is positioned in a supportive rural setting.

Even if you live out in the wild, it is important to have a social centre within reach. Out-of-town superstores have knocked the heart out of many country towns and villages, and have made an impact on the chi of these places, but those that continue to thrive usually have an excellent yin-yang balance. They provide sport and leisure facilities for young people and a good community life, which are the yang activities in the yin setting of the countryside.

In the fields and woods, chi is good and there are many opportunities to restore the balance in our busy modern lives. Intensive farming methods can be harmful, however, so look out for telltale signs such as few songbirds or no hedges before purchasing a property.

Positive Aspects	Possible Negative Aspects
Natural smells	Agrochemicals
Leisurely pace of life	Isolation
Walks	Flooding
Trees	Travel distances & access
Wildlife	Limited public transport
Fresh food	Landfill
Air quality	Military training areas
Relaxed lifestyle	Bad weather
Outdoor life	Effluent pipes
Happy people	Amenities closed in winter

rivers and lakes

Energy is usually very good near water, especially near slow-flowing rivers that meander through the countryside. Proportion is important, so if the water is balanced by an undulating landscape and plenty of green vegetation it will feel comfortable. A stream feeding into a healthy pond is ideal as it will accumulate chi and also attract wildlife to visit your garden. The energy near lakes is different, reflecting the breathless movement of the wind across the water and the sudden appearance and disappearance of water sports activities at weekends.

If you decide to live in a flood plain you will need to make enquiries about the likelihood of floods in the area, especially following those of recent years.

coastal areas

Being beside the sea gives most of us a sense of wellbeing. This is partly due to the beneficial effects of negative ions in the air, which create an invigorating atmosphere. Waves can, however, adversely affect some people, depending on their animal sign – Rabbits, for example, tend to feel uneasy near the sea.

△ A house situated next to a slow-moving river will benefit from good chi flow.

In the summer, the teeming beaches full of holiday-makers are yang. In winter the towering seas are also yang, but the deserted seaside towns and isolated bays are yin. It is a good idea to visit the area in both seasons as they are so different. The elements of wind and water are never so much in evidence as when the storms lash the sea against the rocks. A peninsula is difficult to live on because the chi there dissipates in the winter when it is hammered by the elements.

▷ A tranquil bay in summer looks very different in winter.

ROADS TO HOME

Living in rural areas may mean that you have to commute to work and spend quite some time in the car. The daily journey, and the roads on which you travel, will have a big impact on your life, so check both when considering your new home.

Travelling to work in an easterly direction in the morning and returning in a westerly direction with the sun glaring on the windscreen could affect our moods considerably. This can be particularly dangerous on narrow roads. Wonderful views can make us feel euphoric and energized, although care must be taken not to lose concentration when driving. Scenic roads can be tricky in adverse weather conditions.

Where trees overhang a road they can afford a welcome relief from the glaring sun. However, long stretches may cause nausea and headaches brought on by the dappled light.

Narrow country lanes with high banks or hedges funnel chi and afford no relief for the driver. Where they twist and turn, the driver's vision is extremely limited. Regular use will become a strain.

House styles

The position of our homes within their environment and how they fit in with the surrounding buildings can affect how comfortable we are living there. At a simple level, if our home is a big detached house in a road of smaller terraced houses, then we will be set apart from the rest of the community. Similarly, if the house is very different from its neighbours it may not fit into its environment. Strict planning laws in some areas have preserved the 'spirit' or

▽ This painted terraced house is not in sympathy with its neighbours.

△ A balance of Metal, suggested by the circular lawn, and Water in the curved path.

chi of towns and villages, and such places tend to have a sense of community. Where building has been unrestricted and tall blocks spring up between two-storey houses with no regard for the character of the environment, then the area's chi dissipates and its sense of community is lost.

When we make alterations to our houses or decorate them, we should be mindful of the impact on the neighbourhood. If ours is the only stucco house in a row of brick houses, we isolate ourselves and change the chi of the area. If all the houses in the neighbourhood are of a certain era and we decide to change the style of the windows or substantially alter the architectural detail, we again damage the

BALANCING THE ELEMENTS

Element	Helped by	Harmed by	Weakened by	Weakens
Wood	Water	Metal	Fire	Earth
Fire	Wood	Water	Earth	Metal
Earth	Fire	Wood	Metal	Water
Metal	Earth	Fire	Water	Wood
Water	Metal	Earth	Wood	Fire

△ The intrusive tower blocks have completely changed the nature of this area.

energy of the environment. Doors, chimney stacks and porches all add to the character and overall proportion not only of our house, but of the neighbourhood.

house shapes

The best-shaped house from a Feng Shui point of view is square. The square is a well proportioned space, and is the symbolic shape for Earth, which gathers, supports and nourishes. Rectangular buildings are also well regarded. An L-shaped building is considered inauspicious since it is said to resemble a meat cleaver and the worst position to have a room is in the 'blade'. If a teenager has a room in this position, they may feel isolated and may get up to all sorts of things undetected. An older relative with such a room may feel unwanted. Where houses are not a uni-

FIVE ELEMENT CURES FOR CORRECTING IMBALANCES

Wood: Posts, pillars, tower-shaped plant supports, green walls, trees
Fire: Pyramid-shaped finials, wigwam-shaped plant supports, garden buildings with Fire-shaped roofs, red walls, lights
Earth: Straight hedges, rectangular garden buildings, flat-topped trellis, terracotta troughs, or terracotta walls
Metal: Round finials, round weather vanes, metal balls, white walls
Water: Wavy hedges, water features, black or blue walls

BUILDINGS AND THE FIVE ELEMENTS

Wood: Tall thin apartment blocks and offices are often Wood-shaped.

Earth: Earth-shaped buildings are long and low such as bungalows.

Fire: Fire buildings have pyramid-shaped or pointed roofs.

Fire: Wood-shaped windows and Earth-shaped lines give balance.

Metal: Metal buildings are domed, such as these African huts, and some religious buildings in the West.

Water: Water buildings are those which have had sections randomly added to them over the years.

form shape, we need to make them more regular, in reality or symbolically, as we will investigate later.

orientation

The direction in which a building faces will also affect its chi. North-facing buildings with the main windows at the front will feel cheerless since they will not receive any sun. The energy can become stagnant and it is important to warm the house with colour. Houses that have the main windows facing south and south-west will receive strong yang energy and will need cool colours to compensate. Houses facing east receive early morning sun and vibrant energy. In the west, the energy is falling. Directions determine room placement within the house.

Entrances, paths and front doors

The main entrance to our home is very important. It represents the image we present to the world and can also indicate the view we have of ourselves. When we return to our home, we need to be drawn into our own nurturing space through a pleasant environment, however small. If we live in an apartment, we need to distinguish our own special part of the block and make it unique in some way, by using a colourful doormat, for example, or introducing plants.

entrances

Front gardens can fill up with an accumulation of stagnant energy unless we are careful. In house conversions where the grounds are not managed, the situation can be difficult since no-one is in overall charge of the garden. As a result, packaging, old furniture, chunks of wood and other assorted rubbish can pile up. Often, dustbins are sited in the front garden and can seriously affect how we feel when we return home. Bins should be placed away

△ Tree guardians mark the entrance to this attractive house. The effect that is created is very welcoming.

from the front entrance, preferably behind a hedge or fencing. If one resident clears up, others may follow suit.

paths

These should gently meander through the garden to help us unwind at the end of a long day, or welcome us back from a trip. Straight paths from the street to the front door carry chi too quickly and we do not have time to change gear. Ideally there should be an open space in front of the entrance where chi can gather, but often these are filled with parked cars and there is no distinction between home and work.

▽ A meandering path enables us to shed the cares of the day before arriving home.

ENTRANCES

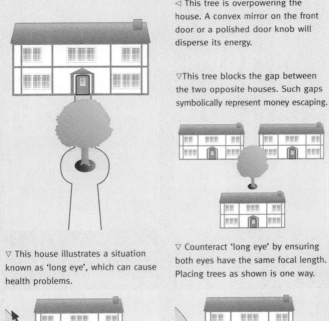

◁ This tree is overpowering the house. A convex mirror on the front door or a polished door knob will disperse its energy.

▽This tree blocks the gap between the two opposite houses. Such gaps symbolically represent money escaping.

▽ This house illustrates a situation known as 'long eye', which can cause health problems.

▽ Counteract 'long eye' by ensuring both eyes have the same focal length. Placing trees as shown is one way.

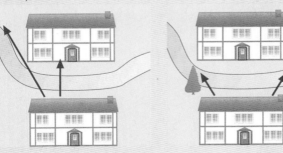

PATHS

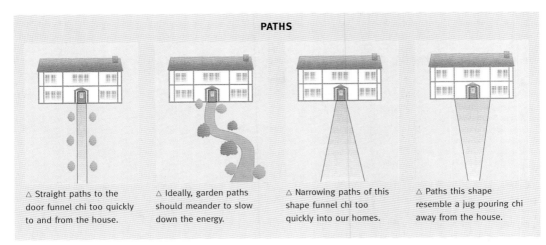

△ Straight paths to the door funnel chi too quickly to and from the house.

△ Ideally, garden paths should meander to slow down the energy.

△ Narrowing paths of this shape funnel chi too quickly into our homes.

△ Paths this shape resemble a jug pouring chi away from the house.

▽ A balance of the Five Elements, but taller plants would improve the proportion.

Squeezing past a car to enter the house is claustrophobic, as are very small enclosed porches, creating restriction which may be mirrored in our approach to life.

front doors

These should be well-maintained and clean. A tub of plants on either side is welcoming but they should not restrict the space or act as an obstruction. House numbers should be visible by day and night and doorbells should be in working order to maintain harmonious relationships with

◁ Plants either side of the poles would improve these well-maintained apartments.

▽ A plant pot on the left would help to balance this front entrance.

callers. The chi of an area can be severely depleted if visitors whistle, shout or use their car horns. The colour the door is painted should reflect the compass direction they face and be balanced according to the Five Elements.

departing

What we see when we leave our homes can also colour our day. Large objects like telegraph poles and trees directly in line with the front door send 'poison arrows' of chi at the house, as do the corners of other buildings. If tall hedges or fences restrict our vision from the house we may become insular or feel depressed.

▽ The Metal-shaped pot plants on either side of this door are full of energy.

Inside the home

Even if the external environment of your home is less than perfect, you can still use Feng Shui to enhance specific areas of your home and help to improve certain aspects of your life that you are not satisfied with.

inside the home

Beneficial positions

Having selected a protected site in which
to live, it is desirable that the house is orientated in what is considered in Feng Shui
to be an auspicious direction, which will
support its occupants. Those people who
fall into the east category should face their
houses toward the east directions; west
group people should face the west directions. It is very likely that there will be a
mixture of east and west group people
within a family or others sharing a house.
The people who are compatible with the
house will feel most comfortable in it.
Others should ensure that principle rooms
fall into their favoured directions or at least
that their beds, desks and chairs are
positioned correctly.

positioning yourself

Once you know your 'magic' numbers, it
is possible to design the interior of your
house so that you position yourself in
directions which are beneficial to you.
Beds should be orientated so that the top
of your head when lying down faces one
of the four beneficial locations. In the same
way chairs that you sit in should also face
one of your beneficial locations.

▷ **We need to relax at the end of the day. A
room with windows facing west is good, or a
position favoured by our 'magic' number.**

▽ **We aim to locate our rooms in good
directions and decorate to suit the elements.**

△ The compass direction your house faces is
dependent on where the main entrance is, and
is the starting point for positioning yourself
inside the house.

FIND YOUR BEST AND
WORST DIRECTIONS

1. Check your magic number on
'The Magic Numbers' table.
2. Check the 'Best and Worst
Directions' table to determine prime
places for you to sit, sleep and work.

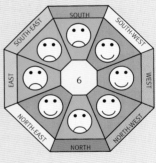

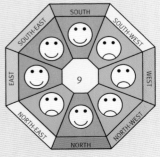

BEST AND WORST DIRECTIONS

Numbers on the faces indicate:

1. Abundance and happiness, if all other aspects are in order. This is where to site the main door and as many of the principal rooms as possible, and the top of the bed.

2. Health. The place for the bedroom, and the top of the bed during illness.

3. Family harmony. This is the best position for the family rooms.

4. The self. This position aids perception and thought processes, the place for a study or a desk.

5. Mishaps. In this position, things will not go according to plan.

6. Arguments at home and work. Not the place for family rooms.

7. Legal and health problems. Do not site principal rooms here.

8. Disaster. Avoid this direction. Place storerooms and toilets here.

Drawing the plan

It is now possible to begin to apply the principles we have learned. In order to position ourselves to our best advantage, we need to determine the compass readings for our homes.

YOU WILL NEED

A compass with the eight directions clearly marked
A protractor – a circular one is best
A scale plan of your home. If you own your home you will already have one. If not, it will be necessary to draw one, in which case you will also need a tape measure and graph paper
A ruler
A lead pencil and five coloured pencils – green, red, yellow, grey, dark blue
A tracing of the Bagua

to draw a plan

Using graph paper, take measurements for each floor, marking external and internal walls, alcoves, staircases, doors, windows and permanent fixtures such as baths, toilets, kitchen units and fireplaces.

take a compass reading

1 Take off any watches, jewellery and metal objects and stand clear of cars and metal fixtures.
2 Stand with your back parallel to the front door and note the exact compass reading in degrees.

3 Note the direction, eg 125° SE, on to your plan as shown in the diagram. You are now ready to transfer the compass readings on to your Bagua drawing.

▷ Use this table to double check that your heading in degrees corresponds with the direction your front door faces, since it is possible to misread the protractor.

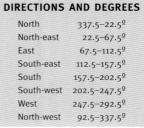

DIRECTIONS AND DEGREES	
North	337.5–22.5º
North-east	22.5–67.5º
East	67.5–112.5º
South-east	112.5–157.5º
South	157.5–202.5º
South-west	202.5–247.5º
West	247.5–292.5º
North-west	92.5–337.5º

▽ Draw a scale plan of your home and mark on it the positions of windows, doors, alcoves and all internal fixtures and fittings as well as bed and desk positions. A compass, protractor, ruler, coloured pencils and a tracing of the Bagua diagram will allow you to survey your home.

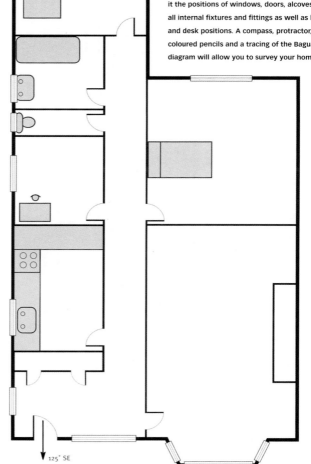

125° SE

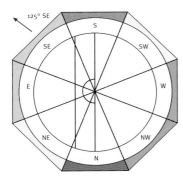

125° SE

△ When you have worked out the compass reading for your front door, transfer it to the Bagua, as shown.

▷ The next step is to find the centre of your home, and then transfer the shape of the Bagua to the plan.

transfer the compass reading to the bagua

1 Place the protractor on the Bagua diagram so that 0° is at the bottom, at north, and mark the eight directions.

2 Having found the compass reading for your home, ie the direction faced by your front door, check it matches the direction; if not you may be reading the wrong ring. Mark the position of your front door.

3 Double-check the direction by looking at the 'Directions and Degrees' table. When you have done this you will end up with a Bagua diagram such as the one above, with the front door position marked. You are now almost ready to place this template on to your home plan.

EAST-WEST DIRECTIONS

Just as people fit into east or west categories, so too do houses. Determine whether your house belongs to the east or west group of directions by checking the direction in which the front door faces.

EASTERN DIRECTIONS: north, south, east, south-east

WESTERN DIRECTIONS: north-east, south-west, north-west, west.

transfer the directions to the plan

1 Find the centre of the plan. Match the main walls across the length of the plan and crease the paper lengthways.

2 Match the main walls across the width and crease the paper widthways. Where the folds cross is the centre of your home. If your home is not a square or rectangle, treat a protrusion of less than 50 per cent

of the width as an extension to the direction. If the protrusion is more than 50 per cent of the width, treat the remainder as a missing part of the direction.

3 Place the centre of the Bagua on the centre point of the plan and line up the front door position.

4 Mark the eight directions on the plan and draw in the sectors.

5 Transfer the colour markings.

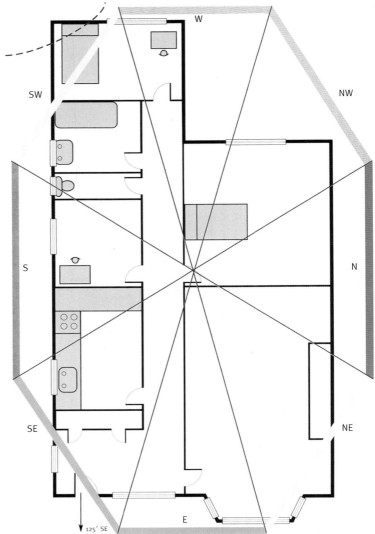

125° SE

Edges, corners and slanting walls

Certain structural details are problematic in Feng Shui. Often the result of conversions, they affect chi and can cause discomfort for the occupants of the house.

edges

Wherever the chi flow in a room is disrupted, difficulties occur. Anyone who has ever walked down a windy street flanked by high buildings will know that the gusts are always worse at the corners of buildings where the wind whips up into a spiral. Where major structural work has been undertaken and walls have been knocked down, a room is often left with supporting pillars. These are not conducive to the free flow of chi because they are usually square and have four corners which point, knife-like, into the room, and they can also interfere with vision.

If there are edges we should aim to soften them. Plants are one solution and fabrics are another. Wherever possible, make columns rounded as this creates an entirely different feel.

Having the edges of furniture pointing at us when we are relaxing on a chair or sofa, can make us feel uncomfortable, as can the edges of bookshelves and fireplaces. Keeping books in cupboards is a solution, but the pleasure of plucking a book from a shelf would be lost and the cupboards would become harbingers of tired energy. Instead, we can use plants to soften shelf edges near where we sit.

△ Round pillars are less obtrusive than square ones. The plant softens the effect.

△ A plant will enliven an awkward corner and move the chi on.

◁ Plants can be used to soften shelf edges near to where we sit.

corners

The corners of rooms are often dark, so it is a good idea to place something colourful there, like a vase of silk flowers for example. Alternatively, you can use something that moves such as a lava lamp or a water feature. Putting plants in dark corners where stagnant chi accumulates will help the chi to move on. Spiky plants are particularly good for moving on chi, provided they are away from chairs where they could direct 'poison arrows' towards the occupants. Uplighters or round tables with lamps on them are other options for dark corners.

Alcoves on either side of a fireplace are often filled with shelves, which help to prevent stagnant areas provided they are not crammed full and some gaps are left.

△ Here, in one place, we have several methods of introducing movement into a dark corner – an octagonal table, a plant, a corner cupboard and a little shelf.

▽ This slanting wall will not adversely affect anyone sleeping in this room as there is plenty of headroom.

THE FLOW OF CHI IN A LIVING ROOM

1. The chairs need to be repositioned as the fireplace corners shoot 'poison arrows' at those sitting in them.

2. The edges of these built-in shelves will affect anyone sitting here unless the edges are softened with plants.

3. A round table with a lamp will move the chi on in this dark corner.

4. The corner of this pillar will send a 'poison arrow' at the occupant of the chair; the chair can be moved or the edge of the pillar softened.

5. Anybody who chooses to sit in this seat will be unaffected by the pillar as it is a safe distance away.

6. Uplighters in these corners of the room will lift the energy.

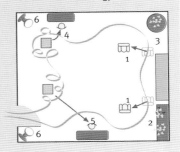

slanting walls

These are becoming increasingly common as expanding families in small houses convert attic space into rooms. Attic rooms with sloping ceilings are often turned into children's bedrooms or home offices. Sleeping or working under a slope depresses personal chi and these areas do nothing to aid the regenerative process of sleep nor creative processes during the day. Sloping ceilings also create a visual imbalance in a room. Mirrors and lights may help to create the illusion of lifting the slope and paint can achieve the same effect. Such rooms are better used as hobby or play rooms or for any short term activity.

If possible, it is preferable to have a smaller room of a conventional shape created instead of a room with sloping walls, even it means sacrificing some of the floor space. A good solution is to fill the sloping walls in with built-in cupboards for storage. Where roof windows are installed to let light into attic conversions, make sure it is possible to see more out of them than just a patch of sky.

▽ Placing storage cupboards under the eaves gives an attic room a more regular shape.

Beams

Not recommended in Feng Shui, beams can be oppressive when positioned over a bed, stove or desk and suppress the chi of the people living beneath them. Proportion, however, is everything. In a barn conversion or a self-build eco-house, the ceilings are high and often vaulted so the beams do not seem to press down on the occupants. The reverse problem occurs when people and small-scale furniture rattle around in vast spaces and are unable to gather chi around them. However, beams in normally proportioned houses do tend to upset the flow of chi in a room, especially if we position ourselves in unsuitable places under them. Simply by moving the

▽ The oppressive effect of these beams is reduced by painting them a light colour.

dining table, desk or bed, we can often overcome any difficulties.

Many people dream of owning a country cottage, complete with roses round the door, log fires and beams. Traditionally it has been the custom to paint beams black so that they stand out, but when these cottages were built it is highly unlikely that this was their original colour. In the same way that pollution and time turn pale sandstone buildings in cities to a tobacco brown, so cooking and fires down the ages have transformed pale oak beams into charcoal-coloured wood. Interior fashions change, however, and it is now more common for beams to be painted the same colour as the ceiling, a welcome trend which makes all the difference to low-ceilinged rooms.

△ These beams are unobtrusive because the roof is so high. Avoid sitting under the low crossbeam running across the room.

Another way of reducing the effect of beams is to use uplighters underneath them, which give the illusion of 'lifting' the beam. Small, light-coloured hanging objects will lighten a beam. Do not hang large, dark or heavy objects below a beam, or anything that collects dust. False ceilings can be attached to beams, either the conventional type or translucent ones with light behind. In larger spaces, such as

▽ Sloping walls and a beam across the bed make this an inauspicious bedroom. The insecurity of the window behind the bed adds to the effect.

△ Exposed beams that are painted the same colour as the ceiling give a lighter airy feel than if they are left in natural dark wood.

◁ This modern living room is made inauspicious by the sloping walls and the dark beam running down the centre of the room.

restaurants, beams have been successfully mirrored, but this would not look good in most homes. Muslin or other fabrics will hide them, but these will harbour dust and create stagnant chi unless washed regularly. Traditionally, bamboo flutes tied with red ribbon were hung from the beam to create an auspicious octagon shape.

Beams over a bed are believed to cause illnesses to occupants at the points where they cross. A beam that runs along the length of the bed can cause a rift between the couple that shares it. When beams are situated over the stove or dining room table, they are thought to hamper the fortunes of the family.

If beams are over a desk, they may hinder the creative flow of the person who works there, and may even be a cause of, or contributory factor to, depression. It is certainly better not to sleep under a beam, and sitting in a chair under a beam or under a gallery, or any length of time, is not a comfortable experience.

Doors and windows

The doors of our home represent freedom and our access to the outside world; but they are also a barrier, acting as a means of protection, supplying support and comfort. Windows act as our eyes on the world. Both play an important role in Feng Shui and if our access or vision through them should not be impeded in any way.

doors

Open doors allow us access to a room or to the outside world. Closed doors shut off a room or our entire home. If either of these functions is impeded, then the chi flow around the house will suffer. Doors

▷ The uplifting view from this window has not been restricted by curtains or blinds.

CURES FOR PROBLEM DOORS

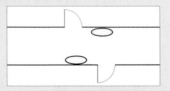

△ If doors are located opposite each other, place an obstruction such as a table to slow down the chi.

△ Where doors are out of alignment, create a balance by positioning mirrors or pictures on each side.

△ Where there are three or more doors in a row, break up the perspective with low-hanging lights or curved tables to slow down the chi.

△ Where an opened door restricts the view into a room, position a mirror to correct this. Doors were traditionally hung in this way to prevent draughts. This practice may also have arisen because of the desire to preserve modesty in Victorian times.

which squeak, stick, have broken latches, or handles too close to the edge so we scrape our knuckles whenever we open them, should all be repaired or altered. Keep a wedge close to doors that might slam irritatingly in the breeze. Ideally, a door should not open to a restricted view

▽ Stained glass panels in doors permit light and lift the energy in dark spaces.

of the whole room on entering, but doors in old houses used to be hung in this way to prevent through draughts or, some speculate, to preserve modesty during the decorous Victorian era.

windows

Sash windows which only open halfway restrict the amount of chi that can enter a room. Some double-glazed units only open halfway, with the same result. Ideally, all windows should open fully, and outwards. Beware of windows which have fixed double-glazed panels with only a small opening section at the top. These can cause fatal accidents if fire breaks out; they are usually fitted with safety glass, so it is virtually impossible to smash them. If

△ Adding an attractive stained-glass hanging can offer some privacy while creating a lively energy in the room.

▽ This stencilled decoration allows privacy in a bathroom, while at the same time letting in as much daylight as possible.

△ **Tied-back curtains are ideal here as they do not restrict the pleasant view.**

these have been fitted in your home, it is advisable to remove them as soon as possible, particularly in children's rooms. Safety is, of course, paramount in children's rooms and measures should be taken to ensure that they cannot open and fall out of windows.

The top of a window should be as tall as the tallest person in the house. Everyone should have a view of the sky through the seasons or they will lose their connection with the natural world. Drooping blinds which prevent this view lower the chi of a room considerably, and slatted blinds send cutting chi into the room.

If you feel the need to keep your curtains closed during the day, the chances are that you are depressed and feel vulnerable. Net curtains, although necessary in some areas, and preferable to curtains, blur the view out of the window. Experiment with other solutions, such as large plants, coloured glass or window stickers to prevent the outside world looking in. The aim should be to see out as much as possible. South-west-facing windows will, however, need some screening in summer, particularly in a study or kitchen.

Too many windows can create excessive yang since they blast the house with chi, while too few windows restrict its flow and are yin. Windows too near the

△ **The seating in this room impedes access to the window, and can be easily rearranged.**

floor in attic rooms feel unstable and a solid object or low table should be placed in front. It is preferable for bathrooms to have windows with an air flow. If this is not available, a water feature containing aromatic oils should be used and an extraction unit installed.

Too many windows in the dining room are considered to be especially inauspicious since the aim is to gather chi around the dining table and the food prepared for friends and family.

▽ **This lovely etched bathroom window allows the occupants privacy, but still permits the maximum amount of light.**

Materials

The materials with which we surround ourselves affect us on a physical level by how they feel and what they look like. They also affect us on a psychological level through their energy. Like everything else, materials have elemental qualities that affect

▽ A wooden floor makes the room look attractive and warm.

HARMFUL CHEMICALS ARE FOUND IN

Wood preservation treatments: use safe alternatives

Cavity wall foam

Paint: use natural pigments

Vinyl wallpaper and paints: use untreated papers and paints

Synthetic carpets and treated woollen carpets: use natural untreated materials

Plastic floor tiles and coverings: use linoleum or rubber

Adhesives: use non-chemical and acrylic alternatives

Upholstery foam: use natural fibres

Processed wood products: use solid or recycled wood

Cleaning materials: use natural alternatives

Food: Select organic food

Fuels: keep consumption to a minimum

Water supply: dispose of hazardous chemicals safely

△ Natural materials such as wood, wicker and cotton fabrics look fresh and inviting.

the chi of the part of the home in which they are used, and they can also have a profound effect on our health and well-being.

Hard, reflective surfaces such as those used in the kitchen have a yang energy and chi moves across them quickly. Soft materials and those with depth of colour or texture are yin and can be used to slow chi movement down.

materials and health

Our choice of materials for fabrics and soft furnishings, furniture, decorating materials, and cleaning and washing agents can play a part in our health and well-being.

Each of us takes responsibility for our own health and that of our families whenever we choose materials for use inside our homes. Many substances present in the products we select can cause life-threatening illnesses over time and many are known to be responsible for allergies.

While investigating the air quality inside spacecraft, scientists at NASA discovered that some plants are useful in extracting harmful substances from the atmosphere. This is a very good reason for introducing plants into our homes, in addition to their other virtues. The list above shows plants which have been found useful in cleaning the air.

◁ Furniture made out of wicker and natural cotton is strong and comfortable, and because they are natural materials is also biodegradable.

Materials and their colours and shapes can be used to enhance, weaken or support an area's energy according to the relationships of the elements.

WOOD

Playing a crucial role in most houses, wood's strength supports the structure of a house, yet its grain suggests fluidity and movement. Polished woods conduct chi quickly but stripped pine seems to absorb it. Wood is ideal for use on floors as it is easy to clean and does not harbour dust mites, which can cause allergies.

BAMBOO, WICKER AND RATTAN

These natural products fall into the Wood element category. In contrast to the yang characteristics of highly polished wood, these materials tend to be yin and thus slow down chi.

COIR, SISAL, SEA GRASS AND RUSH MATTING

These are popular because they are natural products. They make attractive floor coverings but are difficult to clean; this must be done regularly or they will harbour dirt and insects.

FABRICS

These can be made of natural fibres, like cotton and linen which belong to the Wood element, or from man-made fibres. Unless they are treated with chemicals for fire or stain resistance, natural fibres are preferred since man-made fibres create static electricity and deplete beneficial negative ions. Fabrics can encourage stagnant chi if they become faded and dirty.

PLASTICS

Like other man-made materials, plastic falls into the Fire element category as it has been produced using heat. Plastics can block chi and produce harmful vapours and chemicals which may affect health, so they should be kept to a minimum.

METAL

Objects in the house that are made from metal speed up chi flow. The reflective surfaces suggest efficiency and action, and metal is therefore useful in the kitchen and in stagnant areas such as bathrooms. Being smooth and reflective, glass is often classified in the Metal element.

GLASS

Often classified as the Metal element, glass shares some of its qualities. However, glass has depth, and light reflecting on it suggests patterns which flow like Water. Sand is used in the production of glass, so it can also suggest Earth. It depends on the energetic quality of the particular glass and the use to which it is put.

CLAY AND CERAMICS

These two related materials fall into the Earth element category. They can be yin or yang in nature, depending on whether or not their surfaces are shiny. Glazed surfaces are more yang and they conduct chi quickly.

STONE AND MARBLE

Floors and walls made from stone fall into the Earth element category. They tend to be yin since their surfaces are non-reflective and the patterning on them gives them depth. Stone floors are stable and are particularly useful in kitchens. Marble is yang because it is smooth and polished. The natural patterns in marble also suggest the flow of the Water element.

Mirrors

Mirrors have been described as 'the aspirin' of Feng Shui and they have many curative uses. They should always reflect something pleasant, such as an attractive view or a landscape, which will bring the vibrant energy of a garden or scene into the house. When placing a mirror to enhance a space or 'cure' an area, be aware of what is reflected in it or a problem may be created elsewhere. Mirrors should never distort or cut into the image of a person as this symbolically distorts or cuts their chi. They should always have frames to contain the chi of the image.

Mirrors are useful in small spaces where their affect is to apparently double the size of the area. Don't hang them opposite a door or a window since they merely reflect the chi back at itself and do not allow it to flow around the home. Mirrors opposite each other, with never-ending reflections, indicate restlessness and are not recommended. Other reflective objects can be used in the same way as mirrors; for example, highly polished door furniture, metal pots, glass bowls and shiny surfaces.

▽ A mirror will make a small space seem much larger. Do not position it directly opposite a door or window.

△ This hallway is already light but the mirror makes it positively sparkle. Mirrors create an illusion of space and depth.

irregular spaces

Where part of a house is 'missing', in other words irregularly shaped, mirrors can be used to effectively recreate the missing space and make a regular shape.

stagnant areas

Use mirrors in dark corners and at bends in passages to help the chi to circulate around these awkward places.

long corridors

In long corridors where chi moves too fast, mirrors can slow it down. Position several mirrors in a staggered way to reflect pleasant images placed on the opposite wall.

mirrors to deflect

Convex mirrors are used in Feng Shui to deflect fast-moving chi or the influences of uncomfortable features outside the

THE DO'S AND DON'TS OF MIRRORS

Do
Have frames around mirrors
Keep them clean
Replace broken ones
Reflect your whole image

Don't
Have joins or mirror tiles
Hang mirrors opposite each other
Place them opposite the bed
Place them opposite doors
Place them directly opposite windows
Hang Bagua mirrors indoors

THE BAGUA MIRROR

The markings on the Bagua mirror are a kind of shorthand, representing the energies of the Cosmos.

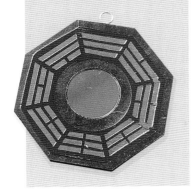

house, for example, corners of buildings, telegraph poles and trees which overpower the front of the house. Convex mirrors will also deflect unwanted influences inside the house, but because they distort images position them in places where they will not reflect people.

bagua mirrors

Bagua mirrors are used to protect a house from malign energies which may attack the occupants. They can often be seen outside Chinese homes and shops. They are used on front doors to deflect the influences of negative energy sources – harsh corners, tall objects and other features. Bagua mirrors represent a yin energy cycle and, as such, should never be hung inside the house or they will affect the energies of the occupants.

△ If a house is not of a perfect shape, a mirror hung inside will symbolically reflect the missing area.

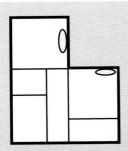

The Wealth area of this house is missing. Place mirrors to symbolically repair the shape and energize the missing space.

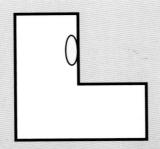

Use a mirror to repair the shape of an L-shaped room by symbolically drawing in the missing area.

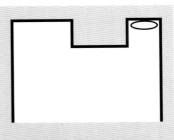

A mirror placed in this gloomy corner, reflecting a view or plant, will enliven a dark space and prevent energy stagnating.

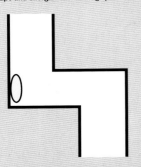

Place a mirror to reflect a bright picture on the opposite wall and thus bring energy to this dark area.

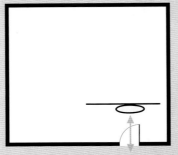

A mirror in this position will not allow the chi into the house or room and will reflect it back through the door.

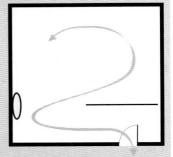

This is a better position as it draws the chi into and through the living area and does not act as a barrier.

Plants

Houseplants play an important role in Feng Shui because they bring a life-force into the home and help to keep the air fresh. Depending on their shape, plants create different types of energy. Upright plants with pointed leaves are yang, and are useful in the south and in corners to move energy. Round-leaved and drooping plants are more yin and calming, and best placed in the north. Plants should be healthy – sick, diseased plants, and those which shed leaves and flowers, profusely will create stagnant energy.

colour and shape

Plants with shapes and colours that correspond to the Five Elements are ideal. Care should be taken when siting spiky plants to ensure that they are not directing harmful energy towards a chair where someone may be sitting.

△ Colourful plants will brighten any area and increase Wood energy. Plants in these colours will benefit an Earth area.

INDOOR BULBS

SPRING: Dwarf tulip, Dwarf narcissus, Crocus, Hyacinth (above)
SUMMER: *Scilla peruviana, Albuca humulis, Calochortus subalpinus, Rocoea humeana*
AUTUMN: Nerine, Autumn crocus, Cyclamen, *Liriope muscari*
WINTER: *Iris reticulata, Chionodoxa luciliae,* Muscari, Cymbidium

△ The money plant has been adopted as the Feng Shui plant. Its leaves resemble coins and Metal energy.

▷ This trained ivy plant brings a lively energy to a room. It would look best in the west or north-west areas.

PLANTS THAT REPRESENT THE FIVE ELEMENTS

△ Geraniums are easy to grow on a sunny windowsill and represent Fire.

FIRE: Geranium, Cordyline, Begonia, Bromeliad, Poinsettia, Aspidistra.
EARTH: Slipper flower, Marigolds, Sunflowers and other yellow plants.
METAL: Money plant, Jasmine, Fittonia, Oleander, Calathea.

△ All the elements are here, captured in both the colours and the shapes of this attractive pot of lillies.

△ Summer jasmine is often grown in an arch shape. Its delicate white flowers have a beautiful scent.

WATER: The Water element can be introduced by standing plant pots on blue or clear glass nuggets.
WOOD: All plants are representative of the Wood element.

flowers

Cut flowers look beautiful in a vase but, once picked, they are technically dead and often stand forgotten in stagnant water. The cut-flower industry uses vast amounts of energy in heating greenhouses, transportation and the manufacture of chemicals. Although there are occasions when only a beautiful bunch of flowers

▽ Use a pretty flowering plant in the house like this Cymbidium as an alternative to cut flowers.

will do, consider the possibility of choosing a potted plant instead, as it can be planted outside afterwards.

Dried flowers are also technically dead and possess a stagnant energy, particularly when their colours have faded and they are full of dust. As an alternative, pictures of flowers, or brightly painted wooden replicas and well-made silk flowers are all acceptable to symbolize growth and stimulate energy.

the feng shui plant

The money plant (*Crassula ovata*) has been adopted as the Feng Shui plant. The name helps, but the round succulent leaves are representative of Metal energy. Use them in the west and north-west. If used in the south-east (the Wealth area), their Metal energy will be in conflict with the Wood energy of that direction.

▷ This bright arrangement would do well in the south-west – an Earth area.

USE PLANTS TO

Hide a jutting corner
Move energy in a recessed corner
Harmonize Fire and Water energy in kitchens
Slow down chi in corridors
Drain excess Water energy in the bathroom
Bring life into the house
Enhance the east and south-east, and support the south

Lighting

Life on Earth depends directly or indirectly on the sun. Our bodies are attuned to its cycles and in every culture the daily rhythms of light and dark are built into the mythology. In China, the yin-yang or Tai Chi symbol reflects the cycles of the sun: the white yang side representing daytime and the dark yin side night-time. In the

▽ Stained glass is very decorative and provides privacy in a room which is overlooked.

△ Our bodies need plenty of sunlight in order to stay healthy.

▷ Muslin filters the light in rooms where the sun's glare is too strong, or offers privacy.

modern world, many of us spend a lot of time inside buildings and our rhythms become out-of-tune with the natural cycle of the sun. In northern countries, which have little sunlight, a condition known as SAD (Seasonal Affective Disorder) is prevalent. It is treated with light that imitates the ultraviolet and infra-red rays of the sun.

The correct type and level of light is very important to our general health and wellbeing. In our homes, natural light is essential, but its quality varies throughout the day according to the way our houses face. Natural light can cause glare or create shadows and we often have to subdue it or enhance it by artificial means. Light can be reflected off shiny surfaces or blocked by curtains or filtered by net or muslin curtains, blinds or frosted or tinted glass. Being aware of how natural light comes into our homes enables us to position our furniture and arrange our activities to make the best use of it, and control it as much as possible.

artificial lighting

In rooms where we are active, such as kitchens, offices and workrooms, and where safety is important, for example on staircases, direct lighting is necessary. In rooms we relax in – living rooms and bedrooms – we can use softer lighting which can be reflected or diffused. To highlight particular areas, such as a picture, chopping board or desk, task lighting can be used.

The position of lighting has a profound effect on the occupants of a house. If shadows are cast where we read or prepare food, or the lights flicker, or light glares on to the computer or TV screen, we will constantly be irritated. Harsh lighting can also affect our moods.

The quality of light is important. Ordinary light bulbs produce light which veers towards the red end of the spectrum, with little blue or green light. Fluorescent light is the opposite; it emits higher electromagnetic fields than other sources and its constant subtle flicker can cause headaches. Full spectrum lighting was designed to copy natural daylight as much as possible, but unfortunately contains slightly higher levels of ultraviolet radiation than ordinary light sources.

Energy production is a drain on the world's natural resources. Recent developments designed to reduce this include CFL (compact fluorescent lamp) bulbs, which not only last longer but also use less

▽ Soft wall lighting helps us to relax at the end of a stressful day.

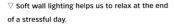

△ Glass bricks have been used here instead of a solid wall. They can be very useful if you want to open up dark areas.

▷ Use uplighters to transform dark corners. Placed under heavy beams, they serve to lighten their negative effect.

electricity, and are useful for halls and landings. Tungsten-halogen lamps give a bright, white light that is close to daylight, high-voltage varieties are too bright for task lighting but useful as uplighters; the low-voltage varieties can be used for spotlights. These bulbs are also energy-efficient.

Electrostress

We are becoming increasingly aware of the negative effects of electromagnetic radiation on the human body. The effects of exposure to ionizing radiation in X-rays and ultraviolet rays in sunlight are now well-known. The low-frequency radiation which surrounds power lines has also been linked to childhood illness. Such radiation also exists around electrical appliances. Non-ionizing radiation emitted by household appliances can be equally harmful over time. Cathode ray tubes in televisions and computer monitors are particularly harmful because both adults and children now spend so much time in front of them. It is wise to sit as far away as possible from the screen. Lap-top computers should not be used on our laps as we would then be connected to an electric circuit. The electromagnetic field around ionizers has a particularly large range so it is not a good idea to place them in bedrooms.

We live in an electrical 'soup'. Radio, TV and microwave emissions pass around

△ Placing a Boston fern next to the television screen has been shown to absorb some of the radiation it emits.

◁ Round-the-clock working and satellite links to the rest of the world have resulted in Hong Kong having higher-than-average electromagnetic activity.

▽ Mobile phones are convenient and allow us to conduct business outside, but pose a health risk if used constantly. A lap-top computer should not be used on our laps.

◁ Microwave ovens can damage your health if they leak. Have them checked annually as you would other household fixtures. They are not well regarded in Feng Shui.

▷ A gadget-free bedroom is essential for a healthy body and peace of mind. While we sleep, our body cells can regenerate naturally, a process which works best if unimpeded by any harmful external influences.

and through us wherever we live. There are few places left on Earth where this is not the case. Satellites connect continents instantly and we can communicate with people across the world, but at a price. Recent research into the use of mobile telephones indicates that frequent use can affect us. The radiation from the appliances we use every day of our lives has been linked to various cancers, allergies, Parkinson's disease, Alzheimer's disease, cataracts, ME and even the total breakdown of the immune system.

Despite our awareness of the effects of radiation, we are so dependent on appliances and communication technology that we are unwilling, or unable, to live without them. We should therefore take precautions. At night, electric blankets should never be left on when we are in bed; if we must use them, they should be unplugged from the mains before we get into bed. Water beds are connected to the electricity supply, so in Feng Shui terms they display the conflict of Fire (electricity) and Water. We need to feel secure when we sleep and the constant motion of a water bed is not a natural way to rest.

Microwave ovens are potentially the most dangerous of all household appliances. If you must have one in your kitchen, it should be used with great care. They have been found to emit low-frequency radiation far in excess of that known to cause lymphatic cancer in children, and are also thought to corrupt the molecular structure of food.

Apartments that have under-floor or overhead heating systems should be avoided as they can create the effect of living in an electromagnetic box.

PRECAUTIONS

Use mobile phones as little as possible and make lengthy social calls from a land phone

Fit screen filters to VDUs

Sit, and make sure children sit, at least 2m (6ft) away from the television screen

Sit as far away from the computer as possible when not working

Limit children's use of the computer

Do not use the computer and television as substitute babysitters

Do not stand near a microwave when it is on

Dry your hair naturally instead of using electrical appliances

Choose gas or wood-burning stoves and heaters rather than electric

Keep all electrical appliances away from the bed

Do not have wiring under the bed

Do not use storage heaters in bedrooms

▽ Storing electrical equipment out of sight will help us to relax.

△ Children sleep better if they are not surrounded by stimulating equipment.

▽ A wood-burning stove lends an attractive focus to a room.

The senses: sight

△ Skyscapes are so beautiful that we should make sure we can capture a view of them in our homes if possible.

What we see affects us positively or negatively, or even subconsciously so we may not even be aware of the effect. If we surround ourselves with wonderful views, bright colours, interesting food and a clean and clear environment we are more likely to lead full and happy lives, because our surroundings will reflect a positive attitude to life, and will stimulate all our senses. The reverse is equally true.

Most homes have problem areas – dark corners which would benefit from light, rooms with columns or L-shaped rooms where the corners point at us – but we can disguise them with plants and materials to soften the edges. There may be things outside which affect us and we may want to keep their influence out.

We can attempt to deflect the problem with mirrors and other reflective objects, or create a barrier, such as a hedge or shrub, to keep it at bay. There is a difference between this type of positive, or yang, barrier designed to keep the negative exterior forces out and a yin barrier which we sometimes create to keep our own negative energies in – tall hedges and walls and drawn curtains. Wherever the ancient Chinese had a wall, there would be a window, or 'Moon Gate', in it through which to see the world beyond and open up future possibilities. Think of this as a good principle to try and follow.

◁ 'Moon Gates' were built into walls in China to afford a glimpse of the world outside.

△ This intricately decorated window can be found in a temple in China.

▽ Crystals are used to bring a sparkle to stuck energy. Suspend one in a window and the light will shine through it, creating a rainbow effect on a wall or ceiling.

SIGHT ENHANCERS

Natural light, Lamps,
Candles, Glass and crystal, Colour,
Still water, Moon Gates,
Reflective metals,
Windows, Mirrors

crystals

Colour resonates with us on both a conscious and a subconscious level, and can affect our moods. The combination of crystal and light gives a lively dancing pattern which will enliven a dark room if the crystal is hung in a window. Where energy is stuck, crystals can help to move it on.

Crystals should be used with care. They have many facets which break light up into tiny segments and can do the same to other energies. If the specific energy of an area is not working, do not hang up a crystal to repair it – or the problem will be exacerbated. A small crystal is adequate for the average home, but larger ones would be needed for a large area.

▷ Coloured glass panels in a window add life to a colourless room. They also provide privacy and so are ideal for a bathroom or for ground floor rooms.

▽ This lovely room has been transformed by the balanced pairs of stained glass windows. Little extra decoration is needed.

coloured glass

Glass, when painted or stained, makes a bolder statement than crystal and its effects can be stunning. Many urban houses have side doors which look out on to a wall and there is a temptation, if they are overlooked by a window from a neighbouring house, to keep a blind permanently down. Replacing the blind, or the plain glass in a door, with coloured glass that supports the elements of the area will bring a wonderful, transforming energy into a dark room. Stained glass is suitable for most rooms.

The senses: sound

Each of the Five Elements governs a different musical quality and sound. We all connect to a particular sound and in Chinese medicine the tone of our voice is categorized according to the elements and used in diagnosis. We each have our own favourite sounds. Gentle background music, the rustle of leaves, bird songs – all have a therapeutic effect. Where noise is rhythmic – a dripping tap, music from a neighbour's party, even someone sneezing at regular intervals – it can grate on our nerves.

Pleasant sounds in the right place and at the right time can soothe and refresh. Bubbling water will create a peaceful ambience and slow us down. If we want to bring life to a place, honky-tonk music, drums and cymbals will fulfil the purpose. Background sounds are comforting and the sound of passing traffic or a ticking clock can be reassuring.

wind chimes

Feng Shui sees wind chimes as an enhancer and it is interesting to note how people respond differently to the noise they make, and their various tones. Take care when

▽ **The vibrations from Tibetan bells will energize a room.**

using wind chimes near fences in a built-up area, since your neighbours may not enjoy their sound as much as you do.

Wind chimes are used to slow energy down. You might need to do this, for example, where a staircase faces the front door. However, the chimes will have the desired effect only if they are activated as the door opens. Chimes are very effective in the kitchen where people often stand at the sink or stove with their backs to the door, because it is comforting to know that the chimes will sound if anyone enters.

Chimes should be hollow to allow the chi in. They can be used to enhance the Metal (west or north-west) area of a building. Do not use chimes in a Wood area (east or south-east), because in that position they are detrimental to the energy of the area.

▽ **The deep-toned, soothing ticking of a grandfather clock is a reassuring sound.**

△ **Here wind chimes help to balance the negative effect of a sloping ceiling.**

water

The sound of gently bubbling water can be relaxing and there are many delightful indoor water features available. Water should be placed in the north, the east, and in the south-east. In addition, until 2023, the south-west is particularly auspicious. Fish tanks are recommended, but must be clean, and contain living plants and natural features. Neglected tanks and unhealthy fish will have a negative effect. The preferred number of fish is nine, one of which should be black to absorb any negative chi.

SOUND ENHANCERS

Wind chimes, Moving water, Music, Clocks, Rustling leaves

The senses: touch

Too often disregarded, touch is as vital as the other senses and is linked to our primeval desire to be in contact with the Earth. No mother can forget her first contact with a new baby – skin on skin is the most basic yet the most magical feeling there is. The tactile sensations in our homes affect our feelings of comfort and security. A scratchy plant that brushes our ankles as we return home will colour our evening, and a cold or harsh feel underfoot as we step out of bed affects the start of our day.

People who have impaired vision develop their other senses and touch becomes much more important. Guide dogs provide physical contact as well as being their owner's eyes. Isolated elderly people are said to live longer if they have pets to stroke.

When we are depressed, physical contact such as a hug from a relative or partner plays an important part in the healing process. Those who are deprived of physical affection as children often have difficulty making relationships.

△ No mother ever forgets her first skin-to-skin contact with her new baby.

The materials with which we surround ourselves in our homes make a considerable impact on us. Few people can resist the urge to stroke a beautiful wooden bowl, although they might pass by a steel sculpture without touching it. Visitors to stately homes are asked to refrain from stroking fabrics and priceless furniture, but it is an irresistible urge, especially if the furnishings are particularly sumptuous. If we clothe ourselves and cover our furniture in fabrics which feel soft and luxurious, it will positively affect the way we feel. The yin-yang balance in our homes is revealed in the sense of touch. Yang rooms like the kitchen and study are full of yang metal objects which are utilitarian, we would never dream of connecting with these except on a working basis. In yin rooms (bedrooms and other rooms for relaxation) we put on warm and comfortable clothing and snuggle into soft beds and sofas.

△ Velvet furnishings and accessories feel wonderfully luxurious.

◁ Different textures provide sensual appeal and give a room character.

TOUCH ENHANCERS

Plants, Wooden objects, Fabrics, Pets, People, Fruit, Smooth objects

The senses: taste

This is not as easy as the other senses to describe in terms of Feng Shui yet it forms as great a part of our wellbeing as any sense. The Chinese see the tastes affiliated to the Five Elements as an integral part of life. If we are to change our perceptions and lifestyles, part of the process includes how we treat our bodies. If the chi is to flow unblocked, then we need to live in a holistic way in every aspect of our lives.

'We are what we eat' expresses the view that our diet directly affects our health. The frantic lifestyles that many of us lead mean that we often grab what we can, and eat it on the run, without taking nutritional balance, or proper digestion, into account. Modern medicine may come up with the cures, but if we eat healthy balanced diets then we are less likely to become ill in the first place.

△ Eating fresh, ripe fruits keeps us healthy – and tastes wonderful.

Using yin and yang and the Five Elements in the kitchen is a science in itself. Chinese herbal medicine balances the constitution using the same techniques as Feng Shui does to balance an environment. (Chaucer's red-faced, lecherous Summoner in *The Canterbury Tales*, a lover of onions and leeks, is a classic case of an excess of the Fire element.) Being aware of the balance of elements in our food, and the poor nutritional value of the

◁ Spend time preparing home-cooked meals rather than resorting to store-bought foods.

pre-cooked fast food products which we now consume, enables us to take charge of all aspects of our lives. The benefits and disadvantages of genetically engineered food products are currently being debated, but we do not need scientific reports to tell us that we should make time in our lives to use natural ingredients. It is unwise to rely on packaged food when we do not know the accumulative effects on our bodies of the chemicals they contain.

SUPPORTIVE FOODS

Once we have consulted the 'Chinese Animals' table and discovered which element governs our sign, we can see below which food types support us. Using 'The Relationships of the Five Elements' table, we will then be able to see which of the elements are beneficial to us and which are not, and adjust our eating habits accordingly.

Wood	sour
Fire	bitter
Earth	sweet
Metal	pungent
Water	salt

The senses: smell

Large stores know only too well the power of the sense of smell. Who can fail to be tempted by the aroma of freshly baked bread at the supermarket entrance, pumped through grills to lure us into the store where the bakery is almost always in the farthest corner?

Animals excrete pheromones to attract their mates and to mark their territory. Our homes also have a unique smell and most of us, if blindfolded, could tell which of our friends' homes we were entering. First impressions make an impact and if

△ A herb path by the back door will smell wonderful and give us pleasure.

△ The smells of freshly-baked bread and natural foods heighten our senses.

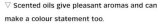

▽ Scented oils give pleasant aromas and can make a colour statement too.

our homes smell less than fresh, this can affect how comfortable we and our visitors feel there.

There is something very different about the subtle smell of lavender as we brush past it in the garden on a warm evening after rain and the artificial lavender-scented air-fresheners sold commercially. Natural smells affect us in a way that manufactured scents never can, with the added advantage of not causing us respiratory problems or polluting the atmosphere. There is nothing to beat the flower-perfumed fresh air which wafts through an open window from a garden, balcony or window box. Many cultures use incense to sweeten the air, and we are now beginning to rediscover the long-lost knowledge of the benefits to health and wellbeing of certain aromatic oils.

SMELL ENHANCERS
Fresh air, Aromatic oils, Plants, Fresh potpourri, Fruit

Colour

The Tao teaches that out of the interplay of yin and yang all things come. Yin is the blackness which absorbs all colours and yang the whiteness which reflects them. They give rise to the Five Elements and their associated colour representations, from which arise the whole spectrum of colours. Colour is vibration and we each respond to it on many levels, consciously and unconsciously. Colour affects how comfortable we are in different environments and can affect our moods. Our use of colour also affects how others perceive us. Colour is used to cure physical ailments and can be used symbolically to enhance spaces or evoke emotions.

When we use colour we are also working with light since light contains all colours, each with its own frequency. Every light situation is different – each home and each room within it. The light

△ This room works wonderfully well. All the elements are there but not contrived.

quality depends on the aspect, the size of the windows and how they are decorated, artificial light sources and the size of the rooms. The materials we use on floors and in decorations and furnishings have the ability to reflect and transmit light or to absorb it. We can use colour to create illusions – of size (dark colours absorb more light than lighter ones); of depth (natural pigments draw light in or reflect it according to the time of day and the season); and of movement (spots of colour around a room create movement and energy there).

Light quality varies around the world. In Africa, where the sun beats down under a bright blue sky, pigments, fabrics and skins in earth colours such as browns, beiges and terracottas are used to great effect. In Britain, where the climate dictates more of a seasonal, indoor life and the light is much less vibrant, the same colours signify a closing in and, used to excess, can lead to a level of withdrawal

and depression. Similarly, the intense colours of Indian silks and the warm tones of the Mediterranean palette have to be used with care when they are introduced in countries where light quality differs. However, they can play a useful role in moving the energy and, with thought, can be effective.

▽ Mediterranean colours make us think of sunshine and holidays.

▽ African colours – browns, beiges and terracottas – predominate here.

BEWARE PEACH

Using the colour peach in your bedroom is asking for trouble if you are married. 'Peach-Blossom Luck' is a well-known concept in China, meaning a husband or wife with a roving eye. A married person may be drawn into adultery. A single person, however, will have an active social life but will probably be unable to find a life partner.

◁ In this conservatory, the Metal and Wood elements are in conflict.

▷ The colours green (Wood), red (Fire) and yellow (Earth) balance the Five Elements.

the Five Elements

The five colours associated with the elements evoke the quality of the energy of each one. We use them to highlight areas of our lives we wish to concentrate on, and the Bagua diagram gives us the associated colours for each direction. In Feng Shui, balance and harmony have prime consideration, but we should decorate our homes according to our personal tastes or we will never be comfortable there. We should also remember the purpose of the room and the element associated with the direction it is in. Then we can achieve true balance and harmony. It would be treating the subject superficially to ensure that a room has, say, a cushion in each of the Five Elemental colours. A more subtle approach would be to put a single red tulip in a glass vase in the south of an all-white room, this would bring in the Wood element in the green stem, and Fire in the red flower. The Metal element is represented by the white room, the Water element by the light moving through the glass vase and the Earth element in the sand used to make the glass, and as the medium the flower grew in.

THE COLOURS

White represents a fresh canvas, and black symbolizes a clean slate, upon both of which we can create a picture with the colours below.

RED: Red is stimulating and dominant, it reduces the size of rooms and increases the size of objects. It is useful as an accent colour. Unsuitable for dining rooms, children's rooms, or kitchens, it is associated with warmth, prosperity and stimulation, but also anger, shame and hatred.

YELLOW: Yellow is associated with enlightenment and intellect, it stimulates the brain and aids digestion. Its positive qualities are optimism, reason and decisiveness, its negative qualities are craftiness, exaggeration and rigidity. Suitable for hallways and kitchens, but not bathrooms.

GREEN: Green symbolizes growth, fertility and harmony; it is restful and refreshing. Its positive associations are optimism, freedom and balance, and its negatives envy and deceit. Good in therapy rooms, conservatories and bathrooms but not in family rooms, playrooms or studies.

BLUE: Blue is peaceful and soothing. Linked with spirituality, contemplation, mystery and patience, its positive associations are trust, faithfulness and stability. Negatives are suspicion and melancholia. Use blue in meditation rooms and bedrooms, but not in family rooms or studies.

PURPLE: Encouraging vitality, purple is dignified and spiritual. Positive associations: excitement, motivation and passion, negatives: mournfulness and force. Use in bedrooms and meditation rooms but not bathrooms or kitchens.

PINK: Pink is linked with purity of thought and has no negatives. Suitable for adults' and childrens' bedrooms but not kitchens or bathrooms.

ORANGE: A powerful and cheerful colour, orange encourages communication. Positive qualities are happiness, intellect and concentration, negative is rebelliousness. Use in living rooms and hallways, but not in a small space or bedrooms.

BROWN: Brown suggests stability and weight. Its positives are safety and elegance, while its negatives are dinginess, and aging. Good for studies but not for bedrooms.

WHITE: White symbolizes new beginnings, purity and innocence. its positive qualities are cleanliness and freshness, its negatives cold, lifelessness, starkness. Use for bathrooms and kitchens, not suitable for children's rooms.

BLACK: Black is mysterious and independent. Its positive qualities are intrigue, and strength, while its negatives are death and evil. It should not be used in children's rooms, studies or living rooms.

Clutter

Not merely items or belongings, clutter is also a state of mind. It can be the things we haven't done that prey on our minds, like unreturned telephone calls and appointments not made, or the ideas and perceptions we hoard which prevent us from doing the things we really want to do. Everything we do not use or wear, or which we are keeping in case it comes in handy one day, constitutes clutter. Inherited objects, and those given to us as presents which we do not like but feel guilty about parting with, are also clutter.

For one reason or another, perhaps due to our upbringing or past experiences, or because we doubt our own abilities, we hang on to situations and ideas which do not let us move on. We may stay in a job thinking we are indispensable or we are

△ This low-beamed cottage room looks oppressive, with its fussy decoration and too many disparate ornaments.

▽ A similar room but far less cluttered gives a lighter, more airy feel.

△ Any extraneous objects would look out of place in this cool, clutter-free bedroom, a perfect place to unwind.

doing it out of a sense of loyalty, but often it is because we are afraid to take the leap and change direction. We may stay in a relationship through fear of emotional upheaval, or not accept a job away from a familiar area through fear of the unknown. All these attitudes clutter our thought processes but by clearing out our physical clutter we see the benefits of 'letting go', which will help us to clear out the mental clutter restricting our development.

clearing out

'Things' or 'stuff' constitute a major problem in most homes, and it accumulates by the day. Useless kitchen gadgets, empty gift boxes to recycle, presents we hate or have outgrown, inherited objects which fear of embarrassment or guilt will not let us part with, and an endless list of other items. We do not need these things in our lives if we are to open up and let new

experiences in. Give them to charity shops or sell them at car-boot sales and buy something you really want.

Most of us hold on to clothes 'in case' we might need them, grow back into them or our children might like them one day. It is far better to live for today and create space for something new which we will enjoy wearing now.

Books are difficult to get rid of as many people believe it is a sacrilege to throw them out. If books sit and gather dust for years on end, unread and not referred to, they too constitute clutter and stuck energy and we should move them on. The world is changing fast and information becomes out of date almost before it is in print. Should we require a fact in ten years'

△ If these overladen shelves are thinned out, there will be room for new books.

time, the information will be accessible elsewhere. Magazines and newspapers also constitute clutter. We are unlikely to read last week's, or even yesterday's, paper and we can always extract any information we require from magazines provided we file it immediately in a place where we are likely to find it again.

Clutter represents stagnant energy and isn't just made up of unstored belongings, the list is endless – blown light bulbs we keep forgetting to replace, dead wasps and dropped leaves on the window ledge, scum marks round the bath, the unfilled pepper grinder in the kitchen, a squeaking cup-board door. Separately, each of these requires only a few minute's attention, but put together, their effect can make years of difference to the quality of our lives.

Do not attempt to rid the whole house of clutter in one go. Start in a small way with a drawer, and complete the whole task of clearing out, tidying and getting rid of unwanted items before moving on to the next.

△ There is no clutter here, but enough objects and colours to make the space interesting.

ENERGIZING OUR HOMES

When we move into a new house, or have had an unpleasant experience in our home, the energy there can become stuck and feel heavy. We can lighten it to some extent by clearing out all the clutter and by cleaning everywhere thoroughly.

Vibrations are important and we resonate at a level which is in harmony with the natural vibrations of the Earth. The senses also work at a vibrational level and if we can improve their quality in our homes we will feel the benefit. Often the

▽ Candles represent Fire. Use with care in the South and to support the West.

△ Burning aromatic oils or incense raises the energy in a room.

vibrations which have caused the previous owner to behave in a certain way will have the same effect on us and we should take note of any problems before moving to a new home.

There are various methods we can use to improve the vibrations in our homes. Having cleaned and rid the house of clutter, open the windows and make a noise in every room. Bells, gongs and clapping all raise the vibrational level. Take particular care to go into the corners, where energy is likely to be stuck. Natural light can be represented by candles placed in each corner of the room and in the centre. Smell can be introduced in the form of incense or aromatic oils. Spring water, charged by the vibrations of the moon, can be sprayed around to introduce negative ions back into the air.

▽ Candles in the corners and centre of a room will help move any stuck energy.

Using the Symbolic Bagua

We all wish at certain times in our lives that some aspect was working better. By focusing on a particular aspect of our lives, we can often stimulate the energy to make things work well for us. Used as a template that we can place on the plans of our home, the Symbolic Bagua gives us a tool for focus with its division into eight life sections. The eight life sections of the Bagua are: Career, Relationships, Family, Wealth, Helpful People, Children, Knowledge and Fame and each area has its own enhancers. By using some of the methods described on the following pages we can hopefully harness some of the 'magic' of Feng Shui for ourselves.

The enhancements used in Feng Shui are designed to focus the mind. For example, we can create the belief that it is possible to stabilize something in our lives by using heavy objects such as stones or pictures of mountains. We can move on a 'stuck' situation by creating or alluding to movement, for instance, using water or wind-blown items. Whatever image we use must have meaning for us in that we can see it physically and relate to its symbolism. Thus we should use images from our own cultures and experiences. Whatever we use, it should not clash with the element of the direction but if possible should strengthen it.

career

This concerns itself with where we are going in life, either in our jobs or in our journeys through life. It can also mark the beginning of a project. ENHANCERS INCLUDE: moving images, a photograph of an aspiration such as a university, or a company brochure if applying for a job.

relationships

These play an important part in our lives. Getting on well with people and having the support of partners, family or friends play a major role in a happy life. ENHANCERS INCLUDE: double images for

△ A perfect arrangement for a table in the Relationships area of a room.

romance, two vases or candlesticks, a photograph of yourself with your partner or group images of friends, a poster or photograph, or a collection of something. Plants are useful to improve the chi, and ribbons or wind-activated objects will energize it as they move, provided there is a breeze blowing. Do not use them if there is no breeze.

family

Our families, past as well as present, will have coloured who we are, how we relate to the world around us and will have contributed to our health and wellbeing.

▽ Framed photographs can be placed in the Family area of a room.

ENHANCERS INCLUDE: Family photographs and documents, and heirlooms.

wealth

This is often taken to be monetary wealth, but it also covers the richness of our lives, fulfilment and the accumulation of beneficial energies around us. Feng Shui cannot help you to win the lottery but if you have worked hard and followed an honest and ethical path towards self-fulfilment, then the magic

△ Chinese coins for the Wealth area – the circle symbolizes Heaven, the square Earth.

may work for you. If this happens, you will probably not want to win the lottery anyway and other, more rewarding bounty may come your way. ENHANCERS INCLUDE: coins, plants, empty bowls and movement, for example, an indoor water feature.

helpful people

Interaction with others is an essential part of life, and this area is a very important one. If you are willing to help others and need some help in return, this is the area to focus on. ENHANCERS INCLUDE: telephones and telephone directories, and business cards.

children

Not quite the same as family, since children are the future rather than part of the past. This area also covers personal

△ **Family photographs can be placed in the Children area.**

projects – the tasks and jobs you nurture from their conception to their conclusion. ENHANCERS INCLUDE: photographs of children, project details, and your artistic and other achievements.

knowledge

This is the area for wisdom and education that is sought after and which can enrich our lives. ENHANCERS INCLUDE: books, framed words of wisdom and pictures of mentors.

HOME ENHANCER

To nurture supportive energy, create a feature that represents all Five Elements. Fill a glass or crystal bowl (Earth) with blue glass nuggets (Earth and Water), top up with water and a floating candle (Fire) and some flowers or petals (Wood). Add coins (Metal) to the bowl to complete the cycle.

THE POWER OF FENG SHUI

Feng Shui works in mysterious ways and the results of any action taken may not be quite as expected. Our actions trigger the energy required to achieve the outcomes we seek. This may not correspond to what we think we need or offer a quick fix. A consultant will offer solutions having ensured that everything is balanced. If we decide to undertake some of the recommendations and not others there will be no balance. Instigate one change at a time and wait before introducing the next. The following case study illustrates the unpredictable nature of Feng Shui.

Richard and Anne had lived in their house for ten years and had never settled. Through lethargy they had let it run down and now could not sell it. The electric lights blew regularly and there was evidence of a water leak outside the house. The only decorating they had done was to paint the living room walls a deep pink which, together with the red carpet laid throughout the house, resulted in Fire overload.

Richard and Anne did not want to spend money on a new carpet, so they were advised to paint the walls white to drain the Fire. They had already installed a large fish tank in the Wealth area since they wanted their money to move. They put several recommendations into practice, but not the major one – the walls. The result was that the energies took over. Within a week, the washing machine flooded the ground floor, ruining the carpet and forcing out the Fire energy, the overloaded electrical system finally blew and the fish in the tank died. The Chinese use fish as a sacrifice to human bad luck, believing they soak it up on behalf of the people.

Thus Feng Shui achieved its objectives and moved the energy on. Richard and Anne were left with no choice but to fix the electrics and change the carpet, and this time they chose more wisely. The changes made the house sellable and they were able to move.

fame

Not notoriety for its own sake, but recognition of an undertaking well done. ENHANCERS INCLUDE: certificates, newspaper cuttings, products of achievement.

the centre of the bagua

The centre is a special place. In a house it is where the occupants meet and where the energies accumulate and flow on. It should be treated well, be bright and welcoming, and not be cluttered. Do not introduce a light fitting with five bulbs here; glass and crystal light fittings will stimulate the area far better. A round rug often works well.

the right time

Most of us will have heard or read of people who have used Feng Shui and received rewards – a job, a long-awaited child, or a partner. We may be tempted to take Feng Shui on board and tweak every area of our homes in order to achieve perfection. Life is not perfect, however, and it is constantly changing. Essentially, the energies of the various directions change over time. Thus if we activate a particular area when the energies are good, things will be fine. If we leave whatever we have done when the energies are inauspicious, then we will create problems.

The adage, 'If it ain't broke, don't fix it' applies, only make changes where they are necessary. Remember also that when using these symbolic measures the compass directions and their related elements are still important, and need to be kept in balance with any changes made.

Investigating your home

The following Feng Shui case study can only offer a glimpse into the kind of analysis which takes place when investigating a home, but gives a good example of the process, and its outcomes.

William and Julia and their son Steven moved into their apartment a year ago. Julia feels comfortable there but William and Steven do not, and Steven has gradually become very run down and cannot concentrate on his schoolwork. William does some freelance work at home to supplement his income, but has not been getting many clients lately. There is tension and the couple's relationship is suffering. A Feng Shui consultant investigates the birthday of each person, their animal, the corresponding element and the compatibility of the animals.

William is a Fire – Rooster, Julia is a Metal + Rat and Steven a Water – Pig. This indicates that while William and Julia have a workable relationship with Steven, William and Julia's relationship can be difficult. According to the Five Elements relationships, Fire (William) is weakened by Metal (Julia), who in turn is weakened by Water (Steven). Being a Metal Rat with yang characteristics, Julia is quite strong and domineering so can hold her own. As a Fire Rooster, William can be inflexible and is not easily swayed by others' emo-

▽ **This bed is well balanced by the matching tables and lamps on either side.**

△ **The position of the bed is crucial. It should be protected behind and face an auspicious direction for the occupants.**

tions so may not be sympathetic to Steven. Fortunately, as a Water Pig, Steven accepts that things are difficult and is perceptive enough to steer clear when necessary.

Next, the consultant looked at the magic numbers, the corresponding east and west directions, each person's favourable and unfavourable directions, and the compass direction of the house.

William is a 7 and belongs to the west group. Julia, a 4, belongs to the east group and Steven, an 8, belongs to the west group. The house faces south-east, an east group direction, and is therefore most supportive of Julia. William's best direction is north-west, which is missing from the house. His office falls between the south and south-west sectors. The south-west is his second-best direction and the south his sixth. Steven's room has geopathic stress by the head of his bed. His best direction is south-west and his second is north-west. Julia's best direction is north and the second south. The consultant then looked at the shape of the house, Steven's room, William's desk position and William and Julia's bed. He made recommendations listed below.

KEY TO DIAGRAM

1. A mirror symbolically completes the house shape. A metal frame represents the element of the area.
2. The head of the bed was re-positioned to face south-west, Steven's best direction, and to remove him from the stressed area.
3. Steven's desk now faces north-west, his second-best direction. This also enables him to see the door and protects him from the fast-moving chi along the long passage. The bookcase and plant also protect him from the chi in the passage.
4. Semi-circular tables with silk flowers slow the chi further. The passage was too dark for live plants.
5. William's desk now faces north-west, his best position. A plant behind him prevents stagnant energy from building up in the corner. A plant on the desk deflects fast-

moving chi through the door and hides the point which would symbolically stab him as he enters.
6. The 'mouth of chi' to the stove, the point of entry of the energy source, and symbolic of wealth, comes from the south, Julia's second-best position.
7. In this room the bed is best in Julia's best position, north. A mirror should not reflect the bed, so a small mirror has been used here (see 1).
8. Two square tables, signifying containment, are placed on either side of the bed.
9. A picture of a couple is placed here to symbolize togetherness in the symbolic Relationships area.
10. Stones have been placed on the bathroom and toilet windowsills.
11. A plant supports William's personal Fire element.

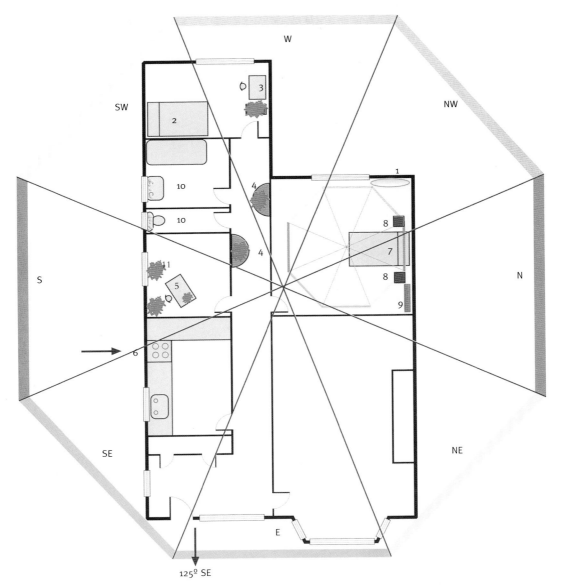

▽ **A floor plan of William and Julia's apartment after the changes were made. The numbers correspond with the captions in the box, left.**

W

NW

SW

N

S

NE

SE

E

125° SE

Putting the principles into practice

Now that you are familiar with the basic principles of Feng Shui, it is time to look at your home, room by room, and see if it is possible to arrange them differently to create spaces that will nourish you.

Halls, lobbies and staircases

When we step though the front door, the first impression we have of a house is the hall. If it is light and spacious with a pleasant, fresh smell, and is clean and tidy, then our spirits will rise. A long dark corridor, the smell of last night's cooking and a stack of newspapers in the corner will set the tone for the whole house. If the energy channels of the house are restricted or blocked, this can have a knock-on effect. Those who live with narrow, dark hallways may suffer restriction mentally or as a blockage in one of their body channels. Psychologically such a place is depressing. It is possible to deal with this by using bright colours and mirrors, and banning clutter. Coat hooks and shoe cupboards or racks make our homecoming easier. If the first things we see on returning is a mess we will not look forward to coming home.

the view from the door

If a door opens immediately on to a wall, people will feel overwhelmed and they will feel life is a struggle. A landscape picture hung on the wall will attract the eye will help overcome this, and give the illusion that we are being drawn on into the main part of the home. An entrance opposite the back door or window will funnel chi straight out. Keep doors closed, place

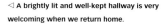
◁ A brightly lit and well-kept hallway is very welcoming when we return home.

▽ Plenty of coat hooks and storage space prevent the hall from becoming cluttered.

plants on windowsills or install coloured glass into the back door window to reflect chi back into the room.

If the first room seen from the door is the kitchen, it will inevitably be the first port of call on returning home. Food will be on our minds before we do anything else. Children will tumble in on returning from school with outdoor clothes and school bags to raid the fridge. An office opposite the door will encourage us to make it a priority to go in and check the answerphone or for emails. Work will be on our minds and we will not be able to relax into the home coming.

Toilet doors should be kept closed at all times, according to Chinese wisdom, so that we do not watch our wealth being flushed away, and a closed toilet lid is an extra precaution.

HALL CLUTTER
Coats, Shoes, Bags, Junk mail, Free papers, Laundry, Items to take upstairs

▽ In this spacious hall, natural finishes, and a variety of shapes, colours and textures create an energetic space.

communal lobbies

In buildings which were once large houses but are now small flats, or in badly managed apartment blocks, the communal entrance lobby is often a problem. There are two ways of approaching a dirty, messy, badly decorated lobby: negatively, by blaming others, or by taking positive action. Stuck personal chi is often a contributory factor to stuck energy in a house so it is in the interests of all the occupants to move it.

▽ Plants either side of the entrance welcome the residents of this apartment block.

CASE STUDY

Nancy lived in a house that had been converted into four flats, with a communal hallway and staircase. The turnover of residents was high and the communal areas were a mess. Approaches to the landlord and other tenants failed, so Nancy painted the hall herself and put up a shelf with a box for each flat into which she sorted the mail and free papers. A bright poster and a plant completed the project. Almost immediately, the neighbours became more friendly. The turnover of tenants slowed down and within two years Nancy and her neighbours bought the property and set about renovating it. The house was transformed into a desirable place to live.

△ The front door of this house opens directly on to the stairs. There is no barrier against the chi, which enters through the door and rushes through the house too quickly.

staircases

Often the front door of a house or apartment opens straight on to the staircase. Again the chi will be funnelled without having the chance to circulate so it is a good idea to block the view of the stairs by using a plant, a bookcase or other piece of furniture. If this is not possible, a round rug or a crystal chandelier will gather the chi in the hall. A wind chime which sounds as the door opens will also help to slow down the chi.

Some attention should be paid to how staircases and hallways are lit and decorated. Low ceilings can feel restricting and make the moving of furniture difficult, and a steep stairwell causes problems when decorating, but overcoming these difficulties and making the best of your hall and staircase will pay off.

The staircase should be in proportion to the dimensions of the rest of the house. Steep stairs conduct chi too quickly. Modern conversions often have spiral staircases leading to the bedroom area. These are considered inauspicious in Feng Shui because they resemble a corkscrew through the home. Wrap some ivy or green silk around the staircase and make sure a light shines from top to bottom. Stairs with open treads allow the chi to escape. Place plants, real or symbolic, representing Wood energy underneath.

△ A large plant placed in this position makes all the difference to the flow of energy. It masks the corner of the stairs from view of the front door and slows down the chi.

CHI FLOW IMPROVEMENT IN A HALLWAY

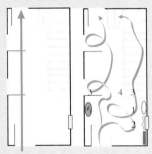

BEFORE   AFTER

1. Muslin curtains create a pause between the outside and the house.
2. Hooks and racks for coats and umbrellas block the view of the stairs from the door and hide outer garments from the inside.
3. At the foot of the stairs a mirror reflects a plaster plate with a painted landscape, which has the effect of drawing visitors deeper into the house.
4. The bottom of the stairs becomes part of the energy flow, instead of being bypassed, so there isn't an inevitable rush to the kitchen by people coming in.

Living rooms

A living room is used for a number of activities – for relaxation, as a family room where games are played, and an entertainment room for watching television and playing music. In some homes, particularly in apartments, the living room may have a dining area attached, or part of it may be used as a study or office space. The arrangement of the room is therefore important if these diverse functions are to be supported successfully.

▽ **Natural materials, lots of colour and a pleasant view give this living room an energetic feeling.**

Living areas should be welcoming, and the colour scheme can help this. Proportion is also important. In barn or warehouse conversions with large open-plan spaces and high ceilings, it is preferable to create small groupings of furniture rather than attempt to create a single room within the space. In small rooms, try to keep bookcases and built-in wall units low, otherwise the room will feel top-heavy and appear to close in.

It is especially important to be able to screen off study or office areas so that work is not constantly preying on the mind when we are trying to relax.

seating

Living rooms are inevitably yin spaces full of comfortable, fabric-covered seats which also represent yin. Chairs and sofas with high backs and arms are protective and represent the Tortoise, Dragon, Tiger formation offering support to those who sit in them. A footstool nearby marks the Phoenix position.

Those sitting in the room should, where possible, not sit with their backs to the door. Guests should feel welcome when they come, so offer them the prime positions facing the door. In rooms where chairs and sofas are not backed by a wall,

▷ All these chairs are supportive, adding to the peaceful energy of this elegant room.

create stability behind the seating by placing a table or bookcase there. It is always best if furniture has round edges rather than pointed. If the bedroom leads off the main living area, make sure that the furniture is not sending a 'poison arrow' into the room from a corner. Keep doors from a living room closed.

BACKS TO THE DOOR

If you have a visitor who does more than their fair share of the talking, position them with their back to the door to reduce their dominance. Uninvited guests who you would like to leave as soon as possible should also be placed outside the main group.

△ In this living room the yellow Earth colour on the walls and lamps is welcoming, but the blue Water energy drains it.

▽ Plenty of Earth colours on the walls and in the furnishing fabrics make this a nurturing and cosy living room.

SEATING ARRANGEMENTS

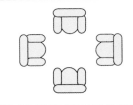

△ This seating arrangement is suitable for a harmonious family or social gathering. The 'circle' is used in all cultures for community gatherings.

▷ In this arrangement the table is sending a 'poison arrow' into the bedroom. Re-position the furniture to prevent this.

▽ The television arrangement spells death to social chat and family unity.

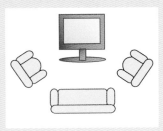

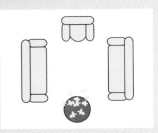

△ This arrangement is useful for a meeting or important discussion, as it focuses people on whatever is taking place, but also has space to allow the energy in.

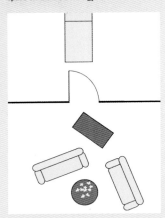

fireplaces

In previous centuries fires were used for cooking, warmth and protection, and were carefully tended. The communal fire was the focal point of family life. These days a real fire is less common, and when it is present it is often a secondary heat source, lit only at festival times or at weekends, rather than a vital source of life. A coal or wood fire, however, always makes a room feel welcoming and draws family and friends towards it.

Since a fireplace is an opening into the room, a mirror above it is beneficial to symbolically prevent the chi from escaping. A fireguard will be necessary, especially where there are children. Plants positioned on either side of the fireplace represent Wood energy, which will symbolically feed the fire and enhance its gathering qualities.

The chimney wall often juts into the living room, creating alcoves on either side. Be aware of this when placing chairs as people sitting in them may be the recipients of harmful chi from the corners. Soften any jutting angles on the mantelpiece with hanging plants.

lighting

A variety of lighting is necessary, particularly if the room is used for a number of purposes. Bright lighting is required for family activities and for children playing, and also in north-facing rooms which get

△ A cosy living area has been created in the middle of this vast space.

little natural light. In addition, there should be softer lights; uplighters in the corners or wall lights, and task lighting if there is a desk in the room.

screens

Ideally, kitchens and dining rooms should be separated in some way from the living room. Where they are linked, screen them off with sliding doors, or a curtain, or food will become too important and grazing habits will be encouraged.

▽ A larger sofa would give more support in this well-proportioned room.

A BALANCE OF LIGHT

△ Here the blue (Water) energy is overpowering the green (Wood) energy and the red (Fire) energy.

△ The red lamp makes an enormous difference, restoring the balance of the various energies in the room.

△ The additional colours and the mixture of
whites turn this into a warm room.

televisions and stereos

Always arrange the seating so that it does
not allow the television to be the main
focus of the room. Where the TV is the
focal point, instead of a warm, gathering
fire, the family will sit in rows and communication will be negligible. (However,
this is better than each child having a television in their bedroom, which can result
in a total breakdown of the social aspects
of family life.) Position stereos as far away
from seating as possible to avoid electromagnetic radiation.

accessories

If the living room is painted in a single
colour, small areas of stimulation are necessary to keep the energy moving. Too
much fabric can harbour dust and fade,
creating stagnant energy, but curtains do
help to create a cosy feeling. Undressed
windows or windows with blinds can be
harsh and, being rectangular, add to the
Earth energy of the room. In rooms that
have many rectangular features and are also
decorated in Earth colours the energy will
feel sluggish and can make the occupants
feel depressed. Keep family rooms well-
ventilated and allow in as much natural
light as possible.

◁ A small television set is far better for the
family's social interaction than a large set that
will dominate the room.

▷ Natural materials and fresh colour give this
room a good feel.

paintings and objects

We should always be aware of the effect of the images with which we surround ourselves, since they reflect our inner selves. Gruesome images and spiky objects can reflect inner turmoil, whereas bells, rainbows and pictures of the seasons will reflect inner peace. If we live alone our living rooms will reflect our desire for a peaceful haven or our need for companionship and we can use the space to create positive atmospheres.

Images and artwork displayed in family spaces should be cheerful and reflect pleasant and harmonious themes. Ideally, photographs of the family should be displayed in this room. If one child is more artistically talented than the others, in the interests of family harmony, his/her achievements should not be spread all round the room or the other children will feel that they are failures by comparison. Guns, swords and other weapons have no place in the living room.

It is important that the contents of the home, especially the communal areas, should be balanced and reflect the lives of all the occupants. If our working lives are hectic, our living rooms will reflect our desire for a peaceful haven. Lonely people should, however, use this room to reflect their need for companionship and remove all single images – such as pictures of lone figures; ornaments should be grouped in

△ This is a room designed for sitting and chatting. The round table ensures the conversation will not get too serious.

▽ We should surround ourselves with positive images. The clean lines of this carved wooden bird make the energy soar.

▽ This oval urn prevents stagnation in an otherwise gloomy corner.

LIVING ROOM CLUTTER

Newspapers and magazines
Full ashtrays
Used cups
Children's toys after bedtime
Fallen plant leaves
Unpaid bills and unanswered letters on the mantelpiece

pairs, and the room should be used to create a positive energy.

Where we share our homes with friends, with a partner, or as part of a family, we need to create personal spaces within which we feel comfortable and where we can express ourselves. Relationships with those whose horoscopes or numbers conflict with our own are common and we will be familiar with the phrase 'opposites attract'. Formulae may suggest, however, that one partner should live in an east group house and the other a west group house. We have to be practical. Where the energies of a house favour one occupant more than the other, it is important to take this into account and enable the other to express themselves within the house and to position themselves in favourable directions in bed and when working and relaxing.

▷ **We should position ourselves in favourable directions surrounded by supportive images.**

CASE STUDY

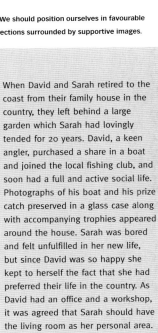

When David and Sarah retired to the coast from their family house in the country, they left behind a large garden which Sarah had lovingly tended for 20 years. David, a keen angler, purchased a share in a boat and joined the local fishing club, and soon had a full and active social life. Photographs of his boat and his prize catch preserved in a glass case along with accompanying trophies appeared around the house. Sarah was bored and felt unfulfilled in her new life, but since David was so happy she kept to herself the fact that she had preferred their life in the country. As David had an office and a workshop, it was agreed that Sarah should have the living room as her personal area.

1. Sarah, a Water Rooster, was being overwhelmed by too much water. A large plant in the North symbolically drained some of the Water energy.

2. Born in 1934, Sarah's magic number is 3, making her best direction south, so the seating was arranged accordingly.

3. David's fishing trophies and photographs were placed in his study and, since she did not want to hurt his feelings but did not like having dead animals in the house, Sarah compromised and suggested that the prize fish could go into the bathroom and not be banished to the workshop. Sarah framed some watercolours she had painted at their former home and hung them on the wall instead.

4. To dispel the idea that this was to be Sarah's lot for the rest of her retirement, and particularly since the windows faced west and the setting sun, the growth energy of the east was stimulated with a picture of the rising sun.

5. A mirror placed in the south-east, also representing Wood, reflected the garden and drew it into the house to

support Sarah's love of and affinity to the countryside.

6. After reading a Feng Shui book, Sarah decided to try to activate the Relationships area to see if she could find new friends. Using the Symbolic Bagua, she put up a poster of a group of people chatting, which was also reflected in the mirror, thus doubling the effect.

When the changes had been made, a neighbour visited and admired Sarah's watercolours and suggested she should sell them. With the money Sarah bought a greenhouse where she now grows exotic plants which she paints portraits of and sells. Interestingly, the picture of the rising sun is, according to the Symbolic Bagua, in Sarah's Offspring or Projects area. She has made lots of friends and has a full and busy life.

Dining rooms

△ This wonderful dining room has a lovely view of the garden. Small shelves would protect diners from the axe-like glass overhead.

The dining room is a social area where family and friends can meet, talk and enjoy good food together. As snacking and 'grazing' typify modern eating habits, the dining room has diminished in importance. For the Chinese it is a centre of wealth, where a full table, often mirrored to apparently double the quantity, is indicative of the financial standing of the family.

Dining room colours should be bright and stimulating to whet the appetite. Dull,

▷ If there is a window behind the dining table, it is important that the chairs have backs to them for support.

lifeless colours should be avoided as they suppress the appetite. Lighting should be chosen with care to complement the food and not cast shadows over the table. Candles can be romantic, but may get in the way when people are serving themselves or become irritating if they are too tall or flicker. Beware of pictures and ornaments that conjure up inappropriate images – hunting scenes or a china pig collection are not suitable if you have vegetarian

△ A lovely setting for a meal. The candles are low enough not to get in the way or prevent people seeing each other properly.

▽ An excellent dining room – the chairs are backed by a wall and the mirror reflects the table, doubling its apparent size.

△ Kitchen diners make a good setting for an informal meal, and round tables are ideal as they encourage lively conversation.

▷ Low candles such as these pretty shell candles are safer than tall ones at the table.

friends. The best images to display are ones of fruit, landscapes, or of peope dining. If mirrors are used, position them so that diners will not feel uncomfortable.

High-backed solid chairs, preferably with arms, represent the supportive Tortoise, Tiger, Dragon formation. Sitting positions are considered to be very important. The prime positions in the room have a solid wall behind them and a view of the door. The most vulnerable positions are those with a door behind them, followed by seats with their backs to a window.

Table shapes are also important and can affect the quality of the meal. Round tables tend to make your guests leave early because the chi spins round them, while square tables allow more stability. Rectangular tables are difficult as those at either end tend to feel left out. The best shaped tables are octagonal, which not only enable guests to interact with everyone else on the table, but also represent the Cosmos as reflected in the Bagua.

balanced eating

Much has been made of balanced eating recently but this is not a new concept. Since ancient times, diet has formed part of the same philosophy as Feng Shui. Meals are planned to create a yin-yang balance and with the nature of the Five Elements in mind. Some foods are regarded as having yin qualities and some yang, and different tastes are associated with the Five Elements.

We should learn to recognize the signals that our bodies and our state of mind give out and recognize whether we are becoming yin (feeling tired and slowing down) or yang (unable to relax and stressed). Once we have developed our awareness we can concentrate on maintaining a balance in our diets by ensuring we eat the same proportion of yin foods – such as alcohol, citrus fruits, chocolate,

△ With proper ventilation and heating, conservatory dining rooms can create light, spacious areas for eating in all the year round.

◁ In such a large area as this your guests might feel slightly ill-at-ease. High-backed chairs would help dispel any nervousness. A round table is a good shape for this room.

coffee and sugar – and yang foods – such as cheese, eggs, meat, pulses and salt.

Yin and yang attributes are attached to each of the Five Elements, and in Chinese medicine herbs and other remedies, including food, are recommended in order to maintain a healthy and balanced body. In northern countries (yin) there is a tendency and need to consume more cooked foods (yang) while in southerly areas (yang) more raw foods are consumed. Eating native products in season is highly recommended in Chinese medicine.

TASTES AND THE ELEMENTS

Wood	Fire	Earth	Metal	Water
spring	summer	late summer	autumn	winter
sour	bitter	sweet	pungent	salt
yin	yang	yin	yin	yang

THE BAGUA AND FAMILY SEATING

We have seen that each sector of the Bagua can represent several things. The sectors are associated with particular manifestations of the energy of one of the Five Elements – in its yin or yang form. Each also represents a certain type of energy reflecting a direction, season or time period. The Symbolic Bagua suggests the journey of life, with each sector representing a particular aspect – career, wealth, relationships and so on.

Here we look at the energies of each sector in terms of the family, using the Bagua in seating plans at the dining table. The diagram (right) shows the arrangement of family members around the Bagua. Each represents the energy of the direction they fall within, and this can add further insight into the qualities of the energy in that location. Bear in mind that we are looking at centuries-old imagery; house-husbands and executive mothers should appreciate that this is an energetic quality, not stereotyping.

FATHER: Representative of solidity, the leader and the head of the household. Sometimes called the Creative energy.
MOTHER: Complements the Father. A nurturing, supporting energy. Also known as Receptive energy.
ELDEST SON: Also known as the energy of Thunder and the Dragon, whose energy erupts from below and soars upwards.
ELDEST DAUGHTER: Called the Gentle energy, this energy is perceptive and supportive and represents growth.
MIDDLE SON: Sometimes called the Abysmal energy, which suggests hard work without much reward.
MIDDLE DAUGHTER: A Clinging energy, representing a fire, bright and impenetrable outside but burning-out and weakness within.
YOUNGEST SON: Also called the Mountain energy, suggesting a firm stillness and waiting.
YOUNGEST DAUGHTER: Also known as the Joyful, or the Lake, which suggests a deep inward energy or stubbornness and a weak, excitable exterior.

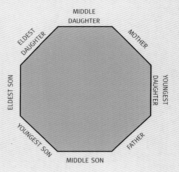

THE DINNER PARTY

This is an extreme example of using the Bagua, but it is included simply to show the potentially powerful effects. Imagine that an executive is retiring from your company and you and a rival are up for the job. You arrange a dinner party and invite your boss, your rival and an employee who you have taken under your wing. Using the Bagua to seat everyone will ensure that you get the job. Out of respect, the boss and his/her partner are in the prime positions. When the boss is not giving any attention to the spouse of your protégé (with his back thus turned to your rival) and is concentrating on eating, the people he/she sees when they look up are you, your partner, and your protégé. Your rival, seated in the worst position, representing hard toil for no reward, and his partner, are too far apart to support each other. The attention of the boss's spouse is taken up by the protégé's spouse, and your partner opposite. After several attempts at conversation, with no support, your rival's spouse gives up. The result is that you get the job, and your protégé moves into your shoes.

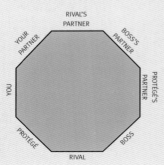

◁ Influence situations by using ancient interpretations of the energies of the Bagua.

▷ Whatever the occasion or intention a decorated table with well-presented, nourishing food will be supportive.

Kitchens

putting the principles into practice

The kitchen, perhaps the most important room in the house, is multi-functional, and therefore often the most difficult room to deal with. Apart from its primary purpose for storing, preparing and consuming food, it is a meeting place for family and friends, a children's play area and occasionally even an office. More than any other room, the kitchen holds clues to a person's lifestyle. As our health centre of our lives, and our home, it is important that it functions well and supports us.

The direction a kitchen faces has a powerful effect on its function. In ancient China, kitchens were open to the south-east to catch the breezes that would help ignite the cooking stove. This practical application of Feng Shui reflects the principle of living in harmony with nature. When we have discovered in which direction our kitchen lies, we can use 'The Relationships of the Five Elements' table to help us create balance.

A red kitchen facing south will be overloaded with yang Fire energy which needs to be drained. 'The Relationships of the Five Elements' table shows that Earth drains Fire, so incorporating a stone floor or some stone pots would be appropriate. As the Fire element is far too dominant, representation of the Water element in the form of a picture of water or a blue blind or tablecloth would also considerably lessen the effect. Plants would not be advisable here since they belong to the Wood element, which feeds

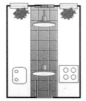

△ Left: Chi rushes through this kitchen, creating a feeling of discomfort.
Right: Ceiling lights and plants by the window slow down the chi and contain it.

△ Task lighting is ideal in kitchens. Here it gives focus in a high-ceilinged room, where other lights would cast shadows.

Fire and makes it stronger. In the case of all kitchens, the Fire element, represented by the cooker and electrical cooking appliances, is in conflict with Water, represented by actual water and the refrigerator. A delicate balance has to be maintained.

Some modern kitchens are so streamlined that everything is tucked away out of sight and nothing is on display. Since the major features consist of only one or two colours or materials, the kitchen can appear lifeless. Sometimes a dash of red, or a green plant can bring a room to life. Ideally, kitchens should contain something from each of the elements.

the stove

The cooker, or stove, is considered to be of great importance. Where possible, the energy source which flows into it, the electric socket or the gas pipe, should be in your most auspicious location. It is important not to feel vulnerable while standing at the stove. The reasoning behind this is that, since food is the prime source of nourishment and health for the family, it is important that the cook should not feel jumpy or the food will be spoiled through lack of concentration.

A reflective surface positioned behind the cooker, or a well positioned chrome cake tin or toaster nearby, will enable the cook to be aware of anyone entering the room. A wind chime or other sound device activated by the door opening will also serve the same purpose.

△ The kitchen stove is the heart of the home and should face in an auspicious direction.

△ If you cook with your back to the door, shiny objects can reflect the space behind you.

△ Keep your cooking area as clutter-free as possible.

chi flow in the kitchen

As elsewhere in the house, chi should be able to circulate freely round the kitchen. It cannot do this if the kitchen door is in direct line with the outside doors and windows since it is channelled straight through. If this is the case, you should aim to slow it down by physical or psychological barriers. The simplest method is to keep the door closed. Barriers could include freestanding shelves, vegetable trolleys or large plants. More subtle methods such as mobiles or lampshades hung from the ceiling, and colour can be used to create visual and psychological barriers. Barriers can be detrimental, however, and a tall fridge or cupboard by the door will block the flow of chi into the room.

Fast-moving chi is not the only problem. Stagnant chi is particularly harmful in a kitchen. It can occur in a room with

△ Smooth, rounded lines allow the chi to move gently around this lovely kitchen.

◁ In a kitchen where the chi flows straight out of the window, try placing some red glass bottles or ornaments, plants or another barrier on the windowsill to slow it down.

▽ Eye-level cupboards over the cooking area are oppressive; open shelves would be better.

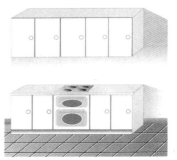

CASE STUDY

This typical modern kitchen has both good and bad points.

1. The cooker, sink and refrigerator are in an ideal triangle formation.

2. The corner of this work surface has been rounded off so there are no 'poison arrows' which otherwise would have pointed at the chairs.

3. The energy is not moving in this corner. A plant or mirror here will help to move the chi along.

4. The chairs have their backs to the door and are vulnerable. A large plant or vegetable basket would act as a barrier. Alternatively, the table and chairs could move out of the corner so the door is visible from each chair.

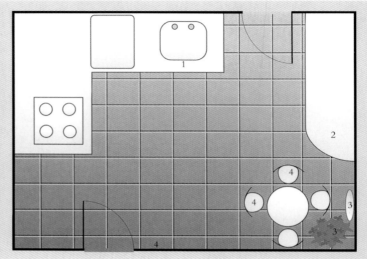

no window and poor circulation, or in a room with dark inaccessible corners. One cause of this is having too much furniture in the room, which impedes movement. If we bump into a table each time we need

KITCHEN CLUTTER

Rotting fruit and vegetables
Out-of-date packets and jars
Unlabelled boxes in the freezer
Unused gadgets
Rarely used electrical appliances
Over-full waste bins
Odd pieces of crockery
Plastic bags
Bits of string
Laundry
Crumbs
Fallen plant leaves
Things which 'might come in handy'

to get to the refrigerator our body chi will not flow as it should because we are forever twisting to avoid it. At the end of a long day, a ready-made meal may seem an easier option than dodging the furniture to obtain fresh ingredients from the

refrigerator. Rather than put things away, we may leave out milk bottles and food, which can have health risks as well as cluttering up the kitchen.

Piles of newspapers, overflowing rubbish bins, crumbs and stains on work surfaces all represent stagnant chi. Another undesirable feature of many apartment kitchens is the cat-litter tray. Bathrooms and toilets are not desirable near a kitchen because of the antipathy of the Water element to the Fire element of the kitchen, as well as for more obvious reasons. If we take trouble with the location of our own toilets and bathrooms, we should also give serious thought to those of our pets.

Pointed corners are a feature of most kitchens – the edges of appliances, the corners of work surfaces, knives, shelf edges and the edges of slatted blinds all send out chi that makes us feel uncomfortable. Knives should be kept out of sight in a drawer, and work surfaces should have rounded edges, if possible. Among the worst sources of this inauspicious chi, known as 'poison arrows', are wall cupboards, which even when shut can be oppressive. There is a tendency to store far too much in the kitchen – out-of-date jars,

gadgets we never use taking up valuable surface space, a dinner service we only bring out on special occasions or when the person who gave it to us visits. If we examine the contents of the kitchen, we will probably be able to throw out or relocate many items to give us more space and enable the chi to flow. There are many useful storage systems available which help us to make optimum use of the space.

▽ **Efficient storage systems reduce kitchen clutter; review the contents regularly.**

△ **Waist-high cupboards by a work surface are preferable to overhead ones, which can be oppressive, especially in a small kitchen. Keep any frequently used equipment to hand and store cooking equipment, rather than crockery or food, inside cupboards that are adjacent to an oven.**

the healthy kitchen

Kitchens appeal to all our senses. Magazine pictures tantalizingly portray them as rooms featuring bowls of fresh fruit and views over lawns and flower beds. Healthy, freshly prepared meals can be seen on tables where friends and family gather to socialize. Delicious smells, tastes, merry sounds, abundance and happiness radiate from these pages but the reality is often different. Modern kitchens, far from supporting and stimulating us, can unbalance and affect us negatively. The noise from kitchen gadgets, the contamination of food by substances used in packaging, dangers posed by the cleaning agents we use on our work surfaces, the chemicals used in food production, all serve to assault our senses and diminish our wellbeing.

△ **There is plenty of Wood element in this country-style kitchen, which provides excellent levels of energy.**

CASE STUDY

Mary's kitchen was dark and oppressive. The small area in front was a particular problem because the staircase formed a deep slope, and the space on the left was too narrow for conventional units. The main area felt claustrophobic, with work surfaces and wall cupboards sending out chi in the form of 'poison arrows'. The cooker could not be moved to face Mary's best direction but this was considered secondary to getting the chi flow right.

1. Red, yellow and green opaque glass was used in the south-facing door and window overlooking a brick wall to stimulate the south Fire element. The light coming through the glass sent a rainbow effect into the room which stimulated the chi there.

2. The plants on the windowsill were placed to stimulate the Wood element of the East.

3. The work triangle is in place, so there is no conflict between the Fire and Water elements.

4. Pale yellow cupboards and a terracotta container in the north-east introduced the Earth element.

5. Stainless steel pans hung in the north-west stimulate the Metal area.

6. Cupboards were used to make the oddly shaped room regular. The one on the right was built over and around the washing machine and drier. Glass doors were put in front of the window to enable the coloured light to shine in. Mary placed her china collection on glass shelves here.

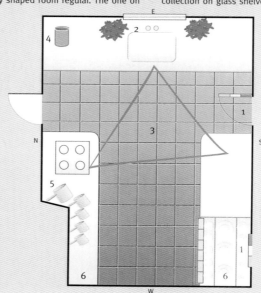

Bedrooms

The bedroom is considered to be one of the most important rooms of the house in Feng Shui. Adults spend a third of their lives in bed, while children and teenagers often spend even more than this. We must therefore be certain that the rooms we sleep in are suitable for relaxing and regenerating us, as well as for encouraging romance in our lives.

beds

A bed should face in one of our auspicious directions, which means that the top of our heads should point that way when we are lying down. Where partners have different auspicious directions, there has to be a compromise; for example, if the house is a West group house and favours one partner, then the bed direction should favour the other.

The best bed position is diagonally opposite the door. The element of surprise is never recommended in the bedroom. If the occupants of the bed do not have a reasonable view of the door, a mirror should be placed to reflect anyone entering. Having the foot of the bed in direct line with the door is known as the 'mortuary position' in China because coffins are placed in that position when awaiting collection.

Doors and windows situated opposite each other are not considered auspicious. If a line of chi between two windows – or a door and a window – crosses the bed, it is thought to cause illness.

△ Four-poster beds can be claustrophobic if they have heavy wood and elaborate fabric canopies and drapes, but this elegant bamboo bed without any excess curtaining gives a very light effect.

▽ The symmetry of the tables and lamps at each side of this bed is perfect. Each side of the bed should have identical furnishings.

▽ Here the view of the garden is auspicious, but less spiky ornaments behind the bed would be better for relaxation.

▽ This soft, dreamy room is very restful. Do not have too many books in the bedroom as they are mentally stimulating.

furnishings

Images in the bedroom should be in pairs, particularly in the Relationships corner of the room. Images of a solitary figure in a single person's bedroom indicate loneliness, as does a single bed. It is possible to feel isolated and insecure within a marriage. If this is the case, hang a picture of a couple on the wall and display pairs of objects. Photographs of parents, children or friends have no place in a couple's bedroom.

Mirrors in the bedroom should not face the bed. The Chinese believe that the soul leaves the body as we sleep and will be disconcerted to come across itself in the

△ Headboards offer support and this magnificent carved wooden headboard is a particularly fine example.

▽ This is an attractive bedroom but the mirror should not reflect the bed. En suite bathrooms are not recommended either.

Ideally, beds should be raised off the floor with enough space for air to circulate underneath. Storage drawers full of old clothes and crates of old magazines and other items stored beneath them create a stagnant chi which is not desirable.

Beds should be made of natural materials which can breathe. Wood is the usual choice although bamboo is also used. People belonging to the Metal element often favour metal beds. Since metal conducts heat and electricity, be very careful to keep electrical equipment and heaters away from the bed. Water beds are not recommended because they cause conflict between Fire and Water, as well as creating instability while we sleep.

Headboards offer support but should always be tightly secured. They represent the Tortoise position, and as such, should be higher than the Phoenix, or the footboard. Beds should be backed by a wall, not a window, which feels insecure and can let in draughts.

Where a double bed is in a confined space and one occupant has to climb over the other to get in or out, harmony will not prevail. The best position for a bed is with a wall behind and enough room on either side for a small table or cupboard. These bedside tables or cabinets should always be symmetrically balanced at either side; one will not do.

CASE STUDY

Although Joe and Amy had a comfortable house, lovely children and were blessed in all aspects of their lives, they revealed separately that they felt lonely and isolated. A look at their bedroom revealed all. On a shelf opposite the bed sat a TV, video and stereo system. Joe enjoyed watching videos in bed and waking up to his favourite rock bands. Amy disliked Joe's choice of videos and her collection of self-improvement books on relationships and stress sat on the next shelf. On the top shelf were photos of the children, and a box of toys for when they came in early in the morning was on the bottom shelf. On the walls to either side of Joe and Amy's bed were wistful images of a solitary man and a solitary woman. Following the Feng Shui consultation, the toys were removed to the children's rooms, where they were encouraged to play on waking. The two pictures were placed side by side, where the wistful gaze could turn into a lustful glance, and the TV, video and stereo were relocated. Joe is no longer worried that Amy is miserable and unfulfilled as she no longer has need of her books.

△ A dressing room is ideal as it frees the bedroom for rest and romance.

mirror. A modern interpretation might be that most of us are not at our best in the mornings and would not want our tousled image to be the first thing we see on waking. It would be much better to see a picture of the sun rising or a fresh green landscape. Street lights outside the room can also create reflective images in a mirror, which may disturb us when we are half-asleep. In contrast, strategically placed mirrors facing a wonderful view will draw it into the room.

The bedroom should not become a storage area or an office, nor serve any function other than romance and sleep. If you have space in your house, dressing rooms are ideal since they remove most extraneous things from the bedroom. Most bedrooms, however, contain wardrobes and drawer space. Keeping these clear of clutter means we can close them easily and make sure we have plenty of room to hang up our clothes. Garments strewn over chairs constitute clutter, and worry us as we know we will have to deal with them eventually. The worst form of storage is an overhead cupboard linking wardrobes on either side of the bed. This acts in the same way as a beam and can leave those under it feeling vulnerable. The same applies to anything hanging over the bed.

electrical equipment

Electrical equipment in the bedroom is not desirable for two reasons. First, it detracts from the main functions of the room.

▽ The beam over this double bed symbolically divides the couple occupying the bed.

CLUTTER IN THE BEDROOM

Pill bottles
Cosmetics
Used tissues
Piles of clothes
Old unworn clothes and shoes
Full waste bins
Piles of unread books
Notebooks and work
Mobile phones
TVs and music systems

morning and are more punctual for work when they are forced to get out of bed to turn off the alarm.

It is surprising how many people have telephones sitting on bed-side tables. They should not be there, they have no place in a bedroom as they prevent relaxation, especially if late night social calls are common. The best place for mobile phones outside office hours is in a briefcase, switched off; everyone is entitled to some time for themselves.

▷ A harp has been placed in the Wealth corner of this room to counteract the sloping wall and lift the energy of the room.

Secondly, the harmful electromagnetic waves that are generated can have an adverse effect on those sleeping there. Ionizers positioned close to a bed present the most serious threat, but even clock radios send out waves over a considerable distance.

Electric blankets are a real problem because they encase the bed in an electromagnetic field. They should be unplugged from the wall before anyone gets into bed. All electrical items should be on the opposite side of the room from the bed, and this includes electrical clocks. One advantage of this is that it makes the snooze button redundant. People find more time to eat a proper breakfast in the

▽ Cramped spaces under slanting walls are not recommended in Feng Shui as they restrict the flow of chi.

BED POSITIONS

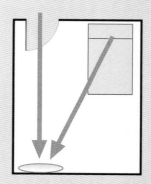

1. If the bed is positioned so that the occupant cannot see who is entering, place a mirror opposite the door.

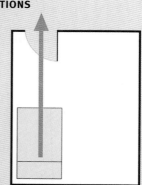

2. When the foot of the bed is in direct line with the door, it is known in China as the 'mortuary position'.

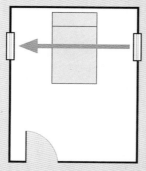

3. A line of harmful chi crosses this bed from two facing windows.

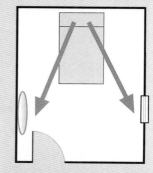

4. A mirror opposite a window can draw in wonderful views.

The nursery

Medical research has shown that pollutants in decorating materials and furniture may be responsible for breathing difficulties and cot deaths in susceptible babies. Decorate the room for a new baby as long as possible before it is due and air the room thoroughly. If this cannot be done, put the baby in the parents' room until the smell of fresh paint has disappeared. Decorating materials should be manufactured from natural products and cot bedding preferably made from natural untreated fibres.

stimulating the senses

We can help small children to distinguish colours and shapes by providing them with suitable stimulation. A mobile hung above the foot of a baby's cot will keep it fascinated for a long time and provide comfort before it falls asleep. Do not place one directly over the head of the baby as this can be threatening.

Very small children could be suffocated if furry toy animals fall on their faces so keep these out of the cot but place them where the baby can see them, perhaps on

▷ This is a bright, cheerful room with plenty of stimulation for a baby.

▽ Bright colours and shapes give lots of visual appeal during the day.

▽ A chalkboard gives a child scope for freedom of expression.

▽ This large chest will take many toys and keep the room free from clutter.

△ This first bed for a young child has a canopy to keep it cosy.

△ Brightly decorated furnishings in this bedroom lift the energy in a dark corner.

a nearby shelf. A bright wall frieze can also occupy a baby's attention, as can a large colourful poster.

Sound can be introduced in a number of ways. Fractious babies who do not sleep well may be soothed by taped music, and the sound of voices from a radio may help the insecure to fall asleep. Musical mobiles can be useful in lulling a baby to sleep, but they might be disturbed if you have to keep rewinding the mobile. Babies soon learn to do things themselves and the look of wonder on its face as a child discovers it can make something happen is magical. By tying bells and rattles to the bars of the cot we help the child on its way to independence, but these are best not left in the cot at night or they will disturb its sleep.

The sense of touch is stimulated by numerous textures – furry, soft, hard and smooth. Allow your child access to a variety of experiences but secure playthings to the cot or you will be forever picking them up from the floor. Do not be tempted to introduce manufactured smells to small children as they are too strong. The familiar smell of a mother or well-loved teddy is far better. At teething time, ensure that all materials which can be put into the mouth conform to safety standards and that cot paint is lead-free.

possible hazards

Pets can be a problem if they snuggle up to the baby for warmth or become jealous of the attention it receives from the parents. Suitable safety precautions should be taken inside the home as soon as the baby

is born. As children begin to crawl, and later to walk and climb, parents need to ensure that all fires and electrical sockets are securely covered, that windows are secure and that stairs have barriers at the top and the bottom.

▽ Wood energy, symbolized by the frieze of trees, suits the growing child, who needs to be allowed freedom of expression.

Children's rooms

Bedrooms for children can be a challenge as they often need to fulfil two functions – sleep and play. Although parents aim to ensure that sleep takes place at night and play during the day, a look at some children's rooms indicates why they do not always get it the right way round as there is no division between the two. Children's rooms should also support them and their needs as they grow. Where a room is shared, each child should have a private space within it that they feel is their own.

The energy of the east with the rising sun in the morning is ideal for children. The west with the setting sun at night is good for hyperactive children who cannot settle, although this direction is normally better for elderly people to sleep in.

▽ Plenty of storage space means that toys can be neatly stacked away.

The heads of beds should face their supportive directions, although this is not always possible when there is more than one child in the room. It is more important that they should feel safe, and a view of the door is essential for children. Rooms with dark corners which house strange shapes and cast shadows on the walls can prove disturbing for young children with vivid imaginations.

beds

Wooden beds are preferable because they do not pick up electromagnetic radiation. Bunk beds are not considered suitable since they depress the chi, both of the child on top who is close to the ceiling and the one underneath who has a body above, often a fidgety one. Canopies over the bed have the same effect and can also harbour dust. Cupboards and beams can also have a

△ A stark, but restful child's room. The bed would be better backed by the wall.

debilitating effect. Children's beds should have a headboard and should not back on to a window or a door.

decoration

As children grow, mentally as well as physically, part of the learning process is to be able to make choices. Children instinctively know the type of energy they require to support them and should be

CLUTTER IN CHILDREN'S ROOMS

Broken, irreparable toys
Outgrown toys
Books they never look at
Outgrown clothes
Dry felt-tip pens
Games and jigsaw puzzles with pieces missing

△ **A reassuring first bed for a young child, as the canopy offers protection.**

isolate them from their families and hamper their social interaction outside. Apart from this consideration, the electromagnetic radiation from TVs and computers is a cause for concern in children's bedrooms, particularly as these rooms are often quite small and so confine the electro-pollution. Where possible, keep all electrical items out of children's rooms and relocate them in other areas such as family rooms or playrooms.

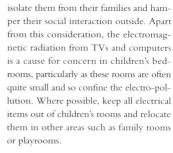

▽ **Low windows can create a fear of falling, the puppet theatre here acts as a screen.**

allowed to design their own bedrooms and have a major say in the decoration and colours, even if it is not to the parents' taste. We can always shut the door and we should respect it when it is shut. Children need their privacy as we do and if we set an example by knocking and asking permission to enter, then we can expect the same in return.

If there is a family room or playroom elsewhere, then excessive stimulation in the form of toys should not be a problem in the bedroom. Where the room serves a dual purpose, create a separate sleeping area and provide storage for toys to be put away out of sight at night.

furnishings

If the floor is hard, a soft rug by the bed is welcoming in the morning and will give a gentle start to the day. Furniture with curved corners helps to prevent minor accidents. If your child has chosen the colours themselves, you can select shades

and hues to suit the child's personality – cooler ones to balance an active child and brighter ones to stimulate a more reticent personality.

It is disturbing how many children, even very small ones, have their own television sets in their rooms as this must inevitably

▽ **A child's room should give her or him the space and facility to read and be creative.**

Teenagers' rooms

Teenagers' rooms are evolving places where children who are growing into adults can express themselves – their happiness, their loves, their hurts and their anger. The latter may be directed against us if we attempt to curb their individuality and try to impose our personalities and values on the private space that will nurture them through to adulthood.

The needs and the tastes of a 13-year-old are very different from those of a 17- or 18-year-old, and some aspects of the room may be changed on almost an annual basis to reflect this. Some principles will remain constant, however. We can introduce our child to the basic principles of Feng Shui and persuade them to place

△ The high, sloping ceilings in this attic room do not impinge on this modern room.

▽ This is a pretty room for a young teenage girl beginning to move away from childhood.

their beds in an auspicious position and think about colour and the flow of chi around their rooms. These principles may help them as they grow into the some of the trials of being a teenager.

Older teenagers' rooms are multi-functional and usually act as bedroom, study, sitting room and entertainment area for them and their friends. It is no wonder

TEENAGE CLUTTER
Food wrappings
Unwashed clothes
Overflowing waste bins
Do not touch anything else
in a teenager's private space

△ Black and white – a bold colour choice – is popular with teenagers.

that their occupants sometimes become confused. Teenagers need our support when they ask for it, even though they do not welcome unsolicited advice. They require their own space, physically and intellectually, but they also need positive affirmation from adults. Hold out against a television in the bedroom and encourage the use of family rooms. A computer in the study will draw teenagers out of their bedrooms.

▽ The bright decor and pretty feel of this room might not suit an older teenager.

Marie, aged 16, was going through an 'awkward' phase. Her mother, Ella, struggled to get her out of bed in the mornings to catch the one bus guaranteed to get her to school on time. Every morning was a battle, and resentment festered throughout the day and affected family harmony in the evening. Homework was left undone and Marie's studies were suffering.

A Metal Ox, Marie could be stubborn and, although a girl of few words, she occasionally exploded. Her arrogant manner irritated her father, a Fire Ox, who didn't take kindly to being opposed or to Marie's surliness. He became impatient with his wife, an Earth Goat, who knew Marie needed support and was torn between them in arguments.

Ella decided to take action and offered to redecorate Marie's bedroom and let her choose the decor. Marie chose purple for her room and Ella, who knew purple to be stimulating for the mind and good for raising self-esteem, agreed.

1. Marie chose a multi-coloured bead curtain for the window.

2. They turned her bed around so that she could see the curtain.

3. Ella removed the old square bedside table, since the square shape symbolizes containment, and bought a round one.

4. The alarm clock was placed on Marie's desk so she no longer had access to the snooze button and had to get up to turn it off.

5. To go on the new round table Ella gave Marie a framed photograph showing the family boarding a plane to go on holiday; this energized the 'Family' area of the Bagua.

6. Taking a chance, Ella purchased two huge silk sunflowers and suggested they would look lovely in the top right-hand corner of the room – the Earth 'Relationships' area of the Bagua represented by the magic number 2.

Now when Ella calls Marie in the morning, she draws the blind and opens the window slightly so the bead curtain moves and tinkles, stimulating the chi. When the alarm rings later Marie has to get out of bed to turn it off, but she is already awake. Family harmony has been restored and they meet on friendly terms more often. Feng Shui is a mixture of common sense and psychology as well as harnessing unseen forces of the universe.

483

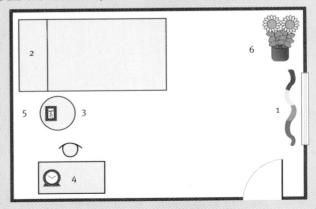

Bathrooms

The position of the bathroom is considered to be important in Feng Shui because water is synonymous with wealth, and thus the disposal of waste water symbolizes the dispersal of the family fortune. Changing climatic conditions have highlighted how precious a commodity water is, and that measures should be taken not to waste it. Conservationists recommend saving water from baths and sinks to water gardens. Dripping taps are symbolic of wealth running away. When we consider that a dripping tap, leaking at a rate of one drip per second, wastes 1,000 litres (264 gallons) per year, we can see the sense in applying ancient rules to modern problems. Baths and sinks that have clogged up plugholes and waste outlets, apart from being a constant source of irritation, can also be a health risk so it is important that we fix them as soon as possible.

△ This spacious and opulently decorated bathroom, although well-appointed, is free from any unnecessary clutter.

▽ There won't be any need for morning queues for the family that enjoys this large, well-equipped, and airy bathroom.

position

Bathrooms should be positioned well away from the front door as this is not an image we want visitors to our homes to subconsciously take away. It is most important not to have bathrooms close to kitchens for health reasons, but they should also be away from dining and sitting areas so that guests won't be embarrassed to use them.

toilets

It is not desirable to see the toilet on entering the bathroom and, if possible, it should be situated where it is hidden from view. Screens can be utilized or the toilet positioned behind the door. Toilet doors should be closed and the seat closed.

Bathrooms are considered to be linked to the body's plumbing system, so a large bathroom using too much water can lead to health problems concerned with evacuation, while cramped bathrooms are connected with restriction in bodily functions. Large bathrooms are also associated with vanity and perhaps an excessive obsession with cleanliness, whereas small

bathrooms are restricting and can cause accidents as people manoeuvre round.

mirrors and cabinets

The use of mirrors can give the illusion of more space. Generally, mirrors opposite each other are not considered to be auspicious in Feng Shui because they conjure up an image of constant movement away from the self, with no grounding influences. However, unless we spend a vast amount of time in front of the bathroom

▽ Use plants and coloured towels to balance the Water element in a bathroom.

△ Screens can be used to hide the bathroom from an entrance or en suite bedroom.

▷ The reflective materials in this bathroom help to counteract its heavy ceiling. A large plant or dash of colour would also help.

▽ Curvy, watery lines and Metal shapes work well in this unusual bathroom.

mirror, this is acceptable if it improves the suggestion of space. Mirror tiles are not recommended, or those which in any way cut the image. Fixed mirrors are preferred to those which jut out from walls and normal mirrors are preferred to magnifying mirrors that distort the image.

Bathroom cabinets are places where stagnant chi can easily accumulate. Most cosmetics have a limited shelf life and many cabinets contain items dating back years. There is a limit to the number of eye baths, tweezers and combs that are required in a lifetime.

en suite bathrooms

The growing trend to have en suite bathrooms attached to bedrooms is not in accordance with Feng Shui rules. Where possible, create a separate room for the toilet or else make sure the bathroom area in the bedroom has an efficient and well-maintained ventilation system. En suite bathrooms that have been built into the bedroom often leave the room in an L-shape with a corner of the bathroom jutting into the bedroom, so action needs to be taken to ensure that this does not point at the bed.

CLUTTER IN THE BATHROOM

Full waste bins
Empty bottles and toothpaste tubes
Unnecessary soap dishes
Unpolished mirrors
Out-of-date medication
Untried cosmetic samples
Bath oils and perfumes that
are never used

△ A good balance of natural materials with the right colours, elements and plants raises the energy in this bathroom.

▷ Keep any clutter in the bathroom down to its absolute minimum, and keep any soap dishes or holders clean and unclogged.

relaxation

Very few of us find the time to relax sufficiently and this often affects our health, both physical and mental. The bathroom is one of the few places where we can escape from the world and be alone. Bathrooms should be decorated so as to enable us to wind down at the end of a busy day, or allow us some peaceful moments in the morning.

irritability and to create a peaceful mood. The bath is an ideal place for self-massage while taking a bath or having just had one. Try stroking one of these oils towards the heart to stimulate the circulation.

Taoists consider that the nutrition we receive from the air when we breathe is more valuable to us than food and water. As we inhale we draw in energy, which provides energy; when we exhale, we cleanse and detoxify our bodies. The art of breathing properly has been part of the Chinese health regime for centuries, and is based on internally balancing yin and yang and creating the correct chi flow within the body. It is thought that illness occurs when the correct chi flow is not maintained. Use your time in the bathroom, especially during long baths, to practise controlled breathing.

Meditation is another very effective relaxation technique. The Chinese call it 'sitting still and doing nothing', which is a deceptively simple description of an art that can take years of practice to perfect. Whether our aim is to reflect on the day or to let our minds wander freely and wind down, the bathroom is the ideal place.

△ An ideal bathroom – it would be difficult to resist rushing home to relax in this at the end of a hard day.

▷ The huge mirror doubles the space in this elegant bathroom. A frame to the top and bottom would contain the chi.

The colours we use to decorate the bathroom affect how we feel there. Blue is a soothing colour, associated with serenity and contemplation. Colour therapists believe that it lowers the blood pressure, promotes deeper exhalation and induces sleep. Green, on the other hand, rests the eyes and calms the nerves. Whatever colours we choose, we can create a space to relax and soothe ourselves by playing gentle music and by adding a few drops of essential oils to the bathwater. Bergamot, lavender and geranium alleviate stress and anxiety, while camomile, rose, lemon balm and ylang ylang are used to alleviate

Conservatories

Building a conservatory is a popular way of extending our homes and it acts as a mediating space between the garden and the house. Ancient Chinese architects designed homes and gardens to interconnect and regarded each as being essential to balance the other. Glimpses through windows and latticed grilles gave views over lakes and vistas, and gardens were planted right up to the house.

Some conservatories are used for plants or as garden rooms, and are places to sit in to relax. Others have become an integral part of the home, taking on the role of dining room, sitting room and in some cases kitchen. Depending on its purpose and aspect, the conservatory can be decorated in various ways.

the conservatory kitchen

A conservatory that is designated as a kitchen can become very warm in the summer and adequate ventilation will be necessary. It is not considered auspicious to have a glass roof in the kitchen because the symbolic wealth, the food, will evaporate away. Practically speaking, it is not comfortable to work with the sun, or with the rain, beating down above, and a blind or fabric should be put up to block the

△ A conservatory is a glorious place to relax in all weathers.

▷ An indoor garden which opens into a family kitchen, the conservatory provides an ideal outlook when eating or preparing meals.

▽ This conservatory opens into the kitchen, enabling the cook to join in the conversation.

sky. Choose fabrics that are easy to clean and ensure that they do not hang too low and are not highly flammable. The same conditions apply to conservatory kitchens as to conventional ones. If working with the door behind you, place a sheet of metal or a large shiny object so that you can see anyone entering the room.

the conservatory dining room

The conservatory dining room should be treated in the same way as a conventional diner, but there are difficulties. The conservatory room often opens directly into

the kitchen and occasionally also into the main living area. There will be doors to the garden and two or three of the walls will be glass. This makes it very difficult to sit with support from behind, so it is important that chairs have high backs, and preferably arms, to provide this. Depending on the aspect, the evening sun may cause glare so protective measures, such as blinds, should be available. Conservatories can be very warm and fans can help to move the air around. A water feature in the conservatory is not conducive to good digestion and should be turned off during meals.

the conservatory living room

Whether it is used as a living room or simply a small space that faces the setting sun that you use for enjoying an apéritif at the end of the day, the conservatory will be a tranquil spot so long as adequate shade and ventilation are provided.

A water feature works well in the kind of space that is simply for sitting in, it will cool the air when necessary, and add a soothing sound. You do need to make sure that it is placed in an auspicious spot according to the Five Elements. North is

◁ What a healthy way to dine – absorbing energy from the landscape as much as the food and company.

▽ Curtains are not really necessary when you have a wonderful view like this.

△ A wide variety of different foliage plants adds interest to this small conservatory area.

auspicious as it is the Water position. If the conservatory sits in the east or south-west, then this is the spot for a water feature, as in this position it will symbolize present and future prosperity.

Balconies and window boxes

Many apartments have balconies which are purely cosmetic and act as barriers between neighbouring apartments when the doors are opened. Others are larger but do not really enable outdoor living as such, having no room for tables and seating. Some apartments have neither but may have an external windowsill on which to put pots or window boxes. All these small spaces bring the natural world inside our homes.

The outlook in many urban apartments is bleak. The most auspicious sites overlook a park or a river, but most overlook a busy road or even a brick wall. Many apartments overlook the windows of other

▷ Flowers in a window box are guaranteed to lift the spirits.

▽ Even in a small space there is usually room for a windowsill display.

CASE STUDY

A flower-lover who lived on the seventh floor was so troubled by pigeons nibbling his plants that he decided to give up trying to grow them. He purchased lots of green silk plants and ivy strands, and a collection of flowers to represent the seasons. Set in the original planters these lasted several years, and few people could tell the difference.

▷ Silk plants are very effective in awkward sites and don't need watering.

WINDOWSILLS

A kitchen windowsill, inside or outside, is a useful place to have a herb collection and bring not only the sight of the natural world into your home but also the smell and the taste.

The window box on the far left contains nasturtiums, pansies and marigolds, all of which are edible. The window box in the picture on the near left contains chervil, coriander, fennel, garlic, purple sage, French tarragon, savory, oregano and basil – an entire herb garden in a box.

apartments and we can be overlooked by dozens of eyes as we wash up or stand on our balconies. The Four Animals formation suggests that we need to define our space. By placing a window box on our windowsill we not only define the Phoenix position, we also fill our homes with the Wood energy of growing plants. Recent studies have shown that hospital patients who overlook a garden or green fields recover more quickly than patients who look out on to other buildings or busy urban streets. A healthy display of green plants to greet us in the morning will spur us on for the day ahead and welcome us home in the evening.

Growing plants on a balcony can be problematic. Compost (soil mix) is heavy and can be difficult to transport to the apartment and also to dispose of later.

△ This green oasis in a bustling city is shaded by an awning which, with the well-maintained plants, creates a protected space.

◁ Even a small outdoor space such as this will provide plenty of energy.

Cosmetic balconies, those that are built for decoration rather than sitting out, may not be able to cope with heavy weights and we must be mindful of this when choosing containers and plants. Bulbs can be a useful solution since they require a comparatively small amount of compost. A succession of bulbs throughout the year will connect us to the seasons, which is auspicious in Feng Shui. Providing we keep them watered until the foliage has died down, we can lift the bulbs and store them for the following year. Depending on the direction in which the balcony faces, the colours of the bulbs may be chosen to correspond to the direction or to focus on a life aspiration, using the Bagua, but this is not essential.

It is preferable to plant shrubs and miniature trees and to use annual plants as spots of additional colour, rather than attempting to uproot plants and dispose of them several times a year.

The home office

putting the principles into practice

Home offices differ from studies in that they are more yang because they have more contact with the outside world. For this reason, they are better placed close to the entrance so that work does not impinge on the whole house and visitors do not have to walk through the living accommodation. Home offices can be difficult places, particularly when situated in the main body of the house. There is always a temptation to take time out to do household tasks, or for the family to drop in. Although home working allows flexibility, it demands a high level of self-discipline in order to work for long enough but not too long, to allow time

▽ A garden studio or office, removed from the main house, is an excellent idea.

△ This luxurious office space is obviously designed for meetings with clients.

▷ If the chair and desk positions in this study were to be reversed it would open up a view of the outside world.

for social activities. A balance has to be maintained. Ideally, home offices should be placed where visitors have access via a separate door and apart from the main house, in a wing or even in a separate building in the garden.

office position

The ideal position for the office is in your best direction or in one of the other three favoured positions. The south-west is not propitious for office locations since the energy levels are falling there. Wherever it is situated, some care in the north will be advantageous.

Any 'poison arrows' should be deflected or hidden, using mirrors or screens. Metal supports Water, so hollow metal wind chimes would be helpful. Water is also auspicious in an office but do not use the area for large displays of plants as they will drain the energy.

desk positions

Desk locations are the same as those for the study but if there is a colleague or some other person working in the home office the desks should not face each other. If there is a secretary, he or she should sit nearer to the door to protect the employer from having to deal with mundane matters. Both desks should have the support of a wall behind, and suitably supportive chairs that follow the favourable Four Animals formation. If a desk is close to a door, use a plant to protect the occupant from unfavourable chi.

When visiting clients are received in the office, the owner's chair should always be backed by the wall facing the door and the clients should be seated in the subordinate position in a smaller chair,

THE BAGUA AND DESKS

Use the Bagua to arrange your desk according to Feng Shui principles.

1. This represents Career or the start of the day and should always be clear to open up possibilities.

2. The Relationships area is suitable for brochures and details of people with whom you will come into contact in the course of your project.

3. A plant here in the Elders area will help to freshen the air and symbolize longevity and stability.

4. Accounts and paying-in books should be placed here in the Wealth area, but not cheque books, which represent money going out.

5. Use this central area for the task in hand and then clear it away. Do not leave things to pile up here.

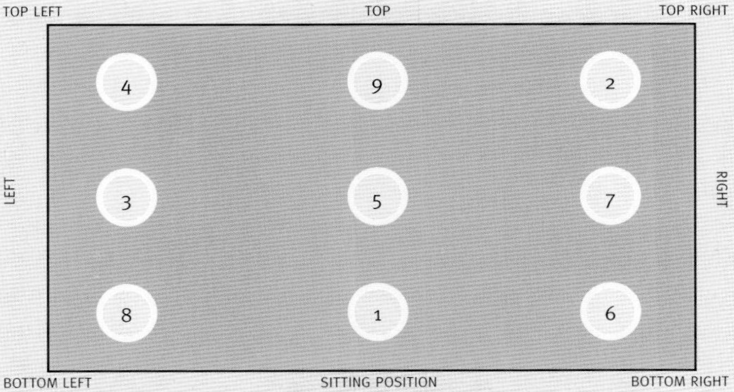
TOP LEFT
TOP
TOP RIGHT
4
9
2
LEFT
3
5
7
RIGHT
8
1
6
BOTTOM LEFT
SITTING POSITION
BOTTOM RIGHT

6. The Helpful People area is the place for the telephone and address book.

7. The Children or Projects position is ideal for putting the current project files.

8. Knowledge and Wisdom – the place to store reference books.

9. The Fame area and the Phoenix position. A crystal object here will denote the boundary of your desk, and of the current project. An uplifting image on the wall in front will represent future possibilities.

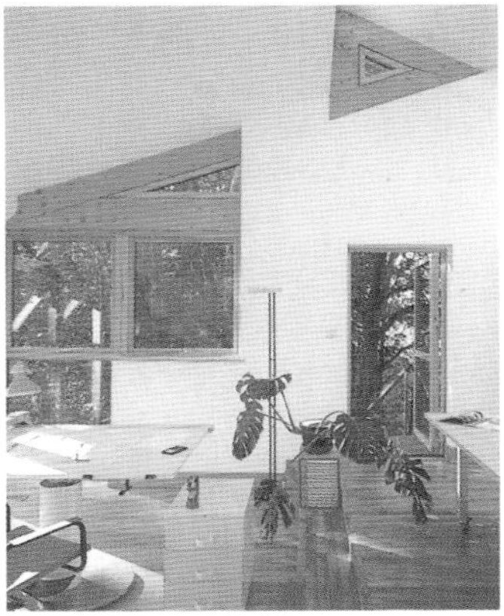

△ **This studio's view would be improved if the foliage outside wasn't so dense.**

with their backs to the door. Having sorted out the best location for the furniture in the office, focus on the contents of the desk, either using compass directions or symbolically.

Take care that any measures taken are not in conflict with the element of the area. Task lighting should always be diagonally opposite the writing hand to prevent shadows.

the office environment

Be aware of the approach to the office from outside and check for dustbins and other obstacles, overhanging branches and anything which will detract from your entrance. Inside the house, the same attention is necessary. Clients who come to visit you will not want to clamber over toys or other paraphernalia, which present an unprofessional approach.

It is important, particularly when the office is a section of a room that is used at other times for another purpose, to mark the boundaries – by a screen, piece of furniture or even a rug. Inside the space, aspirational images, landscapes, good task lighting and bright colours all make a psychological contribution to success.

▽ **This uncluttered desk is arranged following Feng Shui principles.**

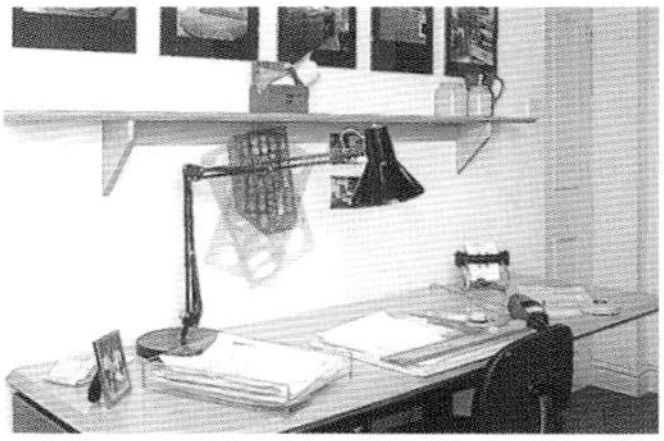

FINANCIAL TIP

Tie three Chinese coins together with red thread or ribbon and place them in the back of your accounts book for good luck.

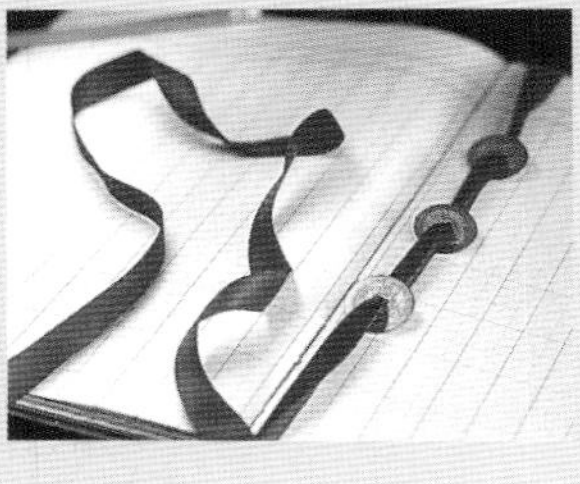

A clutter-free office environment is essential and work spaces should be clear of everything but the task in hand. Do not have stacked filing trays which, symbolically and literally, allow the work to mount up. Deal with letters, emails and telephone calls the same day, note conversations and dates meticulously, and file as you go. Discard catalogues as new ones arrive as well as all out-of-date paperwork.

Home study or studio

The home study may be used by one or more members of the family to study for school or college examinations, for continuing education later in life or for pursuing a hobby or interest. It should be situated in a quiet part of the home, if possible. If study areas form part of another room – the bedroom, sitting room or even the kitchen – care should be taken to ensure that the activities of the two areas are kept quite separate, for example, by screening. It is not a good idea to use a bedroom as a home study, because it will no longer be a place to relax in.

▷ Screens can be used to conceal work equipment in bedrooms and living rooms.

DESK LOCATIONS

The three desk positions below have the support of a wall. You can also see the door and anyone entering. The desk on the right is directly opposite the door. The three desks below right are vulnerable from behind and would make the worker feel nervous.

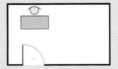

Good: facing the door

Good: diagonally opposite the door

Bad: back to the door

Good: with a view of the door

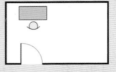

Bad: facing a window

Good: you can see who is entering

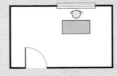

Bad: back to a window

desk positions

The position of the desk is crucial if maximum benefits are to be gained from studying and it should be placed to avoid any areas of damaging chi.

The view from a study window should be pleasant but not detract from work. A view of the neighbours' swimming pool and barbecue area will not be conducive to work. Sitting opposite the windows of a neighbouring house is not recommended since it can cause discomfort, as can facing telephone wires or having roof points

▽ An ideal solution – the folding doors allow light and air in during the day, and you can close down the office at night.

aimed at the office. If there are distractions outside, the window should be covered by muslin, or something similar, to admit light but keep distractions out. Plants placed on the windowsill might serve the same purpose. Studies should have a good supply of fresh air in order to prevent tiredness.

When a considerable amount of time is spent in one position, the furniture should be ergonomically correct. Chairs should fit comfortably under desks and the seat should be at the correct height for writing and using a keyboard. If a conventional computer is used, it should be placed as far away as possible from the chair to reduce the radiation from the screen. Where possible, use a lap-top computer. Trailing wires are dangerous and cause irritation, so tie them together and tape them

△ It would be difficult to work in this room. The stacked bookshelves are also reflected in the mirror and are overwhelming.

◁ A Mayan chime ball hung in the window deflects the 'poison arrow' created by the roof of one of the buildings outside.

CLUTTER IN THE STUDY
Piles of used paper
Piles of unread journals
Out-of-date books
Cluttered hard drive
Noticeboards with out-of-date information
More than two adhesive notes
Broken equipment
Run-down batteries

out of the way. Printers should be positioned to ensure the paper can eject easily. Plants in the study help to improve the air quality and also add some yin balance to the yang machines.

order in the study

The study should be as streamlined as possible and there should be a place for everything. Cupboards, shelves and bookcases will keep books and equipment off the desk surface. Coloured files and filing boxes store information and prevent paper mountains appearing on the desk and floor. Coloured adhesive bookmarkers avoid piles of open books and journals stacking up on the desk, but the marked items should be read in a day or two otherwise the stickers will be a constant reminder of things left undone.

Journals can pile up. You should try to read them immediately and discard them if they contain nothing of interest. If it is necessary to keep them, a small card index in subject order with the journal title, date, article title and page number will help you to quickly locate the items you want.

Once a piece of work has been completed and recognition has been received for it, it is unlikely that it will ever be referred to again. Consider whether a paper copy is really necessary. If not, store all completed work on floppy discs, which take up considerably less space. Remove past work from the computer hard drive to free up space, clear your mind, and improve performance.

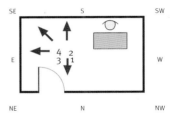

△ Ensure you face your best direction (or one of your other three favoured directions).

Crystal and stone reference guide

These lists are best used as a reminder of the general areas of function rather than a rigid framework that must be adhered to at all times. The names of the crystals in the book are common throughout the English-speaking world. However variations do occur, due to the older names used in jewellery or mining that can sometimes be misleading. The chemical formula of a mineral remains a constant identification regardless of common names around the world and lists the constituent elements of a mineral and the relationship each atom has to the others. The formula for quartz, for example, is SiO_2, which indicates that every atom of silicon (Si) is bonded with two atoms of oxygen (O).

The colours listed here for each crystal are those most commonly found. Although colour is one of the best identifiers of a stone, most minerals can occur in most colours, and beginners can become confused, so other

Crystal/Stone	Chemical Formula	Colour
Amazonite	$KAlSi_3O_8$	Green, blue striated
Amber (fossil resin)	$C_{10}H_{16}O + H_2S$	Yellow, brown, green, red
Amethyst	$SiO_2 + Fe$	Violet-purple
Apophyllite	$KCa_4Si_8O_{20}(F,OH).8H_2O$	Clear, green, grey, pink
Aquamarine	$Be_3Al_2Si_6O_{18}$	Blue
Azurite-malachite	$Cu_3(CO_3)2(OH)_2 + Cu_2CO_3(OH)_2$	Dark blue and green
Black Tourmaline (Schorl)	$Na(Mg,Fe,Li,Mn,Al)_3Al_6(BO_3)_3Si_6O_{18}(OH,F)_4$	Black
Bloodstone	SiO_2	Green with red spots
Blue Lace Agate	SiO_2	Blue, banded
Botswana Agate	SiO_2	White, grey banded
Calcite	$CaCO_3$	Colourless, all colours
Carnelian	SiO_2	Red-orange
Celestite	$SrSO_4$	Grey-blue, clear
Chrysocolla	$(Cu,Al)_2H_2Si_2O_5(OH)_4.nH_2O$	Green to blue
Citrine	SiO_2	Yellow-brown
Clear Quartz	SiO_2	Colourless
Corundum	Al_2O_3	All colours, white streak
Danburite	$CaB_2Si_2O_8$	Colourless
Diamond	C_4	Colourless, all colours
Emerald	$Be_3Al_2Si_6O_{18}$	Bright green
Fire Opal	$SiO_2.nH_2O$	Red, orange
Fluorite	CaF_2	All colours
Garnet	SiO_4 plus various metals	Red, brown, green
Gold	Au	Yellow, orange
Green Aventurine	SiO_2	with inclusions Green, blue
Haematite	Fe_2O_3	Metallic grey/black

identifying qualities such as crystal shape (crystal system) and hardness can be useful to know. Crystal system is not always easy to recognize because of the many variations within each system. However, certain characteristics of each system can really help identification. Mohs' Scale of Hardness is a scale of relative hardness. Minerals of 1 or 2 are extremely soft and easily scratched. A hardness of 3 to 5 can be dulled or scratched easily and so are rarely used in jewellery. Most gemstones range from a hardness of 6 (like moonstone) to 8 (like emerald). Stones harder than 8 are rare: corundum (ruby and sapphire) has a hardness of 9 and only diamond has a hardness of 10.

The influence each stone has with an individual's energy systems will depend on the state of health. However, the general qualities of each stone will suggest that they will work well in certain broad areas.

Crystal System	Hardness	Chakra	Subtle Body
Triclinic	6–6.5	Heart, throat	Mental, etheric
Amorphous	2	Solar plexus	Mental
Trigonal	7	Brow, crown	Emotional, mental, spiritual
Tetragonal	4.5–5	Heart, crown	
Hexagonal	7.5–8	Throat	Etheric, mental
Monoclinic	3.5–4	Throat, heart	Etheric, mental, astral
Trigonal	7–7.5	Base	Etheric, astral
Microcrystalline trigonal	7	Heart, base	Etheric
Trigonal	7	Throat	Emotional, mental
Trigonal	7	All	
Hexagonal	3	All	
Trigonal	7	Sacral	Etheric
Orthorhombic	3–3.5	Throat, crown	Soul
Monoclinic or orthorhombic	2–4	Heart, throat	Emotional, mental
Trigonal	7	Solar plexus	Causal
Trigonal	7	All	Etheric, emotional
Trigonal	9	Crown, solar plexus	
Orthorhombic	7	Crown	Spiritual
Cubic	10	Crown	Mental
Hexagonal	7.5–8	Heart	Astral, etheric, emotional
Amorphous	6	Base, solar plexus	
Cubic	4	Brow	Etheric
Cubic	6.5–7.5	Base	Etheric, astral
Cubic	2.5–3	Heart	Emotional, mental, spiritual
Trigonal	7	Heart	Etheric, mental, emotional
Trigonal	5–6	Sacral, solar plexus	Etheric

Indicolite	$Na(Mg,Fe,Li,Mn,Al)_3Al_6(BO_3)_3Si_6O_{18}(OH,F)_4$	Blue, blue-green
Iron Pyrites	FeS_2	Metallic yellow
Jade – Jadeite	$NaAlSi_2O_6$	Clear, rich green
Jade – Nephrite	$Ca_2(Mg,Fe)_5Si_8O_{22}(OH)_2$	Green
Jet	Organic carbon	Black, dark brown
Kunzite	$LiAlSi_2O_6$	Lilac, clear, green
Kyanite	Al_2SiO_5	Blue
Labradorite	$(Na,Ca)Al_{1-2}Si_{3-2}O_8$	Grey, green iridescent
Lapis Lazuli	$(Na,Ca)_8(Al.Si)_{12}O_{24}(S,SO_4)$	Deep blue with white and gold
Magnetite/Lodestone	Fe_3O_4	Black
Malachite	$Cu_2CO_3(OH)_2$	Greens with black
Milky Quartz	SiO_2	White
Moldavite	Rock silicates	Green
Moonstone	$KaSi_3O_8$	Pearly/cream
Moss Agate	SiO_2	Clear with green/brown inclusions
Obsidian	Igneous rock with inclusions	Black, grey, red-brown
Opal	$SiO_2.nH_2O$	Various
Red Coral	$CaCO_3$	Red, orange, pink
Red Jasper	SiO_2	Red
Rhodocrosite	$MnCO_3$	Pink, orange, cream
Rhodonite	$(Mn^{+2},Fe^{+2},Mg,Ca)SiO_3$	Pink with brown or black
Rose Quartz	SiO_2	Pink
Rubellite	$Na(Mg,Fe,Li,Mn,Al)_3Al_6(BO_3)Si_6O_{18}(OH,F)_4$	Pink, red
Ruby	Al_2O_3	Red
Rutilated Quartz	TiO_2 (in SiO_2)	Yellow-brown
Sapphire	Al_2O_3	Blue, violet-blue
Selenite	$CaSO_4.2H_2O$	Pearly
Smoky Quartz	SiO_2	Brown, black
Sodalite	$Na_4Al_3Si_3O_{12}Cl$	Blue with white veins
Spinel	$MgAl_2O_4$	Scarlet, pink
Sugilite	$KNa_2(Fe^{2+},Mn^{2+},Al)_2Li_3Si_{12}O_{30}$	Lilac, purple
Tektite	Rock, silicates	Brown, black
Topaz	$Al_2SiO_4(F,OH)_2$	All colours, clear
Turquoise	$CuAl_6(PO_4)_4(OH)_8.4H_2O$	Light blue–turquoise-green
Verdelite	$Na(Mg,Fe,Li,Mn,Al)_3Al_6(BO_3)_3Si_6O_{18}(OH,F)_4$	Green
Zircon	$ZrSiO_4$	Brown to clear

Trigonal	7.5	Throat, brow	All
Cubic	6.5	Solar plexus	Astral
Monoclinic	7	Heart	Astral, etheric, emotional
Monoclinic	6–6.5	Heart	Astral, etheric, emotional
Amorphous	2.5	Base	Etheric, emotional
Monoclinic	6.5–7.5	Heart, throat	Etheric
Triclinic	4–7	Throat	All
Triclinic	6–6.5	All	All
Cubic	5.5	Throat, brow	Etheric, mental
Cubic	5.5–6.5	All	All
Monoclinic	3.5–4	Heart	Etheric, emotional
Trigonal	7	All	Emotional
Amorphous	5	Heart, throat, brow, crown	All
Monoclinic	6–6.5	Sacral, solar plexus	Emotional
Trigonal	7	Heart	Emotional, mental
Amorphous	6	Base, sacral, crown	Mental
Amorphous	6	Sacral, solar plexus, crown	Emotional
Hexagonal or trigonal	3	Heart	Etheric
Trigonal	7	Base	Etheric
Trigonal	3.5–4.5	Base to heart	Emotional, mental, astral
Triclinic	5.5–6.5	Heart	Emotional
Trigonal	7	Heart, throat	Emotional, mental, astral
Trigonal	7–7.5	Sacral, heart	Emotional, astral
Trigonal	9	Heart	Mental, spiritual
Tetragonal	6–6.5	All	All
Trigonal	9	Solar plexus, heart, throat, crown	Emotional, mental
Monoclinic	2	Sacral, throat, crown	Emotional, soul
Trigonal	7	Base, sacral	Solar plexus
Cubic	5.5–6	Throat, brow	Emotional, mental
Cubic	8	Base	
Hexagonal	5.5–6.5	Crown	Astral, causal
Amorphous	5–5.5	Base, brow	Etheric, astral
Orthorhombic	8	Solar plexus	Etheric
Triclinic	5–6	Throat, all	All
Trigonal	7–7.5	Heart	All
Tetragonal	7.5	Base	

Correspondence charts

THE SYMBOLISM OF COLOURS

Red: blood, passion, the life essence, power, physical energy, courage, bringing change in difficult circumstances. Associated with Mars, battle, the element of Fire, the south, projective energy

Pink: love and kindness, reconciliation, peace and harmony, compassion, gentle emotions; associated with family, children and friendship, receptive energy

Orange: abundance, fertility, health, joy, attraction, luck; marks the boundary between the self and others; associated with the sun, projective energy

Yellow: communication, the intellect, learning, concentration, also movement, travel and change; associated with Mercury, the element of Air, the east, projective energy

Green: the heart and emotions, love, also nature, gardens and growth, money and prosperity, employment; associated with the Earth element.

Blue: wisdom, patience, possibility, the healing of the spirit, idealism, truth and justice; associated with the moon, the element of Water, the west

Purple: royal and priestly colour, a link with the higher dimension, wisdom, inspiration, magic, religion and spiritual strength; associated with Osiris

Violet: temperance, spirituality, repentance, transition from life to death

Brown: Earth and Earth spirits, instinctive wisdom, the natural world; practical and financial matters, the home, stability, old people, animals; a protective force.

Grey: compromise and adaptability, psychic protection and secrecy

White: divinity, potential, the life-force, energy, purity; contains all other colours; associated with the sun; helpful for new beginnings, clear vision and originality

Black: death and regeneration; conclusions that lead to new beginnings, marking a boundary with the past, banishing and releasing negativity, shedding guilt and regret; associated with Saturn, the Roman god of limitations, suffering and transformation

Gold: worldly achievement, wealth, long life and ambition, confidence and understanding; associated with solar deities.

Silver: dreams, visions, intuition, hidden potential; associated with the moon and lunar deities

THE SYMBOLISM OF CRYSTALS AND STONES

Agate: good for grounding and protection

Amber: good luck stone, draws out disease and clears negativity and depression

Amethyst: peace, protection and spirituality; promotes harmony and balance in the home, clears negativity; disperses electro-magnetic emissions from electrical appliances; heals at all levels; helps with meditation and peaceful sleep, can inspire dreams

Angelite: heals anger, restores harmony, helpful in telepathic communication, connecting with angels and spirits

Aventurine: healing at all levels, dissolves blockages, balances the emotions, green aventurine attracts good fortune and increases perception; pink aventurine heals relationships

Azurite: mental clarity and renewal

Black onyx: protects against negative energy, helps emotional stability, encourages connection with reality

Carnelian: aids creative flow, grounds in the present, inspires confidence, courage and motivation

Chrysocolla: soothes and calms, eases fear and guilt, attracts luck

Chrysoprase: emotionally uplifting, attracts abundance and success, spiritual energy

Citrine: prevents nightmares, enhances self-esteem and mental clarity, brings abundance and material wellbeing; useful for areas where bookkeeping is done

Clear quartz: amplifies energy, spiritually and emotionally healing and empowering, aids meditation; can be used to dispel negative energy and harmful emissions from electrical appliances

Emerald: physically healing and protective, lends insight and security in love

Garnet: stimulates energy, aids expression, strengthens love and friendship

Haematite: aids concentration, reasoning, memory and self-discipline; healing and protective

Herkimer diamond: releases energy blockages, helps with dream recall

Jade: promotes clarity and wisdom; balances the emotions, facilitates peaceful sleep, attracts prosperity

Jet: lifts depression and wards off nightmares; brings wisdom, health and long life

Lapis lazuli: strengthens will, awareness, integrity in relationships; aids the release of emotional wounds

Malachite: healing, absorbs negativity, stimulates creativity and strengthens intuition; useful for work areas

Moonstone: wishes, intuition and new beginnings; restores harmony in relationships, calms emotions and induces lucid dreaming

Moss agate: connects with earth spirits, brings abundance and self-confidence

Obsidian: place in a room for protection and grounding; dissolves anger and fear; snowflake obsidian has a softer effect, restores balance and clarity

Opal: visionary, attracts inspiration and insight

Pearl: enhances purity, clarity and grace

Peridot: warm and friendly, heals wounded self-esteem

Pyrites: provides protection and defence against negative energies; harnesses creative thinking and practicality

Red jasper: connects with earth energy, emotionally calming

Rhodonite: fosters patience, selflessness

Rose quartz: heals emotional wounds, restores love of self and others; brings peace and calm; can be placed at an entrance to 'greet' visitors; keeps the atmosphere positive

Ruby: amplifies emotions, releases and dissolves anger, attracts loyalty, awakens passion

Rutilated quartz: releases energy blockages

Sapphire: symbolizes peace, gives protection and prophetic wisdom

Smoky quartz: lightly grounding and balancing, counteract hyperactivity, fosters self-acceptance and awareness of divine protection

Tiger's eye: creates order and harmony, stability, attracts beauty and abundance

Topaz: symbolizes light and warmth, heals and absorbs tension, attracts love and creativity

Tourmaline: grounding, healing and protective, absorbs negativity and brings discernment and vitality; green tourmaline for success; pink tourmaline for peaceful sleep; watermelon tourmaline for sexual energy; yellow tourmaline for wisdom and understanding

Turquoise: symbolizes protection, blessing and partnership

Zircon: aids healing and sleep

THE SYMBOLISM OF PLANTS AND HERBS

Angelica: burn dried leaves for protection and healing

Anise: keeps away nightmares

Apple blossom: for love and friendship

Basil: gives protection, repels negativity and brings wealth

Bay: guardian of the house, protection against illness; burn leaves to induce visions

Bergamot: attracts success and prosperity

Blessed thistle: brings spiritual and financial blessings; if fresh, brings strengthening energy to a sickroom

Boneset: drives away evil

Cabbage: brings good luck

Catnip: encourages a psychic bond with cats, attracts luck and happiness

Chamomile: for meditation and relaxation; use in prosperity charms to draw money

Chickweed: for attracting love or maintaining a relationship

Chilli: assures fidelity and love

Cinnamon: aphrodisiac; draws money, protection and success

Clove: banishes hostile or negative forces and helps to gain what is sought; burn in incense to stop others gossiping

Clover: for love and fidelity

Coltsfoot: brings love, wealth and peace

Comfrey: for safety when travelling

Cyclamen: for love and truth

Dandelion: enhances dreams and prophetic power

Eucalyptus: healing and purifying

Fennel: protects from curses: hang round doors and windows

Gardenia: for peace and healing

Garlic: for magical healing, protection and exorcism; especially protective in new homes

Ginger: for success and empowerment

Grape: for fertility and garden magic; attracts money

Hibiscus: attracts love and aids divination and dreams

Honeysuckle: strengthens the memory, helps in letting go of the past

Hops: improves health and induces sleep

Hyacinth: for love and protection

Hyssop: purification; hang up in the home to dispel negativity

Jasmine: brings good fortune in love, friendship and wealth; raises self-esteem; induces lucid dreams

Juniper: calms and brings good health; berries are burned to ward off evil

Lavender: purifying; brings peace and happiness, love and sweet dreams

Lemon: attracts happiness, relieves stress

Lettuce: induces sleep, assists in divination

Lily of the valley: brings peace, harmony and love

Lime: increases energy, encourages loyalty

Lotus: emblem of enlightenment, elevates and protects

Magnolia: assures fidelity

Marigold: enhances visions and dreams; renews personal energy

Mistletoe: for protection, love and visionary ability; hang on the bedpost for beautiful dreams

Mugwort: for clairvoyance, scrying and dream interpretation

Mullein: gives courage, keeps away nightmares

Nettle: wards off curses, allays fear

Olive: brings peace of mind and fidelity in love, fruitfulness and security

Orange: attracts peace, power and luck

Orris: attracts love and romance

Passion flower: fosters friendship; brings peace and understanding

Pennyroyal: increases alertness and brainpower; brings peace between partners

Pine: grounding and cleansing; use for a fresh start

Rice: attracts fertility and money

Rose: blesses love, domestic peace, generosity and beauty

Rosemary: protects the home; brings mental clarity and sharpens memory

Sage: brings wisdom, fertility, healing and long life

St John's wort: burn leaves to cleanse and protect

Strawberry: for love and luck

Sweet pea: for friendship and courage

Thyme: for courage and confidence

Tuberose: for eroticism and romance

Valerian: brings love and harmony, helps fighting couples to find peace

Vervain: attracts money, protection; transforms enemies into friends; brings inner strength and peace

Violet: contentment and love

Willow: use leaves and bark for healing and to empower wishes

GODS AND ANGELS

Agni: Hindu god of fire

Amaterasu: Shinto sun goddess

Aphrodite: Greek goddess of love and beauty

Apollo: Greek god of the sun, medicine and music; patron of the Muses

Arianrhod: Celtic mother goddess, keeper of time and fate

Artemis: Greek goddess of the waxing moon, protector of women

Athene: Greek goddess of war, wisdom and the arts

Auriel: archangel, earth

Bastet: Egyptian goddess of love and fertility; represented with the head of a cat

Brigid: Celtic triple goddess, fire deity and patron of the hearth, healing, prophecy and inspiration

Cassiel: angel who assists with overcoming obstacles

Ceres: Roman goddess of earth and agriculture

Ceridwen: Welsh mother, moon and grain goddess

Cernunnos: The Celtic horned god of fertility

Cybele: Phrygian dark moon goddess who governs nature, wild beasts and dark magic

Demeter: Greek goddess of the earth, corn and vegetation; represents abundance and love

Diana: Roman goddess of hunting and the moon; represents chastity, protects women in childbirth

Epona: Celtic horse-goddess of fertility and healing

Freya: Norse mother goddess of love, marriage and fertility

Gabriel: archangel of the moon; associated with the west

Gaia: primeval Greek earth deity, prophetess of Delphi, goddess of dreams

Ganesha: elephant-headed Hindu god of wisdom and literature, patron of business

Haniel: archangel of divine love and harmony, beauty and the creative arts

Hathor: Egyptian sky-deity, goddess of love, joy and dance, usually represented as a cow

Hecate: three-headed Greek goddess of the waning moon, who rules magic, sorcery, death and the underworld

Hermes: Greek messenger god; represents consciousness, transition and exchange

Hestia: Greek goddess of the hearth and stability

Indra: Hindu god of war; associated with weather

Ishtar: Mesopotamian goddess of sexual love, fertility and war

Isis: Egyptian mother-goddess, wife of Osiris; represents life, loyalty, fertility and magic

Ixchel: Mayan goddess of storms and protector of women in childbirth

Janus: Roman guardian of the entrance and god of transition

Jizo: Japanese protector of children and travellers

Kali: destructive aspect of the Hindu mother-goddess

Kuanyin: Chinese goddess of compassion

Lakshmi: Hindu goddess of abundance, wealth and harmony

Lugh: Celtic sky-god; associated with the arts

Luna: Roman goddess of the full moon

Maat: Egyptian goddess of truth, justice and order

Mercury: Roman messenger god; associated with speech, breath, wind and magic

Michael: archangel of the sun; associated with rulership, marriage, music

Minerva: Roman goddess of wisdom

Mithras: Roman god of light

Nephthys: sister of Isis, guardian of the dead Osiris

Neptune: Roman god of the sea

Osiris: Egyptian god, judge of the dead, husband of Isis; symbolizes regeneration of nature

Pan: Greek horned god of wild things; half man, half animal

Parvati: Hindu mother-goddess, consort of Shiva

Raphael: archangel of the air element; associated with communication and business

Re: Egyptian sun god and creator

Sachiel: angel ruling justice and financial matters

Samael: protective archangel; helps with matters that require courage or perseverance

Selene: Greek goddess of the full moon

Shang Ti: Chinese supreme god

Shiva: Hindu creator god, whose meditation sustains the world

Sophia: divine knowledge and wisdom

Sul: Celtic sun goddess

Sunna: Norse sun goddess

Surya: Hindu sun god

Tara: Tibetan goddess of wisdom and compassion

Thoth: Egyptian god of wisdom and the moon

Tsao-chun: Taoist kitchen god

Uriel: archangel of high magic

Venus: Roman goddess of love and beauty

Vesta: Roman goddess of the hearth

Vishnu: Hindu protector of the world

Zeus: Greek supreme god

Suppliers and useful organizations

Crystal healing suppliers

UK
Burhouse Ltd, Quarmby Mills
Tanyard Road, Oakes
Huddersfield HD3 4YP
Tel: +44(0)1484 655675
Email: sales@burhouse.com
Web: www.burhouse.com

Charlie's Rock Shop
Unit 14, 1929 Shop
18 Watermill Way
Merton Abbey Mills
London SW19 2RD
Tel: +44(0)208 544 1207

Crystals
25 High Street, Glastonbury
Somerset BA6 9DP
Tel: +44(0)1458 835090
Web: www.crystalshop.co.uk

Earthworks
Unit 1, Fleetsbridge Business Centre
Poole, Dorset
BH17 7AF
Tel: +44(0)1202 677317
Email: info@earthworksuk.com
Web: www.earthworksuk.com

Evolution
117 Fore Street
Exeter
Devon EX4 3JQ
Tel/Fax: +44(0)1392 410759

Simon & Sue Lilly
PO Box 6
Exminster
Exeter
Devon EX6 8YE
Tel/Fax: +44(0)1392 832005
Email: info@greenmantrees.demon.co.uk
Web: www.greenmanessences.com

USA
Crystal Magic
2978 West Hwy 89A
Sedona AZ 86336
Tel: (928) 282-1622

Multistone International
135 South Holliday St
Strasburg VA 22657
Tel: (540) 465-8777
Web: www.multistoneintl.com

Rosley's Rocks and Gems
2153 N. Sheffield Ave
Chicago
IL 60614

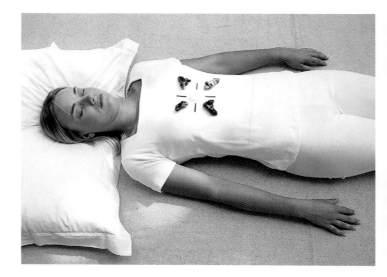

Tel: (800) 844-1498
Web: www.crystalmaster.com

AUSTRALIA
CK Minerals Pty Ltd
PO Box 6026
Vermont South VIC 3133
Tel: 61 3 9872 3886
Email: info@ckminerals.com.au
Web: www.ckminerals.com.au

Living Energies
Shop B80, Chadstone Shopping Centre
Chadstone VIC 3148
Tel: 61 3 9568 2188
and
Shop 113 Warringah Mall
Brookvale NSW 2100
Tel: 61 2 9907 1716

Crystal Living
Shop 270, Lower Level
Garden City Shopping Centre
Cnr. Logan and Kessels Rds
Upper Mount Gravatt QLD 4122
Tel: 61 7 3420 6700

Prosperous Stones
Shop B3 Bay Village
Hastings Street, Noosa QLD 4567
Tel: 61 7 5445 4622

Colour healing suppliers

All products are available internationally.

Green Man Essences
PO Box 6
Exminster, Exeter
Devon EX6 8YE, UK
Email: info@greenmantrees.demon.co.uk
Web: www.greenmanessences.com
Suppliers of colour/light essences.

AuraLight
'Unicornis', Obi Obi Road
Mapleton QLD 4560
Australia
Email: info@auralight.net
Web: www.auralight.net
*Manufacturers of two layers of colour
in bottles.*

Aura-Soma
Dev Aura, Little London
Tetford, Lincs LN9 6QB, UK
Email: info@asiact.demon.co.uk
Manufacturers of two layers of colour in bottles.

AvaTara
Pitt White, Mill Lane
Uplyme, Dorset DT7 3TZ, UK
Manufacturers of two layers of colour in bottles.

Colour healing international groups

Colour Therapy Healing
The Colour Therapy Information Resource
High Banks, 108 Limmer Lane
Felpham, West Sussex PO22 7LP
Tel/Fax: +44(0)1243 585609
Web: www.colourtherapyhealing.com
*An independent source of information on all
aspects of colour therapy, including international
practitioner listings and useful links.*

International Association of Colour
46 Cottenham Road
Histon, Cambridge
CB4 9ES, UK
A contact for colour therapy schools worldwide.

Irlen Institute
5380 E Village Road, Long Beach
CA 90808, USA
Web: www.irlen.com
Colour overlays for use in education.

Iris International School of Colour Therapy
4 Dart Villas, Totnes TQ9 5ET, UK
Tel: +44(0)1803 868037
Email: info@iriscolour.co.uk
*Lectures and training in holistic design and colour
therapy, run by international author, designer and
healer, Suzy Chiazzari.*

Feng Shui organizations

UK

The Feng Shui Society
377 Edgware Road
London W2 1BT
Tel: +44(0)7050 289 200
Email: info@fengshuisociety.org.uk
Web: www.fengshuisociety.org.uk
*This is an organization representing all the different
approaches to Feng Shui, and serves as a focus for
the exchange of information.*

AUSTRALIA

Feng Shui Society of Australia
PO Box 4816, Mulgrave
Victoria 3170
Tel: (03) 9517 8960

USA

American Feng Shui Institute
108 North Ynez, Suite 202
Monterey Park CA 91754
Tel: 626 571 2757

CANADA

The Feng Shui Association of Canada
4841 Yonge Street
Shepherd Center
PO Box 43236, North York, ON
M2N 6N1
Web: www.fengshuiassociationofcanada.ca

Acknowledgements

The publishers would like to thank the following individuals for their contributions and also to thank the listed agencies and photographers for permission to use their images in this book:

Key: t = top, b = bottom, r = right, l = left, m = middle

CRYSTAL HEALING:
Thanks to Kay Harrison of 'Evolution', Exeter and 'Crystals' of Exeter, and also to Charlie, at Charlie's Rock Shop, London, for lending crystals and minerals for the photography.

Natural History Photographic Agency: 15t, Peter Parks; Simon and Sue Lilly: 30br.

COLOUR HEALING:
AKG: 150t. The Art Archive: 119bl. David Noble: 156b. Elizabeth Whiting: 102bl, 106bl. Robert Harding Picture Library: 97tl, 101b, 103tr. The Ronald Grant Archive: 125b. Scala: 96br, 97br. Sonia Halliday: 126ml. Laura Lushington: 121tl. The Stock Market: 95br, 100tr, 101tr, 104bl, 114t, 122ml, 125tl. Sue and Simon Lilly: 158t, 159. Sylvia Corday: 93br, 94br, 126tl.

THE CHAKRAS:
All artworks created by Gary Walton, except for the following: Penny Brown 173, 178, 179, 186; Samantha J Elmhurst 175.
Additional images were supplied by the following libraries:
The Artarchive/British Library: 170 and 174,

Attitudes practised by Hindu devotees in Asanas and Matras 18th century.
Fortean Picture Library: Pair of cosmic men of traditional Nepalese/Tibetan style depicting the seven chakras; private collection, purchased in Nepal. Werner Forman Archive: 231, Ceramic tiles from the Alcazar of Seville, Islamic, 14th century.

SPACE CLEARING, ALTARS AND SHRINES AND FENG SHUI:
Abode UK: 475br, 482t, 483tl.
A-Z Botanical Collection Ltd: 415br (Mike Vardy). The Garden Picture Library: 415bl (Morley Read). Robert Harding Picture Library: 479tl (IPC Magazines), 481tl (IPC Magazines), 482b (IPC Magazines), 483bl (IPC Magazines). Houses and Interiors: 414tr (Roger Brooks), 422bl (Roger Brooks), 422tr (Roger Brooks), 426tr (Mark Bolton), 427bl (Mark Bolton), 430tr (Roger Brooks), 459l (Verne), 462bl (Mark Bolton), 472tr, 488tr (Mark Bolton), bl (Mark Bolton).
Hutchinson Library: 382br (Robert Francis), 384tr (Merilyn Thorold), 387tr (Melanie Friend), 400bl (T. Moser), 400br (Lesley Nelson), 401tl (F Horner), 402t (Edward Parker), 402bl (Sarah Errington), 402r (John G Egan), 403bl (Tony Souter), 408tr (Pern.), 408r (P W Rippon), 408bl (Robert Francis), 409tl (Tony Souter), 409bl (Carlos Freire), 409tr (G Griffiths-Jones), 416t, 417tl (Phillip Wolmuth), 417t (L Taylor), 417t, 417m, 417br (Andrew Sole), 442b (Sarah Murray), 443tl (Lesley Nelson), 445t (N Durrell McKenna), 494bl (N Durrell). Images Colour Library: 385b, 386b, 387bl, 388tr, 389 no. 2, no. 5, 399br, 403tr. The Interior Archive: 382tl (Schulenburg), 383tr (Schulenburg), 418tr (Schulenburg), 422r (C Simon Sykes), 428bl (Schulenburg), 429t (Schulenburg), 441tr (Henry Wilson), 448 (Schulenburg), 450tr (Schulenburg), 451tl (Schulenburg), cbl (Schulenburg), 417t (Simon Upton), 458bl (Schulenburg), 458b (Schulenburg), 461tr (Schulenburg), 463bl (Schulenburg), 464br (Henry Wilson), 466t (Tim Beddow), 468bl (Schulenburg), 471r (Schulenburg), 474tr (Schulenburg), 474b (Schulenburg), 476l (Schulenburg), 479tr (Schulenburg), 480bl (Schulenburg), 484tr (Henry Wilson), 484bl (Schulenburg), 485bl (Schulenburg), 485br (Schulenburg), 487tl (Schulenburg), 487br (Schulenburg), 493tl, 254br (Schulenburg). The Stock Market: 388br, 389 no. 1

(K Biggs), 410tr, 410bl, 410br, 411b, 411t, 412tl, 412m, 413tl, 438t (David Lawrence), 440br, 441tl, 441tr, 442t, 489b. Tony Stone: 440bl (Angus M Mackillop). Jessica Strang: 494r. Superstock: 396tr, 396m, 397br. View: 383m (Phillip Bier), 389 no. 1 (Dennis Gilbert), 417tr (Phillip Bier), 419l (Chris Gascoigne), 428tr (Phillip Bier), br (Phillip Bier), 429bl (Phillip Bier), 439tr (Peter Cook), 462tr (Phillip Bier), 468bl (Peter Cook), 470tr (Chris Gascoigne), 473tl (Phillip Bier), 489tl (Phillip Bier), 494t (Chris Gascoigne), 495l (Peter Cook).
Elizabeth Whiting Associates: 416m, 417m, 417tr, 418br, 422r, 434tr, 434bl, 435tr, 438bl, 443r, 443br, 444bl, 450bl, 450l, 451tr, 458t, 443t, 465tr, 467tl, 476br, 490tr, 491r, 491bl, 492t, 493tr, 493bl.

Index